THE
INDISPENSABLES

Also by Patrick K. O'Donnell

The Unknowns:
The Untold Story of America's Unknown Solider and
WWI's Most Decorated Heroes Who Brought Him Home

Washington's Immortals:
The Untold Story of an Elite Regiment Who
Changed the Course of the Revolution

First SEALs:
The Untold Story of the Forging of America's Most Elite Unit

Dog Company:
Boys of Pointe Du Hoc—Rangers Who Landed at D-Day
and Fought across Europe

Give Me Tomorrow:
The Korean War's Greatest Untold Story—The Epic Stand
of the Marines of George Company

They Dared Return:
The True Story of Jewish Spies behind the Lines in Nazi Germany

The Brenner Assignment:
The Untold Story of the Daring Spy Mission of WWII

We Were One:
Shoulder to Shoulder with the Marines Who Took Fallujah

Operatives, Spies, and Saboteurs:
The Unknown Story of the Men and Women of World War II's OSS

Into the Rising Sun:
In Their Own Words, World War II's Pacific Veterans Reveal
the Heart of Combat

Beyond Valor:
World War II's Ranger and Airborne Veterans Reveal the Heart of Combat

THE INDISPENSABLES

The Diverse Soldier-Mariners
Who Shaped the Country, Formed
the Navy, and Rowed Washington
across the Delaware

Patrick K. O'Donnell

Atlantic Monthly Press
New York

FIRST EDITION

Published simultaneously in Canada
Printed in Canada

First Grove Atlantic hardcover edition: May 2021

Library of Congress Cataloging-in-Publication data is available for this title.

ISBN 978-0-8021-5689-1
eISBN 978-0-8021-5691-4

Atlantic Monthly Press
an imprint of Grove Atlantic
154 West 14th Street
New York, NY 10011

Distributed by Publishers Group West

groveatlantic.com

21 22 23 24   10 9 8 7 6 5 4 3 2 1

To the Marblehead soldier-mariners, especially the forgotten African Americans, and diverse members of the regiment, who sacrificed everything for an idea—the United States. You are the greatest generation.

CONTENTS

PROLOGUE

Delaware River, Christmas Day, 1776

Trailing blood in the snow, the largely shoeless army marched to the boats at night in the midst of the storm as sleet pelted their bodies. At the Delaware's edge, the Marblehead men packed General George Washington's army into the vessels. They began crossing the fast-flowing, ice chunk–filled river—an impossible task for even the most experienced sailors. With the morning rapidly approaching, every moment counted to maintain the element of surprise against the Hessian garrison at Trenton. Despite the odds, Colonel John Glover's soldier-mariners pressed on.

In the winter of 1776, a pall of gloom and the prospect of capitulation hovered over the nascent United States. The Continental Army had endured one crushing defeat after another. The ragtag fighting force had attenuated from over eighteen thousand strong to several thousand men. With most enlistments set to expire on December 31, 1776, it would shrink to mere hundreds, largely barefoot and starving. As Washington direly confided in a letter to his brother, "I think the game is pretty near up."[1]

To turn the tide, the commander in chief staked the entire war on a desperate gamble, engaging in some of the most difficult maneuvers of the Revolutionary War: a night attack, an assault river crossing in the middle of a nor'easter, and a strike on the British-controlled town of Trenton. The ominous countersign "Victory or Death" marked the gravity of the operation.

In these extreme circumstances, Washington turned to the only group of men he knew had the strength and skill to deliver the army to Trenton—John Glover's Marblehead Regiment. The indispensable men miraculously transported Washington and the bulk of his army across the Delaware in the heart of the raging storm, without a casualty. Two sizable portions of the army not guided by the Marbleheaders failed to cross that night. But the courage and nautical talent of the Indispensables allowed the army and the mariners to play a vital role in the land battle that changed the course of the Revolutionary War. Through their own initiative, without orders, the Marbleheaders captured a crucial bridge at Trenton that sealed the fate of the battle as a decisive American victory.

On numerous occasions, the American Revolution would have met an early, dramatic demise had it not been for the SEAL-like operations and extraordinary battlefield achievements of this diverse, unsung group of men and their commander. Their powerful ideas and influence shaped the Revolution and a young country. Marbleheaders formed the origins and foundation of the American navy, and Marblehead captains smuggled or seized crucial supplies—including precious gunpowder, an absolute necessity, without which the Revolution would cease to exist. The creation of a navy contributed to the formation of a sovereign and independent country.

Prior to the Revolution, Marblehead faced a deadly epidemic spurring profound political divisions that would play a role in the Revolution. Experience gained from that event would have an impact on one of George Washington's most consequential decisions: to inoculate the army. When a virus threatened the Continental Army's very existence, an uncelebrated Marblehead fighting surgeon would rise to the occasion and save the troops.

Marbleheaders played a leading role forging an elite unit: the Commander in Chief's Guard or Life Guard—who protected Washington. A motley group of mariners from Massachusetts, the Indispensables, had pasts checkered by smuggling and privateering. A more diverse collection of individuals than any other unit in the Continental Army, the Marblehead Regiment included free African Americans and Native Americans within its ranks, making it one of America's first multiethnic units. This inclusiveness and unity, which tragically would not be seen again in America's armed forces for nearly two centuries, created a dynamic military unit that produced remarkable results. This book is a *Band of Brothers*–style history of the events and people who spearheaded and shaped the pre-Revolution and the Revolution. Rather than providing a regimental history, *The Indispensables* focuses on their actions and humanizes these extraordinary individuals. This narrative is a microcosm that reveals a broader story—at sea, on land, and, to a lesser extent, on the home front and in the legislature. At numerous inflection points within the Revolution—the Battle of Brooklyn, Pell's Point, Trenton, and others—the Marbleheaders were at the right place at the right time to change history forever.

Their story begins in the spring of 1769.

CHAPTER 1

SEEDS OF REBELLION

April 1769, Atlantic Ocean near Cape Ann, Massachusetts

As the deck of the American brig *Pitt Packet* rose and fell with the passage of the waves, British lieutenant Henry Panton called out, "Are all here?"[1]

Most of the crew of the American merchant ship had assembled on deck after the Royal frigate the HMS* *Rose* intercepted the vessel and sent over a boarding party. However, four crewmen—Michael Corbett, Pierce Fenning, John Ryan, and William Conner—had hidden themselves in the forepeak, a small space near the main hold.

The crew of the Marblehead, Massachusetts–based vessel, most of them men of Irish descent, responded with sullen silence. On their way home with a load of salt from Cádiz, Spain, they knew Panton intended to press some of them into service with the Royal Navy. Being "impressed," as it was known, meant being forcibly pressed into service—and it often ended in an early death for those unlucky enough to be taken. In essence, Britain intended to kidnap these civilians, uproot them from their families and livelihoods, and force them into near slavery. The Royal Navy paid impressed sailors a pittance and held their pay for six months to discourage desertion. The incredibly harsh discipline on board the ships spurred large numbers of the men in the navy, both volunteers and those forced to serve, to desert.

"Search the ship," Panton commanded.[2]

---

* The term "His Majesty's Ship" (HMS) did not come into general use until after the Revolution but is used in this book for clarity.

The boarding party quickly found the concealed crew members, but the Marbleheaders had no intention of coming quietly. Brandishing the weapons they had chosen for themselves—a fish gig, a musket, a hatchet, and a harpoon—they boldly refused to yield. "I know who you are. You are a Lt. of a Man of War, come with a pressgang to deprive me of my liberty," Corbett said. "You are determined to deprive me of my liberty, and I am determined to defend it. You have no right to force Us. We have retreated far as We could. We can go no farther."[3]

Sensing their determination, the British lieutenant resorted to violence almost immediately. He and the press-gang with him attempted to push and shove the sailors; however, the Marbleheaders refused to budge, putting their makeshift weapons to good use. In the confusion of the brawl, one of the British officers fired his pistol, which hit one crewman in the arm.

Appalled, Corbett shoved Panton hard enough that the officer staggered backward a few steps. Using his foot, Corbett then drew a line in the salt that had spilled over the deck in the tussle. "If you step over that mark again, I shall take it as a proof of your determination to impress me," he said, "and by the eternal God of Heaven, you are a dead Man."[4]

"Ay, my Lad," Panton replied mockingly, "I have seen a brave fellow before now." In a move calculated to offer as much insult as possible, he paused to take a pinch of snuff before he "resolutely stepped over the line."[5]

Incensed, Corbett hurled his harpoon with the practiced skill of an experienced mariner. It struck true, slicing through Panton's carotid artery and jugular vein.

As his blood swiftly fountained from his neck, covering the wooden planking, Panton cried, "The Rascal has killed me!"[6]

Stunned by the death of their leader, the press-gang retreated to the *Rose*, but swiftly returned to the *Pitt Packet* with a larger group of marines. The American crew members continued to resist; but, eventually, the greater numbers of the British prevailed (although some colonists later insisted that the crewmen would never have been overpowered had they not been drunk at the time of the incident). Instead of pressing* the sailors into service as originally intended, they sailed to Boston, where Corbett faced trial for murder.

None other than future Founding Father John Adams, one of the foremost attorneys in the colonies, represented Corbett at the trial. In court, the witnesses "all agreed in every Fact and Circumstance. Not contradictory Testimony, British Sailors and American Sailors all agreed."[7] A council that included the governor of Massachusetts considered the evidence and returned a surprising decision: "Justifiable Homicide, you are accordingly acquitted and discharged from your Imprisonment. . . . The Court is unanimous in this Opinion."[8]

While history has largely forgotten this incident, at the time, it attracted considerable attention on both sides of the Atlantic. Adams later wrote, "I was amused with the feelings of the Sailors of the Crew of the *Rose*. I met many of them in the Street and on the floor of the Court House, who could not conceal their Joy at the Acquittal of my Client. Some of them thanked me for my noble Conduct as they called it, in behalf of those brave fellows. One of them a Boatswain who had been a Witness, and given his Testimony with remarkable coolness and candor, to the Satisfaction of every Body, said to me 'Sir I have been almost constantly employed for twenty Years in Work of this kind, impressing Seamen, and I always thought I ought to be hanged for it, but now I know it, yet I can't help it.'" Adams concluded, "I don't believe

---

* Navies throughout history employed impressment to force individuals to serve, but the Royal Navy's notorious use of the practice contributed to sparking a revolution and war. Starting in the seventeenth century and ending with the completion of the Napoleonic Wars, the Royal Navy fueled its massive expansion through impressment. As the British Empire grew, the need to protect its commerce and colonies required a larger navy. Armed bands of men, "press-gangs," roamed port towns, kidnapping or compelling men into service. The Royal Navy stopped and boarded ships and forced unwilling sailors to serve. The navy's voracious appetite for bodies to crew its ships did not discriminate among Americans, Englishmen, and foreigners. Crew lived a hard and cruel dog's life for a pittance aboard ship, performing work that often proved fatal. While the practice may have been a source of cheap labor, impressment ultimately led to resentment, riots, and damaged Americans' view of Great Britain. Impressment became a contributing cause for the War of 1812.

there is a Jury in England at this day who would not justify a Sailor in Resistance and condemn an officer for an Impressment."[9]

This event, which some have said was one of the first instances of Americans fighting back against British oppression, serves as a symbol of shifting tides of public sentiment at the time.* Similar to Corbett, the colonists increasingly felt that they had been backed into a corner and victimized by unjust British rule. Like the sailor, they were primed to lash out. Those who, like the crew of the *Pitt Packet*, made their home in Marblehead, Massachusetts, were particularly vociferous in their defiance.

Nestled between a peninsula known as the Great Neck and a stretch of rockbound coast sixteen miles northeast of Boston lies one of New England's finest ports—Marblehead, Massachusetts. At the time, the crowded, bustling town ranked second only to Boston on the list of the most heavily populated and prosperous towns in New England. The pungent odor of fish wafted among the more than five thousand souls[10] crammed into hundreds of clapboard houses, many of them ramshackle, set in grimy, meandering streets. "The Houses being built on the Top, on the sides, & at the bottom of rocks," as one visitor described it.[11] Scattered among the disheveled homes stood magnificent mansions funded by the thriving fishing trade.

In Marblehead, fortunes were made and lost on the sea. By the 1770s, Marblehead's economy relied on fish, specifically New England's most profitable commodity: cod. Catching and trading fish formed a significant portion of the Massachusetts economy.† The commodity and its trade would build affluence and establish families, and their livelihood's reliance on the ocean and ships played a crucial role in amphibious operations and a navy. British efforts to control and regulate trade,

---

* Nearly a year later, John Adams would represent the British soldiers who fired upon Americans at the Boston Massacre. Adams always put the law above his personal beliefs. He considered this incident more important than the Boston Massacre.

† The activities represented approximately 35 percent of the Massachusetts economy.

and to impress sailors, eventually stimulated resistance, and Marblehead became a major influencer in the Revolution, second only to Boston.

The prominent merchant families of the town, the Glovers, Lees, Ornes, Gerrys, and Hoopers, amassed their wealth by risking the perils of the icy waters of the North Atlantic. Marblehead fishermen sailed in schooners typically thirty to sixty feet in length, from thirty to seventy tons each, with crews of seven to eight and captains skilled in the art of navigation and leadership. They fished some of the most treacherous waters in the world—the Grand Banks. An area off Newfoundland larger than the state of Maine, a two-thousand-mile round trip from the mainland, the Grand Banks were singularly brutal. Men fought against the sea to wrest their living from it with little more than determination and their bare hands. A single fish could weigh from five to one hundred pounds or more. Life at sea was grueling: from 1768 to 1769, more than 120 Marblehead sailors lost their lives to the sea.[12] Twenty-three ships sank in the raging storms of the Atlantic. Such conditions produced hardened men who could surmount almost any adversity.

Life on board the schooners also formed bonds of teamwork, fellowship, and discipline. The cruel nature of the sea demanded that sailors work together for joint survival. Captains could rely upon men to obey orders. The sailors knew that if they did their jobs well, they could succeed. No area in the world teemed with cod like the Grand Banks. Each of the roughly 150 schooners operating from the town caught an average of more than one hundred thousand pounds of fish a year.[13] Working around the clock, part of the crew fished while the others gutted the catch, maximizing the productivity of every second spent on the waves.

After the ships returned to port, shoremen dried, salted, and barreled the catch. Each schooner required a shore crew and ground space to cure their fish. Nearly a quarter of Marblehead's population, 1,000 to 1,500 individuals, worked in the fisheries. The constant stench of fish permeated not only the wharves but every area of the town, as the shoremen used beaches, fields, and even the open spaces between the houses to cure fish.

The economic realities for fishermen could be as vicious as the treacherous waters they braved. Most fishermen did not own their own boats; Marblehead's merchant families controlled and owned the fleets. To incentivize them, captains commonly paid men based on the amount of fish they brought in, rather than providing base wages. Their purchasing power depended on their credit. Men would often go into cycles of debt determined by the size of their expected catches. Taxes and regulations directly affected the fishermen's pocketbooks and ability to feed their families, giving Marbleheaders cause to despise bureaucrats in London, nearly three thousand miles away.

In the winter months, when temperatures plunged too low to brave the sea, the men had to find other work. Some crews sailed south to trade. Others would adopt various skilled trades, becoming sailmakers, riggers, and cobblers. Some would remain idle, falling prey to vices such as gambling and drinking. Marbleheaders frequented the many watering holes that sprouted up around town, such as the Three Cod Tavern. Life at sea spawned men who worked hard and drank harder.

The challenges presented by this hostile lifestyle instilled a distinct character into the inhabitants of the town. "Life at sea encouraged risk taking and a numbness to tremendous danger, overcoming daily hazards forged through hard work, teamwork and enterprise. A spirit of general equality of condition and common wants prevented any claim of superiority, and produced a social feel, which united most of them in one great family," noted one contemporary observer.[14]

Marblehead was progressive for the time, with a mix of people from different races and socioeconomic backgrounds. While slavery existed in the town, free people of various races and national origin lived together side by side. In fact, the Marblehead Regiment would become something of a haven for black soldiers and Native Americans. A mix of European immigrants and longtime residents worked alongside black freemen, and most attended church together.

Only about 2–3 percent of the Massachusetts population was black. Massachusetts, however, was progressive for colonial times, and blacks could challenge their masters in court. Marblehead itself was fairly cosmopolitan. Free African Americans and Native Americans lived and worked in the town alongside a smaller population of enslaved African Americans.

Over 1,700 African American and Native American men served among the tens of thousands of soldiers involved in the Revolutionary War from Massachusetts.[15] Of the 4,800 black Americans living in Massachusetts in 1776, the highest concentration—some thousand—resided in Essex County,[16] which encompassed Marblehead and nearby Beverly. Slavery was on its way out in Massachusetts and would be abolished there in 1783. For the eighteenth century, Essex County was ahead of its time.

Men of color fought side by side with their white brethren. Two young men typified those who joined the Marblehead Regiment: nineteen-year-old John Rhodes Russell, a sailor from a seafaring family and Emmanuel "Manuel" Soto, an African American freeman of similar age. Together, joined by a unity of purpose, the two young men and other members of the diverse regiment participated in some of the greatest inflection points of the Revolution and changed history.

On one hand, the seaside town was extremely provincial, centered on large families and focused on citizens' ties to the town's history, but it also had its worldly elements, rooted in its international trade.

Within the town, the very wealthy lived alongside the much less fortunate. They knew from experience that the fickle seas could easily strip the rich of their fortunes, but that it was also possible for those from humble beginnings to rise to the upper echelons of society. John Glover did just that and became one of the most important leaders of the Marblehead Regiment.

A short, stocky redhead with handsome, defined features, Glover was thirty-seven years old in the spring of 1769. Born the son of a carpenter on November 5, 1732, in Salem, Massachusetts, he was only four when his father died, leaving his mother to raise him and his three brothers. On October 30, 1754, John Glover, just shy of twenty-two years old, married Hannah Gale. Five months later, on March 23, 1755, John Glover Jr., was born. This firstborn of their eleven children would embody many of the qualities of his father, possessing his leadership, tenacity, and courage.

John Glover worked as a cordwainer (shoemaker) in his early teens and twenties until he opened a tavern in Marblehead. Glover harnessed his combined artisanal and entrepreneurial skills to finance his transition from shoemaker to self-made wealthy merchant mariner. His brothers, Jonathan, Samuel, and Daniel, also rose to affluence and positions of respect in the town as successful craftsmen, ship captains, and purveyors of rum. Marblehead respected and elevated self-made individuals.

Like many of Marblehead's other distinguished families, the Glovers not only owned fishing vessels but also engaged in trade with southern American colonies and the lucrative foreign trade with the West Indies and the Iberian Peninsula. Building precious relationships that would become invaluable when setting up military supply lines, the Marblehead merchants traded cod, lumber, and goods manufactured in New England to the West Indies for rum, molasses, and sugar. They traded fish to Spain and Portugal in exchange for fruit, wine, salt, and weapons. In the southern colonies, they obtained wheat, turpentine, and tobacco for cod. With the fortune John and his brothers garnered, the Glovers became part of Marblehead's ruling aristocracy. He expanded his empire to include several wharves and warehouses, first in Marblehead and later in nearby Beverly.

In 1759, during the French and Indian War, Glover was commissioned as an ensign in the 3rd Military Foot Company of Marblehead. As befitted a man of his station in the community, he routinely dressed in the finest clothes and wore a brace of pistols. He would later add a Scottish broadsword to his military accoutrements. But the military experience became much more than an opportunity to show off fine clothes. The war endowed Glover with military training and leadership that would be invaluable in the rebellion against Britain. A group of influential merchants, including Glover, began meeting at the Tuesday Evening Club, where the polite conversations often turned into divisive politics.

CHAPTER 2

MARBLEHEAD'S LEADING FAMILIES

Tuesday Evening Club, 1769, Marblehead, Massachusetts

In one of the two halls on the second floor of Joshua Prentiss's home, a group of Marblehead's elite met to talk about politics. Built in 1724 by a local schoolmaster, the stately home witnessed numerous such meetings and history.* At this weekly meeting of the Tuesday Evening Club, John Glover and several other distinguished gentlemen enjoyed "a good fire, pipes, tobacco, wine and good punch," an environment Glover lauded as "the place to talk matters over."[1] A familiar cast of characters sat in the comfortable chairs around the room, sipping libations while discussing their frustrations or satisfaction with British rule.

Sporting a triple chin, a paunch, and a long white wig, thirty-eight-year-old Azor Orne was one of Glover's closest confidants as well as an outspoken critic of the Crown. Descended from a family of wealthy merchants and sea captains, Orne had expanded his fortune thanks to his own successful trading activities. He also owned a great deal of property in the region. From an early age, Orne had an avid interest in local politics, and before the War of Independence, he frequently served as a selectman, a leadership position in Marblehead. Increasingly active in the provincial government, Orne at one time served on no fewer than 179 different committees.

---

* The house also served as the gathering place for the local Freemasons and later for Marblehead's Committee of Safety.

One of Marblehead's first families, the Ornes moved to the town from Salem in 1704, when at the age of twenty-seven their patriarch, Joshua Orne, married Elizabeth Norman, the granddaughter of one of Marblehead's original selectmen. They raised ten sons and two daughters. Joshua Orne started as a cordwainer, rose to justice of the peace, and eventually became the first of four generations of Ornes to serve in the Massachusetts legislature. The Ornes had a love for the name Joshua, which reappeared in the family throughout several generations. Joshua Sr.'s eldest son, known as Deacon Joshua, perpetuated the family business—trade and politics. He became a wealthy merchant and philanthropist who also served as a legislator. By the 1770s, two of Deacon Joshua's sons, Azor and Joshua, had become extremely successful and prosperous merchants. Azor would always regret his lack of a college education, while his half brother Joshua graduated fifth in his class at Harvard and wrote his thesis on the denunciation of the slave trade.[2] They both named their sons Joshua.

Azor's son Joshua seemed to be cut from the same cloth as his father. He, too, would become a fervent Patriot, leaving Harvard to join the Marblehead Regiment.

The prominent men who took part in the Tuesday Evening Club were largely Whigs or Patriots. An intellectual and political movement and a party in Britain, many American Whigs were imbued with the convictions of English philosopher John Locke that all individuals were born with certain inalienable rights and liberties,* encompassing the natural law philosophies of the Enlightenment. For many "American Whigs terms like 'Interest,' 'Liberty,' and 'Life' held special meaning. . . . [They] found 'Interest' to be inseparable from 'Life' and 'Liberty.' Most believed that the only way to protect one's liberty was to own property. Without property or liberty, a person could not achieve independence."[3]

---

* To avoid confusion, the term "Patriot" will often be used in place of "Whig," which applied to the politics of the time. The Founders also referred to themselves as Patriots.

Loyalists (generally supporters of the Crown, traditionalists, or in some cases those who simply who did not support American Whigs) were often deeply entrenched within the ranks of the affluent and also powerful members of society. Some Marbleheaders remained in the middle when passions flared among camps. In the coming years, "Join or Die" became the Whigs' passionate rallying cry, while others did not choose a position or remained silent.[4] Politics in the Tuesday Evening Club, and in society in general, were malleable; events changed hearts, minds, and affiliations. Individuals often shifted between the two camps or remained undecided.

Another prominent Tuesday Evening Club member was Elbridge Gerry. Slight of build and birdlike, Gerry, with his protruding forehead, sharp nose, and sharper intellect, was instantly recognizable. Nervous at times, he had a "singular habit of contracting and expanding the muscles of his eye" that lent an "unusual sternness."[5] A fierce debater, his opponents would often label him a "grumbletonian."[6]

Scrupulous, principled, powerful, and an ardent abolitionist, Gerry would become a signer of the Declaration of Independence, delegate to the Constitutional Convention, Massachusetts governor, and United States vice president. Although he was a man who despised the concept of "political parties," as he believed their existence was anathema to the best interest of society as a whole, Gerry, correctly or incorrectly, is forever remembered for the term "gerrymandering."* The youngest but the most educated and well connected of the Marblehead leaders, Gerry was a brilliant, passionate, and radical ideologue of Marblehead and an acolyte of firebrand Samuel Adams. His love for liberty was infectious.

Republicanism drove Gerry's beliefs and values. As one of his biographers described, "Republicanism held a special meaning for men in late eighteenth-century America, for it described the image of the

---

* In 1812, Gerry, a man who did not believe in political parties, then governor of Massachusetts, signed the bill that redrew the Massachusetts state senate districts. Gerry was not the originator of the bill.

ideal society which they hoped to achieve and live in. Republicanism postulated the establishment of an organic state in which citizens would sacrifice their private desires for the public good and the interests of society as a whole. Virtue, or the unselfish devotion to the public good, was to be the aim. A republic was to be maintained by a combination of elements: morally virtuous citizens, virtuous leaders, and a constitutional arrangement that would prevent the centralization of power and ensure the preservation of private liberty."[7] Gerry infused these abstract philosophies into his life. An intellectual powerhouse, he would emerge a key influencer in the Revolution.

Elbridge's father, Thomas, emigrated from England to Marblehead in 1730 and, like the patriarchs of other first families, built a fortune operating ships out of the flourishing port. Unlike other Marblehead families, who displayed opulence, the Gerrys believed in the austerity and minimalism derived from their Congregationalist roots.

Though slight of build, the native son of the fiercely independent seaside town loomed large in his love of liberty and his aversion to those who might threaten it. His ancestry, education, upbringing, and associations all combined to create a perfect storm of radical fervor that would fuel his considerable efforts in the fight for American liberty. Elbridge Gerry entered Harvard before the age of fourteen and graduated in 1762 with his bachelor's degree before receiving a graduate degree in 1765. He then entered the family business and became immersed in colonial politics. He served as a representative to the General Court in 1772, where he met Samuel Adams. His friendship and correspondence with Adams and Founding Fathers, such as John Adams, and other radicals, throughout his career propelled Marblehead and its prominent families to the forefront of colonial politics. The Gerry family operated and owned one of the most profitable fishing and merchant fleets in Massachusetts, and they built international relationships with the most powerful trading interests around the world—something that would prove instrumental in the coming years. Despite their cosmopolitan ways, the Gerrys were strict Congregationalists, however, and they eschewed any extravagant displays of wealth.

Unlike the Gerrys, at forty-eight rotund Jeremiah Lee was, by most estimates, the wealthiest man in Massachusetts and perhaps one of the richest men in the colonies before the Revolution, and he liked to show it. Lee had thirteen siblings. His father, Samuel Lee, was an enterprising merchant and justice of the peace who moved to Marblehead in 1743. Jeremiah followed in his father's footsteps and grew his fleet of trading vessels. While many well-to-do colonists were loyal to the Crown, Lee was always a staunch Patriot. Married to Martha Swett, Lee had amassed great wealth and built one of the most elegant homes in North America at the time. The Lee family intertwined with the Glovers, the Ornes, and even their archrivals in business, the Hoopers, via marriage. Lee's cousins and nephews would play key roles in the Marblehead Regiment.

Before the war, his favorite nephew, William Raymond Lee, worked in the accounting room of his uncle's sprawling enterprises. Groomed by his uncle, the dashing and charismatic William eventually managed the entire business empire. He and his wife even lived in his uncle's mansion for a time until, "desiring to live in less splendor,"[8] the couple moved just a short distance away to the mansion belonging to William's grandfather, Samuel Lee, a renowned architect and builder, who was involved in the family's trading business and served as justice of the peace and a selectman. Creative as well as business-minded, William invented a new kind of cartridge box and proved to be a natural military tactician. Washington would later note he "may undoubtedly be called a martinet in military matters."[9]

Impressment, magnified by the Michael Corbett trial, deepened the political fractures within the town between the Loyalists and those with ideas considered radical.

One of those ardent Loyalists, Robert "King" Hooper, was among the most eminent and affluent men in the area. A representative to the General Court, "for many years, he was on intimate terms with various members of the British government and military."[10] Hearing impaired, the dark-haired, triple-chinned shipping magnate declined a seat in the council in 1759 due to his deafness.[11] His wealth was matched only by the massive debt that his aggressive business tactics racked up in the tens of thousands. Hooper owned scores of vessels, including the schooner *Pitt Packet*, which was involved in the 1769 incident; however, despite the ordeal of the long Corbett trial, Hooper remained loyal to the Crown. And, despite Corbett's Patriot leanings, he remained employed by Hooper.

Often working alongside Corbett, forty-one-year-old Loyalist Ashley Bowen was employed as a captain, sailor rigger, and maker of ships' sails and colors by all of the major families within the town. British impressment of American sailors did not incense Bowen as much because he experienced it firsthand, having served with impressed fellow crew members on his first vessels. Having volunteered to serve in the Royal Navy during the French and Indian War, Bowen, a midshipman, and thirty-two volunteer sailors from Marblehead participated in the siege of Quebec. After hostilities ceased and the men were discharged from service, Bowen and the Marblehead men boarded the ship *Thornton* for the journey home with Bowen in charge. On the journey, "Mr. Bowen was exposed to great difficulty and danger, as nearly the entire care of the sick devolved upon him, and he was obliged to personally superintend the burial of the dead."[12] Bowen brought most of the men home, but thirty-five died at sea. Bowen was proud of his service, and his participation made him a loyal patriot to the Crown, strengthening his belief in the greatness of the Royal Navy—he considered it invincible. Despite changing times and threats to his livelihood, Bowen regularly could not obtain work because of his Loyalist sympathies. Despite the economic hardships brought on by his political leanings, he stood by the courage of his convictions.

The growing wealth of the Marbleheaders and other colonists did not go unnoticed by the Crown. After many years of war, Britain needed to raise more money, and the colonies, with their successful trade and lack of political influence, seemed like an ideal place to obtain it. From three thousand miles away, Parliament enacted the Sugar Act of 1765 along with the Acts of Trade and Navigation. These and other edicts continually frustrated Marblehead's merchants. Affecting their pocket-books, the bureaucracy, about which they had no say or control, caused the tempers of the Marbleheaders to seethe. Some of the laws and taxes were aimed directly at Marblehead in particular. In 1762, one of the first red-wax-sealed writs of assistance from the Crown specifically targeted the town and stationed a customs official in Marblehead endowed with the "Power to Enter into Any Ship, Bottom, Boat, or Any Other Vessell, as also into Any Shop, House, Warehouse, Hostry, or Any Other Place whatsoever, to make diligent Search into Any Trunk, Chest, Pack, Case, Truss, or Any other Parcell or Package whatsoever."[13]

The Stamp Act was a tax that required printed material be pro-duced on stamped paper from London, and affixed with a revenue stamp. The tax further galvanized the ire of Patriots who considered it an act of economic warfare. Marblehead's leading merchants responded with an embargo. Samuel Adams and other Sons of Liberty, a secretive organization opposed to the Crown's policies, played a crucial role in fighting the Stamp Act.

In 1765, forty-two-year-old, deeply religious Samuel Adams quit his job as a tax collector. A member of Boston's elite, he received his master of arts from Harvard. Sam was bad in business and even worse with money; nevertheless, his father made him a partner in the family malt business that supplied that crucial ingredient to brewers. The Bostonian was then elected to the position of tax collector; he was too lenient when taxing his fellow Bostonians and racked up a massive £3,500 debt he personally owed to the city. Adams quit his tax-collecting position in early 1765 to fight the Stamp Act. His charisma, dynamic personality, and skill in performance shined "[through his] good Voice, and [he] was Master of Vocal Musick. This Genius he improved, by instituting sing-ing Societys of Mechanicks [craftsmen], where he presided." Through song and fiery oratory, Adams, called the "Psalm Singer with the gifted face," wooed converts to his cause and ideas. He sometimes recruited members of the church choir, "& embraced such Opportunities to ye inculcating Sedition,"[14] wrote one Loyalist. A radical Whig, philosopher, and rabble-rouser, Adams, and the Sons of Liberty, bent and changed history. The Boston Sons of Liberty expanded to other charters around the colonies and joined the Stamp Act Congress in appealing to the House of Commons. The Americans' nonimportation and nonexportation policy and political campaign proved successful, and Parliament then passed the Townshend Acts, imposing a tax on goods imported from Britain to the colonies. Their efforts not only cut off tax revenue collection, but also caused unemployment in British industry dependent upon American raw materials and closed the colonies to British imports. Each additional tax and regulation, combined with the impressments of Marblehead sailors, added fuel to an already combustible situation.

As tensions and resistance to the economic warfare mounted, and the Crown sent troops to Boston, an atrocity would soon have a profound effect on the families of Marblehead.

CHAPTER 3

MASSACRE AND TEA

March 1770, Marblehead, Massachusetts

It began, "A few minutes after nine o'clock four youths, named Edward Archbald, William Merchant, Francis Archbald, and John Leech, came down Cornhill together, and separating at Doctor Loring's corner, the two former were passing the narrow alley leading Mr. Murray's barrack in which was a soldier brandishing a broad sword of an uncommon size against the walls, out of which he struck fire plentifully."[1] The story appeared in the March 12, 1770, edition of the *Boston Gazette* and made its way the fifteen or so miles to Marblehead. In its few short pages, John Glover and others read the account of the event that came to be known as the Boston Massacre.

The pages revealed how the young men and the soldiers pushed and struck at one another with a variety of makeshift weapons. Then, "on hearing the noise, one Samuel Atwood came up to see what was the matter; and entering the alley from dock square, heard the latter part of the combat; and when the boys had dispersed he met the ten or twelve soldiers aforesaid rushing down the alley towards the square and asked them if they intended to murder people? They answered Yes, by G-d, root and branch! With that one of them struck Mr. Atwood with a club which was repeated by another; and being unarmed, he turned to go off and received a wound on the left shoulder which reached the bone and gave him much pain."

Soon more people came out into the streets, and the soldiers responded by charging with their bayonets. Agitated, the Bostonians, many of them young men, yelled in defiance and, "it is said, threw snow balls. On this, the Captain commanded [the Redcoats] to fire; and more snow balls coming, he again said, damn you, fire, be the consequence what it will!"

It was over within minutes. "By this fatal manoeuvre three men were laid dead on the spot and two more struggling for life," the *Gazette* reported. "The dead are Mr. Samuel Gray, killed on the spot, the ball entering his head and beating off a large portion of his skull.

"Mr. James Caldwell, mate of Capt. Morton's vessel, in like manner killed by two balls entering his back.

"Mr. Samuel Maverick, a promising youth of seventeen years of age, son of the widow Maverick, and an apprentice to Mr. Greenwood, ivory-turner, mortally wounded; a ball went through his belly and was cut out at his back. He died the next morning.

"A lad named Christopher Monk, about seventeen years of age, an apprentice to Mr. Walker, shipwright, wounded; a ball entered his back about four inches above the left kidney near the spine and was cut out of the breast on the same side. Apprehended, he will die.

"A mulatto man named Crispus Attucks, who was born in Framingham, but lately belonged to New-Providence and was here in order to go for North Carolina, also killed instantly, two balls entering his breast, one of them in special goring the right lobe of the lungs and a great part of the liver most horribly."

Thirty-five-year-old Renaissance man and doctor Benjamin Church performed the autopsy on Attucks, the first man killed in the massacre. Church wrote,

> I found two wounds in the region of the thorax, the one on the right side, which entered through the second true rib within an inch and a half of the sternum, dividing the rib and separating the cartilaginous extremity from the sternum, the ball passed obliquely downward through the diaphragm and entering

through the large lobe of the liver and the gall-bladder, still keeping its oblique direction, divided the aorta descendens just above its division into the iliacs, from thence it made its exit on the left side of the spine. This wound I apprehended was the immediate cause of his death. The other ball entered the fourth of the false ribs, about five inches from the linea alba, and descending obliquely passed through the second false rib, at the distance of about eight inches from the linea alba; from the oblique direction of the wounds, I apprehend the gun must have been discharged from some elevation, and further the deponent saith not.[2]

A graduate of Harvard, Church received his medical training in London and returned with an English wife to the colonies, where he emerged as one of the most accomplished surgeons in Boston. Church was able to conduct cataract surgery by "couching on the eyes"[3] on fifty-six-year-old Mrs. Hodges, restoring sight from blindness. As skillful with words as with a scalpel, Church published a poem titled *The Choice* in 1757: "Life without storms a stagnant pool appears, / And grows offensive with unruffled years / . . . / Whatever station be for me design'd; May virtue be the mistress of my mind."[4] Known for his biting sarcasm, Church also penned a parody, a tune called the "Massachusetts Song of Liberty." A radical Whig, Freemason, and member of the Sons of Liberty, Church was a close friend of Samuel Adams. He traveled in all the right circles of Whig politics and emerged as one of the leading men in Boston. The surgeon appreciated the finer things in life and built an elaborate summer home, along with a mountain of debt, which forced him to seek additional sources of revenue. Known for his dalliances outside his marriage, he sought the company of the fairer sex, later including a "Girl of pleasure"[5] in Marblehead.

Church confirmed the murder of the American in his autopsy. The massacre roiled the citizens in Marblehead and throughout Massachusetts, and forced open the growing political fissure between the Loyalists and the Whigs of the town. "So enraged are the people at the late horrid Massacre in Boston, that it is thought, if a proper Signal should be given, not less than Fifteen Hundred Men, from this Town [Salem] and Marblehead, would turn out at a Minute's Warning, to revenge the Murders, and support the Rights of the insulted and much abused Inhabitants of Boston," a Salem resident wrote.[6] But instead of retaliating with physical violence, the citizens of Marblehead put economic teeth behind their anger, unanimously passing a binding agreement of nonimportation of tea on May 10, 1770. The agreement included language affirming their "highest indignation and resentment, that a lawless, ignorant, and bloody soldiery should attempt of its own authority to fire upon and destroy so many of our brethren in ye town of Boston, and we hereby declare a readiness with our Lives and Interest, at all times to support ye civil authority of this Province in bringing to justice all such high-handed offenders against ye wholesome laws of this Land."[7] Many colonists boldly put aside their short-term financial self-interest and waged economic war against the greatest trading power in the world at the time, such as they had done successfully several years earlier when opposing the Stamp Act.

Life in Marblehead became increasingly uncomfortable for citizens of the town who were loyal to the British and those still sitting on the fence. Town representatives secured signatures from 712 Marblehead families in favor of the nonimportation agreement, but also recorded the names of the seventeen families who refused to sign. Seven of those apparently relented, and the town voted that the names of the remaining ten families should be published in the *Essex Gazette* as "unfriendly to the community." Officials were instructed not to "approbate any of them to the Sessions for license to sell spirituous liquors."[8]

The Glovers, the Gerrys, and the Ornes, three of the most prominent Marblehead families and strident Whigs, from this point forward took the lead in the town's political affairs. Elbridge Gerry, though only twenty-six at the time, had become a patriotic zealot, fueled by his close friendship and correspondence with Boston radical Samuel Adams. As one contemporary newspaper phrased it, when "the taxation question appeared to be settled and the tea had not yet been spilled, when business was brisk and prosperity reigned without prohibition,

Gerry wrote as though the chains of despotism were clanking in the lanes of Marblehead."[9] The provincial press largely favored the Whigs, allowing men like Gerry to disseminate their ideas.

Extensive communication between the Marblehead zealot and Samuel Adams, in fact, spawned the idea of creating committees of correspondence to sway public opinion in response to British atrocities. The committees coordinated and disseminated the Whig response to British actions, acting as a de facto shadow authority superseding the Crown's power. As Adams wrote to Gerry, "I was at first of your opinion, that 'it would be most proper for a committee from Boston, united with committees from two or three other towns, . . .' and I mentioned it to several gentlemen of the neighboring towns." Adams entreated him to encourage Marblehead to appoint its own committee. "This would at once discover a union of sentiments thus far, and have its influence on other towns. It would at least show that Boston is not wholly deserted."[10]

Gerry assured Adams, "I think the friends of liberty here will be able to hand you something soon."[11]

Less than a month later, the Marbleheaders answered Adams's call. Elbridge's father, Thomas Gerry, moderated the meeting that created Marblehead's Committee of Correspondence. Elbridge may have been the most vocal advocate for action, but politics was a family affair. Elbridge, his father, and his brother would all sit on the committee. Of the eight seats on the Marblehead Committee of Correspondence, six would be held by members of the three eminent Whig families: Captain John Glover, the three Gerrys, and brothers Azor and Joshua Orne Sr.[12]

Not all of the merchant families shared the same level of passion, however. Twenty-nine families, "though firm friends of their country[,] . . . were unprepared to indorse the language of the resolutions adopted at these meetings" and signed a protest published in the *Essex Gazette* claiming the resolutions "did not fairly represent the sentiments of the people of Marblehead."[13] Jonathan Glover—John Glover's brother—and Jeremiah Lee, shockingly, were both among the dissenters, perhaps hoping to straddle the political fence and not muddy their names publicly in the eyes of the Crown. Trust and loyalty were apparently malleable. Origins of civil war simmered below the surface. The next town meeting, however, resolved the matter. According to the *Essex Gazette*, "The Whigs and Tories had a warm Engagement, and the latter being worsted were put to immediate flight."[14] Jonathan Glover later publicly recanted. Gerry assured Adams in his next letter, "We have little or no difficulty with the enemies of our constitution. . . . The Whigs here are very happy in falling in with your sentiments."[15] Ultimately, correspondence with each other did little to salve the colonists' grievances against Britain, and the feelings of discontent and outrage continued to spread, escalating toward the Boston Tea Party.

Fittingly, at least two men with ties to Marblehead took part in that act of rebellion. Although born into a Loyalist family, thirty-year-old Marblehead doctor Elisha Story felt, like many of his countrymen, that "taxation without representation" was immoral. Story's father was the Register of the Court of Admiralty, which meant that he helped enforce the unpopular Stamp Act of 1765. Story's father's office "was broken into at the time of the Stamp Act riots, on the supposition that the stamps had been deposited there for distribution, and all the books and papers carried into King Street, and burned."[16]

Story joined the Sons of Liberty, the clandestine organization tied to Samuel Adams that resisted the Crown and played a major role in eliminating the 1765 Stamp Act. Sons conversed with one another using a secret language and donned medals around their necks, and some wore hats with pins engraved with "45" to commemorate the Jacobite uprising in 1745. Annually on August 14, the Sons gathered for a massive outdoor dinner near Boston's Liberty Tree, a famous elm in Boston Common, where the group conducted its first act of defiance against the Crown in 1765.

Thirty-two-year-old Harvard-trained doctor Joseph Warren, a specialist in smallpox inoculations, played a leading role in the group. With piercing blue eyes, a keen mind, and a magnetic personality, Warren was also Grand Master of the St. Andrew's Lodge of Masons. Most of the Sons were Freemasons, and from their ranks sprang the core leadership of the organization and part of Samuel Adams's Boston Committee of Correspondence. After Warren lost his wife in April, he hurled himself into the Sons of Liberty, working closely with his mentor, Samuel Adams. Powerful members of the group included fellow widower, silversmith, and industrialist Paul Revere; Doctor Benjamin Church; and John Adams. Wealthy Bostonian and ardent Patriot John Hancock often financed many of the Sons' efforts.

The Sons typically met at the Green Dragon Tavern, located on Union Street's west side in the North End. A massive brick building operating since 1712, it was owned by the St. Andrew's Lodge. Here, the Sons of Liberty leadership, including Marbleheaders Elisha Story and Gabriel Johonnot, proclaimed "to oppose the vending of any tea sent by the East India Company . . . with our lives and fortunes," a mortal pledge, and the men "determined the tea shipped by the East India Company shall not be landed."[17]

Son of Liberty Johonnot would soon be joined by marriage to the Marbleheaders. Born into a wealthy family in 1748, he was descended from a family of French Huguenots, one of the first thirty to settle in Boston. His father, Zacherie, a wealthy distiller, was also one of the Sons of Liberty. However, like Story, Gabriel lived in a divided family. His older brother, Peter, a staunch Loyalist, would later serve as a messenger for the British. Gabriel, by contrast, was an active participant in the Boston Tea Party.[18] He had married the daughter of Reverend Samuel Cooper of Boston in 1766 at age eighteen, but after her passing, he married Sarah Bradstreet of Marblehead and first became acquainted with the men he would later serve beside throughout the war. Involved in the heart of the American Revolution from the beginning, Johonnot served on the committee appointed by the Sons of Liberty to interact with consignees regarding shipments of tea sent to Boston by the East India Company "and require them [consignees] to promise not to land or pay duties on tea sent by said company."[19] They considered the consignees Crown officials, and many of them were related to Governor Thomas Hutchinson, including two of his sons.

The Sons believed in liberty, from both individual and societal perspectives: "It referred to not only the autonomy of each person's rights, but also the integrity of the group, and especially to the responsibility of a people to regulate their own affairs," as one historian explained. The popular slogan "No Taxation without Representation" linked to the Boston Sons' motto, "Equality before the Law," and their ideas of equality.[20] The group found the tea tax particularly abhorrent since it validated Parliament's right to tax the colonies at will and could give rise to more Crown-dominated monopolies foisted upon them. On a pragmatic front, the act also cut into the profits of some Whigs smuggling tea into the colonies. Parliament passed the Tea Act in 1773 as a bailout of sorts for the nearly bankrupt East India Company. The firm had racked up millions of pounds of debt and had tons of tea rotting in warehouses. The Tea Act allowed the company to assign its own agents or consignees and cut out the middlemen and auctions, thereby allowing them to sell tea directly to the market, creating a monopoly. Tea became a symbol of the Crown's oppressive economic policies.

The Sons singled out three tea-carrying ships owned by the East India Company, fitting targets for their wrath. The East India Company was a juggernaut. Immersed in politics, the company operated a monopoly under a Royal charter that eventually controlled half the world's trade, employed its own armies, emerged as one of London's most powerful financial institutions, and effectively operated as a Crown enterprise. The Sons of Liberty spent weeks protesting the arrival of the ships and demanded the return of the tea to Britain with no duty or tax paid on it. When one of those ships, *Dartmouth*, arrived in Boston Harbor in early December 1773, Story stood guard to prevent it from unloading its precious cargo.[21] Then, on the fateful night of December 16, he donned his disguise at the Chase and Speakman Distillery.

That frigid winter evening, Johonnot, Story, and scores of other Sons of Liberty darkened their faces with charcoal and wore headdresses to camouflage their identities, a scheme devised by fellow Patriot and Bostonian Sarah Bradlee Fulton. In Boston Harbor, they boarded two stranded tea-laden vessels prohibited from unloading their tea by the Patriots and forbidden from returning to England by Governor Hutchison. Story, along with his fellow "Indians," pried open and unceremoniously dumped 342 chests, £9,000 worth, of tea into the water in protest of Britain's sole remaining tax on tea. The men worked for several hours, did not destroy any property but the tea, and replaced a padlock they had disabled.[22] One Tea Party member who tried to pocket a small portion of the tea was ostracized, manhandled, and forced to return the stolen goods by his peers. The Boston Sons of Liberty in 1773 did not believe in random, wanton destruction of property, but upheld their principles of the pursuit of freedom in their act of defiance against the Crown as they conducted themselves in an orderly manner. Troops stationed in nearby Castle William in Boston Harbor witnessed the destruction of the tea but did not intervene—they had not received orders from the governor for assistance. But when Hutchinson discovered what transpired, he initially considered their actions treason. Destruction of the tea was analogous to crossing the Rubicon. As John Adams, also a member of the Sons of Liberty, described a day later, "The die is cast. The people have passed the river and cut away the bridge. Last night three cargoes of tea were emptied into the harbor. This is the grandest event which has ever happened since the controversy with Britain opened. The sublimity of it charms me! . . . The town of Boston never was more still and calm on Saturday night than it was last night. All things were conducted with great order, decency, and *perfect submission to government*. No doubt we all thought the administration in better hands than it had been."[23] Adams and the Sons of Liberty had a taste of self-governance.

The Sons of Liberty's actions in Boston Harbor had consequences; in the coming months, the Crown would come down hard on Boston, closing the harbor to commerce and leveling a host of punitive measures on the colonists. Bold protest and Britain's harsh reaction galvanized both sides of the conflict. On the British side, many were appalled at the act of defiance and felt the action must be punished severely. On the Patriot side, communities throughout the American colonies united in their sympathy and support for Boston and their fear of a similar fate.

Backed by the alliance of the Glovers, Ornes, Lees, and Gerrys, the Patriots in Marblehead gained momentum. However, their fervor would suffer a severe blow. The town was already facing attack from an insidious force that could not be stopped by weapons: smallpox.

CHAPTER 4

A VIRUS AND THE REVENGE
OF THE LOYALISTS

May 1773, Atlantic Ocean

William Matthews of Marblehead laughed and talked with the crew of the French vessel that had pulled up alongside his own in the Atlantic. As was common between fishermen, Matthews arranged a small trade. He obtained a piece of highly prized Castile soap and, in a decision that would have deadly consequences, carried it back with him to port.

The practical fisherman's wife used the soap to wash what was likely the smelliest thing in the house at the time—the clothes he had been wearing on the fishing trip. Two weeks later, "she broke out and swelled to a great degree . . . poisoned."[1] The "poison," contained in the soap, spread to the women who cared for Mrs. Matthews, despite bathing in "salt water and liquor of elder."[2] The scourge of smallpox had arrived in Marblehead on June 1, 1773.

Those infected with the variola virus, known as smallpox, undergo several stages: high fever, rashes, and pustules that form like peas under the skin. The affected are highly contagious.

The Selectmen of Marblehead first attempted to contain the illness by quarantine. Poles flying a red flag designated "pest houses" near the waterfront in a desperate effort to isolate the sick. "All dogs running at large on the streets were to be killed immediately."[3] Authorities constructed fences around the homes of the infected. The plague spread, leaving death in its wake. It often left those who survived horribly disfigured by scars—remnants of the hideous pustules on their faces.

Before Edward Jenner discovered the first successful smallpox vaccine in 1796, physicians employed inoculation to combat the disease. This procedure involved lancing a pustule and then inserting the contaminated knife under the skin of a healthy person. The patients often received a smaller dose of the virus that allowed their bodies to combat the disease and eventually become immune. But they could also manifest a full-blown case of smallpox. The uneven nature of the results of the procedure led to fear. Individuals played a game of Russian roulette—would inoculation protect or kill?

By August 1773, as smallpox ravaged the town, the flow of ships out of the busy port threatened to propel the disease beyond borders of Marblehead. Whig families, and initially Loyalists as well, devised a controversial solution: build an inoculation hospital. Democratically, the families called a town meeting and approved the construction of a private hospital on Cat Island, a small speck of land in the harbor. John and Jonathan Glover, Elbridge Gerry, and Azor Orne fronted the money to buy the land and construct the building. However, when the time came to fund the enterprise, Robert "King" Hooper and other Loyalists demurred and became vocal opponents of the hospital. Local politics, funding, and personal animus to the Patriots derailed bipartisan support.

John Glover hired Doctor Hall Jackson, who had extensive experience with the disease and specialized in smallpox inoculation. The owners charged a fee for the inoculation procedure to subsidize the costs of the hospital and doctor and initiated a series of processes to minimize spreading the disease. The founders went out of their way to avoid the appearance of profiting from the venture and covered the cost of one of every ten indigent Marbleheaders who wanted treatment but could not afford it.

Glover and his fellow investors used two boats to ferry patients and provisions to Cat Island: *Mercury Cruiser* and *Noah's Ark*. To avoid contamination, they erected a fence on the vessels to separate the crew from the patients. No one was allowed to depart the island without clearance from the physicians and a permit from the selectmen.

The three-story hospital contained ten rooms with beds and a kitchen. A small building near the dock had two rooms separated by a door, an eighteenth-century version of an airlock. Here, after being cleared by doctors for departure, the patients would be fumigated, cleaned, and supplied a fresh set of clothing before boarding the boat back to the mainland.

Loyalist diarist Ashley Bowen satirically compared the treatment of the hospital's first patients to a military operation. "This day at noon Colonel Orne with a body of volunteers and a number of invalids landed at Cape Pus on the NW end of the Isle of Cat and laid siege to the Castle of Pox. General Jackson, Commander-in-chief; . . . this siege will last thirty days. By an express from Castle Pox, General Jackson had a smart engagement and wounded nearly one hundred of Colonel Orne's body of volunteers the first evening they landed."[4]

The editor of the *Essex Gazette*, on the same page politically as the hospital proprietors, wrote a glowing review of the hospital and its procedures: "One Hundred and Three in number . . . the patients are all daily displaying the signal of Health from the middle of the Island, and are all in high spirits."[5]

For Glover, inoculation became personal when his daughter Hannah fell ill with smallpox. She survived the ordeal, and Glover brought the rest of his family to Cat Island for inoculation. Hannah received treatment from local doctor Nathaniel Bond, later fighting surgeon with the Marblehead Regiment. A graduate of Harvard Medical School, Bond was a close friend, associate, and apprentice of Doctor Joseph Warren—a Son of Liberty and close confederate of Sam Adams and John Hancock. Both doctors shared an expertise in smallpox. Bond was also a contemporary and friend of the brilliant doctor and Son of Liberty Benjamin Church.

In a letter confiding to Warren about a specific medical case, Bond wrote, "Last night I was up till after 8 oC with a Patient under the Bilious Cholic."[6] Bond also revealed his darker side, their mutual membership in a secret society called the Spunker Club. Known as Resurrectionists, the Spunker Club was a group of eighteenth-century Harvard medical students who snatched bodies from graveyards for their anatomy studies. In colonial Massachusetts, medical students were permitted to dissect the bodies of executed criminals, but the demand greatly exceeded the supply, causing some students and doctors to resort to sneaking into graveyards, digging up graves, and stealing corpses under the cover of night to study in their classrooms the next morning.

The first two groups of patients on Cat Island survived inoculation; however, the third group may have caused a new outbreak in town. Tories, led by Jeremiah Lee's archrival, King Hooper, seized on the incident to clamp down on the hospital, attempting to put it out of business. Hooper and his forces took over the town meeting and implemented new regulations. They required patients to linger for a painful thirty-day waiting period after inoculation before reentering the mainland and insisted they land first in a remote area of the town. When a group of inoculated patients attempted to enter a public wharf before the expiration of the thirty-day waiting period, an enraged mob hurled rocks at the craft and "beat or pushed them off two or three Times."[7] On January 12, 1774, the mob torched *Mercury Cruiser*—demonstrating mob violence could be hijacked by either side.

Several days later, eagle-eyed Marbleheaders spotted several men stealing contaminated clothes from Cat Island. "They were accordingly watched . . . they picked up a Quantity of Cloathing, near the Hospital, that put out for airing."[8] As they attempted to escape in boats, the clothing-nappers hurled the infected items overboard in the wake of their pursuers. After apprehending the thieves, the mob loaded the four men in a cart and tarred and feathered them "in the most extraordinary Exhibition of the Kind, ever seen in North America." Waving a large white flag, a fifer and four drummers escorted the cart and paraded through the streets of Marblehead to Salem. Some thousand people witnessed the "the exquisitely droll and grotesque Appearance of the four tarred and feathered Objects of Derision, exhibited a very laughable and truly comic scene."[9]

King Hooper called another town meeting to stamp out the disorder. With the Loyalists having the upper hand, they quashed a motion proposing that the hospital be purchased from the Glovers, Ornes, and Elbridge Gerry. Attendants resolved to form a committee to inspect the hospital, and the owners conceded they would shutter the facility once the current patients completed their treatment.

The inspection committee visited the hospital, and the following evening, about twenty men blackened their faces and, "in disguise,"[10] silently rowed over to Cat Island armed with incendiary tubs of tar. They set fire to the hospital with eleven patients sleeping inside "without any attempt to wake the people."[11] Running from the flames, the thugs aimed an "andiron at [one of] the victim's head[s]," clipping him in the shoulder and dropping the man to the floor. "One of the Patients with a Child at her Breast was driven to the Smoke-House fainting several times as she went. And others were turned out, cold as it was, with scarcely any thing to cover them."[12] Miraculously, none of the patients died in the conflagration. The flames reduced the hospital to ashes, resulting in a £2,000 loss for the Patriot investors.

Obtaining a court order, the proprietors served a writ on two of the arsonists, and the deputy sheriff arrested and jailed the men in Salem. "Almost as soon as the keys were turned upon them," angry mobs assembled. "400 to 500 armed themselves with clubs, sticks of Wood, &c." The crowd stormed the jail "and burst open the doors . . . with Iron Crowbars, Axes, &c they soon beat their Way through four of Prison-Doors, each of which was very strong, and well secured with many large Locks." In less than ten minutes, the throng freed the two men, carrying off the two prisoners in "Triumph, and went to Marblehead where they soon dispersed."[13]

At midnight, the mob descended upon John Glover's home. Forewarned, Glover had transformed his house into a fortress and placed two loaded cannon in the foyer behind the front door. When the masses arrived, Glover threw open the front door and appeared with torch in hand. The primed cannon by his side, Glover readied to ignite the touch-hole of each piece of ordnance. With steely determination, the stout, diminutive merchant "commanded the mob, in his military style, to halt, or they were dead men."[14] Glover stood his ground; the rabble dispersed.

The turnabout of events and the erosion of the Patriots' influence in Marblehead delighted Hooper and the town's Loyalists. But the law in Salem did not forget the incident and the destruction of their jail. Within a day, the sheriff organized a posse of scores of armed men to march toward Marblehead to seize the prisoners and those who had destroyed the jail. Six hundred to eight hundred Marbleheaders assembled to oppose them and "were determined to repel, to the last extremity, any force that should be brought against them."[15] Glover, Orne, and Gerry emerged to defuse the situation. The Patriots agreed to drop the charges against the men, "demands [a potential civil lawsuit] they might have on the county or sheriff,"[16] and claims for damages to the hospital.

Gerry and the other proprietors of the hospital had their homes surrounded and their lives threatened. The loss of property and unexpected violence rattled Gerry. The event had a profound impact on his psyche for the rest of his life. Citizens could be as tyrannical as despots—the tide turned and when the crowd attacked the very people who supported them, the Whigs were stunned and disgusted. Gerry wrote to his mentor Sam Adams for advice on dealing with the throng. Adams sagely responded, "The tumult of the people is very properly compared to the raging of the sea. When the passions of the multitude become headstrong, they generally will have their course: a direct opposition only tends to increase them; and as to reasoning, one may as well expect that the foaming billows will hearken to a lecture of morality and be quiet. The skilful pilot will carefully keep the helm, as to prevent, if possible, her receiving injury."[17]

A priority of any government should be the protection of its citizens. Gerry, Glover, and Lee found their lives threatened by an ungoverned throng and awkwardly and desperately asked Royal governor Thomas Hutchinson for protection—none was offered. The event fractured the Whig coalition. In the wake of the riots, John's brother, Jonathan, even pledged his allegiance to the Crown, and signed a letter praising Hutchinson. Glover, Orne, and Gerry withdrew from the Marblehead

Committee of Correspondence, despite pleas from Samuel Adams. The Loyalists now controlled Marblehead politics, setting back the Whigs' cause in Marblehead. In his resignation letter, Gerry described the mob: "We should probably have continued in ye same Pursuit until Time has determined ye event of our Struggles; had not ye later prevalent disorders put an End in this place to all order and Distinction & rendered public Officers of every degree obnoxious to ye Controul of a savage Mobility."[18]

But threats to his life were not the primary factor in his withdrawal from politics. "When faced with the choice of remaining with Marblehead's Committee of Correspondence—an extralegal body from the British point of view and one containing possible seeds of American independence . . . He resigned. In doing so, he demonstrated that in his mind republicanism was more important than any thoughts of an emerging Americanism,"[19] according to one of Gerry's biographers. Gerry's absence from politics would not last long. He resumed his role on the Committee of Correspondence in June and was elected to the Massachusetts Provincial Congress just in time for a series of events that would shape history.

CHAPTER 5

BOSTON PORT ACT

May 13, 1774, Boston Harbor

General Thomas Gage stepped off the HMS *Lively* onto the wharf at Boston. Having returned to England the previous year, he and his family were in London when the colonists hurled tea in the harbor the previous December. Gage returned to become the new military governor of the Province of Massachusetts Bay.

The second son of an English nobleman, Gage had married American Margaret Kemble. A great beauty and the social equal of her husband as the daughter of a wealthy businessman and a descendant of the illustrious Schuyler family, Margaret had well-known sympathies for the colonists. In 1775 she told one gentleman that "she hoped her husband would never be the instrument of sacrificing the lives of her countrymen," and she is strongly suspected of eventually providing life-saving intelligence to the Patriots.[1] During the general's assignment in Boston, the Gages and their eleven children did not reside in the city but instead were hosted in good friend King Hooper's summer home—an elegant three-story Georgian mansion called The Lindens* in the town of Danvers, closer to Marblehead than to Boston.

---

* The Lindens is now the oldest house in Washington, DC, and located near an estate owned by former president Barack Obama on Kalorama Road. During the height of the Depression, George Morris purchased Hooper's home for $10,000 and shipped its pieces in six train cars. Architects painstakingly reassembled the mansion in Washington.

In the aftermath of the Boston Tea Party, Parliament had deemed the well-liked fifty-five-year-old general who had served with George Washington during the French and Indian War to be the best replacement for the unpopular Thomas Hutchinson, who had been recalled to London. The British general's unenviable task would be to implement the series of bills passed in March 1774 that were so extreme in their scope the colonists labeled them the "Intolerable Acts"; London called them the Coercive Laws. Designed to punish the Tea Party and bring Massachusetts into line, the new laws abrogated the charter of Massachusetts, banned most town meetings, formed a new court system, shut down Boston Harbor, and allowed Americans to be tried for crimes in London.

Bells tolled on June 1, 1774—a day the colonists had designated as one of fasting and prayer throughout the colonies, as a sign of defiance and resistance—when General Gage executed the terms of one of the most egregious of the Intolerable Acts: the Boston Port Act. He closed Boston Harbor, stationing warships to block all traffic in and out of the port, throwing thousands out of work, and starving the city both literally and economically until the citizens of Boston could pay for the tea cargo destroyed in the rebels' protest. Later that month, he further dissolved the local government under the authority of the Massachusetts Government Act, eliminating citizens' autonomy, and made himself a virtual dictator. The Justice Act attacking their right to a fair trial, and the Quartering Act, forcing them to house British soldiers, rounded out the hated pieces of legislation.

In instituting the Intolerable Acts, Gage misread the Americans. He advised Parliament that isolating the radicals would squelch the fire of their rebellion. "America is a mere bully, from one end to the other, and the Bostonians by far the greatest bullies," he wrote. On the other hand, as an Englishman, his deep respect for English law led some to criticize the governor as too lenient in his treatment of the colonists. As Lord Percy wrote, "The general's great lenity and moderation serve only to make them [the colonists] more daring and insolent."[2] Months later, Edmund Burke observed in his address to Parliament, "In this character of the Americans, a love of freedom is the predominating feature which marks and distinguishes the whole. . . . This fierce spirit of liberty is stronger in the English colonies probably than in any of the people of the earth. . . . The temper and character which prevail in our Colonies are, I am afraid unalterable by any human art. We cannot, I fear falsify the pedigree of this fierce people and persuade them that they are not sprung from a nation in whose veins the blood of freedom circulates. . . . An Englishman is the unfittest person on earth to argue another Englishman into slavery."[3]

Instead of isolating the radicals as the British hoped, the Intolerable Acts increased sympathy for Boston. Support for the city began to unify the colonies as nothing yet had—if the Crown could disenfranchise Massachusetts, none of the colonies were safe. One provision of the punitive Boston Port Act, now largely forgotten, had an enormous potential impact on seaside Marblehead. The act designated Marblehead the primary port of entry for all North American trade by transferring the customs house from Boston to Marblehead for an indefinite period of time until British officials judged Boston safe from rebels. Loyalist diarist Ashley Bowen recalled the atmosphere: "There were soldiers planted here in guard boats. . . . Our streets were filled with strange faces and Boston full of British troops. Sad Times! JCA [Jesus Christ Almighty]."[4]

This unexpected turn of events forced the citizens of Marblehead to choose between their own immediate prosperity and the common cause of liberty. The citizens of Marblehead rose to the challenge, refusing to profit from the misfortunes of their fellow men. They maintained the embargo on British goods and threw their support behind the city by signing the nonimportation agreement regarding goods from Britain that the citizens of Boston requested. This unifying sympathy for the plight of the colonial rebels in Boston catapulted the Whig leaders, Elbridge Gerry, Azor Orne, John Glover, and Jeremiah Lee, back to the forefront of Marblehead politics and neutralized the power of the Loyalists, silencing some of their voices by labeling them traitors and refusing to do business with them. Salem diarist Doctor William

Bentley noted the enormous power the men[5] wielded: "These three men gave a character to Marblehead in the last generation or for the last thirty years. . . . The leading men had power nowhere else known in N. England."[6]

Political revolution that flowed from Boston and Marblehead became the zeitgeist; and a majority of colonists in New England supported it.

Twenty-eight Marblehead merchants went above and beyond, signing the nonimportation resolution and offering their wharves and storehouses: "We hereby offer to our oppressed, but much respected brethren of Boston . . . the free use of our stores in this town. . . . We likewise assure them of our readiness in seeing to the lading and unlading of their goods in this town, . . . showing how much we sympathize with and respect them. . . . And [we] hope soon to see them relieved from their distress, and the liberties of America founded on a permanent basis by an indissoluble Union."[7] One historian noted, "The inhabitants of Marblehead tendered the use of their wharves to the Bostonians, one of their number, Elbridge Gerry, the future Vice President, saying that the resentment of an arbitrary ministry would prove a diadem of honor to the oppressed town."[8] Driven by his sympathy for the Bostonians, the urging of his mentor and friend Samuel Adams, and his ever-present fear of uncontrolled centralized power, Gerry devoted himself to the business of distributing the food, supplies, and other goods for the support of the unemployed people of Boston that poured into Marblehead from across the colonies. Across Massachusetts, the rebellious colonists continued to hold town meetings, despite Gage's explicit prohibitions: "Whereas by a late Act of Parliament, all Town-Meetings called without the consent of the Governor . . . are illegal, I do hereby strictly prohibit all Persons from attending . . . any Meeting not warned by law, as they will be chargeable with all the ill Consequences that may follow thereon, and answer the same at their utmost Peril."[9]

In reaction to their refusal to obey, Gage made a show of force at one Salem meeting in August. Gage assembled troops outside and simultaneously summoned the Patriot leaders to his office in Salem at the time of the meeting. When they admitted to organizing the meeting, he detained them, only to be embarrassed the next day when "upwards of three thousand [armed] men assembled there from adjacent towns, with full determination to rescue the Committee if they should be sent to prison," warning the governor that "'if he committed them he [Gage] must abide by the consequences'—for they would not be answerable for what might take place."[10] To back up his proclamations, Gage stationed a regiment of British troops in Salem Neck and Marblehead. The presence of troops caused constant friction. One zealous Redcoat bayoneted and wounded Marblehead captain John Merritt,[11] which caused an immediate outcry from the Americans. Only a swift trial and punishment of the soldier temporarily quelled the unrest.

Gage's actions and the incident further emboldened the Americans. "The towns through the country are so far from being intimidated, that a day in the week does not pass without one or more having meetings, in direct contempt of the Act; which they regard as a blank piece of paper and not more," wrote Boston merchant John Andrews. "They had one directly under his nose at Danvers, and continued it two or three howers longer than was necessary, to see if he [Gage] would interrupt 'em. He was acquainted with it, but reply'd—'Damn 'em! I won't do any thing about it unless his Majesty sends me more troops.'"[12]

CHAPTER 6

GUNPOWDER

"On Courage I know we have in abundance, conduct I hope we shall not want, but powder—where shall we get a sufficient supply?" John Adams wrote in a letter to his wife, Abigail.[1] In every mythic quest, the hero must search for some elusive artifact essential to accomplishing the mission. For the American revolutionaries, that Holy Grail was gunpowder.

On the eve of the Revolution, most colonists had guns. Many used firearms to hunt for food, and many had weapons left over from the French and Indian War. However, gunpowder to fire those weapons was extremely scarce. The Patriot leaders realized their predicament early on as the political revolution rapidly moved closer to armed rebellion. Powder enabled or curtailed success on the battlefield. Without it, any revolution would find itself crushed before it began. Adams summed up the desperate search: "Every Thing, has been done, and is now doing, to procure the *Unum Necessarium*," the one necessity.[2]

The first person to discover gunpowder was actually searching for something much different. In China around AD 850, an alchemist whose name has been lost to history was mixing together various elixirs with the hope of finding ways to extend life or create gold. Accidentally, he created the *huo yao*, the "fire drug." A book first printed in 850 titled *Classified Essentials of the Mysterious Tao of the True Origin of Things* warned of gunpowder's lethality: "Some have heated together sulfur, realgar and saltpeter with honey; smoke and flames result, so that their hands and faces have been burnt, and even the whole house where they were working burned down."[3] It did not take long for these early experimenters to find a use for the powder. Artisans soon began staging spectacular shows to impress the emperor. "Suddenly a noise like thunder *phi li* was heard, and the setting off of *pao chang* (*firecrackers*), and then the fireworks (*yen huo*) began," described the centuries-old tome *Dreams of the Glories of the Eastern Capital*.[4]

Soon the Chinese adapted the knowledge gained from creating these elaborate displays to the creation of implements of war. Gunpowder-propelled arrows and the first explosive bombs soon appeared on the battlefield wielded by Chinese armies who laid their enemies low. Rockets, flamethrowers, and fire lances followed. The Chin dynasty later packed bamboo with the fire drug and added projectiles, creating the earliest antecedent of the modern gun.

But creating gunpowder was far from easy. Mixing the gunpowder ingredients was an art form and often proved perilous. A single spark had the potential to blow up its creators or an entire house. In addition, not only was the process dangerous, but finding one of the ingredients was incredibly challenging.

Gunpowder is the mixture of three major components: sulfur, charcoal, and the most elusive and difficult to produce, potassium nitrate, or saltpeter. Also called "salt of stones," potassium nitrate forms naturally in privies, old bat guano in caves, and manure piles. But finding these hidden treasures required large gangs of people hunting for it. And in the early years, alchemists extracted the nitrates in various ways, but the time-consuming process was uneven and laborious.

It was not until the fourteenth century that craftsmen figured out a way to develop saltpeter artificially. In a truly foul process, they combined dung piles with urine-laden soil and boiled them together. Half a year later, the process resulted in saltpeter.

In the open, gunpowder burns quickly, but in a contained space, it explodes. The saltpeter furnishes oxygen needed for rapid combustion, and the remaining charcoal and sulfur then burn, resulting in a flash. In a gun barrel or cannon, the confined gas pressure of the explosion builds and releases, thrusting a bullet or cannonball down the barrel, the path of least resistance.

Just how gunpowder and early guns arrived in Europe is unknown; some speculate that they traveled on the Silk Road, and others theorize that the Mongols brought the technology with them during their European conquest. The first-known printed references to powder in Europe occur in friar-scientist Roger Bacon's *Opus Majus*, which was published in AD 1267.

What the Chinese had invented, the Europeans soon perfected, increasing the potency of both the powder and the weapons that utilized it. They developed a surefire recipe: 75 percent saltpeter, 15 percent charcoal, and 10 percent sulfur. They also found that converting corns or grains into powder by grinding them with a mortar and pestle and then moistening the powder rendered it vastly more potent.

While the Chinese had never been able to produce effective small arms, the Europeans were soon manufacturing lethal firearms light enough for a single person to carry. They developed and further enhanced firing mechanisms—first the matchlock, then the wheellock, and later the flintlock. They also discovered that rifling, or etching spiral grooves inside the barrel, greatly improved the accuracy of small arms.

No longer would the muscle and skill of highly trained knights determine potency of an army. Knights relied on swords, an extension of arm strength; now, firearms replaced the brawn needed to thrust a sword or draw a long bow. A common laborer, when armed with a gun, became a warrior. The ability to kill from a distance proved decisive.

Gunpowder cannons also rendered useless the ultimate defensive structure of the Middle Ages: the castle. Cannons firing iron or stone balls could demolish massive fortress walls, destroying in hours or days the citadels that had taken decades to construct. In 1453, gunpowder transformed the Middle East. Before the arrival of firearms, Constantinople's stout walls had fallen only once in 1,500 years. But the twenty-one-year-old Ottoman Sultan Mehmed the Conqueror commissioned Orban, a European engineer, to design a series of gargantuan siege guns, including a twenty-seven-foot super cannon that hurled a half-ton stone ball. Carted around by sixty oxen, the siege gun devoured gunpowder and could fire only seven times per day. Orban's artillery degraded the wall, and assault parties flooded through. History forever changed.

By the 1600s, Europe had mastered the creation of gunpowder, refined small arms and cannon, and developed oceangoing ships to transport the weapons. Once these elements melded together, unstoppable Europe unleashed its power and conquered much of the world.

In 1774, organic American production of gunpowder was virtually non-existent. The colonists had to produce powder domestically, import, or purloin it from Royal sources. While production of the explosive in the colonies in a Massachusetts mill dates to 1639, the Navigation Acts that controlled trade between Britain and the colonies discouraged industrial production in North America. American powder mills that had emerged during the French and Indian War were shuttered, replaced by cheap imports from the mother country and the rich supply of saltpeter from India. Britain imported two thousand tons a year from India. By October 1774, Royal decrees forbade export and import of powder and arms in the colonies, and there was practically no domestic production; the provincials found their supply chains at the mercy of Great Britain. Gunpowder was the lifeblood of any eighteenth-century army. With virtually no production of powder in North America, the revolutionaries would quickly have to find a way to boost manufacturing of the munitions, or else import or purloin the precious stuff.

Meanwhile, Britain had a nearly inexhaustible supply of the raw materials necessary for gunpowder, as well as a stranglehold on commerce that left the colonies at its mercy. Each pound of black powder contained about seven thousand grains, or enough for a single shot from each of forty-eight muskets. Cannon were powder hogs: an 18-pounder gun required six or seven pounds, and a 32-pounder, eleven or twelve pounds of the explosive substance for each shot.[5] To store powder, manufacturers packed it in one-hundred-pound oak barrels with non-sparking copper hoops or in fifty-pound half barrels.

Time was not on the colonists' side. Time also proved to be a major bottleneck; potassium nitrate requires half a year to form. The Patriot leaders simply could not afford to wait that long to have the means to defend themselves. And creating an efficient saltpeter factory required expertise the colonists did not have. One American columnist noted, "Several attempts of this kind have miscarried."[6] By 1775, newspapers and pamphlets printed tips on making powder. However, homegrown saltpeter gardens produced uneven results and, in some cases, poor-quality munitions.* The scarcity of gunpowder even caused Benjamin Franklin to suggest bringing back bows and arrows.[7]

The British were well aware of the scarcity of gunpowder in the colonies as Gage wrote Lord Dartmouth in August 1774, "[I'm planning] a series of missions against the arsenals and powderhouses of New England, designed to remove as many munitions as possible—enough to make it impossible for the people of the region to make a determined stand."[8]

---

* In the coming years, the Americans would find the answer to their gunpowder supply problems in France. The French had developed the most powerful powder in the world, and within three years French powder was the main source of ammunition for the rebels, crucial to the Revolution.

CHAPTER 7

ARMS RACE AND A FLEDGLING GOVERNMENT

In the predawn darkness of September 1, 1774, some 260 handpicked men disembarked from longboats on the rocky beach of Ten Hills Farm. The Redcoats marched in column to their objective: the powder magazine, formerly a windmill, on Quarry Hill in Middlesex County, present-day Somerville, Massachusetts. When the red column reached the stone-siloed structure, the county sheriff, David Phips, handed Lieutenant Colonel George Maddison the keys to the black wrought-iron gate of the magazine. Quickly, the soldiers seized the 250 fifty-pound half barrels of powder and gingerly transported them out of the structure and back to the boats. As the bulk of the party removed the powder, Maddison split part of his force to seize two of the province's field pieces. Within a few hours, it was over; under General Thomas Gage's orders, Maddison had executed the perfect raid. He and his men returned to their British bastion in Boston, Castle William, and unloaded the powder. Although it was technically within his authority to remove the king's powder, Gage's actions triggered significant unintended consequences.

Gage and British military planners recognized how crucial gunpowder was to the rebels, and aimed to seize it to disarm them. In 1774, Great Britain had the mightiest navy and world's strongest empire. Without powder and weapons, any revolution that turned into an armed conflict could be crushed by the empire's superb army—just as it had defeated all insurrections and insurgencies in its long history.

A little more than a month after the raid, the Crown advised its colonial governors to "take the most effectual measures to arresting, detaining and securing any Gunpowder, or any sort of Arms or Ammunitions which may be attempted to be imported into the province."[1] It also banned the importation of powder and weapons. As a result, the colonists would scour the earth for powder, and especially saltpeter, to replenish their stores. The Marblehead men and their contacts in the Caribbean and Spain would prove indispensable to this effort of obtaining and smuggling powder back to North America in the coming months.

Hours after the Maddison raid, the provincials discovered their priceless powder missing. Church bells rang out, and fire beacons last used during the French and Indian War burned brightly. The countryside was alarmed for war. The alert carried with it a rumor that spread like wildfire: six Americans had been killed. Colonists believed another Boston Massacre had occurred.

"[I] never saw such a scene before—all along [the road to Boston] were armed Men rushing forward some on foot some on horseback, at every house Women and Children making Cartridges, running Bullets, making Wallets,* baking Biscuit, crying and bemoaning and at the same time animating their Husbands and sons to fight for their Liberties, tho' not knowing whether they should ever see them again."[2] Thousands descended upon Cambridge Common, many armed and possessing "a Spirit for revenging the Blood of their Brethren & rescue [their] liberties."[3] Numbering over four thousand,[4] militias and groups from all over New England arrived in Cambridge, including many Marbleheaders. One band, led by Marblehead captain Gilbert Warner Speakman, raced to Boston: "The powder's being remov'd, last Thursday night, yet they were down to Cambridge [thirty miles away] by eight o'clock Fryday morning, with a troop of horse and another on foot, both under the command of Gib.[ert Warner] Speakman."[5]

---

* A wallet was a long, narrow sack used to carry items and slung over the shoulder, much like a knapsack.

Disdain for the latest acts of Parliament, seizure of the powder, and reported deaths of Americans enraged the mob. Americans demanded change; they sought the resignation of several officials. In their cross-hairs were Judges Joseph Lee and Samuel Danforth; Sheriff David Phips, who handed over the keys to the powder magazine; Lieutenant Governor Thomas Oliver; and William Brattle, who sent a letter to Gage informing him the storehouse contained Massachusetts's gunpowder. At the courthouse, Judges Lee and Danforth resigned. Brattle fled to the safety of Gage's troops garrisoned at Castle William. After the throng surrounded his house, Oliver surrendered his new position as commissioner but was advised to remain as lieutenant governor out of fear of whom Gage might appoint in his place. The mob preferred the devil they knew.

Fearing violence, Doctor Joseph Warren emerged from the shadows of the resistance and made his way to Cambridge along with other members of the Boston Committee of Correspondence. Dashing, handsome, and a brilliant orator with a magnetic personality, Warren mounted the courthouse steps and addressed the crowd, appealing for calm. He got it. "They were dress'd just as they are at work—every man appeared just as composed as if they were at a funeral," recalled one participant.[6] Charismatic, adventurous, and with a flair for the dramatic, the Boston physician was a Renaissance man who dabbled in a variety of activities, from performing Cato in his Harvard dorm to training in the local militia. The account of the death of six Americans was a hoax. No blood had been shed, Warren assured the crowd. Remarkably, the committee's William Cooper also addressed the crowd and said the powder was old and Gage had a right to take it, until another committee member "tugged on Cooper's sleeve and told keep quiet." The men put an end to the dispute when members of the committee of correspondence also voted to approve a proposition: "They abhorred and detested all petty Mobs, Riots, Breaking Windows and destroying private Property."[7] "There was an awful stillness, silence thro' the Lines and among the body of people,"[8] recalled one participant. Negotiations with the committee were relayed to the crowd, "read publickly at proper Distances till the whole Body of the people were made clear of it."[9] Gage wisely did not dispatch troops to Cambridge. Aghast at the crowds, he noted, "The whole country was in Arms, and in Motion, and numerous Bodies of the Connecticut People had made some Marches before the Report was contradicted."[10] The day nearly ended uneventfully until despised customs commissioner Benjamin Hallowell passed by the crowd in an opulent chaise. "Dam you, how do you like us now, you Tory son of a bitch!"[11] someone yelled. Hallowell sped away, fearing for his life. Scores of horsemen from the throng pursued, and several members of the committee got on their horses and tried to stop the men hunting Hallowell. Violence would ruin the message of their peaceful protests. Eventually, only one man caught up with the customs official. As the horse pulling his chaise stumbled, Hallowell flashed his pistols at his pursuer, mounted his servant's horse, and galloped toward the safety of Gage's troops.

As the afternoon wore on, the azure sky became overcast and tempers waned. In true eighteenth-century fashion, "the Gentlemen from Boston, Charleston, and Cambridge" offered refreshments "for their greatly fatigued Brethren, they cheerfully accepted it, took leave and departed, in high good humour and well satisfied," newspapers reported.[12] By 5:00 p.m., a thunderstorm swept the area and drove the crowd away.

The event would be called the "powder alarm," and in its wake Gage began efforts to call in reinforcements from New York and Quebec and urged his superiors in London to send a staggering twenty thousand additional troops. Revealing his readiness to jettison any lingering qualms about the colonists' rights, Gage wrote, "Nothing that is said at present can palliate; conciliating, moderation, reasoning, is over; nothing can be done but by forcible means."[13] In another missive, he continued, "Tho the people are not held up in high estimation by the troops, yet are numerous, worked up to a fury, and not a Boston rabble but freeholders and farmers of the country. People are daily resorting to this town [Boston] for protection, for there is no security to any person deemed a friend of the [British] government in any part of the country. Even places always esteemed well affected have caught the infection and sedition flows copiously from the pulpits."[14] The political revolution raging in Massachusetts manifested in the enormous crowds—representing the start of a large segment of the population's seizing control of their political destiny. The crowd played a role in the negotiations but trusted its leaders as the powder alarm tilted a political revolution toward military conflict.

After the event, Gage advocated for using overwhelming force to crush the rebellion. "Resistance should be effectual at the Beginning. If you think ten Thousand Men sufficient, send Twenty, if one million (pounds) is thought enough, give two; it will save both Blood and Treasure in the End. A large force will terrify, and engage many to join you, a middling one will encourage Resistance and gain no friends."[15]

Months would pass, as transatlantic communication required a three-to-four-month voyage plus time for the absorption of the message and generation of a response. London promised Gage a pittance of what he requested. Vastly outnumbered and desperate to buy time for more reinforcements, Gage strengthened his defenses in Boston. The powder alarm set in motion an arms race between both sides; the political revolution veered toward military action as the colonists began to take up arms to defend themselves. Gage realized surgical strikes to remove powder and ordnance might ignite the flame of war, but they also might be the best way to squelch that flame.

The timing of the raid and its blowback could not have been worse from Gage's perspective. Responding to the spiraling crisis in Boston, delegates from the American colonies met in Philadelphia for the First Continental Congress. Until dispelled, the rumor of the death of six Americans in the powder raid dominated the meetings.

Organized in 1774 in Philadelphia at the urging of Benjamin Franklin, the First Continental Congress included representatives from twelve of the thirteen colonies (Georgia did not initially participate for fear of losing British protection against hostile Indians among other issues). The Congress unanimously voiced complaints regarding the treatment of citizens by Parliament and their advocacy for a voice in their fates. Congress had never been more united; the Crown's tyranny in Boston could happen to any of them. On October 20, 1774, via the Articles of Association, a nonimportation and nonexportation agreement, Congress declared a boycott on British goods and agreed not to export goods to Britain, Ireland, or other British colonies if the Intolerable Acts were not repealed. The act would take effect on December 1, 1774. Within Marblehead, and other towns in the colonies, the Whigs soon established committees of inspection to enforce the economic rules of the Articles of Association. John Glover led the committee in Marblehead.

The articles also discontinued the slave trade, which Great Britain dominated. Article Two stated: "We will neither import nor purchase, any slave imported after the first day of December next, after which time, we will wholly discontinue the slave trade, and will neither be concerned in it ourselves, nor will we hire our vessels, nor sell our commodities or manufacturers to those who were concerned in it."[16] These are hardly words of individuals fighting to expand and further the institution of slavery. In fact, the heart of the political revolution, Massachusetts, was a hotbed of abolition. In January 1774, Massachusetts passed a similar resolution to Article Two, but Governor Thomas Hutchinson refused to sign it. Fierce opposition to slavery came from New England pulpits. Deacon Benjamin Colman wrote in the *Essex Journal* on July 20, 1774, "Can we lift our faces with confidence before God, by solemn prayer, that he would remove the yoke of bondage from us and set us at liberty from the bondage that lays upon us, while we keep a tenfold heavier yoke on the necks of our brethren, the negroes." Reverend Nathaniel Niles proclaimed in a sermon, "For shame, let us cease to enslave our fellow men, or else let us cease to complain of those that would enslave us. Let us either wash our hands from blood or never hope to escape the avenger."[17] These abolitionists and Marbleheaders such as Elbridge Gerry and Joshua Orne believed America's freedom was coupled with the freedom of enslaved African Americans.

The articles boldly struck at the heart of British trade: the Continental Congress had declared economic war on their imperial rulers, so heavily dependent on the North American economy. In 1774, America boasted one of the highest standards of living in the world. Two-thirds of the white population owned land, in contrast to only one-fifth of their fellow brethren in Britain. Additionally, Americans had one of the highest literacy rates in the world; two-thirds of them could read and write.[18] The American population, about two and a half million, doubled every twenty-five years, combined with explosive economic growth.

Congress also adopted the Suffolk Resolves drafted by Joseph Warren. In September, representatives from Suffolk County, Massachusetts, gathered and drafted a response to the Intolerable Acts, declaring them illegal and a violation of the Massachusetts Charter, and urged the people to form their own government and sanction Britain economically. The resolves proclaimed, among other things, "The most sacred Obligations are upon us to transmit the glorious Purchase, unfettered by Power, unclogg'd with Shackles, to our innocent and beloved Offspring. On the Fortitude—on the Wisdom and on the Exertions of this important Day, it suspended the Fate of this New World, and of unborn Millions.—If a boundless Extent of Continent, swarming with Millions, will tamely submit to live, move and have their Being at the arbitrary Will of a licentious Minister, they basely yield to voluntary Slavery, and future Generations shall load their Memories with incessant Execrations."[19]

To combat the growing rebellion, in October, Governor Gage enforced what was known as the Massachusetts Government Act and dissolved the provincial assembly. Patriot leaders, including Warren, John Hancock, Jeremiah Lee, Gerry, and Orne, met anyway on October 5 in the Salem courthouse. Over the course of several days, they boldly elected representatives and set up an alternative government: the Massachusetts Provincial Congress.

On the chilly afternoon of November 8, thirteen men met secretly at Captain Ebenezer Stedman's house in Cambridge. The powder alarm transformed the Patriots' political revolution into a weapons and powder race, a military insurgency, and, ultimately, a civil war. The leadership of the Patriot movement in the room that night, John Hancock, Doctor

Joseph Warren, and Jeremiah Lee, all agreed: "Voted, unanimously, by the committee of safety, that the committee of supplies be advised to procure all the arms and ammunition they can, at the neighboring provinces on the continent; and, that it is recommended, that the committee of supplies do, and may with safety, engage to pay for the same, on the arrival here of said arms and ammunition."[20]

The Massachusetts Provincial Congress had taken its first step toward organizing its own military, separate from the forces of Great Britain, on October 26 with the establishment of the Committee of Safety and the Committee of Supplies.

Colonel Azor Orne served on the Committee of Safety, the most powerful executive arm of the Massachusetts Provincial Congress, which had the authority to call up the militia and provide for the defense and safety of the colony. Marbleheaders were at the very heart of the decision-making process of the new government, testifying to Marblehead's importance as a hotbed of Patriot politics and making the town a potential military target.

The Committee of Supplies was responsible for arming and supplying the Massachusetts militia and prepared the way for an Army of Observation and other efforts essential to running the extralegal Massachusetts Provincial Congress. Marbleheaders Lee and Gerry leveraged their fortunes, relationships, and trade contacts into military supply lines for the colonists. The provincial government had no money. Congress would rely on credit and take over the Crown's tax functions within the colony, and at times, Gerry, Lee, and Orne dipped into their personal funds.

The Marbleheaders made an enormous contribution to the colony's supply needs—especially its thirst for powder. Lee had forty-five ships and assets valued at over £24,000, making him one of the wealthiest men in the colonies.[21] The Marbleheader channeled those assets to support the Patriot cause. Gerry also employed his large fleet and money to supply the effort, but both men had something perhaps more valuable—relationships. These priceless overseas connections and the ability to purchase military supplies, guns, gunpowder, and commodities such as salt would prove crucial to the Revolution.

Lee and Gerry's most important contacts were with the mega-trading house owned by the Gardoqui family, José Gardoqui and his three sons. The Marbleheaders traded with the Bilbao-based Basque merchants for decades—they named their ships, such as the *Gardoqui*, in their honor and maintained friendships with the patriarch and his sons, including Diego, Spain's future ambassador to what would become the United States. Marbleheaders previously exchanged fish for fruit, salt, and other commodities, and now sought military supplies, weapons, and gunpowder. Spain did not openly trade with the colonies for fear of war with Britain, but it turned a blind eye to trading with individuals with whom it enjoyed trusted, existing business relationships and friendships, such as the ones Lee and Gerry fostered.

In December, Lee wrote to José asking "to procure as many muskets & pistols as can be made ready." Fittingly, Michael Corbett, who hurled the harpoon killing the British officer on the *Pitt Packet*, delivered the letter personally to the family patriarch. The Spaniards delivered the goods and loaded Corbett's ship with "300 Muskets & Bayonets, & about double the number of pair of pistols."[22] These Spanish weapons would arm the Marblehead Regiment.

José pledged his family's support: "[We] are determined at all events to assist you accordingly. We see with the utmost concern the difficulties You labor under." Gardoquis also offered intelligence to the Marbleheaders: "We hourly look out for the London Post, should it bring anything Worth notice, you may depend on being advised."[23]

The Gardoquis were enormously influential and had the king of Spain's ear. Gerry and Lee recognized the importance of this relationship.

These international associations, fostered by the Marbleheaders, also played a crucial role in alliance building. Gerry was one of the first American leaders to promote alliances publicly, "but if foreign force is employed against us, we may be greatly puzzled, unless we endeavor at the same thing, especially by our wants of military stores."[24] In the coming months and years, the Spanish government secretly and nearly exclusively channeled military supplies through the Gardoquis to Gerry.[25] Ultimately, the relationship with the Basque trading house contributed greatly to a blossoming alliance with Spain.*

Each committee had multiple objectives. In addition to organizing and arming local militia and stockpiling military supplies and weaponry, the committees aimed to track and suppress any activities by Loyalists. Ironically, the government established by a cause devoted to freedom and liberty adopted wide-reaching, draconian powers to quash their political enemies. As one team of historians explains, "These committees assumed police, legislative, and judicial powers in all matters pertaining to political conduct—and in those times, nearly everything *did* pertain to politics, not only what people said, but what they produced or consumed. Committees wielded a potent weapon: the threat of social and commercial ostracism at the hands of a populace that did not easily forgive transgressions."[26] The possibility of open civil war drew closer.

Some of the most important decisions of the early Patriot movement flowed from these committees that included Marblehead's leading families and Benjamin Church. Sarcastic and haughty, Church, a forty-year-old physician and colleague of Joseph Warren and Nathaniel Bond, participated in these crucial meetings. Seemingly a firebrand Son of Liberty, based on his speeches and what flowed from his pen, Church cloaked a darker side and worked for another cause. On January 29, 1772, Governor Thomas Hutchinson wrote, "The faction seems to be breaking, the Doctor Church . . . is now a writer on the side of Government."[27] Hutchinson indicated that the Crown paid Church handsomely to write anonymous articles. Beneath his patriotic ardor and arrogance lurked a heavily indebted opportunist who craved wealth. Church sought to align himself with the winning side: he was Gage's most well-placed spy—directly in the middle of the Patriot nerve center. But the good doctor also had a connection to Marblehead—his mistress, Mary Wenwood.

---

* Marblehead relationships played an enormous role in America's alliance with Spain and the arms, powder, and materiel that flowed from the Iberian country. Don Diego Gardoqui later became Spain's ambassador to the United States.

CHAPTER 8

THE MARBLEHEAD REGIMENT

"The madmen of Marblehead are preparing for an early campaign against his Majesty's troops,"[1] scoffed a Loyalist newspaper earlier in 1774, skeptical of the idea that Americans could threaten the most experienced and skillful military professionals on the planet at the time.

The Massachusetts Provincial Congress directed towns in the region to organize companies of minutemen, troops who could be ready at a moment's notice to defend the safety of their neighbors. Each company was to have a minimum of fifty privates and several officers and noncommissioned officers, at least a quarter of whom should be on call at any given time. Congress further instructed that "each of the Minute Men not already provided therewith, should be immediately equipped with an effective Fire Arm, Bayonet, Pouch, Knapsack, Thirty Rounds of Cartridges and Ball, and that they be disciplined three Times a Week, and oftener as Opportunity may offer."[2] Those not furnished with bayonets outfitted themselves with a "useful and efficacious weapon": the tomahawk.[3] Gunpowder remained precious and the most elusive of all the supplies.

Massachusetts militia companies typically included three separate groups: the training band, the alarm list, and the minutemen. Towns expected all able-bodied men between the ages of sixteen and seventy to serve in the training band, which drilled on a regular basis. Those on the alarm list stood ready to serve in case of emergency. About a quarter of those on the training band could be called to duty on short notice at any given time—these were the minutemen.[4]

Far more prepared than most of the neighboring towns, Marblehead already had an active militia. In October 1774, they drilled "three or four times a week, when Col. Lee as well as the Clergymen there are not asham'd to appear in the ranks, to be taught the manual exercise, in particular."[5] The Marbleheaders hired a tutor in military history, "a fencing master taught them the use of the small and broad sword," and a former British Army sergeant taught them the finer arts of war.[6]

Technology drove tactics and determined how the men drilled. Because muskets were so inaccurate, the Marbleheaders drilled laying down concentrated fire in large numbers. In battle, soldiers of the time lined up in rows, three ranks deep, and fired en masse; therefore, everyone in the front ranks who had a clear line of sight to the opposing side pulled his trigger at the same time. This massed fire improved the odds of hitting the enemy.

As formidable as they would appear, most of these volleys were not very successful. "It was just possible for a good marksman to hit a man at 100 yards; a volley could be fired with some chance of obtaining hits on a mass of troops at two hundred yards; but at three hundred yards fire was completely ineffective."[7] One trial in France showed just how inaccurately muskets performed: 60 percent hit the target at 82 yards, 40 percent hit at 164 yards, and a mere 23 percent at 300 yards. An observer wrote, "Powder is not as terrible as believed. Few men in these affairs are killed from in front while fighting. I have seen whole salvoes fail to kill four men."[8] The reality is that parade ground trials did not translate into battlefield actuality: men had adrenaline surging, smoke obscured lines of sight, misfires occurred with regularity (sometimes as high as 25 percent), and often the enemy was barreling down with fixed bayonets. In the chaos, men sometimes broke from fear, and even a well-trained soldier could not get off as many well-aimed shots in combat as in a trial setting.

Loading a musket involved several practiced steps. Marbleheaders carried cartridge boxes that held twelve to thirty-six prepared cartridges. The cartridges were tubes of paper with the same diameter as the musket bore. Each contained a ball and a premeasured amount of black powder, and they were crimped on the end. To fire, the soldier would pull out a cartridge, rip off the top of the paper with his teeth, pour a small amount of powder into the priming pan, pour the rest of the powder into the musket barrel, and then insert the ball and paper into the barrel and ram them down. Only then was the musket ready to fire. Under the best possible conditions, a well-trained and well-supplied soldier could load and shoot four or five times per minute. In the heat of battle, distracted by the smoke and sounds of conflict and with adrenaline surging through his veins, a soldier often forgot or skipped essential steps in the intricate process, which could lead to misfires that had deadly consequences.

The local paper, the *Essex Gazette*, reported that the militia held a field day early in October and "the military Spirit prevails greatly."[9] That led Loyalists to complain and object vociferously. But military preparedness was not the only purpose of the training. It also became a social event. After each drill, they typically swaggered en masse to a local tavern where "the Wine and Punch went round" as Patriot speakers passionately denounced the Crown.[10]

In reality, the Marblehead militia was far from ready to challenge the British forces. Complicating matters, many of the current militia officers had been appointed by Governor Thomas Gage or one of his predecessors and, therefore, presumably owed their loyalty to the Crown. In one of many public meetings in November, the town voted it "not expedient" for these officers to continue in their posts. To that end, the Patriots declared that the regiment would assemble to elect new officers who were "friend[s] of this country."[11] The Whigs set up a committee consisting of three members of each company and charged them with informing the officers of their removal.

The existing officers—and their Loyalist friends—objected strenuously. The town sent a second committee to notify them that, in the opinion of the majority of the local residents, they could "not hold or execute their commissions without hostile designs against the liberties of America."[12] Most resigned, albeit grudgingly, but a few doggedly refused.

This turn of events sent the town into an uproar. People flooded the town meetings, and they could not all fit into the usual building. After a series of rowdy and rancorous discussions, the local populace voted in favor of a resolution that advised the militiamen to disregard any orders issued by Loyalist officers; it forbade the officers from attempting to

muster the militia. That effectively left the officers without men to follow their command and ended the debate about leadership of the militia.
Far from pacified, however, many Loyalists in the town continued to
resist the measures passed by the Patriots of Marblehead.

To suppress this defiance and enforce the Continental Congress
resolution that prevented importation of British goods, the town established a committee of inspection, which included John Glover, "composed of fifteen patriotic citizens, whose zeal for the cause of their
country was a sufficient guaranty that the duty would be faithfully
performed."[13] Many of those chosen for this committee would also
become officers in what would later become known as the Marblehead
Regiment* or would play other essential roles in the Revolution.

The militia privates, whose ranks included many of the able-
bodied men in the town, initially formed seven companies (numbered 1
through 7), chose Colonel Jeremiah Lee as their new commander,
assisted by Colonel Azor Orne, Lieutenant Colonel John Glover, and
Major John Gerry, brother of Elbridge Gerry. The regimental staff,
Lee, Glover, Orne, and Gerry, mirrored the Whig leadership within
Marblehead. Status, wealth, experience, and leadership drove assignment
to the staff officer positions. With Lee and Orne as the titular heads of
the regiment, plucky, stocky John Glover, the most experienced officer,
actually played the leading role of commanding the men—a position
he would officially assume in the coming months.

Several other men would play major roles throughout the war. For
most of the Revolution, the second-in-command was Lieutenant Colonel
Gabriel Johonnot. Serving as adjutant was Caleb Gibbs, a twenty-six-year-
old Rhode Island native with a Roman nose, distinguished features, and
a commanding presence who had relocated to Marblehead.[14] An accomplished seaman, Gibbs had helped the Sons of Liberty smuggle goods into
Boston past the British blockade. Washington would later single him out

---

* At the time, the regiment fell under the militia, but in the spring of 1775, Congress
redesigned the unit as the 21st Regiment, and later the 14th Continental Regiment,
a.k.a. Glover's Regiment or the Marblehead Regiment.

for several important positions, and the two men became close friends. Doctor Nathaniel Bond also trained in the militia and would become the regimental surgeon and later command a company.[15]

The Marblehead Regiment was blessed with considerable talent. Natural leaders who spent their lives ordering men in extreme hardships, sea captains commanded many of the companies, as they were well practiced in making split-second, lifesaving decisions involving one of the most brutal forces of nature: the ocean. Many of the men they commanded were weathered from the sea and worked as a team on the cramped quarters of fishing schooners, where each man depended on the other: race was eclipsed by survival.

The Regiment would ultimately boast ten companies; each company typically incorporated a captain, a lieutenant, an ensign, several sergeants and corporals or noncommissioned officers, and roughly forty to fifty privates. Fluctuating in number over time, the regiment expanded and contracted based on enlistments and battle casualties, eventually topping five hundred. During 1774–1775, the variegated regiment contained almost entirely Marblehead residents. Based on later muster rolls, the soldiers in the regiment averaged twenty-three years of age and five feet five inches in height, and John Glover furnished the majority of their arms. The rolls recorded roughly a third as being "dark complexion," a third not labeled, and another third as "light complexion."[16]

The Marbleheaders were one of the first and most diverse regiments in the colonies and, later, the army. Their diversity would prove to be their strength as they would work together as a team to overcome seemingly impossible situations, unified by their belief in a cause greater than themselves. Others noted this strength. One contemporary observer later wrote, "The only exception I recollect to have seen, to these miserably constituted bands from New England, was the regiment of Glover from Marblehead. There was an appearance of discipline in this corps; the officers seemed to have mixed with the world, and to understand what belonged to their stations. Though deficient, perhaps, in polish, it possessed an apparent aptitude for the purpose of its institution, and gave a confidence that myriads of its meek and lowly brethren were incompetent to inspire."[17]

Privates and noncommissioned officers have engaged in the bulk of
the combat in wars throughout history; they made up the majority of the
men in each company. Teen soldier Private John Rhodes Russell and others
trained alongside many individuals of color, among them Manuel Soto,
Caesar Glover, and Romeo.[18] Caesar Glover was a thirty-five-year-old freeman and "labourer." Impoverished before the war, he would end his life in
the same manner. Yet his service to the country was unflinching. Caesar
would fight in all the regiment's campaigns and several years beyond.[19]
Also enlisted in the regiment, Manuel (or Emmanuel) Soto marched and
fought side by side with Romeo and Caesar Glover.[20] Many men of color
who were not on the rolls would also fight in the Revolution—scores
served.[21] African American, Native American, and Hispanic members of
the Marblehead Regiment were integrated with their Caucasian brothers.
They would unite to drill and march, sleep next to one another, endure all
the same hardships, and eventually some would die in combat together.

Many of the prestigious families of Marblehead contributed multiple members to the regiment. Brothers, cousins, and best friends trained
side by side. John Glover's son, John Jr., commanded a company. Sons
and fathers prepared for war, such as the Bowdens, the Folletts, the
Grants, and the Blacklers.

Jeremiah Lee brought his favorite nephew and the operations manager of his business, William Raymond Lee, on board as a staff officer.
A round-faced but distinguished man with a sharp nose and thin lips,
William R. Lee, a brilliant tactician, would play a major role in the
regiment's success. His first cousin, Joseph Lee; his second cousin,
Seward Lee; his brothers-in-law, John Glover Jr. and Marston Watson;
and his relative by marriage Joshua Orne would all serve together.[22]
The regiment was truly a family with deep ties of blood and friendship,
a latter-day band of brothers trained for war.

As the men drilled, General Gage, the Marbleheaders, and their
fellow Americans raced to arm themselves. Marblehead received intelligence that the British would strike Fort William and Mary in Portsmouth, New Hampshire, to seize the valuable cannon and powder stored
there before the colonists could secure it.

CHAPTER 9

THE FORGOTTEN FIRST SHOTS: THE RAID ON FORT WILLIAM AND MARY

December 1774, Marblehead, Massachusetts

John Gerry, brother of Elbridge Gerry, dipped his pen into his inkwell and prepared to convey vital information about the Crown's suspected plans to disarm New England. By way of its informants in Salem (who had heard the news from informants in Boston), the Marblehead Committee of Correspondence had learned that King George III had signed an order in October banning the export of arms, gunpowder, and military supplies to the colonies. Gerry warned officials in Portsmouth on December 12, "the contents [of the intelligence received from Salem] are alarming and a full discovery of what we have long apprehended, We would recommend the immediate removal to you of your Military stores, as undoubtedly the design of . . . is universal and the [powder] of so Great a Quantity as you possess would almost tend to our ruin, We have taken the necessary Precautions ourselves. . . ."[1]

Aware that Fort William and Mary in Portsmouth, New Hampshire, had considerable stores of gunpowder, Gerry assumed that the Redcoats would head there next to seize the stockpile. His pen scratched as he scrawled his missive, and he hastily sealed his letter with wax before handing it off to an express rider, who would make the arduous trek through the snow and sleet to get the information into the hands of John Langdon, a member of the Sons of Liberty and local Patriot leader.

Born in 1741, Langdon was the son of a prosperous farmer and shipbuilder whose family had lived for generations in the area that became Portsmouth. The younger Langdon went to sea in his youth, and by the age of twenty-two captained his own ship. Over time, his fleet and his trading business grew, and he became one of New Hampshire's wealthiest residents. However, when the British began imposing new restrictions on trade, Langdon's income diminished. He became one of the earliest and most vocal dissidents, calling on his fellow colonists to rebel against the British government.

Although the locals referred to Fort William and Mary as "the Castle," in truth, it was little more than a decrepit piece of crumbling stonework. Its walls reached no higher than six to eight feet—in the places where they hadn't fallen down. The nickname likely referred not to the appearance of the fort but to its location on New Castle Island, which sat in the mouth of the Piscataqua River, the boundary between New Hampshire and Maine. Fort William and Mary had stations for up to thirty artillery pieces, but only a few cannons were kept in readiness while the majority remained in storage. Even if more guns had been available, the stronghold did not have the personnel to man them. In 1774, the New Hampshire Assembly had authorized funds for only one officer and three men at the fort.

However inadequate its defenses may have been, Fort William and Mary was still one of the only fortifications of any size in that part of the colonies. As a result, the British used it to store their invaluable supplies of gunpowder, as well as weapons. It was this that Langdon and his like-minded Patriots hoped to secure.

Additional intelligence arrived on December 13, buttressing the claims made by Gerry. None other than the legendary Paul Revere rode the sixty-six miles from Boston through a snowstorm carrying word that the Crown had advised all royal governors to seize the forts in their territory and place them in the hands of loyal troops. The forty-one-year-old industrialist, renowned Boston silversmith, and powerful Freemason was a key member of the Sons of Liberty and had close ties with Joseph Warren, John Hancock, and Samuel Adams. In addition, spies in Boston had seen troops leaving secretly, "suspected for yo[ur] place [Portsmouth] to take possession of the Fort there; there; we are informed tha[t] our Brethren in NewPort having received some intimation of such design, have already dismantled their Fort & remove[d] the Cannon to a place of security, in duty to our Brethren of Portsmouth, we have sent this early intelligence of the design of our Enemies," the letter said.[2] Revere delivered his message to the local Patriot leaders, who immediately convened an emergency meeting in a Portsmouth tavern. They agreed to meet again the next day, but that wasn't urgent enough for Langdon and some of the other men, including future Marblehead mariner Winborn Adams.

With large groups of Patriots meeting openly in public places, the royal governor of New Hampshire, Sir John Wentworth, sensed trouble. Descended from some of the earliest settlers in New Hampshire, Wentworth came from an upper-class family and had earned degrees from Harvard. Despite being a close personal friend of John Adams, he was fervently loyal to the king. Upon hearing of the unfolding plot, on December 13 he sent an urgent surreptitious message to the provincial officer in charge of the fort, Captain John Cochran, advising him to "exert the utmost vigilance in maintaining your command" and "refuse admission to any number of Men under any pretense whatsoever." Wentworth even desperately urged Cochran to "engage three or four good men, I would have you enlist them."[3]

At noon the following day, the unrest reached a boiling point. Langdon and his comrades had rallied a group of Patriot supporters. Preceded by a fife and drums, they marched through the streets of Portsmouth boldly proclaiming their intention to seize the fort. A report in a Loyalist New York paper noted, "Two or three warm zealous members, having the good of their country at heart more than the others, and thinking any further deliberations on so important an affair unnecessary, gave out their orders early the next morning for the drums to be beat to raise volunteers to go and take the King's fort."[4]

Dismayed by this turn of events, Governor Wentworth fervently dispatched the local justice of the peace and sherriff John Parker to admonish and warn the throng "[that] they were going about an Unlawful Act to take away the Powder out of his Majesty's Fort, and that it was the highest Act of High Treason and Rebellion." The exasperated Parker further "exhorted and enjoined them to desist."[5] In reply, Langdon laughed and mocked the men and continued leading the Patriots toward the fort, eventually clambering into boats that would transport them to the island. More men from both the New Hampshire and Maine sides of the river joined the mob, and a crowd several hundred strong disembarked near the Castle.

In Portsmouth, the governor's attempts to stop his citizens had reached near-comic proportions. He first demanded that the sheriff send an underling to determine what was happening on the island, but everyone refused to go. Having no other options, Wentworth decided to venture to the fort himself. However, no one—not even the bargemen he employed—was willing to row him out to Fort William and Mary. The Loyalist governor next attempted to call out the local militia. This, too, failed; most of the local militia sided with the rebels and were taking part in the raid on the fort.

Langdon's boisterous march through the streets was only part of a larger plan of attack. Before the parade began, a much smaller group of merchants and salty sea captains paid an ostensibly innocuous visit to Captain Cochran. On that cold December day, the officer graciously invited them to come in and sit by the fire. At first, Cochran, who himself was a former ship captain, "had no suspicions of any Plot or Intentions against himself or the Fort or any thing therein."[6] First two and then five men gathered by the fire to swap tales of their seagoing days. Then four or five more began approaching, and the captain "first began to suspect there was some unlawful Scheme contriving."[7] Cochran queried the men as to why they suddenly felt the need for a visit. Quick on the uptake, Cochran's wife, Sarah, approached. Whispering in his ear that she worried he was being betrayed, she thrust "his Pistols well-charg'd" into her husband's hands.[8] At gunpoint, Cochran began interviewing the men one by one, inquiring about their intentions. During the interrogations, more men arrived, swelling the ranks of the visitors. The Patriots on the premises now outnumbered the six soldiers on duty at the fort.

The time for confrontation had arrived. Blurting out the obvious, Cochran told the men he knew they planned to take the fort "by stratagem." Unmasked, one of the men admitted they planned to take Cochran prisoner but said he himself "abhorred such cowardly ways." Not intimidated, Cochran ordered the men out of the fort and, as he later described, "instantly pointed three Cannon towards the Gate and other Places where I thought they would be most serviceable to prevent Persons from Coming in as I then began to be apprehensive a sudden Attack was intended to be made upon the Fort."[9]

Now on high alert, those defending the fort prepared for battle. They accepted help from a local cooper, who offered to defend the fort with them, and they also pressed another local civilian into assistance.

While the plot to seize the fort by stealth unraveled, Langdon's crowd was nearing the gates. Espying a mob approaching from multiple directions, Cochran positioned his men "in the most advantageous Station I could judge of, and ordered them not to flinch on pain of Death but to defend the Fort to the last Extremity, telling them that the Instant I saw any sign of Cowardice in either of them I would drive a Brace of Balls through his Body."[10]

When faced with the reality of the cannon in the fort, the would-be attackers seemed to lose some of their bravado. A handful approached Cochran and asked to be admitted to the Castle. Cochran refused but said he was willing to talk. The Patriots had hoped to be able to take the gunpowder for themselves without a real fight, but hopes for that possibility were dwindling.

Not ready to concede, Langdon asked Cochran to allow him to enter the fort with just one other man, sea captain Robert White. Cochran agreed under the condition that the two men would "go out again without being compelled."[11] Once inside, Langdon boldly apprised the captain that the colonists intended to take the gunpowder. In reply, Cochran demanded to see an order from Governor Wentworth authorizing such an action, for the governor was the only person with the authority to dispose of the powder.

With a smile, Langdon cheekily responded that he "forgot to bring his Orders, but the Powder they were determined to have at all Events."[12] Unamused, Cochran said that if they wanted the gunpowder, they would have to resort to "Violence [and he] would defend it to the last Extremity." Negotiations abruptly terminated, and Cochran ordered Langdon and White out of the Castle, warning the men, "If [you] attempt to come into the Fort [your] Blood be upon [your] own hands, for I will fire on you."[13]

That was apparently the invitation the Patriots had been waiting for. Almost immediately, the mob stormed the fort en masse. True to his word, Cochran fired his guns, sending 4-pound shot hurtling into the colonists, arguably, the forgotten first shots of the Revolutionary War. The attackers dove for cover, and most of the cannonballs landed harmlessly on the ground, although a few lodged in nearby buildings.

Soldiers in the fort followed up with musket fire, which proved equally ineffective. "The balls whistling thro the party cover'd some with the Earth where they struck, went thro a warehouse, another pass'd thro a Sloop, the third lodg'd in an House at Kittery, all well aim'd but the assailants falling under the walls as they saw the Match applied, escaped with life,"[14] revealed one Loyalist. Before they could reload, the throng of Patriots scaled the walls. Unflinching despite the twenty-five-to-one odds, the defenders attempted to fight them off hand to hand. Cochran later testified that he "was pressed upon, but kept them off a considerable Time with my firelock and Bayonet."[15]

Inevitably, the Patriots' greater numbers allowed them to gain the upper hand. Portsmouth mariner Thomas Pickering vaulted from the Castle wall onto the captain and seized him by the throat, setting Cochran enough off-balance that the other attackers could grab hold of him.

The other soldiers in the fort mustered as staunch a fight as their captain. One of them, Isaac Seveay, continued to resist bravely even after the mob had disarmed him. A Patriot shot at the unarmed soldier, but the pistol misfired. The colonist then ordered Seveay to kneel and ask forgiveness for his part in defending the gunpowder. The soldier replied that he would kneel "when his Legs were cut off below his knees . . . but he would not before."[16] Irate, the attackers hurled Seveay to the ground and punched the Loyalist repeatedly in the head. Similar scenes played out elsewhere as many of the soldiers ceased fighting only when their muskets were broken into pieces.

Many of the combatants knew each other personally, and at least one of the Whigs had served in the British Army. A member of the mob told one of the fort's defenders that if he had been wielding a club, "he would knock his Brains out."[17] The melee was a precursor of the civil war that would run throughout the American Revolution, where the brother-against-brother fight was as vicious as the battle against the Crown. As the raid concluded with Cochran and his cohorts captive, the Patriots committed a final act of defiance: they "triumphantly gave three Huzzas, and hauled the King's Colours."[18]

Having taken Cochran prisoner, the Patriots marched him to his quarters, but there they encountered a surprise: the feisty Sarah Cochran, who leaped to her husband's defense. To the shock of the men holding Cochran captive, she "snatch'd a bayonet" and went on the attack, "[and] spiritedly join'd ber husband," becoming the first female Loyalist combatant of the Revolution.[19] As a result of her actions, the Loyalist officer briefly broke free and joined her in the fight. Very soon, however, the captors disarmed the couple and took them prisoner.

Meanwhile, other Americans smashed the heavy wooden doors of the powder magazine with their axes and confiscated about a hundred one-hundred-pound barrels of the precious powder. Adding insult to injury, they snidely left Cochran and the Loyalists a single barrel, loading the rest onto boats to take back to Portsmouth. Given the lack of organic production of gunpowder in the colonies, the powder was priceless and crucial for military operations. It would prove to be critical in upcoming engagements, including possibly Bunker Hill, where this very powder would likely play a role in a key inflection point in the battle.[20]

Now the Patriots faced the challenge of what to do with the gunpowder they had just liberated. To resolve that question, they turned to militia major John Sullivan, who had recently been elected to serve as one of New Hampshire's delegates to the First Continental Congress. The son of Irish settlers, Sullivan was the only lawyer in the town of Durham and a friend of Governor Wentworth. To the ire of his neighbors, Sullivan had handled foreclosures of homes of some fellow Americans. However, his allegiance had shifted, and he had become a vocal opponent of British rule. He split up the stash of gunpowder, sending it to cities like Exeter and Dover, as well as keeping some in his hometown of Durham. After this act of treason, Sullivan was now all in as a rebel.

Stunned by the news of the fort's fall, Governor Wentworth sent an express letter to General Gage and Vice Admiral Samuel Graves, in command of the North American Station of British naval forces, informing them of the extraordinary attack on the Crown and seizure of the powder. Wentworth added that the Patriots planned to seize the cannon at the fort, and he begged for help. The governor also noted, "This event too plainly proves the imbecility of this government to carry into execution his Majesty's order in Council, for seizing and detaining arms and ammunition imported into this Province, without some strong ships of war in this harbor."[21] To secure the fort and reclaim the powder, Graves ordered several warships to sail for Portsmouth immediately.

Alerted that more Patriots were on the way and might hit the fort again, Wentworth tried to bolster its defenses. He ordered the local militia to round up thirty more men, forcibly if necessary, to defend the Castle. Although a militia officer went through the motions of beating a drum and calling for volunteers, he soon dolefully returned to the governor to report that it was impossible to find anyone to help.

Unaware of John Sullivan's role in hiding the gunpowder, Wentworth summoned him and asked whether he believed another raid on the Castle was likely. Sullivan confirmed Wentworth's worst fears and noted that the colonists were worried that the British government planned to use the gunpowder and cannons against New Hampshire's residents. Wentworth called this "a wicked falsehood . . . and a vile calculated report,"[22] and he convinced Sullivan to try to persuade the men not to mount another raid.

Patriots from Portsmouth and outlying towns had been milling around discussing their next move. Some asked for conferences with the governor, all of which were fruitless. Rain started to fall gently, and the crowd converged upon Tilton's Tavern, where Sullivan was paying for libations. As would occur throughout time, history would unfold in a tavern. Honoring his word to the governor, Sullivan first attempted to convince the men to abandon their plans for a second raid. As a lawyer, Sullivan knew that seizing the munitions was treason (even though some of it may have been the colony's property), and filching the Crown's cannon would be a further escalation. But others, including firebrand and Rogers's Rangers* veteran Andrew McClary, spoke forcefully in favor of capturing the cannons and ordnance at the fort before they could be turned against them.

As the night wore on—and the drinking continued—ardent Patriots headed home, while more supporters swelled the ranks of those who remained in the tavern. One brought word that more than sixteen hundred men were on their way to support Portsmouth. Eventually, even Sullivan was persuaded, and he agreed to lead a second raid on the Castle to take the artillery and other military equipment.

Unlike the first raid, there was no attempt at surprise with the second attack. Well in advance, Cochran received word that Sullivan and the others were on their way and intended to seize the remaining munitions.

With Sullivan leading, future Marblehead mariner Winborn Adams and hundreds of other men clambered into shallow-drafted cargo gundalows and rowed down the moonlit Piscataqua River. After a brief but frigid journey, they made landfall on the island. Sullivan strolled up

---

* During the French and Indian War, Rogers's Rangers was a provincial company initially from New Hampshire that expanded into over a dozen companies of Americans attached to the British Army. The Rangers conducted scouting, ranging, and special operations–like activities. Led by Major Robert Rogers, the force proved highly effective. Rogers distilled his tactics into twenty-eight rules known as Rules of Ranging that are still taught alongside a modified version to all modern US Army Rangers.

to the fort along with another compatriot and hailed Cochran. Astonishingly, considering the previous day's drama, the Loyalist captain led the Patriots inside and beseeched Sullivan to reveal who they were and what they wanted. Sullivan responded that he had a large force consisting of men of property (to highlight their stature in the colony). The captain appealed to Sullivan, whom he knew as a fellow Freemason, urging him to relinquish the attack. Cochran later recounted that he hoped "to Acquaint [Sullivan] that If he attempted anything of the kind I would certainly fire upon any Body of Men that should attempt to come within the Fort and that I was prepar'd to defend it."[23] The militia major then dropped the hammer and stated he intended to take anything in the fort belonging to New Hampshire. Specifically, Sullivan referred to seizing the munitions held in the Castle that the colony had purchased. Cochran passionately sparred with Sullivan verbally, and one of the Loyalist soldiers heard "several high threatening Words pass betwixt them."[24]

Cochran had sworn an oath to defend the fort but knew he faced impossible odds. So the Loyalist captain reached an accord: he would let the attackers inside if they would remove only the small number of munitions belonging to New Hampshire. But as soon as the gates swung open, Sullivan's men ransacked the fort and purloined Crown and colony property alike. Struggling through the night, Sullivan's men carried off stands of muskets and manhandled the heavy cannon into the gundalows. With Graves's warships carrying hundreds of reinforcements en route to Portsmouth, Sullivan, Adams, and the rest of the men arrived safely back to Portsmouth. Sensing the pending arrival of the British, Sullivan scotched plans for a third raid and dispersed the captured booty as the men melted back to their homes.

Reveling in their success, the Patriots erected a liberty pole in nearby Greenland, New Hampshire, and vowed to defend their liberty with their lives and fortunes. Sullivan penned a letter to "the inhabitants of British America" that captured the arguments of the Patriots in Portsmouth. Sullivan reminded the readers of how Rome disarmed the Carthaginians, "[These] brave people notwithstanding they had

Surrendered up three hundred Hostages to the Romans upon a promise of being Restored their former Liberties; found themselves Instantly Invaded by the Roman Army. They were told that they most Deliver up all their Arms to the Romans and they should peaceably Injoy their Liberties up on their Compliance with this Requisition." The Carthaginians complied and Rome destroyed their city. Sullivan implored, the question was "whether, when we are by an arbitrary decree prohibited the having Arms and Ammunition by importation, we have not, by the law of self-preservation, a right to seize upon those within our power, in order to defend the liberties which *God* and nature have given to us." The Patriot signed the missive as "The Watchman."[25]

In Newport, Rhode Island, Patriots, upon learning of the Crown's order banning the exportation of arms and gunpowder, ordered cannons and two hundred barrels of powder removed from Fort George and sent to Providence for safekeeping. On December 14, Samuel Ward, one of Rhode Island's delegates to the First Continental Congress, wrote a letter warning the other colonies and summing up the enterprise: "The Spirit & Ardor with which all this was done gave Me ineffable Pleasure and I heartily wish that the other Colonies may proceed in the same spirited Manner for I fear the last Appeal to Heaven [a reference to John Locke] must now be made & if We are unprepared We must be undone. The Idea of taking up Arms against Great Britain is shocking but if We must become Slaves or fly to Arms I shall not hesitate one Moment which to choose for all the Horrors of civil War & even Death itself in every Shape is infinitely preferable to Slavery which in one Word comprehends every Species of Distress Misery Infamy & Ruin."[26] Stung by the acts of aggression and the disaster at Fort William and Mary and Fort George, Gage, using intelligence furnished from Doctor Benjamin Church, plotted his next strike: Marblehead and Salem.

CHAPTER 10

SALEM NEARLY IGNITES
THE REVOLUTIONARY WAR

February 1775, Marblehead Harbor

Oars creaked in the locks and waves gently lapped against the side of their boat as the small party of Marblehead men led by Samuel Trevett rowed toward their goal, the captured American merchant vessel anchored near the twenty-gun British warship HMS *Lively*. The mariners uttered no words as they made the perilous trip under the cloak of darkness.

Born in Marblehead in 1751, Trevett would later be described as "a finished old gentleman of the old school." He was knowledgeable on a wide variety of subjects, and "his extensive and varied information, and the urbanity and politeness of his manner, rendered him a most agreeable as well as an exceedingly instructive companion."[1] However, on this night, his anger at the British was directing his actions.

For weeks, *Lively* had been patrolling the waters off Marblehead. Her mission was to prevent the import of any prohibited cargo, particularly the arms and gunpowder the Patriot leaders so desperately needed to protect themselves against the Crown. Accomplished smugglers, the Marblehead seamen were frequently able to transport contraband under the watch of the Royal Navy. But on this day, *Lively* had found one solitary chest of arms on a merchant vessel heading for port. The commander immediately ordered the ship to anchor itself next to the *Lively*.

Determined that the muskets intended for the Marbleheaders should not fall into the hands of the Crown, Trevett hatched a plot to liberate the munitions. He and his band of mariners prevailed: the British never realized the men had come aboard until they discovered the chest missing the next day. Ultimately, Trevett's captured weapons armed the Marblehead Regiment, and the Crown never recovered them.

Trevett's bold raid came after the *Lively* attempted to impress several Marbleheaders into the service of the Royal Navy. The cruel practice had continued despite Michael Corbett's trial and acquittal six years earlier. In one incident, the town of Marblehead came together successfully to thwart the British and rescue one such man. When a lieutenant from the *Lively* impressed two men from a local vessel, the Marbleheaders gave chase. Ashley Bowen records that "whale boats and a number of rowboats set off with owners to rescue the men and attacked the barge."[2] A local paper reported, "He was surrounded by eight or ten whale-boats manned and armed." The British lieutenant warned the colonists to keep their distance. They did but demanded the men be released. "On his refusal, they pointed their pieces into his boat, and Mr. L——ordered his men to do the same; one of the impressed men took this opportunity and leaped overboard; Mr. Lechmere snapped his piece at the man, which missed fire."[3] The whaleboat rescued the sailor in the water, but the British took the remaining man aboard the *Lively*.

By February 1775, it was becoming painfully obvious that verbal objections and strongly written letters were not going to be enough to convince the Crown to loosen its grip. Tension gripped the colonies as everyone waited for conflict to erupt.

But before they could mount a defense of their cities—let alone go on the attack—the colonists needed cannons and gunpowder, which were in short supply. For that, the colonists turned to two activities in which the Marblehead mariners would play a crucial role throughout the Revolution: smuggling and privateering.

In Massachusetts the newly established Committee of Supply, led mainly by Marblehead men, took on the responsibility of sourcing the all-important guns and powder. Jeremiah Lee, a Marblehead shipowner and merchant who spearheaded the committee, pledged his substantial fortune to the cause. As one of the wealthiest men in the colony, he had the funds and the connections to source weaponry from foreign countries. Under his direction and using his money, the Patriots in Salem had acquired from the Dutch the more than a dozen naval guns that they had concealed in local blacksmith Robert Forster's smithy.

As Britain clamped down on shipments of military supplies to the colonies, Patriot leaders stepped up their efforts to acquire or manufacture weaponry, expanding the arms race to defend themselves. In November 1774, the Massachusetts Committee of Safety appointed David Mason to the post of engineer, an act that Mason would later proudly proclaim was the first military appointment of the Revolution. He immediately began looking for gunpowder and armament. Before the month was out, he had purchased a number of 12-pound guns that the French had left behind in Nova Scotia. Mason contracted with Forster to affix the cannons to carriages so that they could be moved as necessary, and he put his wife and daughters to work preparing five thousand cartridges, packets of boiled flannel filled with gunpowder that could be used to fire the guns. By February, the cannons and cartridges were ready for service—news that soon reached the ears of General Thomas Gage.

Having learned through his network of spies, including the traitorous Doctor Benjamin Church, that rebels in Salem had been furtively amassing artillery and gunpowder, General Gage determined that city would be his next target. To secure the military stores, he selected Lieutenant Colonel Alexander Leslie and approximately 250 men of the 64th Regiment of Foot. They were the ideal force because they had been stationed in Salem a month earlier and knew the town. The son of an earl, the forty-four-year-old Leslie was a lifelong soldier who would lead his men to several British victories during the Revolution. However, his first engagement would fare far less well than he hoped.

Leslie relied on stealth and speed for the operation's success. Gage chose Leslie's regiment in part because its departure was easy to conceal from Boston's residents. Stationed on Castle Island in Boston Harbor, the 64th could easily board the HMS *Lively* away from the prying eyes of those on the mainland. They loaded up quietly after midnight, and in a further attempt to keep the operation covert as long as possible, Leslie ordered his men to remain belowdecks throughout the voyage.

When the ship entered Marblehead Harbor around noon on Sunday, February 26, 1775, the mariners in the area presumed it to be on standard Royal Navy business. They saw only the usual contingent of sailors on deck, so everything appeared routine. The captain piloted *Lively* into Homan's Cove, a secluded spot on the western side of the bay. Knowing the habits of the colonists, Leslie and his men lingered in the belly of the ship until between 2:00 p.m. and 3:00 p.m., when he was convinced that nearly everyone in Salem was at church for Sunday-afternoon services. Then they discreetly disembarked onto the deserted beach, loaded their muskets, and fixed bayonets. They also carried with them various tools—hatchets, spades, coils of rope, and other implements they would use to destroy or carry off the illegal cannons.

On that cold, wintry day, Colonel Jeremiah Lee and other alert Marbleheaders spotted the Regulars. One of them snatched up a drum and headed for the church, beating out the prearranged signal. "To arms! To arms!" he called.[4] "The foe! They come! They come!"[5]

Cocksure, Leslie ordered his fifers and drummers to strike up "Yankee Doodle," in mockery of the Patriots, as the 64th marched double-time in the general direction of Salem.

Colonel Mason, the local Patriot leader who had overseen the acquisition of the cannons the British sought, was alerted and ran into the North Church, adjacent to his house, crying out, "The reg'lars are coming and are now near Malloon's Mills!"[6]

The congregation immediately rushed out into the frigid, damp weather to prepare their defense. A call went up, "To arms! To arms!" Mason rounded up a group of young men to conceal some of the cannons in the woods, while teams of horses transported other guns to nearby towns. Townsfolk rushed to ring church bells and continued to beat drums to call their neighbors to arms. Some removed planks from the South Mills Bridge on the outskirts of town, while others set out for the drawbridge known as North Bridge, a crucial crossing point for the British to attain the guns.

When the advance guard of the 64th Foot reached the South Mills Bridge, they repaired the damage in mere minutes, and the Redcoats were soon storming toward the courthouse, where they briefly paused to speak with "a young tory lawyer,"[7] Samuel Porter, and a merchant, John Sargent, who supposedly waved a white flag from his roof to direct Leslie's march.[8] Upon reaching Sargent, Leslie whispered something in the Loyalist's ear with many of the locals watching. The crowd jeered, and Sargent later supposedly fled Salem and never returned.

The march quickly resumed; the local residents assumed that Sargent had divulged the location of the guns. Leslie and his men were headed straight for the North Bridge, where Mason and an immense crowd of other revolutionaries, including Timothy Pickering, leader of the Salem militia, were waiting. As soon as the Redcoats came into view, the Salemites raised the drawbridge. Quite a few climbed up on top of the upraised bridge and sat there "like so many hens at roost."[9]

Leslie marched to the foot of the bridge, unaware that his passage was blocked. Surprised and indignant, the colonel "stamped and swore, ordering the bridge to be immediately lowered."[10] His display of temper amused the Salem residents, and one of them laughingly asked why he wanted to cross. The angry officer replied that he was following orders and would cross, even if it cost his life and the lives of his men. However, his vow placed Leslie in a predicament. He had no right to fire on the townspeople unless they attacked him and his men first. And short of attacking, Leslie did not have any other means of persuading the local populace to lower the bridge. Knowing this, John Felt, a captain in the militia, jeered, "You had better be damn'd than fire! You can have no right to fire without further orders."[11]

Leslie retorted that he had every right to cross on the king's highway.

"It is not the King's highway," shouted an elderly man. "It is a road built by the owners of the lots on the other side, and no king, country, or town has anything to do with it."

"By God! I will not be defeated!" asserted Leslie.

"You must acknowledge, you have already been baffled," Felt observed with a smile.[12]

While Leslie mulled his next move in consultation with his officers, the people on the bridge vocalized their feelings. "Soldiers! Red jackets! Lobster-coats! Cowards! Damnation to your government!" one man yelled. Another added, "Fire and be damned!" A third noticed that the icy wind was making the soldiers shiver and jeered, "I should think you were all fiddlers, you shake so!"[13]

About this time, some of the colonists spotted a group of gundalows on the west side of the bridge. Hoping to prevent the British from employing them to cross, a few residents quickly knocked holes in the bottoms of the boats. Catching sight of what they were doing, Leslie ordered his soldiers to stop the men from scuttling the craft. The Redcoats brandished their bayonets, prompting one of the Patriots to tear open his shirt and dare the men to impale him. A scuffle ensued, and Joseph Whicher received a small wound. Still, the colonists completed their work, rendering the boats unusable.

Flummoxed, Leslie consulted with his officers regarding their next move. Clearly, none of the residents were going to comply with his wishes without a show of force, but he could not retreat without losing face. He strode back up to the bridge and announced, "I am determined to pass over this bridge before I return to Boston, if I remain here until next autumn."[14] This, of course, did nothing to endear him to the mocking townspeople, who were growing increasingly hostile.

While Leslie contemplated his next course of action, further altercations erupted between the locals and the Redcoats. From a ladder propped against the drawbridge, Mason hollered across the river to

Leslie that soon thousands of local militia would be descending upon the town. The Marbleheaders had mustered behind the rear of Leslie's column. Rugged fishermen, weather-beaten and tough from years at sea, the motley members of the regiment moved into position along the main road and were ready to pounce. "While Colonel Leslie and his officers were debating with the citizens, Robert Wormstead, one of the young men from Marblehead,—who afterward distinguished himself by his daring and bravery,—engaged in an encounter with some of the soldiers."[15] "Five feet and eleven inches in height, uncommonly active and athletick [*sic*], "brave to a proverb, generous to excess, and humane, as he was fearless of danger and death,"[16] Wormstead, a skillful fencer and ensign in the Marblehead Regiment, achieved almost mythological status in an incident separate from Leslie's raid. According to legend, Wormstead took on six British officers at the local watering hole, the Three Cod Tavern, using only a broken broom as a weapon. "Breaking a broom across his knee," Wormstead taunted, "Begone now! Damn ye! I've took your dare, / Licked and disarmed ye and drawn no red! / Let the broomstick teach ye to talk with care / With a tongue that's civil—in Marblehead."[17]

A local minister named Reverend Thomas Barnard appeared and declared that his mission was one of peace. The sun was just about to set. Barnard organized discussions between Leslie and some of the Patriot leaders. Leslie offered a compromise: the Redcoats would promise to march peacefully across the bridge and slightly beyond before turning around and retreating to Marblehead. This way everyone got what they wanted; the Patriots kept the guns safe while Leslie obeyed the letter of his orders, if not the spirit.

The townspeople agreed and soon lowered the drawbridge. True to their word, Leslie and his men marched in formation fifty yards beyond the bridge before making an about-face. However, one of the local inhabitants was not ready to let the British troops off so easily. As the soldiers were turning around, a woman named Sarah Tarrant leaned out her window and yelled, "Go home and tell your master he sent you on a fool's errand and has broken the peace of our Sabbath. What! Do you think we were born in the woods, to be frightened by owls!"

Leslie did not reply; however, one of his men aimed at the housewife with his musket.

"Fire if you have the courage," she taunted. "I doubt it."[18]

The Redcoats left without firing a shot. With their fifes and drums playing, they marched swiftly back the way they had come.

While the action had been unfolding near the bridge, the Patriots in the surrounding towns had not been idle. Messengers had carried the news of Leslie's arrival to other local militia, and by the time Leslie's regiment was leaving, a large crowd of minutemen from the town of Danvers had joined those from Salem near the bridge. A notice in a newspaper read, "Col. Leslie's ridiculous expedition, on the 26th ult., occasioned such an alarm, that the people of all the neighboring towns, as well as those at 30 or 40 miles distance were mustering, and great numbers actually on their march for this place; so that it is thought not less than 12 or 15,000 men would have been assembled in this town within 24 hours after the alarm, had not the precipitate retreat of the troops from the drawn-bridge prevented it."[19] They fell into ranks behind the soldiers, escorting them back to their ship.

As Leslie's regiment passed back into Marblehead, Lee and Glover's men joined the procession, stepping in time with the soldiers in the most sarcastic manner possible. They saw the Redcoats all the way back to their ship, and as the British soldiers backed away, the Marbleheaders looked on in triumph.

Later apprised of the course of events, General Gage called his decision to send Leslie to Salem "a mistake."[20] For the British, it would be much worse than that. The provincials had learned that they could stand up to the soldiers, and rather than punishing the Patriots for their actions, the Redcoats eventually turned tail. The king's soldiers looked like fools—buffoons to be mocked rather than feared.

A letter from John Hancock to Elbridge Gerry summed up the consequences of the Salem Gunpowder Alarm:

We are all extremely pleased at the conduct of Marblehead and Salem. The people there have certainly convinced the governor

and troops that they will fight, and I am confident this movement will make the general more cautious how he sends parties
out in future to attempt the like. . . . Mr. Adams and all friends
are well, and much pleased with your conduct. I hope when the
day of trial comes we shall be enabled to stand firm.[21]

Despite having failed to capture the guns, Leslie had shown great
restraint by withstanding the mockery of the Marblehead and Salem
residents. Guided by the wisdom of Reverend Barnard, cooler heads
prevailed, halting a clash of arms. Without their actions, the Revolutionary War would most likely have started at Salem's North Bridge.
Instead, destiny and the "shot heard round the world" would unfold on
Lexington Green and Concord's North Bridge.

On March 5, 1775, the anniversary of the Boston Massacre, Joseph
Warren orchestrated a dramatic and symbolic display. Harking back to
his theatrical days at Harvard, Warren emerged through a rear window
of the Old South Meetinghouse wearing a toga, evoking the spirit of
Roman leader Cato. Several Sons of Liberty joined Warren, including
Benjamin Church, who had delivered a fiery speech two years earlier
on the anniversary. Orating to a crowd of Bostonians as well as dozens
of British soldiers in the front rows, Warren detailed the horrors of the
massacre. "Stronger language could not have been used, if no threats
had been uttered, or no English officers been present."[22] He did not
advocate for independence but warned, "If these pacific measures are
ineffectual, and it appears that the only way to safety is through fields
of blood, I know you will not turn your faces from your foes, but will
undauntedly press forward, until tyranny is trodden under foot."[23]

Several officers in the audience weren't having it and displayed
their sentiments through an open threat: "After one of the orator's
boldest utterances, an officer of the Welch Fusiliers who was seated
at Warren's feet held up several pistol-bullets in his open palm. Not
at all disconcerted, the speaker quickly dropped a handkerchief over

them." At the conclusion of his address, the officers "struck their canes upon the floor, made insolent noises, and some of them exclaimed, 'Fie! Fie!'" The crowd misinterpreted the cry as "fire" and "panic ensued."[24] Samuel Adams and William Cooper, the town clerk, restored order, but not before Warren had successfully stoked the fire of the Patriots' fury over the memory of the atrocity of the massacre.

Bad news travels quickly. A ship arrived in New England with news that Parliament had passed legislation known as the Restraining Act, which would ban the colonists from fishing in the Grand Banks, destroying their livelihood by throwing nearly all of Marblehead out of work. Most of those living in Marblehead now felt war was inevitable. It was only a matter of time.

The Committee of Supplies had been busy. Jeremiah Lee, Gerry, and Glover raided their warehouses and ships of available military supplies and stockpiled them for the Patriot cause. They brought in war materiel and supplies through their shipping lines and provided funds to David Mason, the fifty-three-year-old craftsman and ornamental painter turned artillerist who was one of the men leading the supply buildup in Essex County and working directly with the Committee of Supply. In a small green notebook, Mason cataloged his munitions.[25] Most of the materiel was secreted away in Marblehead, Salem, and Concord at Colonel James Barrett's farm. Barrett, a wealthy miller and ardent Patriot, commanded the Middlesex County militia, and his hidden arsenal brimmed with cannons and powder, as the local militia leader recorded in "Account of the Provisional Stores sent to Colonel Barrett of Concord, partly in his own custody and partly elsewhere, all under his care." All the powder Barrett inventoried came from Jeremiah Lee:

> "From Colonel Jeremiah Lee of Marblehead, 6 hogsheads [over-sized barrels], containing 35 half-barrels of powder, 6 of which were stored at Colonel Barrett's, 5 at James Chandler's, 6 at James Barrett Jr.'s; 6 at Ephraim Wood's, 6 at Joseph Hosmer's,

and 6 at Jonas Heywood's. Eight hogsheads more were soon received from Colonel Lee, 6 of which were sent the last of March to Leicester."

Lee transported another cache of supplies to Concord. "Containing tents, poles, axes, and hatchets, stored at Abishai Brown's; and also 318 barrels of flour, 68 of which were stored at Ebenezer Hubbard's, 66 at Captain Timothy Wheeler's, 56 at Samuel Jones's, 23 at Isaac Hubbard's, 16 at Jonas Heywood's, 82 at Samuel Whitney's and 7 at Jonathan Heywood's." Lee added in a letter accompanying the supplies, "Don't so much as mention the name of powder, lest our enemies should take advantage of it."

Gerry also furnished a mountain of materiel to Barrett.

"7 loads of salt fish, containing about 17,000 pounds, stored at Elisha Jones's; 18 casks of wine, 20 casks of raisins and a quantity of oil, (which were carried to Stow); and 47 hogsheads and 50 barrels of salt, which were stored in 15 different places in town; 4 loads of tents, tow-cloth, and canteens, stored at Ephraim Potter's; 1 bundle of sheet-lead [used to make musket balls], several hogsheads of molasses and a quantity of linen. From Salem 46 and from Boston 12 tierces of rice, estimated to contain about 35,000 pounds; 20 stored at Ebenezer Hubbard's, 6 at Thomas Hosmer's, 3 at Thomas Davis's, 7 at Stephen Blood's, 7 at Edward Richardson's, 5 at Deacon George Minott's, and the remainder in the town-house."[26]

On March 7, 1775, the Marbleheaders on the Committees of Safety and Supplies once again met. Under the leadership of Jeremiah Lee, the committee outlined the locations of the hidden caches of arms and munitions throughout eastern Massachusetts. With his presence in the heart of the Patriot leadership, the next day Doctor Benjamin Church delivered directly to Gage the priceless intelligence of the hidden locations, including those in Concord. Church wrote, "A disposition to oppose the late parliamentary measures has become general. The parent of that disposition is a natural fondness for old custom and a jealousy of sinister designs on the part of the administration." Church noted the inexperience of the Committee of Safety, "the weakness of the executive power of that body and party from an inadequate knowledge in conducting their novel enterprise." Remarkably, Benjamin Church offered a cogent and prescient analysis on how Americans would fight: "The first opposition would be irregular, impetuous, and incessant from the numerous bodies that would swarm to the place of action. . . . The most eligible mode of attack on the part of the people is that of detached parties of bushmen who from their adroitness in the habitual use of the firelock suppose themselves sure of their mark at 200 yards."[27]

CHAPTER 11

PRELUDE TO WAR: RENDEZVOUS AT BLACK HORSE TAVERN

April 18, 1775, Boston, Massachusetts

"You will seize and destroy all the Artillery, Ammunition, Provision, Tents, Small Arms, and all Military Stores whatever,"[1] General Thomas Gage wrote in his orders to Lieutenant Colonel Francis Smith, a fifty-two-year-old veteran regimental commander. Gage was planning a swift, surgical strike to destroy the Patriot arms buildup in Concord and was vowing to avoid a repeat of the debacles at Fort William and Mary and Salem. With painstaking detail, he enumerated the explicit actions he expected of his troops to neutralize the rebels' cannon and munitions, much of which the Marbleheaders had painstakingly obtained:

> You will order a Trunion [cannon support] to be knocked off each Gun, but if it's found impractical on any, they must be spiked, and the Carriages destroyed. The Powder and flower [*sic*], must be shook out of the Barrels into the River, the Tents burnt, Pork or Beef destroyed. And the Men may put Balls of lead in their pockets, throwing them by degrees into Ponds, Ditches &c., but no Quantity together, so that they may be recovered afterwards. If you meet with any Brass Artillery, you will order their Muzzles to be beat in so as to render them useless.[2]

However, while Gage planned to show no mercy when it came to the weapons and military supplies, he made sure that his men would stay within the bounds of British law and refrain from damaging any of the personal possessions that belonged to the colonists. "You will take care that the Soldiers do not plunder the Inhabitants, or hurt private property," Gage directed.[3] He knew the colonists would seize on any violation of British law as a pretext for further defiance of the Crown. Gage considered himself a man of principle. He viewed himself not as a harsh oppressor who employed arbitrary arrests but rather as the duly appointed king's representative who enforced the rule of law. The royal governor believed that firm resistance would quell the spirit of rebellion fermenting in the colonies and had said the Americans "will be lions while we are lambs; but if we take the resolute part they will prove very weak."[4] Centuries ahead of his time, Gage had a rudimentary grasp of counterinsurgency; however, on a practical level, he wanted to buy time and recognized the weakness of his own military position. Until reinforcements arrived, he had to conduct the raid in a surgical manner to avoid an overwhelming response from the colonists.

Gage had spent weeks preparing for the operation to seize rebel munitions at Concord. In late February, he had sent out two spies disguised in "brown clothes" and wearing "reddish handkerchiefs."[5] He instructed them to "take a sketch of the roads, passes, heights &c. from Boston to Worcester, and to make other observations."[6] From there, they headed to Concord. While the provincials were aware of the men's mission, the spies were able to provide Gage with a detailed description of the topography of the area. The general's agents managed to confirm earlier intelligence regarding additional locations of hidden caches of powder and arms, including in meetinghouses and even below the pulpit in a Lexington church. Gage also had other intelligence sources. His wife Margaret's brother, Major Stephen Kemble, led the military governor's spy operations and maintained an extensive network of Tory sympathizers who provided him with details about rebel activities; he also nefariously pressed provincial children into service as spies. Above all, Kemble had on his payroll Doctor Benjamin Church, who, in his leadership positions, had access to the most sensitive Patriot secrets.

Knowing that secrecy was paramount in seizing the weapon stores, Gage orchestrated a counterintelligence effort designed to prevent express riders from spreading word about the movement of the British troops. He ordered ten officers and ten sergeants to key intersections where they would be sure to encounter any horsemen carrying messages for the provincials. Their mission: "to stop all advice of [the] march getting to Concord."[7] They were also on the lookout for the rebel leaders. However, the sight of finely dressed officers lingering near country roads and inns and asking where they might find John Hancock and Samuel Adams had the opposite effect of what Gage had intended. The suspicious colonists knew something was afoot, and word of the unusual activities quickly spread.

That same day, April 18, about eight miles to the northwest, the members of the Massachusetts Committees of Safety and Supplies were meeting in the Black Horse Tavern in Menotomy, the present-day city of Arlington. Those attending included John Hancock and Samuel Adams, as well as Marbleheaders Charles Lee, Elbridge Gerry, and Azor Orne—the core of the Patriot leadership.

Messages regarding British troop movements were flying across the countryside on horseback, and word of their possible plans had reached the Whig leaders. Fearing that the Redcoats were headed for Lexington and Concord, the committee members moved some of the cannons and supplies out of Concord. When the meeting adjourned, Hancock and Adams headed to Lexington for the night, but Lee, Gerry, and Orne chose to sleep at the tavern, a decision that proved fateful.

Two other committee members, Richard Devens and Abraham Watson, headed east toward Charlestown in a carriage. On the way, they passed through "a great number of British officers and their servants on horseback."[8] Concerned, the Patriots immediately turned their chaise around and rode back through the column of Redcoats at breakneck speed and returned to the inn. They told the three Marblehead men still at the Black Horse about the officers, and Gerry instantly sent a message to Hancock and Adams warning "that eight or nine officers of the King's troops were seen, just before night, passing the road towards Lexington, in a musing, contemplative posture; and it was suspected they were out upon some evil design."[9] When word reached Lexington, the local militia mustered to protect the two Patriot leaders, and scouts ventured out to see if they could acquire any more information about the Redcoats' intentions.

Around 10:00 p.m. on April 18, around seven hundred British regulars under the command of Lieutenant Colonel Francis Smith had loaded up on boats and headed toward Charlestown. Watchful Patriot eyes immediately informed provincial leaders in Boston. No one knows for certain whether the Patriots gathered the information from their observations and connected the dots or whether someone from the British side tipped them off. By some accounts, Gage confided his plans to only one person: his beautiful and charismatic wife. Margaret Gage had been born in America and may have felt conflicted about the growing tension between Britain and the colonies. Without firm proof, many suspect she warned the Patriots.

Regardless of who provided the intelligence, the news quickly reached Paul Revere and William Dawes, two Sons of Liberty who frequently served as messengers. Earlier in the day, when the colonists initially began to worry about the weapons store in Concord, Revere and Dawes had established a signal code to alert the countryside of the troops' arrival. Lanterns placed in the tower of the Old North Church would signal how the British were coming: "one if by land, two if by sea."

Now, with two lanterns blazing in the tower of the North Church, signaling the Redcoats' arrival by sea, Revere rowed across the harbor, narrowly escaping the British sentries, and embarked upon the famous "midnight ride" celebrated in Henry Wadsworth Longfellow's popular poem. As he galloped toward Lexington, he awakened the occupants of nearly every house along the road, rallying other messengers to carry word of the soldiers' movements. Sympathetic colonists pulled muskets out, cleaning and oiling them for the inevitable fight.

Around midnight, Revere arrived at the home in Lexington where Hancock and Adams were sleeping. Gerry's earlier dispatch had alerted the Patriot leaders to the potential threat, and consequently, militiamen guarded the house. The volunteer troops told the messenger to stop making noise because he would wake the family. "Noise!" Revere replied. "You'll have noise enough before long. The Regulars are coming out."[10]

Exasperated, Revere strode up to the house, the parsonage of a local clergyman distantly related to Hancock, and banged on the windows. Instantly, sashes rose all over the building, and heads popped out to see the source of the commotion. Recognizing the messenger, Hancock called, "Come in Revere, we're not afraid of *you*."[11]

Still wearing his spurs, riding boots, and muddy clothes, Revere tramped into the dwelling and delivered his message. He then fell into conversation about the night's events with Adams and Hancock, and the men began to worry that the British had captured Dawes, who should have arrived by then. Dawes showed up about thirty minutes later, which lifted the mood in the room.

Tired from their wild rides through the night, the two messengers rested for about an hour while they discussed the British intentions with Hancock, Adams, and the militia leaders. The group concurred that the regulars must be after more than just the two Patriot leaders, and they rightly suspected that the powder and munitions stored in Concord were the true target of the operation. And that meant they needed to get a warning to the provincials in the neighboring town.

As the church bells of Lexington rang out a warning, Revere and Dawes mounted their saddles once again for a gallop through the night, this time joined by a third man, Doctor Samuel Prescott, a "high son of liberty" they met on the road who volunteered to accompany them to Concord. The trio set out, again calling to each house on the road. However, the British horsemen Gage had dispatched intercepted the group near the town of Lincoln, just two and a half miles outside Lexington. Having barely eluded several capture attempts that night, the Patriot messengers again attempted to flee. "God damn you! Stop!" shouted one of the British officers. "If you go an inch further you are a dead man!"[12]

Prescott, who knew the area well, urged his horse to jump over a stone wall and scramble through a thicket before making his way back to the road and on to Concord. Dawes wheeled his horse around and galloped back into the darkness toward Lexington. With the Redcoats closing in, he rode swiftly toward a farmhouse and, thinking fast, called out, "Halloo, my boys. I've got two of 'em."[13] Assuming they were about to be ambushed, the British soldiers retreated, leaving Dawes free to ride away.

Revere, however, was not so lucky. A group of ten or twelve British soldiers caught the silversmith and took him prisoner at gunpoint. Angry at losing the other two suspicious-looking riders, the Redcoats, in Revere's words, "abused me much."[14]

An officer intervened. "Sir," he asked with all the distinction and courtesy of a British gentleman, "may I crave your name?"

"My name is Revere."

"What?" replied the shocked officer, who, like his fellow comrades, was under orders to find and capture the elusive messenger. "Paul Revere!"

"Yes."

The Redcoats proceeded to question the silversmith, who replied truthfully, if a bit arrogantly, to their queries.

At one point, Revere told them, "Gentlemen, you've missed your aim."

The British told him that he didn't know what he was talking about, that they were out to round up deserters.

"I know better," said the wily messenger. "I know what you are after, and have alarmed the country all the way up." He then proceeded to tell them more about the British mission than they themselves knew. He even went so far as to warn his captors that they would soon be in danger, noting, "I should have five hundred men there soon."

Revere's cheeky manner infuriated his captors. According to Revere, the British major on the scene "clapped [a] pistol to my head and said he was agoing to ask me some questions, and if I did not tell the truth, he would blow my brains out."

The messenger replied that "[I do] not need a threat to speak the truth." He added, "I call myself a man of truth, and you have stopped me on the highway, and made me a prisoner I knew not by what right. I will tell the truth, for I am not afraid."

With this wordy conversation, the silversmith aimed to buy time and keep the Redcoats away from Lexington at all costs. He believed they intended to capture Hancock and Adams, which Revere believed would be a tragic blow to the cause of freedom. He repeatedly emphasized that provincial forces were waiting in the city and that the British soldiers were in danger of starting a war—as well as in great personal peril.

The captors ordered Revere and several other locals they had rounded up that night to mount up on their horses, and they nervously started toward Lexington. "We are now going towards your friends, and if you attempt to run or we are insulted, we will blow your brains out," the major warned Revere.

As calm and insolent as ever, Revere responded, "You may do as you please."

When the group of riders was about a half mile outside town, a gunshot suddenly rang out. Within a few seconds, a volley of musket fire crashed through the darkness, and then the town bell began to sound loudly. "The bell's a'ringing!" one of the prisoners with Revere shouted. "The town's alarmed, and you're all dead men!"[15]

While the shots were likely not the true beginning of the battle, the sounds erupting from Lexington seemed to confirm everything Revere had said. Convinced that battle was beginning, the British officers decided to rush to aid their comrades—but they couldn't very well hurry with their prisoners weighing them down. In an impulsive move, they freed the Americans and drove off their horses before urging their own mounts to trot toward the town.

Now on foot, Revere and the others took a cross-country shortcut through the swamp, hoping to beat the British riders to Lexington and deliver yet another warning that the British were coming.

Just shy of 2:00 a.m. on April 19, the news of the British troop movements reached the Black Horse Tavern, only slightly ahead of the advancing Redcoats. The three Marblehead men, still in their nightclothes, watched from the window as the long column of British soldiers entered the town. The tramp of hundreds of marching feet shod in stiff, square-toed brogans awakened townspeople, and candles soon lit windows throughout Menotomy as the colonists peered out into the road. Perhaps a small group of soldiers peeled off from the main column and headed directly toward the Black Horse; in any event, at one point the Marbleheaders—and the nervous innkeeper—realize their level of danger. According to accounts of the night, Gerry nearly panicked and ran to the front door, intending to flee into the street. "For God's sake, don't open the door!" the innkeeper warned.[16] He quickly ushered the trio out the back door and into the cornfield beyond.

As the men scrambled through the leftover stubble from the previous fall's harvest, Gerry got tangled up and fell. "Stop, wait!" he shouted to Orne. "I can't get up, I'm hurt!"[17] Rather than help their friend to his feet, Orne and Lee joined Gerry on the ground, hoping to avoid the gaze of the Redcoats. The trio of Patriot leaders lay undiscovered in the field for much of the night. However, the cold air overcame Lee. He became ill and never recovered. Before another month had passed, Lee was dead, and the Marblehead Regiment had a new commander: John Glover.

CHAPTER 12

FIRST BLOOD AT LEXINGTON:
DISARMING THE AMERICANS

While Azor Orne, Elbridge Gerry, and Jeremiah Lee shivered in the muddy cornfield, the long column of Redcoats surged forward like a giant centipede that snaked through Menotomy into the frosty night, marching toward Concord.[1] Despite Gage's sub-rosa attempts to cloak the operation in secrecy, church bells and alarm guns rang out along the countryside warning the population of the British advance. Their cover blown, Lieutenant Colonel Francis Smith concentrated on speed to accomplish his mission of disarming the Americans and destroying the cannon and munitions. Without gunpowder and cannon to support a standing army, any rebellion could be crushed, as the British had demonstrated throughout the history of their empire, and most recently during the Jacobite uprising of 1745 in Scotland.

Smith detached six companies of his elite light infantry and a mix of grenadiers of marines,* led by Major John Pitcairn, to forge ahead of the column and secure two bridges that led out of Concord. He also wisely sent a messenger to Boston for reinforcements—the corpulent officer knew he would need them.

First formed during the French and Indian War, the light infantry adopted some of the nimble fighting techniques of Native Ameri-

---

* Smith's force was mixed and included the light infantry and one company of the grenadiers of the marines, and several marine officers integrated into each flank battalion.

cans. An early precursor to special operations forces, the Light Bobs were chosen for their endurance, intelligence, and mastery of firearms. This specialized force trained in "leaping, running, climbing precipices, swimming, skirmishing through woods, loading and firing in different attitudes, and marching with remarkable rapidity." These were "chosen men, whose activity and particular talents for that duty should be the only recommendation to their appointment."[2] British marines, another elite force, mixed in with the Light Bobs.

The light infantry marched ahead of Smith's main force. Paul Revere, after being released, had reached Lexington and warned John Hancock and John Parker's men in Lexington of the British advance. Through the first faint streaks of dawn, the vanguard of the column saw the fields and hills come alive with armed men darting toward Lexington, "a vast number of Country Militia going over the Hill with their arms to Lexington,"[3] one officer remembered.

As the Lights marched toward Lexington, they encountered Lexington resident Benjamin Wellington, who was armed with his musket and bayonet. British lieutenant William Sutherland confronted Wellington to disarm him "& met one of them in the teeth whom [he] obliged to give up his Firelock and Bayonet."[4] After taking Wellington's musket, the British ordered him to return home. Instead, the provincial found another weapon and continued to make his way to Lexington Common. Shortly after the encounter, the British ordered their men to load their arms; before that, they had marched with unloaded muskets. In unison, the men lifted cartridges from their ammunition boxes, tore the tops off the paper cartridges with their teeth, primed the pan, placed the powder and balls down the barrels of their muskets, and resumed the march. Rounding a bend in the road, they saw the darkened silhouettes of Lexington's meetinghouse and homes.

A drumbeat called the Americans to arms. Captain John Parker's militia company reassembled on the northeast corner of Lexington Common. Like Parker, many of the American officers present that day were combat veterans of the French and Indian War. The men had been up all night after Revere's initial warning that the Redcoats

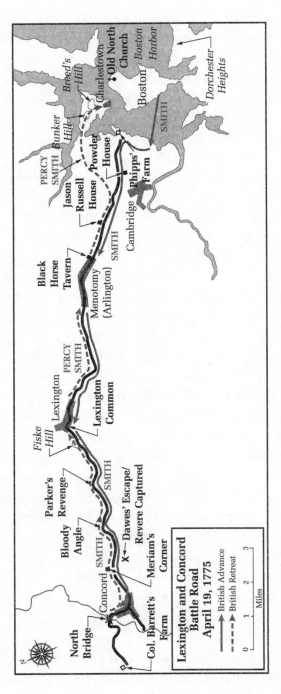

"Battle Road: Lexington and Concord"

were on the march toward Concord. An hour or so earlier, they had sent out their scouts to determine the British position. Only one rider returned, but he said he had not seen anything. Some had then adjourned to the nearby tavern and undoubtedly fortified themselves while others returned to their homes.

Just as Parker's men reassembled, two men tugged and strained on a large chest, teetering across the green in front of the militia. Paul Revere and John Lovell struggled to spirit John Hancock's trunk full of papers off to safety, walking through the center of history in the process. Revere heard Parker address his men: "Let the troops pass by. Don't molest them, without they being first."[5]

Before the meetinghouse at Lexington, the road forked, the left toward Concord, the right lane to the northeast and directly into Parker's men. The soldiers in the front of the column did not hesitate, immediately turning right and marching the vanguard of British troops directly toward the colonists—a decision that would prove fateful and monumental.

One American heard a British officer shout, "Damn them, we will have them!"[6]

Hundreds of yards behind the front of the column, Smith decided instead to turn left toward Concord and his mission, losing sight and temporary control of the forward light infantry companies and marines.

The phalanx of scarlet came into view of Parker's men. Ironically, their force included the same mounted officers who had captured Revere only hours earlier.

The more than seventy Patriots nervously eyed the British as one exclaimed, "There are so few of us, it would be folly to stand here."[7]

Indeed, the Americans were outgunned and outnumbered; a game of chicken ensued.

Parker firmly implored his troops, "The first man who offers to run shall be shot down."[8]

"Stand your ground! Don't fire unless fired upon!"

"But if they want a war, let it begin here."[9]

Major Pitcairn rode toward the group and yelled to Parker's men, "Throw down your Arms, ye Villains, ye Rebels!"[10]

None of Parker's men laid down their arms. But Parker unexpectedly changed his orders "to disperse and not to fire."[11]

Pitcairn barked, "Surround and disarm them."

Another American heard a British officer shout, "Ye villains, ye rebels, disperse; damn you, disperse!"[12]

Some men slowly dispersed, others stood their ground, but nobody laid down their arms. Time seemed to stand still. And then the high-pitched crack of a shot pierced the morning air of the New England common.

Nobody knows which side fired first. The shot could have been accidental, a deliberate provocation, or an impetuous discharge from a trigger-happy American or one of the Crown's troops. Several Americans claimed they saw an officer fire his pistol at them. The actions that followed were spontaneous and electric. Like a tightly coiled spring that had just sprung, the British troops, without orders, let out a series of throated shouts:

"Hazzah!" "Hazzah!" "Hazzah!"[13]

The British charged and fired into Parker's men only thirty to sixty yards away.

Several Americans fought back. Many of their shots went errant, but two balls grazed Pitcairn's horse, and one slammed into the ankle of a British soldier. "The balls flew so thick, I thought there was no chance for an escape, and that I might as well fire my gun as stand still and do nothing," recalled Ebenezer Munroe.[14]

Known for their iron discipline, training, and tactical prowess on the battlefield, the British officers nonetheless lost control of their men. The troops ran wildly through the green.

Horrified by the unfolding bedlam and his men shooting at Americans without orders, Pitcairn rode out into the melee and drew his sword, flashing it feverishly in the air, signaling a ceasefire. In the ensuing chaos, some Americans held their ground, ignoring Parker's orders to withdraw. Although writhing in pain from a gunshot wound, Parker's cousin, Jonas Parker, knocked prone from the force, on his hands and knees, still attempted to reload his musket. One of his fellow Americans heard him declare that "he would never run."[15] Shortly after those words were uttered, a Redcoat charged, impaling the New Englander with a bayonet and disemboweling him.

Meanwhile, Revere and Lovell hauled Hancock's trunk into the nearby woods and paused for several minutes as the fracas unfolded. Before the engagement, a tavern keeper had whisked Samuel Adams and Hancock, against Hancock's wishes, away to a place of safety.[16]

Lieutenant Colonel Smith and the main column of troops arrived in the midst of the chaos. Horrified by the carnage and loss of control, he rode into the center of the action. Smith demanded a drummer and ordered a beat to arms. One British officer vividly recalled, "We then formed on the Common, but with some difficulty, the Men were so wild they cou'd hear no orders."[17] Trained to respond instantly to a drummer's command, the men reluctantly broke off the action and formed into ranks.

As the British troops assembled, through the smoke and haze, the townspeople tended to the wounded and dying. The toll of the battle had been severe. Eight pairs of fathers and sons mustered that day. Five men from that group would never take another breath. Nearly a dozen were wounded.

Lieutenant Colonel Smith addressed his officers and informed them of their mission: Concord. Seize and destroy cannon and munitions the provincials had secreted away. The men fired their weapons and shouted "hazzah!" several times. To bystanders, it seemed like a *feu de joie*. It is also possible the troops cleared their muskets so they remained unloaded to prevent an accidental discharge during the march. But the huzzahs certainly did not win the hearts and minds of the Americans. Either way, expecting more trouble, the officers ordered their men to ready cartridge boxes and move ammunition so it would be easily accessible. The entire countryside had been alarmed and would now be swarming with thousands of hostile Americans.

Despite the renowned iron discipline of the British Army, several of the officers risked their careers and told Smith to abandon the mission: "Give up the idea of prosecuting [this] march." Smith flatly refused and said he "had his orders" and was "determined to obey them."[18]

CHAPTER 13

CONCORD

With the first light of day on their scarlet backs, the British column trudged toward Concord. Along the way, Francis Smith's troops espied an occasional figure or men on horseback darting among the nearby hills. In the distance, they heard the drone and toll of Concord's church bell pressed into service as an alarm. By about 7:30 a.m., the long column of troops that sprawled nearly a quarter of a mile arrived in the town. "The sun was rising and shined on their arms, and they made a noble appearance in their red coats and glistening arms," one minuteman recalled.[1]

Militia and minutemen from Concord and surrounding towns, wielding a miscellany of their own personal arms, proudly assembled on the hill behind Concord's meetinghouse. Patriots in the town planted a liberty pole, and a flag defiantly flapped in the breeze.

Reverend William Emerson, Concord's firebrand preacher, told his flock and fellow Patriots, "Let us stand our ground. If we die, let us die here!"[2] Emerson recalled the British advance, their drums beating a martial tune, "glittering in arms, advancing toward us with the greatest celerity."[3]

The leaders of the militia ordered their men not to fire unless fired upon. After a debate, they decided to withdraw to a hill located by the North Bridge that led into the town, nearly a mile from the center of Concord.

With the center of Concord now under British control, Smith ordered his men, without warrants, to search and destroy any munitions or weapons of war located in the town. As a consequence of intelligence furnished by Thomas Gage's spies and Doctor Benjamin Church, they knew exactly where to start looking.

Major John Pitcairn pounded on the door of the Wright Tavern, owned by Ephraim Jones. The local waterhole also doubled as Concord's jail. When the New Englander refused to open the door, Pitcairn ordered several grenadiers to break it down. Once inside, Pitcairn demanded he reveal where the cannons were hidden. Still obstinate, Jones would not answer. Pitcairn knocked him to the ground, "clapped a pistol to his head,"[4] and threatened to blow his brains out if he did not comply. Under such duress, Jones led the officer to three 24-pounder cannons buried behind the tavern. Unearthing the guns, the British disabled them by destroying their trunnions. Pitcairn then released two prisoners from the jail—one held for being a Tory. Remarkably, after disabling the guns, he sat down and ordered breakfast from Jones—which he paid for—and British regulars sauntered into the tavern and bought shots of rum.

The remainder of the Crown's troops broke into more homes and found caches of lead musket balls. They ransacked a gristmill, dumping barrels of flour (supplied by Jeremiah Lee) and the musket balls into the nearby millpond, and they cut down Concord's liberty pole. The Redcoats could have seized more armaments had it not been for Paul Revere. Having been warned on April 7 of a potential raid, the Patriots moved the contraband, some of which the Marbleheaders supplied, into deeper hiding places. Smith also sent several companies across the North Bridge under the command of Captain Lawrence Parsons to Colonel James Barrett's farm about two miles outside town. The farm had recently contained multiple cannons, but Barrett and his family had moved the guns into neighboring towns and secluded areas.

In Concord, British manhandled cannon carriages and rolled them into a blazing fire. But soon flames from the inferno spread to nearby structures.

In a bizarre juxtaposition, the Revolution paused, and both sides put aside their differences. Locals in Concord and the Crown's troops formed a bucket brigade to extinguish the flames that consumed a nearby townhouse.

On the hill overlooking Concord's North Bridge, the provincials who saw the billowing clouds of white smoke reached a different conclusion. Seeing the plumes, young lieutenant Joseph Hosmer stormed over to Colonel James Barrett, who debated their next move, and said, "Will you let them burn the town down?!"[5] Barrett, who wore "an old coat, a flapped hat, and a leather apron"[6] and whose farm was now being raided by Parsons's troops, looked at the faces of his men. Captain Isaac Davis drew his sword and proclaimed, "I haven't a man who is afraid to go."[7] Barrett ordered hundreds of men forward but warned not to shoot first, wait until fired upon, and then "fire as fast as [they] could." The New Englanders advanced toward the bridge. A fifer played "The White Cockade," an old Jacobite ditty,[8] to annoy the king's troops. The British maneuvered into formation to check the advance. They started removing the planking from the bridge while the provincials shouted for them to leave the bridge alone.

In practically a repeat of Lexington, a shot rang out—later dubbed "the shot heard round the world" by Ralph Waldo Emerson, poet and the son of Reverend William Emerson.

One British soldier fired without orders, followed by two others, and then the front British ranks erupted in a sheet of flame and smoke as they discharged a volley. A British musket ball pierced Isaac Davis's heart, killing him. Two other provincials fell, and many suffered wounds from the fusillade.

One of the Patriot officers shouted, "Fire, fellow-soldiers, for God's sake, fire!"[9]

The skirmish continued for several minutes, during which provincials killed two British soldiers and wounded four of the eight officers present at the bridge. Then, an extraordinary event occurred—the line of elite, handpicked light infantry buckled and finally broke. The Crown's finest troops fled for their lives to avoid armed farmers, mechanics, and tradesmen, all turned citizen-soldiers.

Lights raced back toward Concord, where they ran into Colonel Smith and two companies of grenadiers whom he brought up to check the rout. Barrett's men took up a strong position on the high ground behind a stone wall and observed their adversary. As the Americans and the king's troops eyed each other, an unreal scene unfolded as Elias Brown of Concord, whom Reverend Emerson called a "crazy man," stumbled between the two camps, tipsy and selling hard cider to both sides.[10]

Eventually, Smith decided to withdraw his men into the center of Concord to wait for Parsons's companies to return from Colonel Barrett's farm. The militia commanded by Barrett moved back into the hills. Remarkably, the bridge remained unguarded by either side.

When Smith had sent the companies earlier that morning, he believed mountains of cannon and ordnance were hidden at Barrett's farm. Gage's intelligence pinpointed the munitions at the homestead. Instead, the troops only found Barrett's wife and a seemingly empty house. For days Barrett's family and other Patriots had been moving the precious cannon and ordnance, hiding them in nearby towns and woods. Very early that morning, in the nick of time, Barrett's sons had buried muskets in a recently plowed field. "One guided a yoke of oxen, in turning over the furrows, into which others dropped the muskets that had been stored in the house."[11] They also hid musket balls under the noses of the light infantry by cleverly concealing them in the attic in "the bottoms of barrels which were then filled with feathers."[12] The Redcoats found a few gun carriages that they burned.[13]

Returning empty-handed, the Redcoats crossed back over the now-abandoned North Bridge. To their horror, they espied the dead bodies of two of their men and one soldier who was barely alive and writhing in searing pain. That soldier had his head split open, brained with an ax: blood and brains oozed from his skull. Concord native Ammi White, in a bloodthirsty rage, had earlier bashed the wounded, defenseless soldier's skull. Word of the savage nature of the incident spread like wildfire among the British troops, and the atrocity sparked vicious reprisals from both sides.

Reunited with all of his companies, Smith reorganized his men in the same line of march as at the start of the expedition. Soldiers commandeered carts and wagons to carry the wounded officers. The rank and file had to fend for themselves. Those who could walk did so. Severely wounded privates were left behind. By noon, they set off eastward on the long road toward Boston. Light infantry flankers moved ahead on either side of the column. Smith's mission had failed—only disabling a few cannon, burning a handful of gun carriages, and scattering musket balls—but ultimately, it ignited a revolution that would eventually expand into a global war. Time was running out for the expeditionary force. Exhausted and running low on ammunition, they were still seventeen miles from Boston. A countryside of thousands of enraged colonists lay between them and their safety.

CHAPTER 14

THE BLOODY GAUNTLET

As Francis Smith and his men marched toward Lexington and Concord, Elbridge Gerry, Azor Orne, and Jeremiah Lee made their way back into the Black Horse Tavern from the freezing cornfield where they had been hiding. Gerry later received a note from Hancock:

> Dear Sir, I am much obliged for your notice. It is said the officers are gone to Concord, and I will send word thither. I am full with you that we ought to be serious, and I hope your decision will be effectual. I intend doing myself the pleasure of being with you to-morrow. My respects to the committee. I am your real friend, John Hancock.[1]

The three Marbleheaders were the remaining members of the Committee of Supplies. That morning they and the Committee of Safety had planned to meet at the Black Horse Tavern. Since the tavern lay in the line of march for the British expeditionary force, the men rode to Watertown, where they met Doctor Joseph Warren and General William Heath. A gentleman farmer and a voracious reader of military history, Heath trained with Boston's Ancient and Honorable Artillery Company. A record of the meeting does not exist, but undoubtedly the Patriots discussed next steps, strategy, and tactics on how to deal with the British expeditionary force. After spending the morning with the leadership from Marblehead, Warren and Heath rode to Lexington to join the battle.

*   *   *

Smith's long band of scarlet trundled forward. The walking wounded, with bandaged arms, legs, and heads, marched alongside the hitherto unscathed. The light infantry fanned out in an attempt to protect the flanks of the column. In the distance, the ridges and hills teemed with swarms of men assembling from the towns in the area.

The first mile of the march was uneventful until the column hit a juncture known as Meriam's Corner, where several country lanes merged. Here, minutemen and militia ambushed the British. Using the terrain to their advantage, the Americans hid behind boulders, trees, and stone walls while pouring a deadly volley into the retreating Redcoats. As combat veterans of the French and Indian War, many provincials had firsthand experience in this new American way of war, called skirmishing or bushfighting, forged and advanced during those battles a few years earlier. To counter the Americans, the light infantry advanced on the flanks, sometimes surprising and slaying those who fought from their homes and farms. "We sent out very large flanking parties, who soon scoured the woods and stone walls; and whenever we were fired on from houses or barns, our men dashed in and let very few of those they could find escape,"[2] recalled Captain William Glanville Evelyn. The eldest son of Reverend William Evelyn, a vicar of Trim, Ireland, the Irishman commanded a company of light infantry within the 4th (King's Own) Regiment of Foot. Marbleheaders would encounter Captain Evelyn again.

Perched on a boulder-strewn hill outside Lexington, John Parker and his men patiently waited to pounce on Smith's column. Running low on ammunition and having already sustained dozens of casualties, the Redcoats ran into an ambush that history dubbed Parker's Revenge. Parker's men, some also wounded from the fight on Lexington Green, unleashed a devastating volley. One ball hit Smith in the thigh, knocking him out of his saddle. John Pitcairn galloped up and, with sword drawn, directed the troops to clear the hill, which they did at high cost only to discover another hill and hundreds of fresh Americans to fight through.

At Fiske's Hill, Americans ambushed Pitcairn from behind a pile of rails, killing several regulars around him. The marine officer was thrown from his saddle by the fusillade of lead, and his horse bolted off carrying his pistols. Near the hill sat a farmhouse with a well where exhausted, parched men from both sides attempted to quench their thirst. Here, James Hayward of Acton and a British soldier approached at the same time.

The Redcoat shouted, "You are a dead man!"

Hayward retorted, "And so are you."[3] Both men fired and fell simultaneously, each hit by the other's bullet. The British soldier lay dead. Hayward died the next day.

Fighting for their lives, the expeditionary force marched forward over the dead and dying of both sides. Ensign Henry De Berniere, who had provided Gage some of the intelligence for the raid, recalled, "The whole behaved with amazing bravery but little order. We attempted to stop the men and form them two deep, but to no purpose: the confusion increased rather than lessoned. At last . . . the officers got to the front and presented their bayonets, and told the men if they advanced they should die: Upon this they began to form under heavy fire."[4] In the haze of acrid smoke from gunfire, Lexington's meetinghouse came into view.

Exhausted, out of ammunition, and having sustained many dead and wounded, the men neared the ends of their ropes. "We were attacked on all sides from woods, and orchards, and stone walls, and from every house on the roadside . . . we were attacking fresh posts and under one incessant fire," Captain William Glanville Evelyn recalled.[5] Most of Smith's troops felt like only a miracle could save them.

Suddenly, a cannon boomed. A 6-pound ball crashed through the nearby wooden meetinghouse. Lord Percy, with thirteen hundred regulars in his brigade, arrived to rescue the expeditionary force from "inevitable destruction."[6]

* * *

Elements of the Marblehead Regiment arrived that morning, including officers Caleb Gibbs, Gabriel Johonnot, Joshua Orne,* and John Glover, and battled with the British during their retreat. Former Bostonian Johonnot recalled harassing the British retreat from Lexington: "I entered and devoted to the service of the United States of America, my whole time of service from the memorable nineteenth of April, seventeen hundred and seventy five, Thursday of the first commencement of Hostility against the said United States, by the British government, having on that day volunteered in a company commanded by Capt. John Glover marched and proceeded from Marblehead to harass the British Troops, on their retreat from Lexington, and from that day continued in the Revolutionary Army in the station of Lieutenant Colonel."[7] Undoubtedly, Romeo, the African American freeman who accompanied Johonnot, was there as well. Additionally, other black Patriots from Essex County were likely present, including Manuel Soto.

One Marbleheader's wife recalled that he left their family bed to join the fight. However, many of the rank-and-file members of the regiment missed the battle because they were fishing the Grand Banks.[8] Most of the town's men were at sea, catching cod before the New England Trade and Fisheries Act took effect and destroyed their ability to earn a living. As Ashley Bowen recorded, "This day fair weather sailed many of our fishing schooners [to the Grand Banks]."[9] Bowen further noted, "Sailed fifty of our fishermen for the Isle of Sable and brig *Wolf*."[10] The skeletal Marblehead Regiment moved into position and participated in the heaviest fighting in a string of skirmishes moving from Lexington to Menotomy.

In the British retreat toward Boston, Lord Percy formed a marching square several columns wide, with the light infantry moving ahead working the flanks. Around 3:15 p.m., after several delays, Percy ordered

* Ashley Bowen's diary indicates Orne's presence in Lexington around the time of the battle, so it's highly likely he was also present at the battle.

his men forward: "It began now to grow pretty late, and we had 15 miles to retire, & only 36 rounds."[11] As the columns and flankers surged forward, British fifers and drummers mockingly played "Yankee Doodle."

General William Heath countered with a moving envelopment of Percy's troops, which the English nobleman recalled as "an incessant fire, wh[ich] like a moving circle surrounded & fol[lowe]d us wherever we went."[12]

Minutemen and militia, indiscernible during the battle, swarmed the British from all flanks. Gibbs and the Marbleheaders engaged the British in Menotomy fighting house to house and hand to hand. They joined the battle with men under the command of Major Loammi Baldwin, whose regiment would later fight with the Marbleheaders in a brigade as the war progressed. Baldwin, a true Renaissance man, served as a soldier, engineer, politician, farmer, and botanist. His lasting fame came from the Baldwin apple he developed and propagated in later years.

Inseparable on the battlefield, Heath and Warren fought side by side. In the thickest of the battle, Warren had a pin that held his hair back shot off by a musket ball. "He was seen animating his countrymen to battle, and fighting by their side; and there he was found administering healing comforts to the wounded." Three healers, all close friends—Warren, Bond, and Church—were present that day. Honoring his duty to save lives, Marblehead doctor Nathaniel Bond focused his healing arts on the British soldiers. He later defended his actions to his friend Elbridge Gerry in "a story that in the simplicity of my heart I supposed true I last Wednesday morning for the sole purpose of what I believed to be removing extreme needless distress [tended British soldiers]."[13] The other member of the trio of doctors present feigned urging the militia on, but like so many of his actions, including sprinkling blood on his stockings to create the appearance of having been in the thick of battle, Doctor Benjamin Church's were deceptive.

Americans defended their homes, firing from windows and doors. "The soldiers were so enraged at suffering from the unseen enemy that they proceeded, and put at death all those found in them,"[14] recalled Frederick Mackenzie, an officer in the Royal Welch Fusiliers. The

Americans would not yield, and the British ran into many a man like seventy-eight-year-old Captain Samuel Whittemore, who protected his home in Menotomy[15] as he hid behind a stone wall, killing a soldier and firing his pistol to slay another. While attacking a soldier with his sword, a ball blew off part of his cheekbone. Then the Redcoats bayoneted him numerous times, "shouting we have killed the old rebel."[16] Whittemore lay in a pool of his own blood, having been bayoneted six or eight times, and his hat and clothes "were shot through in many places,"[17] but he would survive and live to be ninety-six.

The British executed several prisoners after they surrendered. Dennison Wallis ran for his life, jumping over a wall after the Redcoats shot the men around him. Wallis had been struck twelve times and left for dead, but lived to tell what he had witnessed.[18] In and around the grounds of Jason Russell's house, a dozen Americans, including its owner, were killed defending the home. Russell, fifty-eight and lame, refused to leave the dwelling, and he reportedly declared, "An Englishman's house is his castle."[19] A macabre scene of the weltering, bayonet- and bullet-riddled bodies of her husband and other Americans greeted Jason Russell's wife when she returned to her home after the battle. She described the floor of the kitchen as a lake of blood "almost ankle deep."[20] Many of the men fighting around the Russell House were from Beverly and would soon become a company within the Marblehead Regiment.[21]

Burning homes, killing livestock, and plundering anything they could cram in their haversacks, including the church communion silver, the British embarked upon an orgy of violence. They lost more men as they pushed east to break through the ambush. After moving through Menotomy and the bloodiest combat, the British still had to cross the Charles River to reach the safety of Boston. As Percy marched into Cambridge, he discerned that the provincials had removed the planks on the bridge over the Charles and a large American force occupied the ground around the crossing point. Instinctively, Percy made a bold decision that saved his troops. He ordered his men to take a less traveled lane that led into Charlestown. A force of Salem men led by Colonel Timothy Pickering could have engaged Percy, but Pickering dithered.

One of the men marching with Pickering was Francis Symonds, who would later become a captain in the Marblehead Regiment.[22]

The exact reasons for his hesitation are not known; however, many Americans still considered themselves British subjects and thought there was time to negotiate and talk.[23] Major Pitcairn commanded the rearguard, which checked the militia as the British force passed over the Charlestown Neck. Lord Percy noted they arrived at Charlestown "having expended almost every cartridge."[24]

A bloodred sun set on the British troops, many of whom had not slept for two days, as they set up defensive positions to cover the evacuation of the wounded and the retreat to Boston on a place ironically known as Bunker Hill.

In the morning, the British would find Boston surrounded by thousands of Americans.

CHAPTER 15

SIEGE, THE ARMY OF NEW ENGLAND, AND MR. GERRY

Private Romeo and core members of the Marblehead Regiment* encamped around Boston. Over twelve thousand Americans, mostly from Massachusetts, cut off the British stronghold from the rest of the colony. Thomas Gage knew his army of 3,200 troops could not withstand an assault, so he feverishly continued strengthening his defenses, erecting an abatis and positioning artillery batteries at strategic points. To shorten his lines, the British general ordered his troops to abandon Charlestown Neck, demolished a series of redoubts, and hastily built V-shaped earthworks known as flèches on and around Bunker Hill.

Terrified the Americans would storm Boston any day, Gage forbade egress out of the city, effectively taking the inhabitants hostage. As an olive branch, he offered to let the women and children leave "upon the condition that Male inhabitants within the Town shall on their Part solemnly engage that they will not take up arms against the King's Troops, within the Town, and should an attack be made from without."[1]

The British general turned the population of Boston into human shields with the hope of preventing an attack or quashing any plans of an internal uprising in the city. He hammered home his point, "that in case the Troops should be attacked . . . and the attack should be aided

---

* This included John Glover, William Raymond Lee, and the bulk of the leadership of Marblehead Regiment.

by the inhabitants of the Town, it might issue in very unhappy consequences to the Town."[2]

As the British prepared for a final stand, the hostages bought Gage precious time until reinforcements arrived. The royal governor proposed a gun control scheme aimed at disarming the inhabitants of Boston. If the Bostonians registered and turned in their weapons to the Crown's troops for safekeeping, then they could freely leave the town—at least that was the promise. Loyalist selectmen voted and approved the plan.

After the vote, a massive line formed outside Faneuil Hall. Over the course of two days beginning on April 24, 1775, the Bostonians, armed to the teeth, turned in 1,652 firelocks, 572 pistols, and over 900 bayonets.[3] Taking their weapons, Gage allowed some residents to leave; however, the flood tide that followed alarmed the Loyalists in the town, and Gage reneged on his promise. The siege continued, and so did the detention of many of its Patriot citizens.

Rather than solidifying British control of the colonies as he had intended, Gage's actions galvanized support for Massachusetts's plight. Other colonies viewed the action as a clear case of tyranny, and more people felt drawn to the Patriot cause. Citizen-soldier militia from the colonies poured into Massachusetts. Americans mobilized for more conflict. But Boston was not Gage's only problem; as commander of British forces in North America, he faced a massive shortage of troops necessary to put down the spreading rebellion. The bulk of Gage's men were in Boston, ten regiments in all (each with a strength of approximately four hundred men). He had only several hundred men left to hold the British colonies in the rest of North America. Gage had four regiments garrisoned in Canada and the frontier, and half of a regiment was stationed in New York[4]—hardly enough to quash the growing rebellion.

Since Lexington and Concord, Elbridge Gerry, Azor Orne, and an ailing Jeremiah Lee played a crucial role in shaping what would eventually become the United States. Marblehead men formed the heart of the

Patriot leadership. The king's troops had attacked Americans. Now the Committee of Safety and the Massachusetts Provincial Congress, led by president pro tempore Doctor Joseph Warren, effectively acted as a provisional government, making crucial decisions. The Massachusetts Provincial Congress made monumental decisions but were careful not to claim official status, which could upset their sister colonies.

On April 21, the Massachusetts Provincial Congress convened in Concord. Momentously, it effectively assumed control of the Massachusetts Bay government, extended lines of communication, and sought the participation of the thirteen colonies. The colonies would ultimately agree to unite at the meeting of the Second Continental Congress in Philadelphia. But for now, the Massachusetts Provincial Congress and the Marbleheaders would be the government for the growing rebellion. Jeremiah Lee and Gerry in particular, played a vital role in forging these relationships among the colonies through their trading contacts.

Gerry, stretched to the limit, participated in the most important committees and their decisions. The Marbleheader "embraced truth when he saw it" and launched himself into the work, employing his "considerable knowledge."[5] Not known for his oratory prowess, Gerry, "stammering in speech," punctuated his statements with an "uncouth delivery broken and interrupted with many a heck & hem & repetition of ofs & ands." Despite his flaws in delivery, "he assumed such a superiority over his opponents."[6] Deliberate and prudent, the Marblehead Patriot was a "Man of immense Worth."[7] Unassuming in character but dynamic in action, he was described as "an instrument for setting this continent in a flame."[8]

While the Marbleheaders met, John Hancock, Samuel Adams, and John Adams traveled to Philadelphia for the long-scheduled meeting of the Second Continental Congress, due to begin May 10, 1774. Before departing on the weeks-long carriage journey, John Adams visited the bloody ground of Menotomy, Lexington, and Concord. He provided a compelling perspective on the current state of affairs as well as the people's state of mind. "I rode to Cambridge where I saw . . . the New England Army. There was great confusion and distress: Artillery, Arms, Cloathing were wanting and sufficient Supply of Provisions not easily obtained. Neither the officers nor Men wanted Spirit of Resolution. I rode from thence to Lexington and along the scene of Action for many miles and enquired of the Inhabitants, the Circumstances. These were not calculated to diminish my Ardour in the Cause. They on the Contrary convinced me that the Die was cast, the Rubicon passed, and as Lord Mansfield expressed it in Parliament, if We did not defend ourselves they would kill us."[9]

Adams was correct about the sorry state of the provincial forces. The delegates to the Provincial Congress faced the all-too-real likelihood that the various volunteer militia and minuteman units would disintegrate. To guard against this possibility, they ordered the immediate formation of a Massachusetts army and officer corps of 13,600 men.

This Massachusetts contribution represented only a part of the larger, thirty-thousand-strong New England Army of Observation that the Committee of Safety hoped to raise.[10] The Marbleheaders on the committee had to meld a diverse conglomeration of unemployed fishermen, dockworkers, tradesmen, and farmers, as well as doctors and lawyers, from a variety of age groups into an American army. Men like John Glover and John Parker, who had priceless French and Indian War experience, led many of the regiments within this growing force.

Organizing and shaping the army, however, fell on the shoulders of Marblehead mariner Colonel Azor Orne, a member of the Committee of Safety, which "regulat[ed] the regiments of the army."[11] The committee officially formed and authorized each regiment, which consisted of ten companies of fifty-nine men, three officers, one captain, and two subalterns. To keep them together, Orne and Elbridge Gerry instituted a formal process of enlistment. The Provincial Congress ordered this to be immediately implemented, and its minutes of April 23, 1775, stated, "That Mr. Gerry give the express going to the press, his order for the enlisting papers."[12]

As Orne and his committee regulated the regiments of the new army, the Provincial Congress organized an artillery corps with Richard

Gridley as chief engineer. The sixty-five-year-old was one of the few Americans with a commission in the British Army.* An expert in the science and art of artillery, he had honed his skills in the French and Indian War. Marbleheaders Samuel R. Trevett and Robert Wormstead commanded a battery of artillery within the unit.

Arming, supplying, and feeding such a gargantuan force constituted an enormous undertaking. Most of the men did not have uniforms and instead wore homespun clothes. The majority of the citizen-soldiers were armed with privately owned weapons. Gerry, Lee, and other merchants and ship captains strained their contacts and put decades of trust and goodwill into motion to purchase priceless gunpowder and arms for the cause. They sent their personal fortunes, as well as cargo goods like salted cod, to trade for the necessary supplies. The Marbleheaders secured America's first foreign aid for the Revolution in December 1774. In July, Gerry pleaded with Bilbao-based José Gardoqui, the patriarch of a mega-merchant house in Spain. "The Ministry in Britain have been endeavoring to keep a Supply of powder from the Colonies, well knowing that they cannot enslave them by any other Means," he wrote. To that end, he sent the vessel *Rockingham* "with £1000 sterg [sterling] in cash, & six hundred & fifty pounds Bills of Exch[ange] on your House." The money was "to be invested in good pistol & Cannon powder—half each."[13]

Gardoqui obliged, but that was only half the battle. On arriving back in North America, the ship had to evade the Royal Navy's squadron blockading Massachusetts. In this case, the smuggling effort failed, and the British seized the goods Gerry had intended for the American army. Fortunately, both Gerry and Gardoqui had scores of ships that traded among the colonies, the Iberian Peninsula, and the Caribbean, including the Dutch island of Sint Eustatius. Dutch shippers "disguised [the powder] in tea-chests, rice barrels, and the like" to confound the

---

* Gridley served in King George's War as well as in the French and Indian War. His British commission was in one of the two regular regiments raised in the American colonies.

Royal Navy in the event they were stopped and searched.[14] Gerry dispatched Captain Michael Corbett to trade 120 hogsheads of fish and shingles and boards to purchase "an Article, so immediately necessary."[15] Corbett exchanged the fish and other commodities and brought back powder. Many Marblehead ships made it through the blockade, carrying their valuable materiel, as well as news of Crown troop movements and other world events.

While the Marbleheaders trained their attention on the weighty matters of colonial politics and outfitting the army, their hometown faced genuine peril. On April 20, the day after the Battles of Lexington and Concord, rumors spread that the British intended to raid Marblehead and other Massachusetts ports. Riders alerted the countryside, and panic ensued. Parts of the coast evacuated. Most of the military-age Marbleheaders manned the siege lines or remained at sea, fishing the Grand Banks; few were left to protect the folks at home.

HMS *Lively* and the brig *Hope* had blockaded Marblehead. With the barrels of their cannons trained on the seaside village, the British demanded the Patriots hand over provisions. The town reluctantly acquiesced.

Concerned about the town's vulnerability in the men's absence, Gerry raised the issue of its defense during the April 22 session of the Provincial Congress. However, Congress had so many fires to extinguish, they tabled the matter. Eventually, Congress would strengthen the defenses of seaside towns like Marblehead and Beverly, and Glover's Regiment would play a role in their defense.

But these external threats were not the only ones Marblehead faced. Internally, the many Loyalists in the town also posed a risk. In response, the Patriots cracked down on neighbors who remained loyal to the Crown.

CHAPTER 16

THE LOYALISTS

Life became impossible for most Loyalists living in Massachusetts. Only those within occupied Boston felt some degree of safety. Loyalists from Marblehead and the countryside streamed toward the city, where they hoped the British could keep them safe. Ashley Bowen noted that within Marblehead, "most of our people [Loyalists] gone out of town with their goods. . . . All of our countrymen have turned their houses into pawnbroker's shops to receive the Marblehead men's goods."[1]

The fates of Jeremiah Lee's business rival, the wealthy merchant Robert "King" Hooper, and his family are emblematic. Hooper ensconced his family in his home in Danvers and largely abandoned his Marblehead holdings. The Loyalist scion never regained his fortune or status and died bankrupt. One of his sons, Joseph Hooper, refused to renounce the Crown. After surviving several attempts to burn his residence, he fled to Europe in the hull of one of his father's ships laden with fish, and his property was confiscated.[2]

In May 1775, the Massachusetts Provincial Congress officially addressed the issue of Loyalists, making Loyalism effectively illegal and requiring that the names of known offenders be published in Cambridge and Salem newspapers. Proactively, the Congress declared, "A number of men, some of whom have, in times past, by the good people of this province, been raised to the highest places of honor and trust, have become inimical to this colony; and merely on principles of avarice here, in conjunction with the late Governor Hutchinson, been trying to reduce America to the most abject state of slavery; and as well as avoid the just indignation of the people, as to purse their diabolical plans, have fled to Boston, and other places for refuge."[3]

The Congress resolved, "Those persons, among whom are the mandamus counselors, are guilty of such atrocious and unnatural crimes against their country, that every friend of mankind ought to forsake and detest them, until they shall give evidence of a sincere repentance, by actions worthy of men and Christians." The new provincial government pushed enforcement down to the local level and to committees of inspection "in every town in this colony, to see this fully enforced, unless in such cases as the Congress shall otherwise direct."[4] While typically not formally forced out, Tories fled their homes, leaving their property to be confiscated by the new government and used to fund the cause.[5]

In a divided country, as this first American civil war continued to develop into a revolution presumably based on liberty and freedom, ironically, liberty generally only flowed one way—toward the Patriots.

But sometimes it didn't.

Doctor Nathaniel Bond, an ardent Patriot who would emerge as the fighting surgeon of the Marblehead Regiment, was wrongly accused of being a Loyalist, despite having "done nothing worthy of the smallest punishment" but only treating wounded British soldiers during the Battle of Lexington. Mob justice descended upon him, causing him to write Gerry. "So strongly and barbarously cruelly represented that I am in danger of my life every moment. Thousands having sworn to kill me at first sight. What I must beg and entreat of you Sir is that you will be kind enough to appeal to the Commanding Officer to send immediately a strong guard to carry me to the camp for a trial by Court Marshall [*sic*]." Bond feared for his life and desperately wanted to clear his name: "I appeal to the Judge of Souls. If you have any faith in my [illegible] or if you should regret to hear of my being hunted to an untimely Grave by murderous hands. . . ." To hammer home the gravity of the situation, Bond ended the letter by saying, "If you cannot attend to the matter you will undoubtedly soon hear that I am gone from this life."[6]

Bond also called his good friend Joseph Warren to his defense. Warren and Bond's friendship dated back to their time at Harvard

Medical School and their shared membership in the secret society of Resurrectionists known as the Spunker Club. After a court of inquiry, the Committee of Safety exonerated Bond: "Doctor Nathaniel Bond, of Marblehead, having been charged before this Committee with having acted an unfriendly Part to this Colony; . . . appears to have been altogether involuntary, and was such as several of our most firm Friends were led into false Rumours spread of the Transactions of the 19th Instant) no Impressions to the Doctor's Disadvantage may remain on the Minds of any Person whatever. Joseph Warren, Chairman."[7]

A member of the Patriot leadership who was not yet suspected was fellow Harvard alumnus Doctor Benjamin Church. As the Congress deliberated and shaped the new government, Church enthusiastically participated on committees where he carefully spun a web of lies and captured some of the Revolution's most important intelligence. From his perch in the Provincial Congress, Gage's top spy had an unparalleled vantage point to view the inner workings of the Patriot nerve center.

Days after Lexington and Concord, the good doctor stunned the Committee of Safety by boldly proclaiming, "I am determined to go into Boston tomorrow." The room was aghast. "Are you serious, Doctor Church?" Warren incredulously retorted. "They will hang you if they catch you in Boston." Paul Revere, who was present at the meeting, questioned Church's loyalty: "I was a constant and critical observer of him, and I must say, that I never thought Him a man of Principle; and I doubted much in my own mind, whether He was a real Whig." However, Church assuaged some of the concerns by planting blood on his stockings after Lexington and Concord. Revere remembered, "I met him in Cambridge, when He shew me some blood on his stocking, which he said spirted on him from a Man who was killed near him, as he was urging the Militia on. I well remember, that I argued with my self, if a Man will risque his life in a Cause, he must be a Friend to that cause; and I never suspected him after, till He was charged with being a Traytor."[8]

The siege on Boston had rattled Church's plan to deliver his intelligence to Gage, so he needed a plausible excuse and means to break through the lines and get into the city. He dug in his heels: "I am serious, and I am determined to go at all adventures."[9]

After considerable debate, Doctor Warren implored, "If you are determined, let us make some business for you," and the quorum "agreed that he should go to git medicine for their and our Wounded officers."[10] Church passed through the lines the next day. For appearance's sake, he was taken prisoner. But once within the arms of the British, he rode in style, as Gage furnished him with a carriage to British headquarters, where he disgorged his priceless intelligence on the inner workings and plans of the Committee of Safety. Remarkably, after the meeting, he walked freely around occupied Boston and returned through American lines with the medicine and, unknown to his fellow Patriots, a sack full of British money for his betrayal as he resumed his powerful position on the Provincial Congress.

A future American traitor approached the Massachusetts Provincial Congress with a bold plan. Benedict Arnold, then thirty-four, a successful, charismatic merchant, and at this stage still very much a Patriot, submitted a daring plan to seize Fort Ticonderoga located in New York near the southern end of Lake Chaplain and seize its supplies, powder, and dozens of priceless cannon. Strategically located but vulnerable, the fortress, known as the Gateway to the Continent, had fallen into disrepair and was defended only by two officers and forty-six men, many of them invalids suffering from disability or disease. After Lexington and Concord, Gage ordered that Ticonderoga and the nearby fortress of Crown Point be reinforced. The Committee of Safety approved the plan of invading another colony, New York, and gave Arnold a commission, two hundred pounds[11] of precious black powder, £100 sterling, horses, and orders to recruit four hundred men for a covert mission to seize the fort. Gerry opposed releasing such a significant amount of the precious powder, and Warren ominously warned that they should not "trifle away this only moment we have to employ for the salvation of our country";[12] nevertheless, Warren released the gunpowder to

Arnold. Unbeknownst to all parties, the precious powder would prove superfluous to Arnold's mission but crucial in a looming battle.

As Arnold prepared to leave, he received word that Ethan Allen and his men, known as the Green Mountain Boys, had already set out to capture the fort. Riding his horse nearly to death, Arnold sped off in hot pursuit of his rival, eventually catching up to the militia commander and demanding command of the mission. Allen, who also sported an oversize ego, demurred, and Arnold faced a walkout by many of the Vermont men, who refused to serve under an interloper. Through successful negotiation on Arnold's part, they reached a compromise: the two men would share joint command.

On May 10, eighty-three men assembled into boats at what is now Shoreham, Vermont, crossed a portion of Lake Chaplain, and assaulted Ticonderoga at dawn. The garrison did not put up a fight. Allen and Arnold first encountered Lieutenant Jocelyn Feltham and demanded Ticonderoga's surrender. Groggy, Feltham inquired by whose authority he had to surrender the fort. According to tradition, Allen responded, "In the name of the Great Jehovah and the Continental Congress."[13] Eventually, Captain William Delaplace, the commander of the British stronghold, meekly emerged from his sleeping chamber with his "breeches in hand." Both Allen and Arnold ordered his surrender. Arnold diplomatically stated, "Give up and you will be treated like a gentleman."[14] Delaplace complied, and the fort, cannon, and cache of liquor transferred into American hands. Arnold tried in vain to restrain the Green Mountain Boys as they went on a drunken rampage. Later, Arnold's men seized Crown Point and raided Fort Saint-Jean, seizing a British sloop. Whether or not the Americans could maintain control of the cannon and forts remained in doubt, but for the time being, the back door into New England had been secured, along with a motley collection of cannons, mortars, and howitzers. The lot consisted of British and French ordnance from different eras, some belonging in a museum, in various conditions: "unserviceable, bad, to good." Arnold reported to Azor Orne and the Committee of Safety that he snared 111 cannon at Crown Point and 86 at Ticonderoga. Included in the haul were thirty thousand flints, thousands of cannonballs, and shells. Powder remained a problem, as the expedition netted only twenty-eight barrels of "damaged powder";[15] however, artillery captured at the forts would prove crucial in a looming battle.

News of the blood that flowed at Lexington and Concord spread through the colonies, traveling by word of mouth, rider, and ship. Word had not reached Virginia by April 21 when the royal governor, Lord Dunmore, ordered twenty British soldiers and marines to conduct a raid in the middle of the night on the Williamsburg powder magazine. Troops seized eighteen half barrels of precious black powder, leaving three full barrels of spoiled powder in the octagon-shaped brick building. Dunmore, like Gage, had been acting on the Crown's orders to confiscate powder and arms from the colonists. Elements of Virginia's militia swiftly mobilized and called on George Washington to lead the militia and demand Dunmore return the powder. Washington demurred and called for caution, unaware of the bloodshed at Lexington and Concord. Eventually, word reached Virginia of the events in Massachusetts, and Dunmore's raid galvanized support within Virginia for the Revolution. The rebellion engulfed the colonies, and Whigs seized royal powder supplies at Charleston in April 1775, and days later in Savannah.

CHAPTER 17

TYRANNY, VICTIMS, AND THE AMERICAN NARRATIVE

Elbridge Gerry listened intently as John Parker recounted the horrors of the cool morning hours of April 19. Smoke, sound, blood, and the chaos of battle came to life as Parker revealed what unfolded on Lexington Green. Who fired first became all-important, distinguishing traitor from victim, aggressor from defender. Americans, still Englishmen, needed to convince their fellow brothers—and the world—that they were the victims. The savvy founders were aware of the necessity of information warfare long before the term was coined.

Just days after the battles, Gerry participated in one of the Provincial Congress's most crucial efforts: gathering depositions to convey to London the American narrative of events at Lexington and Concord. The Patriots knew that if Thomas Gage's report reached the British press first, they would be branded traitors who started the Revolution by firing on the king's troops. The Provincial Congress directed "that Mr. Gerry, Col. Cushing, Col. Barrett, Capt. Stone, Doct. Taylor, Mr. Sullivan, Mr. Freeman, and Mr. Watson, and Esquire Dix, be a committee to take depositions, *in perpetuam*, from which a full account of the transactions of the troops, under general Gage, in their route to and from Concord, &e, on Wednesday last, may be collected, to be sent to England, by the first ship from Salem."[1]

Gerry zealously launched himself into the crucial task. John Adams described his dedication: "If every Man here was a Gerry, the Liberties of America would be safe against the Gates of Earth and Hell."[2] After swearing an oath to tell the truth, the battle's participants answered questions Gerry and his team asked them, and the Marbleheader deposed not only Americans but also captured British soldiers. Twenty depositions he compiled confirmed the American narrative of victimhood—the Americans were victims and the British fired first. On April 23, John Bateman, deposition 13, a British regular in the 52nd Regiment, swore under oath, "There was a small party of men gathered together in that place, when our said troops marched by, and I Testify and Declare, that I heard the word of command given to the Troops to fire, and some of said Troops Did fire, and I saw one of said small party lay Dead on the ground nigh said meeting house; and I testify, that I never heard any of the Inhabitants so much as fire one gun on said Troops."[3]

What he did not ask was why so many Americans risked treason, their lives, their fortunes, and their honor to fight for a nation yet to be born. Of course, they were defending themselves, but a myriad of other reasons also compelled them to action.

One American captured the zeitgeist of the period. In an interview years after the war, Captain Levi Preston shed light on why Americans fought, risking their fortune, lives, and way of life for revolution.

Was it about the Stamp Act?

"I never saw one of those stamps."

Was it about the tea tax?

"I never drank a drop of that stuff; the boys threw it all overboard."

The interviewer asked him about several esoteric concepts that Preston dismissed. Much of it boiled down to the fact that Americans don't like to be told what to do. As he then responded, "Young man, what we meant in going for those red-coats was this: we always had governed ourselves, and we always meant to. They didn't mean we should."[4]

Sovereignty.

Working at lightning speed, Gerry gathered the depositions, and Joseph Warren drafted an elegant letter introducing the colonists' narrative of victimhood to sway public opinion in Great Britain. To hammer home the American viewpoint, Gerry also enclosed copies of the *Salem Gazette* that contained the story of the battles, with black coffins representing the American dead adorning the headline.

Transporting the documents to London became a crucial race against time: the Americans needed to spirit their package across the ocean before Gage's report arrived. Near panic occurred when the Patriots learned Gage's vessel, the hulking 200-ton brig *Sukey*, had left for London with the British version of events days earlier. The Patriots pinned their hopes on the sleek 62-ton *Quero*, captained by thirty-four-year-old John Derby, a well-connected Patriot from Salem whose father, Richard Derby, had stood his ground at North Bridge and defied Colonel Alexander Leslie during the Salem Powder Alarm.

Leaving Salem for Britain on the night of April 28–29, *Quero* miraculously avoided *Lively*'s blockade of Salem and Marblehead and cut through the emerald, churning waters of the Atlantic. The fast ship did not carry cargo, just ballast stones, leaving the vessel light and nimble. Captain Derby would navigate the treacherous waters on one of the most important yet forgotten voyages in American history.

To avoid prowling British agents and ships, Derby had orders to land in Ireland and journey overland to England to deliver his extraordinary news to London-based agents Benjamin Franklin and Arthur Lee. Joseph Warren stressed, "P.S. You are to keep this order a profound secret from every person on earth."[5]

Derby maintained his silence: even his crew did not know the precious cargo or *Quero*'s destination. Despite their efforts to cloak the mission in secrecy, Doctor Church knew about the covert operation from his position as a member of the Provincial Congress. Whether or not he transmitted the vital intelligence to Gage is not known. It is also unclear whether Congress instructed Derby to land in Ireland as a deception; regardless, Derby ignored the order. In twenty-nine days, fast for its time, *Quero* braved rough seas, evaded British military vessels, and even passed by the *Sukey* in the Atlantic to arrive at the Isle of Wight. From there, Derby journeyed to the port of South Hampton and then traveled overland by carriage to London.

Dubbed the "accidental captain," Derby seemed to appear out of thin air with earth-shaking news that would change an empire overnight. He secretly met Arthur Lee, a Virginian educated in medicine and law, and delivered the news to John Wilkes, Lord Mayor of London, "an eccentric and fearless radical" who openly "espoused the contention of the colonies."[6] Depositions and newspaper accounts reprinted in the London press created a sensational tidal wave of public opinion largely favorable to the colonists. Desperate for Gage's report, which had not yet arrived, the Crown tried to discredit the material, but Lee countered the attack in the press with an American broadside.

Meanwhile, the British cast a dragnet to hunt for Derby, but he slipped through their fingers and sailed back to the colonies. After an excruciating twelve-day wait, Gage's report finally arrived, bearing a broadly similar version to the American account—with the major exception of who fired first.

Crown troops killed Americans, and their actions did much to unite the colonies against Britain, including creating some sympathy among the British people. The colonists had achieved a tremendous early propaganda victory as victims.

Derby was not the only Essex County captain returning from a voyage. In May, Marblehead welcomed home its men who had spent weeks fishing the treacherous waters of the Grand Banks. Many would soon become part of the Marblehead Regiment.

Tragically, Jeremiah Lee, the Patriot leader of the Marblehead Regiment, died that month from illness and trauma sustained the night he hid in the cornfield during the Battle of Lexington. Command of Marblehead's militia regiment now passed to John Glover, who ordered a drummer and fifer to march through the streets of Marblehead to drum up, literally, enlistments for the new regiment. Many answered the call, including several free blacks. On June 15, Congress commissioned John Glover, a colonel in the Army of Massachusetts, the new commander of the Marbleheaders to replace Lee.

The unit would also go through a series of designations—first as the 23rd Regiment, later the 21st Continental Regiment, and ultimately the 14th Continental Regiment.[7] The "Marblehead Regiment," "Marine Regiment," and "marines"[8] were also terms used to describe the men.

Glover reported to the Provincial Congress that he had levied ten companies for the regiment, consisting of "505 men, inclusive of officers, and about three-quarters of said number armed and effective; who are willing to serve in the said army. . . . All are now in Marblehead."[9] Only seven of the men came from outside the town,[10] including Captain Francis Symonds from Danvers. One of these was sixteen-year-old Spanish immigrant Francis Grater from Barcelona. Like all of the men in the regiment, he was a volunteer who "enlisted and was never drafted."[11] Samuel Trevett's Marblehead artillery company also drilled and prepared for battle.

The second-in-command of the regiment remained Gabriel Johonnot, aided by two members of the Lee family.[12] About the impressive young officers, William Tudor wrote to John Adams, "This Lieut. Col. Johnnot [sic] of Glover's Regiment, has Fire, Sense and Courage, nor is Major Lee of the same Regiment deficient in either. There is also Jos. Lee a Captain in the same Regiment. This young Fellow is son to the late Col. Jer Lee of Marblehead. He has a young Wife at Home, and his Fortune sets him above any mercenary Inducement. He is here purely from the best of Motives, the Love of Freedom and his Country. There are also several Young Fellows in that Regiment of Spirit and Parts, who will never basely cringe to beg the General to inform Congress they wish for Preferment. I will take another Opportunity to prosecute this Subject."[13]

Companies formed the heart of the regiment. Thirty-four-year-old William Blackler led the 2nd Company while shipmaster John Selman became captain of the 4th, and the experienced sea captain Nicholson Broughton headed the 6th. Broughton's son-in-law, John Devereux, also a shipmaster, would serve as second lieutenant in the 6th Company,[14] while sailmaker Captain William Courtis led the 7th Company, and John Glover Jr. the 9th. Two Marblehead goldsmiths would also command companies: Thomas Grant and Joseph Swasey.[15]

Ensigns played a special role, taking turns carrying the colors of the company or regiment. Initially joining the unit as a sergeant, William Hawks became an ensign and proved resilient, fighting in all of the regiment's campaigns and battles. He would chronicle his experiences in a detailed orderly book. Joshua Orne and later Robert Wormstead joined Hawks in the role of ensign.

Children also served. Some of the youngest members of the regiment were fifers and drummers, whose purpose was to communicate commands over the din of battle to maneuver troops. Each regiment possessed unique drum signals and drilled the men to follow orders dictated by a particular drumbeat. Fifers and drummers played popular tunes when the men marched, which instilled a sense of esprit de corps and fellowship.

Thomas Grant Jr. was a child of ten when he enlisted in his father's company as a fifer. Many of the musicians in the Revolutionary War were children or teenage boys. These father-and-son teams were often assigned to separate companies; however, they fought in the same battles. Some child soldiers were orphans. Often in the vanguard, they would witness the horrors of battle.

On May 25, the time for preparation for battle came to an end when the HMS *Cerberus* arrived at Boston Harbor. Named for the Greek mythological three-headed hound of hell, the ship fittingly carried reinforcements and three British generals—John Burgoyne, William Howe, and Henry Clinton—who would have a profound effect on the Revolution and take part in the battle that would become known as Bunker Hill.

CHAPTER 18

BUNKER HILL

Elbridge Gerry watched with mounting horror as his roommate and friend, Doctor Joseph Warren, methodically laid out his best clothes, cleaned his musket, and sharpened his sword. President of the Massachusetts Provincial Congress and recently commissioned as a major general in the Massachusetts militia, Warren led the community of Patriot sympathizers in Boston. He intended to join the provincial troops amassing on Bunker Hill for the expected battle with the British.

On the morning of June 17, Gerry pleaded with Warren, reminding him of his importance to the cause and warning him that the fight was likely to be a bloodbath. "We [have] not powder sufficient to maintain the desperate conflict which must ensue," Gerry said, "and should all be cut to pieces."

"I know it," Warren replied. "But I . . . should die were I to remain at home while my fellow citizens are shedding their blood for me."

"As sure as you go, you will be slain," Gerry warned.

Warren responded with a familiar Latin phrase: "Dulce et decorum est pro patria mori." ("It is sweet and fitting to die for one's country.")[1]

In the late eighteenth century, the land around Boston, especially the area where the Battle of Bunker Hill took place, looked quite different from the way it does today. In the eighteenth century, open ground sprawled across hills. A little more than three miles east of Hastings House in Cambridge, where Warren prepared for battle, Bunker Hill sat on the Charlestown peninsula, to the north of Boston.* The summit was only 110 feet high but was the highest point on the peninsula. To the north, the Mystic River flowed past, and the Charles River lay to the south and east. A narrow strip of land, known as the Charlestown Neck, connected the western side to the mainland. Bunker Hill was on the west side, fairly close to the neck, and it was the original military objective for both the provincials and the British. But Breed's Hill, a shorter, sixty-four-foot-high summit that was farther east and closer to the buildings of Charlestown, would within days be the scene of some of the most ferocious fighting of the Revolution.

Also in the spring of 1775, attempting to quell the growing spirit of colonial rebellion centered in Boston, Thomas Gage requested reinforcements. Six thousand more Redcoats landed there, accompanied by three generals who would play critical roles in the War of Independence: William Howe, John Burgoyne, and Henry Clinton.

A thirty-year army veteran, Howe was a tall aristocrat with a reputation for fighting bravely when on the field and drinking, gambling, and whoring when off it. Distantly related to the king, he also held a seat in Parliament, where he expressed some sympathy for the colonists' cause. However, when ordered to fight against the provincials, he did his duty to the best of his ability. During the French and Indian War (part of the global Seven Years' War), Howe had pioneered the use of a new type of force: the light infantry or Light Bobs.

Like Howe, Henry Clinton was descended from nobility and had served in the Seven Years' War, where he made close friendships with several Americans he would later face on the battlefield. But unlike the gregarious Howe, Clinton described himself as "a shy bitch."[2] He and Howe frequently disagreed about strategy and tactics, and in hindsight, many historians argue that Clinton's plans might have been more successful had they been followed.

* Today, Charlestown is part of the city of Boston, but at the time of the Revolution, it was a separate town.

The third man in the trio, General John Burgoyne, was also a Seven Years' War veteran. Outgoing and fashionable, he was known for his high living and extravagant attire. On at least two occasions, he sold his officer's commission to pay off debts and support himself. While the military was Burgoyne's primary career, he also wrote several popular plays, and he served in the House of Commons in Parliament.

Looking for ways to tighten their grip, Gage and the other generals decided to send men to seize several high points around Boston, including Bunker Hill, to give them greater control over Boston Harbor and, they hoped, prevent the Patriots from using the high ground to mount an attack.

The provincials had very different plans for those hills. They intended to bring down artillery from Concord and install them where they could fire into Boston and drive the Redcoats out of the city. When they heard that the British had scheduled an attack for June 18, they immediately began building defenses. General Israel Putnam set to work on fortifications on Bunker Hill on June 15. The next day, Colonel William Prescott arrived with 1,200 more men and several more officers, and a disagreement ensued over where to build the fortifications. Prescott argued that his artillery would have better field of fire against a British attack on Breed's Hill, and he had his men construct an earthen redoubt on the crest of the shorter hill.

Several African Americans from Essex County participated in constructing the fortifications, including combatants Cuff Chambers and Jacob Francis.[3] Francis later recounted an anecdote about middle-aged commanding officer General Putnam, affectionately nicknamed "Old Put":

> The men were at work digging, about 500 men on the fatigue at once, I was at work among them, they were divided into small squads of 8 or 10 together, & a non-commissioned officer to oversee them. General Putnam came Riding along in uniform as an officer to look at the Work. They had dug up a pretty large stone which lay on the side of the ditch. The General spoke to

the corporal who was standing looking at the men at work & said to him "my lad throw that stone up on the middle of the breastwork," the Corporal touching his hat with his hand said to the General "Sir I am a Corporal." "Oh." (said the General) "I ask your pardon, Sir," and immediately got off his horse and took up the stone and threw it up on the breastwork himself & then mounted his horse & rode on, giving directions.[4]

The British soon noticed the American efforts to fortify the heights. General Clinton urged his fellow officers to attack as soon as it was light, before the colonists could complete their preparations. The other general officers agreed to move up their original schedule by a day, but they saw no need to launch the assault so early in the morning. They also disagreed with Clinton about the best plan of attack. He wanted to land troops on the neck, the narrow part of the peninsula, to cut off the Patriots' retreat and leave them isolated and vulnerable. The others thought it would be relatively easy to overcome the inexperienced colonial forces so that they could make a more direct attack, landing on the eastern edge of the peninsula, climbing Breed's Hill, and sweeping inward toward Bunker Hill, enveloping the provincial force as they went. Burgoyne was of the opinion that "trained troops are invincible against any numbers or any position of untrained rabble."[5] And Howe added, "The terrain is open, and of easy ascent and, in short, would be easily carried."[6] Clinton was outvoted.

Howe began the assault by bringing one of his greatest military assets—their naval force—to bear. The twenty-gun HMS *Lively*, Marblehead's nemesis, trained its broadside on the as-yet-unfinished redoubt, and the other British cannons in the harbor soon joined in. One of the 9-pound cannonballs decapitated one of the young workers, but Colonel Prescott encouraged the others to carry on. He jumped to the top of the earthen redoubt, waved his hat in the air, and taunted the ships, yelling, "Hit *me* if you can!"[7] Despite the thunder of the artillery and the constant tremors from the balls thudding into the hill, the work continued.

From Boston, General Gage happened to be peering through his spyglass toward the fort at just that moment. Abijah Willard, a Loyalist who, ironically, was Prescott's son-in-law, stood by his side. Willard immediately recognized his father-in-law, and Gage asked Willard whether he believed the older man would fight.

"Yes, sir," Willard admitted. "He is an old soldier; he will fight as long as a drop of blood remains in his veins; it will be a bloody day, you may depend on it."[8]

Meanwhile, the British began the laborious process of assembling their men and ferrying them from Boston to the eastern edge of the Charlestown peninsula in longboats. When they had finally all arrived in the early afternoon of June 17, Howe grew concerned that the Patriots may have brought in more men than expected. He called for additional reinforcements, and the Redcoats on the beach enjoyed a leisurely lunch while they waited for more troops to arrive.

Atop the hill, the Patriots seemed far less sanguine. The officers issued a flurry of orders—some of them conflicting with one another—and the men scurried about, unsure of what to do. A letter written to Samuel Adams explained, "To be plain, it appears to me there never was more confusion and less command. No one appeared to have any but Colonel Prescott, whose bravery can never be enough acknowledged and applauded."[9]

After witnessing the arrival of the British Army, some of the provincial fighters began to have second thoughts and slunk away from their posts. Alarmed by the dwindling numbers of men, the officers sent messages to Patriot leaders in Cambridge asking for more reinforcements. Most of the additional troops never arrived; only one man showed up. However, the appearance of that one man made a huge difference to the troops' morale, for it was none other than Doctor Warren himself.

Despite Warren's intention of heading to Breed's Hill early in the day, a migraine headache left him incapacitated most of the morning. His apprentice, David Townsend, recalled, "[He] was sick with one of his oppressive nervous headaches, and had retired to rest and taken some chamomile tea for relief."[10] Early in the afternoon, Townsend found

Warren still at Hastings House, and the two men set out together for the hill. On the way, they encountered provincial soldiers wounded by fire from *Lively* and other Royal Navy vessels. Warren instructed Townsend to stay and care for the injured, while he continued on toward the battle, immediately going to General Putnam.

"I am sorry to see you here, General Warren," said Putnam. "I wish you had taken my advice and left this day to us, for, from appearances, we shall have a sharp time of it. And since you are here, I am ready to submit myself to your orders."[11]

Warren declined to take command. "I came only as a volunteer," Warren explained. "I know nothing of your dispositions; nor will I interfere with them. Tell me where I can be most useful."[12]

Putnam pointed to the redoubt, noting that Warren would be covered there.

"Don't think I come to seek a place of safety," the doctor protested. "But tell me where the onset will be most furious."

Putnam again pointed to the redoubt, saying, "That is the enemy's object. Prescott is there, and will do his duty, and if it can be defended, the day will be ours."[13]

The president of the Massachusetts Provincial Congress immediately headed for the redoubt, now manned by only about 150 colonists, the rest having deployed elsewhere on the hill or deserted. As cannonballs fired from Howe's artillery and the Royal Navy furrowed into the hill around him, Warren strolled casually across the field, attired "in his wedding suit," which included "a light cloth coat with covered buttons worked in silver," while "his hair was curled up at the sides of his head and pinned up."[14]

The men inside greeted him with "loud hurrahs," even though he came alone. He brought the news that artillery and other reinforcements were on the way, and this bolstered their courage. Like Putnam, Prescott offered to turn over command to Warren, but the doctor demurred. "I shall take no command here," Warren responded. "I have not yet received my commission. I came as a volunteer, with my musket to serve under you, and shall be happy to learn from a soldier of your experience."[15] He added that he only wanted "to give what assistance I can, and to let these damn rascals see that the Yankees will fight."[16]

Warren would soon have a chance to demonstrate just how willing he was to fight, but most of the artillery and reinforcements he promised would never arrive on the battlefield. The exception was an intrepid Marbleheader who would make the British pay dearly for their assault.

The day before the Battle of Bunker Hill, Congress officially assigned Colonel John Glover as the commander of the 21st Regiment. He remained in Marblehead, however, following his orders to recruit more men and defend the city. Captain Samuel Trevett marched over to Breed's Hill with his company and their guns. Trevett led a fifty-one-man artillery company into Charlestown, composed of thirty-nine Marbleheaders, including Lieutenant Joseph Swasey and Sergeant Samuel Gatchell,[17] which had formed only a month earlier on May 8, 1775, with eight enlisted men and five officers. By the end of May, the company's numbers had swelled by several dozen. In an effort to strengthen their bonds and fellowship, the men worshiped together and on Sunday, May 21, 1775, listened to a sermon by the Reverend Mr. Whitewell.[18] Trevett's company engaged in the fighting at Bunker Hill as part of Colonel Richard Gridley's artillery regiment. Gridley, an experienced artillerist from the French and Indian War, unfortunately filled the regimental staff rosters with his incompetent family members, including his son Scarborough.

Trevett quickly showed himself to be more courageous than the other officers in the artillery regiment. His superior, Major Scarborough Gridley, had orders to lead his men across Charlestown Neck to the redoubt on Breed's Hill. But the sight of Patriot dead and wounded who had fallen on the neck to the fire from the British vessels nearby terrified Gridley. Rather than proceeding across the neck, he stopped dead in his tracks. A colonel who was passing by encouraged the major to cross with his men, but still Scarborough refused. "We are waiting to cover the retreat," the major insisted. When the colonel again ordered him forward, "[Scarborough] Gridley proceeded a short distance with his artillery, but, overcome with terror,—unequal to the horrors of the scene,—he ordered his men back . . . to fire with their three pounders upon the *Glasgow* and the floating batteries."[19]

When the fighting began, most of those who had come to the peninsula retreated to the fortifications atop Bunker Hill, which they believed would be safer. By one account, an officer refused to move forward to join the battle even after General Putnam put a gun to his head. However, Marbleheader Samuel Trevett and his men eagerly joined in the fighting.

Disgusted by Scarborough Gridley's lack of bravery, Trevett struck out on his own. In a letter penned many years later, he recounted, "About one o'clock in the afternoon of the 17th of June, 1775, I left Cambridge with my company, for Bunker's Hill." He and the men with him crossed the neck without incident. He added, "When I arrived at Bunker's Hill, on the northwest side, I there saw General Putnam dismounted, in company with several others. I halted my company, and went forward to select a station for my pieces, and on my return, saw Gen. Putnam as before; the American and English forces being then engaged."[20]

Trevett and his men began descending the hill to move their two cannons into position near a rail fence where they could fire on the Redcoats as they disembarked. Accompanying them were two hundred Connecticut militia led by Captain Thomas Knowlton, a fearless thirty-six-year-old French and Indian War veteran who later led a force known as Knowlton's Rangers. Knowlton immediately began reinforcing the fence they hoped would protect them from the British guns. Using rails scavenged from the nearby fields, they built a second fence parallel and very close to the first fence. They then stuffed the narrow strip in between the two fences full of rocks, grass, sticks, and other debris until it slowly turned into a barricade—albeit only partially bulletproof and definitely not cannon-proof.

The rail fence reached nearly to the breastwork of the redoubt. A patch of swampy ground several hundred yards across made it impractical to extend the fence any farther. And while the wetland might slow the British regulars, it would not be enough to keep them at bay. To defend this area, the colonists built a series of three flèches, arrow-shaped defenses assembled from more pieces of rail fence, bundles of sticks, and earth.

As soon as the soldiers completed the flèches, Trevett and his men moved their field pieces behind the fortifications, where they could fire on the British and had some protection from British fire. Meanwhile, another Patriot officer arrived to reinforce Knowlton's men. Colonel John Stark, a forty-six-year-old backwoodsman from the wilds of New Hampshire, adored by his men, fatefully led his 150-man company to positions along the rail fence. A group of Abenaki Indians had captured Stark when he was a young man. When the tribe ordered him to run through a gauntlet of warriors wielding sticks, Stark instead grabbed one of the clubs and attacked. Impressed by his fearlessness, the chief made Stark a member of the tribe, forever cementing Stark's reputation for heroism in the face of seemingly impossible odds. In the French and Indian War, Stark served as an officer in Rogers's Rangers, a colo-nial precursor to America's special operations forces. He led his men to numerous victories but refused to take part in any attacks on the tribe that had adopted him. His experience made him one of the most qualified military officers in the fledgling Patriot forces, leading men who had gotten their first taste of combat at Fort William and Mary. Armed with powder and weapons they had looted from the fort, the New Hampshire men stood ready to repulse a British flanking move and unhinge Howe's entire plan.

Stark's second-in-command was Major Andrew McClary, another member of Rogers's Rangers, who had been present at the tavern in Portsmouth right before the second raid on Fort William and Mary. Born in Ireland, McClary had emigrated to New Hampshire with his family in his teens in an attempt to escape British oppression in their homeland. In addition to farming their land, the McClary family also owned a tavern that hosted town meetings and served as a gathering place for Patriot leaders intent on resisting the Crown. Tall, athletic, and gregarious, McClary was a natural leader and an officer in the militia who had taken part in numerous skirmishes with local Indians. That experience would serve him well as the Battle of Bunker Hill progressed.

By midafternoon, the additional British reinforcements had arrived, swelling the ranks on the Charlestown peninsula to around 2,300 men plus 250 officers and 125 artillerymen.[21] On Howe's command, the Redcoats began their ground assault. To eliminate the threat of marksmen, the British first set fire to the wooden buildings of Charlestown using hot shot—cannonballs heated on forges aboard the warships and fired on the town. Soon billowing black smoke blanketed the battlefield, choking the fighters and lending an apocalyptic aura to the setting. The flames engulfed Charlestown's churches, turning them into "great pyramids of fire."[22]

The warships halted their cannonade, and Howe formed his men into ranks. Two wings of scarlet over one thousand men strong formed on the left and right at the base of Breed's Hill. Artillerymen moved the all-important cannons into position, ready to take aim at the hastily constructed fortifications on the hill. The slight breeze hardly cooled the men from the afternoon sun on the summer day. Sweat poured down Howe's men's faces as they sweltered in woolen coats. Regimental drummers and fifers played while Patriot marksmen began to target the British as they were still moving into position. The first Redcoats fell as Howe addressed the group of light infantry he would personally lead into battle. "I shall not desire one of you to go a step farther than where I go myself at your head. Remember, gentlemen, we have no recourse to any resources if we lose Boston but to go on board our ships, which will be very disagreeable to us all."[23]

A master of battlefield tactics, Howe never intended a direct frontal assault. Instead, the general planned to swing his light infantry and grenadiers around north to a beach along the Mystic River, where the series of rail fences, including those manned by Knowlton, Trevett, Stark, and McClary, formed a feeble barricade. Here he hoped to find a weak spot in the American defense that would allow his men to penetrate

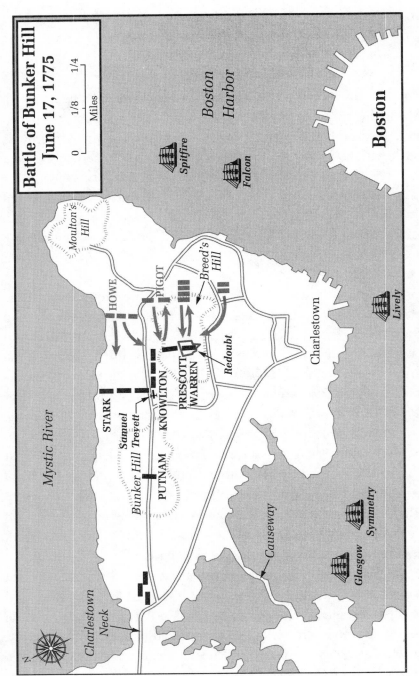

Battle of Bunker Hill
June 17, 1775

Miles
0   1/8   1/4

Boston Harbor

Boston

Spitfire

Falcon

Moulton's Hill

HOWE

PIGOT

Breed's Hill

Lively

Redoubt

Charlestown

STARK

Samuel
Bunker Hill Trevett

KNOWLTON

PRESCOTT
WARREN

PUTNAM

Mystic River

Charlestown
Neck

Causeway

Glasgow

Symmetry

N

"Bunker Hill"

the lines and attack the redoubt from behind. But it would not be an easy climb. Although the weather was mild with temperatures in the seventies, the sun had reached its zenith and was blazing down on the men in their wool uniforms. The Redcoats would be climbing through thick, uncut hay and clambering over rocks and fences. All the while, provincial marksmen would be taking aim, intent on picking them off one by one.

With powder scarce, many of the Patriot officers instructed their men to wait to the last moment to fire. Stark ordered his men not to fire until they could "see the enemy's half-gaiters,"[24] the heavy fabric leggings that covered most of a soldier's ankles. Perhaps a Patriot officer shouted, "Don't fire until you see the whites of their eyes!" a popular expression of the times, though this is likely a myth that crept into the lore of the battle decades later. However, the officers did instruct the colonial fighters to direct their fire low so as not to shoot over the enemies' heads, a common problem when firing from high ground. They also told the men to concentrate their fire on officers.

Behind the Patriot lines, a teenage drummer boy and a fifer played "Yankee Doodle"; the tune the British had mockingly used to taunt the Americans at Salem and Lexington had become the American fight song.[25]

In an inflection point of the battle, Stark's and McClary's men, supported by Trevett's cannon, proved deadly as the massed fire tore into Howe's light infantry. Sniping from behind cover, the colonists took turns firing and reloading and firing again at the oncoming lines of scarlet. The musket balls, typically .69 caliber, smacked into the enemies' bodies with ominous thuds as they tore through flesh and bone—often destroying so much tissue that amputation would be necessary if the soldiers did not die in the field first.

Warren, Prescott, and the other men in the redoubt added to the torrent of lead ripping through Howe's troops. Arranged in lines three deep, the Patriots took turns leaning against the packed dirt wall and firing their muskets into the advancing Redcoats. As soon as one man had fired, he stepped to the back and quickly reloaded his weapon, while two other men took their turns to fire. This resulted in "a continued sheet of fire." One British officer described the carnage: "For near thirty minutes, our light infantry were served up in companies against the grass fence, without being able to penetrate—indeed how could they penetrate? Most of our grenadiers and light infantry, the moment of presenting themselves lost three-quarters and many nine-tenths of their men. Some had only eight and nine men a company left; some only three, four, and five."[26] The provincials were handing some of the Crown's finest troops a beating.

The Patriots fired upon the oncoming Redcoats. Howe's elite light infantry and many men who had fought at Lexington and Concord, including Captain William Glanville Evelyn, surged forward. Stark's and Trevett's fire on the side of the hill cut down many of them like a scythe clearing wheat. "The dead lay as thick as sheep in a fold,"[27] Stark recalled. The charge disintegrated into chaos, and many men broke and ran back down the hill. British officers threatened to run through fleeing soldiers with their swords.

With a determination born from his involvement in countless battles, Howe re-formed his men and again sent a force charging up the right side of the hill. Led by experienced fighters like McClary, Stark's New Hampshire Company once again held its fire until the British were within range. Also fighting near Stark's men alongside the fence rail were future Marblehead Regiment private, fifteen-year-old Jabez Tarr, along with his brother and Benjamin Webber. Tarr's pension file later recorded, "He marched to Mystic; remained encamped there untill [sic] 10th June, at dusk his company joined their Reg.—went on the Breeds Hill—helped build the fort—was in the Battle on 17th June—part of his company [indecipherable] the line on the left wing by Mystic river at the Rail fence. Three more killed two wounded—retreated about 6 o'clock p.m. to Mystic."[28]

Howe's attack, meant as a feint to distract the Americans from the flanking thrust on Knowlton's men, sputtered. After leading the charge, Howe found himself alone on the battlefield—his entire staff either dead or wounded. The general's aide-de-camp had fallen in front of his eyes, and a musket ball had even shattered the wine bottle his servant carried. Remarkably, considering that his flamboyant scarlet uniform made him a prime target for the American marksmen who hunted British officers, he was still standing. "There was a moment, I have never felt before,"[29] he later recalled. The British fell back; the American lines erupted in huzzahs.

It was a do-or-die moment. Howe gathered his men for one final assault and changed tactics. Rather than attack in a highly vulnerable, long, horizontal line, he formed his men into columns. He also abandoned his attempt to flank the Americans by assaulting the fence held by Stark. Seeing a weak point in the American defenses, he trained his artillery on the flèches manned by Trevett and the other provincial troops.

Loading and firing an eighteenth-century cannon was a complex and time-consuming process. First, one of the artillerists would use a wad screw to clean out the barrel of the gun, removing any remaining bits of cartridge residue or other detritus from the last firing. The crew member followed up with a more thorough cleaning with the "sponge," a moistened piece of fleece that extinguished any burning embers. During the cleaning process, the gunner held his thumb, covered in a piece of leather, over the touchhole to prevent a draft that might ignite anything inside the barrel. Next, the matross would collect one of the cartridges, a supply of gunpowder wrapped in flannel that was kept quite a distance from the guns to prevent accidental explosions. They then loaded the cartridge down the muzzle of the cannon and rammed it home into the breach with the ramrod. Next came the shot—the traditional solid cannonball, a canister (a tin can filled with lead or iron balls), or grape (a canvas bag filled with iron balls). At this point, the gunner who had his thumb over the touchhole would finally pull it away and use a priming rod to poke a hole in the cartridge holding the gunpowder. He would insert a fuse in the touchhole and light it with a lint stock which contained a slow match, hopefully resulting in a successful firing. After recoil from the weapon moved the cannon, the crew would then reposition it before starting the process over again. The entire sequence could take over a minute, during which the artillerists were vulnerable to enemy fire.

By this point in the battle, Trevett and his Marbleheaders had mown down countless numbers of the enemy, but with their rapidly dwindling supply of powder, they could do nothing in the face of the British onslaught. The records are not entirely clear, but the Redcoats may have disabled one of Trevett's field pieces, or the Marbleheader may have spiked both of his cannons after running out of gunpowder. In any event, as he and his men were leaving the flèches, they saw two other guns that one of the other artillery officers had abandoned. The British had disabled one beyond repair, but Trevett ordered his company to help him drag the second to safety. Before they reached their goal, a company of Redcoats approached and took aim at point-blank range. Certain that they were about to die, some of the Marbleheaders threw their hands in the air to surrender. The British fired anyway. In a testament to the poor quality of firearms of the era, they hit only one of Trevett's men. The young captain kept his cool, and as the British were reloading to take a second shot, he and his men dragged the cannon off the hill.

His bravery meant that the Patriots saved one of their precious artillery pieces; the others that took part in the battle were lost. The salty Marbleheader later recounted the events with a characteristic lack of fanfare: "I proceeded on with my company, and soon after joined that part of the American force at the rail fence, towards Mystic river, the Americans commenced a general retreat. As I was descending the northwest side of Bunker's Hill, I again saw Gen. Putnam in the same place, putting his tent upon his horse. I asked him where I should retreat with the field piece I had brought off, he replied to Cambridge, and I accordingly marched my company to Cambridge."[30] Unlike the other artillery companies, which had retreated, Trevett's men had continued firing their guns through the fiercest fighting. Robert Wormstead, who had dueled so valiantly around the Salem Powder Alarm and who would soon become Trevett's brother-in-law, "was struck in the shoulder by the fragments of a bursting shell. He narrowly escaped having his head blown from his shoulders, the fate which befell a companion whom he was assisting from the battlefield."[31]

Having overcome the opposition on the front of Breed's Hill, the British continued their uphill charge toward the one remaining bastion of defense: the earthen redoubt on the crest. The Redcoats attacked the fortification ferociously. Toiling through the insufferable heat and nauseating smoke, the soldiers pushed through several lines of rail fences and unmown hay. Inside the redoubt, Colonel Prescott and Doctor Warren urged the provincials to fight on and remain steady in the face of the coming onslaught. "The Redcoats would never reach the redoubt," Prescott told them, "if they would observe his directions: withhold their fire until he gave the order, take good aim, and be particularly careful not to shoot over their head; aim at their *hips*."[32]

Inspired by their leaders, the inexperienced men inside the fortification dropped one Redcoat after another. "After they were well form'd they advanced towards us in order to swallow us up, but they found a Choaky mouthful of us,"[33] recalled one participant. The provincials' efficient fire brought down most of the forward group of the British, but more came behind them and still more after that. "We fired until our ammunition began to fail," recalled one of the Patriot fighters. "Then our firing began to slacken—and at last it went out like an old candle."[34]

With very little ammunition left, the Patriots were running out of options. Several of the men, having depleted their supplies, simply shook their comrades' hands and left the redoubt. Calling on his considerable rhetorical skills, Warren urged the colonists to stay and fight on, even as their numbers dwindled. Just when things were looking the grimmest, Prescott found some gunpowder left behind by one of the artillery crews. He doled it out among the men, warning them "not to waste a kernel of it, but to make it certain that every shot should *tell*."[35] For bullets, the men collected musket balls that had landed in the redoubt, and some substituted nails, small rocks, or whatever bits of metal they could find that might do damage.

The British reformed, now much closer to the fortification on the summit, inexorably closing in on the packed dirt walls. "Fight, Conquer or die!"[36] shouted the grenadiers as they launched themselves into the fortification, swarming up and over the redoubt. The provincials fought back with whatever they could find—bayonets and swords for those who had them, rocks, pickaxes, and fists for those who did not. Gore soon covered the walls and floor of the bastion. "I cannot pretend to describe the Horror of the Scene within the Redoubt, when we enter'd it," wrote one of the British officers. "'Twas streaming with Blood and strew'd with dead and dying Men, the Soldiers stabbing some and dashing out the Brains of other[s] was a sight too dreadful for me to dwell any longer on."[37]

Some of the colonists panicked and fled. One later wrote home, "I was in the fort when the enemy came in, Jump'd over the wall and ran half a Mile, where balls flew like hail stones and Cannon roar'd like thunder, but tho I escap'd then it may be my turn next. Oh may I never forget God's distinguishing Mercy to me, in sparing my Life, when they fell on my right hand, and on my left, and close by me. . . . They were to the eye of reason no more expos'd than myself.—When the Arrows of death flew thick around me, I was preserv'd while others were suffer'd to fall a prey to our Cruel enemies."[38] In Prescott's words, "The Enemy being numerous surrounded our little Fort began to mount our Lines and enter the Fort with their Bayonets, we was obliged to retreat through them while they kept up as hot a fire as it was possible for them to make."[39]

Doctor Warren and Prescott both fought for their lives as they exited the fortification. Prescott parried several bayonet-wielding regulars with his sword, while Warren fought with "a coolness and conduct which did honor to the judgment of his country in appointing him a major general."[40]

Waving his sword in the air in a final attempt to rally his fellow Americans, Warren "bravely defended himself against several regulars," but a British officer recognized the Patriot doctor and leader. The officer's servant is suspected of firing a pistol at point-blank range in a "cowardly manner" and shooting Warren in the face. As Gerry had foreseen, the Battle at Bunker Hill resulted in the death of one of America's most respected Patriot leaders. General Howe, who somehow survived the vicious battle with only a small injury to his foot, found it difficult to believe that the doctor had willingly sacrificed himself and said that Warren "was worth five hundred of their men."[41]

Warren was not the only prominent leader lost in the retreat. Stark's righthand man, Ranger Andrew McClary, veteran of the attack on Fort William and Mary, who was so influential in repulsing the British along the fence line, initially made it off the field of battle. Thirsty, he stopped at a tavern for a drink with his friend and fellow officer Henry Dearborn. According to Dearborn, McClary "soon observed that the British troops on Bunker Hill appeared in motion, and said he would go and reconnoiter them, to see whether they were coming out over the Neck." Having satisfied himself that Howe's men were staying put atop the hill, McClary headed back toward Dearborn. "He was returning towards me, and, within twelve or fifteen rods of where I stood with my company," Dearborn recalled. "A random shot from one of the frigates . . . passed directly through his body, and put to flight one of the most heroic souls that ever animated man. He leaped two or three feet from the ground, pitched forward, and fell dead upon his face."[42]

Despite being falsely accused of ties to the Loyalists weeks early, Marbleheader Doctor Nathaniel Bond sprang into action to treat the wounded. At the end of the day, the Patriots' casualties totaled 115 killed and 305 wounded. Despite the heavy combat, only two Marbleheaders died at Bunker Hill, and three, including Wormstead, sustained wounds.[43]

By comparison, the British lost 1,054 killed or wounded, about half of the total they had brought to the field. They could claim victory by virtue of having driven the colonists off the hill, but it was a Pyrrhic victory at best. Howe felt "the success [was] too dearly bought."[44] The "sad and impressive experience of this murderous day sunk deep into the mind of Sir William Howe,"[45] and his experience at Bunker Hill would inform his decision-making throughout the war.

At first, the Americans did not realize the impact the battle had on the British, and they considered Bunker Hill a catastrophic failure. In the aftermath, the Patriots were looking for scapegoats. Suspicion naturally fell on the artillery commanders who had abandoned their posts. According to committee reports from the Massachusetts Provincial Congress, "General Putnam declared to your Committee, as his opinion, that the defeat of that day was owing to the ill-behaviour of those that conducted the artillery, and that, one of these officers ought to be punished with death, and that unless some exemplary punishment was inflicted, he would assuredly leave the Army."[46] In a great miscarriage of justice, General Putnam wrongly named Samuel Trevett as the artillery captain who had displayed cowardice. The colonial forces arrested Trevett but eventually realized their mistake. By that time, however, Trevett was fed up with the provincials' mistreatment and felt they had besmirched his honor.* He went home to Marblehead and formally disbanded his company, and even though the Committee of Safety asked him to return, he refused. Most of his men joined other units. At least eleven joined their fellow Marbleheaders, including his soon-to-be brother-in-law Robert Wormstead, in Glover's Regiment, which would become part of the newly formed Continental Army led by General George Washington.

---

* According to the *New England Magazine*, "[Trevett] retained the faculties of his mind to the last moment, and on the very day of his decease, gave the usual household directions. In conformity with his express injunctions, he was buried at sunset, without any funeral procession, and with no other ceremony than thirteen tolls of a single bell, probably in allusion to the thirteen States, for whose independence he sacrificed his property and devoted his youth." *New England Magazine*, ed. Joseph Tinker Buckingham et al., 2 (1832):177.

CHAPTER 19

GENERAL GEORGE WASHINGTON ARRIVES IN CAMBRIDGE

On July 2, 1775, George Washington arrived in Cambridge. Six feet two, with reddish-brown hair and blue-gray eyes, the Virginian possessed a commanding presence. His effect on the troops was immediate: "Joy was visible on every countenance . . . and it seemed as if the spirit of conquest breathed through the whole army."[1] Weeks earlier, the Second Continental Congress had commissioned Washington as commander in chief of "the Army of the United Colonies." Eventually, the army would be the "Continental Army." A remarkable leader, gifted in organization, who embraced novel ideas and was willing to place country over self, Washington would emerge as the Revolution's indispensable man.

He went to work immediately. On horseback, the Continental Army's new commander in chief inspected the various defenses and soldiers under his command. The next day, a portion of the troops assembled in parade formation. Washington did not have a full accounting of how many forces he had under arms outside Boston. As the first order of business, he ordered a tally of his men in each unit. Washington's letter to Congress on July 10 expressed his disappointment in the number and quality: "Upon finding the Number of Men to fall so far short of the Establishment and below all Expectation, I immediately called a Council of the General Officers, whose opinion as to the mode of filling up the regiments and providing for the present Exigency, together with the best Judgment we are able to form of the Ministerial Troops, I have the Honor of inclosing. From the Number of Boys, Deserters and negroes which have inlisted in this Province, I entertain some doubts whether the Number required, can be raised here; and all the General Officers agree, that no Dependence can be put on the Militia for a continuance in Camp, or Regularity and Discipline during the short time they may stay."[2]

The commander in chief required a headquarters, and the Vassall House,[3] located in Cambridge, where the Marblehead men billeted, seemed ideal. Washington valued appearance and chose the house for its location and grandeur, which befitted his taste and leadership style. The general also discerned talent when he saw it. Over several weeks, he forged a special relationship with John Glover and the Marblehead Regiment's adjutant, Captain Caleb Gibbs. The Virginian recognized the uniqueness of Glover and his men, who were well led and trained, and experts on the sea, an area about which Washington had little knowledge. Their time together solidified a relationship and trust that would prove invaluable during the most crucial moments of the war. The Revolution's indispensable man had found his indispensable men.

Their location near the siege lines necessitated protection; his headquarters required security from a potential British raid. Washington selected Glover's men for this critical duty. He favored the Marbleheaders, and during the month of July, Washington named Glover, Gabriel Johonnot, and William Raymond Lee officers of the day and "officer of the main guard to-morrow." Gibbs was listed as "Adjutant for the day tom-morrow on July 3, and 21st."[4] To ensure security, the commander in chief issued passwords and countersigns every day to the troops to distinguish friend from foe when operating near the lines. Washington fittingly chose the countersign of "Marblehead" for July 19. The relationship marked the origins of the Life Guard that was formed months later.

To make room for Washington's staff, Glover's men relocated one mile west of Cambridge to the grounds of a tavern. On July 15, Washington recorded their departure from the Vassall House with the receipt, "To cash paid for cleaning the House which was provided for my Quarters & which Had been occupied by the Marblehead Regt . . . $65."[5]

As Washington reorganized his army, the specter of a British attack loomed over his plans. Accordingly, he first prepared the

Marbleheaders: "It is ordered that Col. Glover's Regt. be ready this evening, with all their accoutrements, to march at a minute's warning to support Gen. Folsom of the New Hampshire Forces, in case his lines should be attacked. It is also ordered that Col. Prescott's Regiment equip themselves to march this evening & take possession of the woods leading to Lechmere's Point, and, in case of attack there, Col. Glover's Regiment to march immediately to their support."[6] While no major combat broke out in July, both sides conducted a series of raids and skirmishes, including one that was later recalled by General William Heath: "A little after two o'clock in the morning, a number of volunteers, under the command of Majors [Benjamin] Tupper and [John] Crane, attacked the British advance guard at Brown's house, on Boston Neck, and routed them, took a halbert, a musket, and two bayonets, and burnt the two houses."[7]

Along with the raids, the Marbleheaders also harassed the British with a series of floating artillery batteries on the Charles and Mystic Rivers. The Americans employed flat-bottomed boats along with whaleboats that could carry dozens of men and the artillery. Recently promoted lieutenant William Hawks wrote in his orderly book regarding the origins of the batteries that an order went out for men who were "skilled in the management of Whaleboats" and "whose business will be take care of the Floating Batteries now building & Whaleboats." The next morning Glover's Regiment provided "that one Subalton, one Sargeant, one corporal & Thirty privates Parad [sic] out of Coll. Glover's reg Tomorrow at 8 O'Clock at Cambridge Bridge."[8] Captain William Blackler commanded the floating batteries on both rivers as they fired on the enemy in Boston. Aboard one battery, Marblehead lieutenant William Beubier related "that a gun blasted as they were firing at the Enemy in Boston and Killed and Wounded Several Persons."[9] The Marbleheaders and the floating batteries were at the forefront of an American navy, a concept the Marbleheaders would expand shortly.

Arming over 550 Marbleheaders remained a challenge. On the second day of July, the regiment received an infusion of weapons: "One hundred small arms were delivered to Colonel Glover, for the use of his regiment, amounting as by appraisement, to one hundred ninety-two pounds eleven shillings, which guns he engaged should be returned in good order, unless lost in the service of this colony, as by his receipt in the minute book."[10]

A lack of supply was not limited to the Marblehead Regiment; the army as a whole required everything from additional firearms, bayonets, and equipment to uniforms and, most critically, gunpowder. Washington not only inventoried his men, but also his supplies. "The General was so struck, that he did not utter a word for half an hour. Every one else was also astounded."[11] Washington informed Congress on August 4, "Our situation in the article of powder is much more alarming than I had any idea of . . . [not] more than nine rounds of powder a man."[12]

Washington cracked down on the wanton use of powder and issued his general orders: "It is with indignation and shame, the general observes, that notwithstanding the repeated orders which have been given to prevent the firing of guns, in and about the camp; that it is daily and hourly practised; that contrary to all orders, straggling soldiers do still pass the guard, and fire at a distance, where there is not the least probability of hurting the enemy, and where no other end is answered, but to waste ammunition, expose themselves to the ridicule of the enemy, and keep their own camps harassed by frequent and continual alarms, to the hurt of every good soldier, who is thereby disturbed of his natural rest, and will at length never be able to distinguish between a real and a false alarm. . . . The colonels of regiments and commanding officers of corps, to order the rolls of every company to be called twice a day, and every man's ammunition examined at evening roll calling, and such as are found to be deficient to be confined. The guards are to apprehend all persons firing guns near their posts, whether townsmen or soldiers."[13]

Powder remained the Achilles' heel of the army, preventing it from launching offensive operations or even defending itself, and the commander in chief knew he needed to keep the true nature of the situation from the British. Washington went to great lengths to conceal this weakness, but a deserter entered General Thomas Gage's lines and revealed Washington's great powder shortage. "The fact was so incredible that Gage treated it as a stratagem of war and the messenger as a spy; for coming with the express purpose of deceiving him and drawing his army into a snare,"[14] wrote one participant. Despite Washington's precautions, Doctor Benjamin Church stealthily continued to relay information to Gage. As surgeon general of the army, he might not have known about the shortage of powder; however, he worked in the hospital near Washington's headquarters and was privy to many important meetings.

The Patriots finally uncovered Church's treachery when he attempted to use his Marblehead mistress, Mary Wenwood, as a courier after several other avenues of communication failed him. "The Doctor haveing formed an Infamous Connection, with an Infamous Hussey to the disgrace of his own reputation, and probable ruin of his Family, wrote this Letter last July."[15] Wenwood, "a Native of Marblehead, a very lusty Woman much pitted with the Small-Pox, who generally wears the best of Cloathing,"[16] aroused the suspicion of her former husband, Godfrey Wenwood. She asked for his help in procuring a meeting with the Newport customs officer or the captain of a British warship patrolling Newport Harbor for the purpose of forwarding a communication from Cambridge on to besieged Boston. Wenwood convinced her to give him the letter, which he held for some time before opening it and alerting the Patriots.

The indecipherable language of the letter raised even more alarms. General Washington called for the woman to be arrested and interrogated. "She was then Taken into Custody, and Brought to the Generals Quarters that Night. It was not till the next day that any thing could be got from her."[17] Doctor Benjamin Church finally emerged as the author of the letter. Immediately taken into custody, the surgeon general vehemently denied the accusation of treacherous behavior but failed to produce the key to the coded letter in question.

Elbridge Gerry scrambled to break the code. He enlisted the services of expert decipherer Elisha Porter. Together the two men discovered that Church had used a substitution cipher, replacing each letter of the alphabet with a symbol, and Gerry was able to write to Continental Congress delegate Robert Treat Paine, "The Letter . . . is decyphered; the Contents respect the State of the Army, the Quantity of powder now in our possession, what is expected & where, together with other Intelligence of a black & treacherous Nature."[18]

Church continued to plead his innocence, but a court-martial convicted the Son of Liberty. Authorities then stripped him of his post and confined the doctor to the Vassall House. Evidence at the time proved inconclusive to execute Church, and only decades later would his intelligence reports to Gage surface proving he was a spy, so Massachusetts exiled him instead. His ship left Boston Harbor in January 1778 for the Caribbean: the vessel and Doctor Benjamin Church were never seen again.

As Washington took account of his actual supply, Marbleheaders continued to tap their trading contacts for additional powder that they smuggled in from the Iberian Peninsula and the West Indies. Gerry related to Washington on August 1 the herculean efforts to obtain gunpowder: "We are in daily Expectation of some Powder from the West Indies, but cannot say what Success our plans will meet with; indeed We have exerted Ourselves to obtain It several Ways which may be communicated at a more convenient opportunity. . . . We are ready to exert to the utmost to serve the Cause, provided the Commissary General desires it for the present—the powder shall be sent immediatel[y] if ordered or be made into Cartridges as soon as maybe."[19] The commander in chief on August 4 devised a daring plan to mitigate the gunpowder crisis. "It was proposed to make an Attempt on the Magazine at Halifax where there is Reason to suppose there is a great Quantity of Powder—And upon the Question being severally put it was agreed to by a great Majority. & that the Detachment for this Enterprize consist of three hundred Men."[20]

Getting the men there would fall upon the shoulders of John Glover and require a navy.

CHAPTER 20

WASHINGTON'S COVERT NAVY

At Glover's Wharf in Beverly, teams of carpenters sawed and hacked gun ports into the sides of the *Hannah* and strengthened her main deck to accommodate the weight of four 4-pounder guns and their carriages. For additional security, they also mounted several swivel guns on her gunwhale to ward off a potential enemy boarding party or small boats. Sailors installed topsails and a flying jib to augment her main canvas sails. Within days of initial refitting, her cargo hold contained gunpowder and shot, completing the metamorphosis from fishing boat to a vessel of war primed to audaciously challenge the most formidable force on the high seas: the Royal Navy.

John Glover's 78-ton *Hannah*, likely named after his wife, had sailed for ten years fishing the Grand Banks and trading in the East Indies. In June 1775, before her conversion to an instrument of war, the ship had barely avoided capture by the HMS *Merlin*. While stalking the approaches of Marblehead, the *Merlin* sighted *Hannah*'s white flag containing a blue diamond flying over her masthead. The captain of the British vessel ordered a barge to intercept and board the schooner as the *Hannah* drew near the harbor. A man of action, Glover rowed out from Marblehead to rescue his ship. "John Glover went off and met her, and the Merlin's barge met her at the same time. The officer of the barge ordered her to bring to. Glover ordered her not, and the schooner run under the ships stern, paid no regard to her and run alongside the wharf. All is well that ends well,"[1] recalled omniscient diarist Ashley Bowen. Safely within the confines of the harbor, *Hannah* had, for now, dodged the Royal Navy, but her escape proved to be the first of many close calls.

By the middle of August 1775, Washington had taken the revolutionary step of bringing the war to sea, starting with ordering John Glover to outfit his schooner. Whether the idea of using armed vessels to intercept British ships originated with Glover or Washington is lost to history, but at the time, Glover and his men had been guarding Washington's headquarters in Cambridge, and several of Washington's officers, including Glover and William Raymond Lee, were made officers of the day. Undoubtedly, his relationship with Glover and his proximity to the seasoned sailors of Marblehead played a role in arming American ships, since Washington chose them to arm the first one.

Many advocates had approached Washington regarding arming American ships. Elbridge Gerry had discussed the need for a navy with his close friend, the stout, diminutive, but brilliant John Adams, who considered himself a connoisseur of naval matters dating back to his defense of Marbleheader Michael Corbett, who threw his harpoon at a British officer attempting to press him into service with the Royal Navy. The idea of arming American merchant ships came from multiple quarters. Adams wrote, "Mr [Christopher] Gadsden of South Carolina whose Fame you must have heard, was in his younger Years, an officer, on board the Navy, and is well acquainted with the Fleet. He has Several Times taken Pains to convince me that this Fleet is not so formidable to America, as we fear. He Says, We can easily take their Sloops, schooners and Cutters, on board of whom are all their best Sea-men, and with these We can easily take their large Ships, on board of whom are all their impress'd and discontented Men. He thinks, the Men would not fight on board the large ships with their fellow subjects, but would certainly kill their own officers. He Says it is a different Thing, to fight the French or Spaniards from what it is to fight British Americans in one Case, if taken Prisoners they must lie in Prison for Years, in the other obtain their Liberty and Happiness. He thinks it of great Importance that Some Experiment should be made on the Cutters. He is confident that We may get a Fleet of our own, at a cheap and this would give great Spirit to this Continent, as well as little Spirit to the Ministry."[2]

The commander in chief originally scotched the idea, flatly stating on August 11, "Weakness & the Enemy's Strength at Sea—There wou'd be great Danger that with the best Preparation we could make, they would fall an easy Prey either to the Men of War on that Station or Some who would be Detach'd from Boston. . . . I could offer many other Reasons against it, some of which I doubt not will suggest themselves to the Hon: Board—But it is unnecessary to enumerate them when our Situation as to Ammunition absolutely forbids our Sending a Single Ounce out of the Camp at present."[3]

However, the quest for gunpowder proved instrumental in softening Washington's position on a navy. As John Adams stated in a letter to James Warren, "Every Thing, has been done, and is now doing, to procure the *Unum Necessarium*."[4] In what proved to be a fruitless venture, the commander in chief sent a ship to Bermuda in a desperate attempt to assuage the army's dire need for powder, but it returned empty-handed. Unbeknownst to Washington, Congress also sent a ship and, with the help of Bermudians, raided a remote royal magazine and then rowed over one hundred barrels of powder to two waiting American ships that sailed back to the colonies. Perhaps realizing the suicidal nature of a raid on Halifax to acquire more munitions, which Washington had discussed weeks earlier, the commander in chief resorted to outfitting a vessel to pick off one of the many unescorted ships sailing into Boston to supply Gage's trapped forces.

Only days later, Washington turned to his seafaring officer, John Glover, who had a ship for rent, and for seventy-eight dollars a month, one dollar per each ton of the 78-ton *Hannah*, Washington had the origins of a navy. "The first Armd Vessell fitted out in the Service of the United States," as Glover later explained.[5] An armed ship could be viewed as major escalation in the Revolution. Sovereign and independent nation-states had their own flagged ships. Ultimately, an armed vessel crewed by the Continental Army could also export the powerful groundbreaking ideas and ideals of the Revolution to other nations in a way that a merchant vessel could not. Washington lacked the authority to create a navy; only Congress had that authority. Nevertheless, he created one. The army's thirst for powder outweighed the risk. If Washington's venture failed, it would be a significant liability; therefore, the commander in chief wisely kept the project a secret.

The Revolution would now be fought at sea, as well as on land.

Hannah moored at Glover's Wharf on the western end of Beverly Harbor, located a few miles from Marblehead. Beverly boasted about three thousand residents, several miles of rocky beach, a sandy coast, and a deep, protected port—one difficult to navigate, ideal protection from the roving British fleet, which was unfamiliar with the waters. The town had the facilities to harbor Washington's fleet in Glover's warehouse and wharf, which he had purchased in December 1774.[6] Glover chose his friend and business associate, Marbleheader Nicholson Broughton, to command *Hannah*. Fifty years old and an experienced captain, Broughton led a company within the 21st Marblehead Regiment. Known for his "zeal" and ardor for the Revolution, Broughton lived what he believed. An inscription carved in stone after his death immortalized him as "a man whose life and conversation shed lustre on his religious profession and furnished an example every way worthy of imitation." In four generations, every male member of the Broughton family captained a ship. The family "seemed like descendants of the ancient sea-kings." Even Broughton's thirteen-year-old son, Nic Jr., enlisted in the Marblehead Regiment and "won for himself a renown which is still recognized."[7]

Glover went all in on the endeavor, as evidenced by *Hannah*'s crew. Glover's brother-in-law and former captain of *Hannah*, John Gale, became the ship's master, and twenty-year-old John Jr., Glover's son, her first lieutenant. The men of the regiment had deep bonds forged in friendship and interconnected by the blood of family. As one contemporary later remarked, "Colonel Glover has given the strongest proofs of his good opinion of the Schooner commanded by Captain Broughton, he has ventured his brother[-in-law] & his favourite son on board of her."[8]

Recruiting the remaining thirty-six privates for the crew proved effortless. Volunteers from multiple companies stepped forward, drawn by the allure of prize money as well as the desire to escape the drudgery of siege lines. Washington micromanaged the process from the beginning and issued Broughton specific orders on prize money: "For your own Encouragement & that of the other Officers & Men to Activity & Courage in this Service, over & above your Pay in the continental Army you shall be entitled to one third Part of the Cargo of every Vessel by you taken & sent into Port (military & naval Stores only excepted, which with Vessels & apparel are reserved for the publick Service)—which third Part is to be divided among the Officers & Men in the followg Proportions."[9]

His detailed instructions left no doubt that he intended to keep the operations of his secret navy close to the vest. On September 2, he wrote Broughton, "If you should be so successful as to take any of such Vessels you are immediately to send them to the nearest & safest Port to this Camp under a careful Prize Master directing him to notify me by Express immediately of such Capture with all Particulars & there to wait my farther Direction."[10] The prize master or agent appointed was Jonathan Glover, John's brother. Eventually, Jonathan brought on his friend and business associate William Bartlett as a fellow prize agent who would oversee the thorny nature of adjudicating the status of each prize vessel.

Washington also instructed Broughton "to be very particular & diligent in your Search after all Letters or other Papers tending to discov[er] the Designs of the Enemy or of any other Kind & to forward all such to me as soon as possible," and also commanded prisoners be treated "with Kindness & Humanity as far is consistent with your own Safety—their private Stock of Money, & Apparel to be given them after being duly search'd."[11]

In the third week of August, toughs wearing rounded jackets and tarred fishermen's trousers assembled in Marblehead—men drawn from Glover's Regiment, weathered, salty "soldiers . . . who had been bred to the sea."[12] The motley crew did not go unnoticed by Loyalist Ashley Bowen: "This day fair weather. Came to town a company of volunteers for privateering. They came from Camp at Cambridge and are to go on board Colonel Glover schooner."[13] Another Loyalist bluntly stated, "fishermen gone from Marblehead—good riddance!"[14]

On the morning of September 5, 1775, *Hannah* set sail. With a "fair wind"[15] in her sails, the schooner maneuvered through Beverly Harbor and into the open waters of the Atlantic. Somewhere near Cape Anne, Broughton ominously reported to Washington, "About 5 oClock Saw two ships of War" patrolling the area—the Royal Navy's twenty-gun *Lively* and the eight-gun *Savage*. The Crown's warships immediately "gave me Chace."[16]

Hannah's four 4-pounder guns pulled from storage in Glover's warehouse stood little chance against the *Lively* and *Savage*. A 4-pound shot is precisely that—a 4-pound ball of solid iron. The cannon could hurtle the ball several cable lengths, each being about two hundred yards. Still, much of the ship-to-ship fighting was typically only fifty feet apart because of accuracy and tactics of the day.

"I made back towards Cape Ann but did not go in,"[17] Broughton reported. He sailed near the rocky and dangerous shoals of Cape Anne and barely outran the Crown's ships. Unable to capture *Hannah* and with a lack of mastery of the treacherous waters, *Lively* and *Savage* disengaged the pursuit.

The next morning, Broughton found himself in the Crown's sights again: "I saw a ship under my lee quarter she giving me Chace I run into Cape Ann harbor, I went out again that night about sun sett."[18] *Hannah* once again escaped *Lively*.

But hunting had been good for the British warship, despite *Hannah*'s escape. On September 6, *Lively* pounced on the merchant ship *Unity*, owned by John Langdon, a Patriot and now a member of Congress, who played a key role in the raid on Fort William and Mary. *Lively*'s log stated, "Fired a Shott . . . to a Brig Sent the boat on board. Found her to be from Pescatuway with Lumber bound to St. Vincent Sent a Petty Officer & 3 men aboard her and took her hands out."[19] The captured American vessel, now under British control, sailed toward occupied Boston.

A day later, the hulking 260-ton *Unity* crossed paths with *Hannah*. Broughton hailed the ship: "I told him he must bear away and go into

Cape Ann, but being very loth I told him if he did not I should fire on him, on that he bore away and I have brought her safe into Cape Ann Harbour."[20]

The overjoyed crew thought they had seized a legitimate prize. After examining the ship's papers, Washington realized, to his horror, that his covert navy, whose existence was unknown to Congress, had recaptured an American ship owned by Congressman John Langdon. The commander in chief swiftly ordered the ship and crew immediately released. Broughton objected, arguing the ship had deliberately sailed toward Boston so it could be captured and sell its cargo to the British.

Joseph Searle, a private in Broughton's crew, violently protested the loss of the prize until placed under arrest by Broughton's officers, triggering one of America's first mutinies as the crew seized arms, freed Searle, and stared down Broughton and his officers. An express messenger sped to Washington. The general ordered Glover to send several companies to put down the mutiny. The men did not resist, but one observer acidly noted, "The rascals are brought down here under guard, and I hope will meet with their deserts."[21]

A court-martial on September 22 found the Marblehead men guilty of "Mutiny, Riot and Disobedience of orders." The court sentenced Joseph Searle to "thirty-nine Lashes upon his bare back and be drum'd out of the Army,"[22] and fourteen other crew members to receive twenty lashes each and a variety of other punishments. Showing mercy, Washington commuted the sentences of the other men, and only Searle received the lash.

Moving past this episode, Washington nevertheless saw the tremendous value in the navy—how capturing a single ship could potentially alter the course of the war—and ordered Broughton to raise a new crew and get *Hannah* back out to sea.

On October 10, *Hannah*'s new crew, consisting of more of Glover's men, sailed out of Beverly and went back on the prowl. The Royal Navy took notice and dispatched the sixteen-gun *Nautilus* to blow the nettlesome ship out of the water. Not far from port, *Nautilus* spotted the American warship. Broughton made a hasty retreat back to the relative safety of Beverly, which the British had until now avoided since the harbor had many sandbars and a narrow channel that made for treacherous navigation. During the flight, *Hannah* grounded on mud flats in a cove outside the harbor. "The people speedily assembled, stripped her, and carried her Guns, &c. ashore."[23]

Nautilus pounded the stranded ship, forcing Broughton to abandon his craft. *Nautilus* captain John Collins now ordered part of his crew to their small boats, armed with incendiaries, to burn the *Hannah*. As the British approached, the tide went out. *Hannah* now sat high and dry in a sea of quicksand-like mud inaccessible by the small boats. Meanwhile, the town assembled along with Glover's Regiment and started peppering *Nautilus* with musket fire. When they began to use the 4-pounder cannon they dragged off *Hannah*, Collins retreated. He could not destroy *Hannah*, and his own craft might not survive if he stayed. As the tide continued to recede, the British warship found herself in the same dire situation as the *Hannah*. Collins exclaimed he "found ye ship grounded."[24] Under fire, unable to retrieve his anchors, and suffering casualties, Collins cut the cables and abandoned his anchor. "Rebels kept firing upon us with the above cannon and small arms. Shattered our Rigging, sails and hull."[25] Of the two casualties—one man who lost a leg and another shot through the side by a musket ball—only one survived. That evening when the tide came in, the *Nautilus* floated back to sea to fight another day.

The damaged *Hannah*, however, would never sail as a man-of-war again—but the incident was only the beginning of the story of an American navy.

Chapter 21

Broughton's Odyssey

Despite *Hannah*'s inglorious start, Washington moved forward with building America's first navy, ordering John Glover to arm and raise crews for several more vessels. Confident in his prescient judgment, Washington understood the urgency of the need to stop the supplies flowing in to reinforce British troops and demanded results practically overnight: "Upon the best Terms you can—let them be prime Sailors, put them into the best Order & loose no Time."[1] He warned, "A great Number of Transports are hourly expected at Boston from England and elsewhere."[2]

As the enterprise expanded, Washington brought in the army's muster-master general, Stephen Moylan, to assist Glover in managing the burgeoning navy. The muster-master general had the arduous task of accounting for the men in each of the Continental Army's units.* A tough, husky Irish immigrant, Moylan hailed from a prominent Irish trading family[3] who sent him to Paris and later Lisbon for his education. The well-spoken gentleman with a brogue had a keen mind for international trade and business. Elected before the war as the first president of the Friendly Sons of St. Patrick, an organization of prosperous merchants, Moylan is credited with coining the term "the United States of America" in a January 2, 1776, missive to Joseph Reed, Washington's secretary and aide-de-camp.[4]

---

* Moylan's position involved tabulating all of the muster rolls for the army, a painstaking task.

Moylan's partnership with Glover proved potent, and the duo realized Washington's vision. Moylan extended Washington's direct authority to Glover, as Reed wrote, "Mr. Moylan, the Muster-Master General, is associated with you in this business; and whatever engagements are entered into by you and Mr. Moylan, when you happen to be together, or by either in case one goes to Newbury, the General will fully ratify and confirm."[5] Eventually, Moylan's influence expanded, and Washington made the Irishman an aide-de-camp.

Glover located two schooners for the incipient navy—the *Hancock*,[6] which was previously named *Speedwell* and owned by Marbleheader Thomas Grant; and the *Franklin*, originally Archibald Selman's *Eliza*. The tiny, growing fleet was later dubbed "Washington's cruisers." With *Hannah*'s navy days behind her, Broughton now captained *Hancock*. John Selman, an experienced captain in his thirties and another officer from Glover's Marblehead Regiment, commanded *Franklin*. Washington ordered his tiny fleet on a mission that once again revolved around the quest for precious gunpowder. Congress received intelligence that two unarmed brigantines had sailed from England to Quebec containing powder. Recognizing their limited window to intercept the British warships, Washington immediately ordered Glover to equip the two vessels for the mission.

On October 5, a month after *Hannah*'s maiden voyage as a ship of war, Washington finally informed Congress of his secret navy. His announcement came at a most opportune time since Congress had recently received intelligence on the powder brigs. But when Congress actually took up a motion to arm vessels, some members balked. Samuel Chase, a boisterous representative from Maryland, denounced the plan: "It is the maddest Idea in the World, to think of building an American fleet. Its Latitude is wonderful. We should mortgage the whole Continent."[7]

However, other members of Congress, including Silas Deane, John Adams, and New Hampshire Patriot John Langdon, who was involved in capturing gunpowder at Fort William and Mary, boldly embraced the idea. Despite having his merchant ship *Unity* seized and recaptured by *Hannah*, Langdon ardently advocated for an American fleet, once again proving the wisdom of the politically savvy Washington in promptly returning the vessel weeks earlier to the member of Congress, who graciously sent a reward to Marblehead officers for the ship's recapture.[8] The motion passed, and Congress assigned a three-person committee to estimate the cost of the enormous undertaking. Christopher Gadsden, who had been in contact with Adams months earlier, now joined the committee in Adams's place. Both men also consulted Elbridge Gerry for his expertise in maritime matters; the group would morph into the Marine Committee. On October 13, 1775, today considered the birthday of the US Navy, a congressional resolution* officially authorized the fitting out of armed vessels to intercept enemy shipping. As the navy expanded, Washington would brief Congress again and reveal the existence of six ships being fitted out for war, and the committee acquiesced. Despite the resolution's authorization, Congress did not formally approve funding for the navy until November 30, 1775, when "the Congress approve[d] the General's fitting out armed vessels to intercept the enemy's supplies."[9]

Congress wanted an expanded navy to guard trade routes, raid British holdings, conduct special missions, and, it was hoped with the larger gunned vessels, challenge British warships directly. Coupled with Washington's cruisers, authorizing and building the Continental

---

* Charles Francis Adams, *The Works of John Adams, Second President of the United States*, vol. 5 (Boston: Little, Brown, and Company, 1865), 9. "*Resolved*, That a swift sailing vessel, to carry ten carriage guns, and a proportionable number of swivels, with eighty men, be fitted, with all possible despatch, for a cruise of three months, and that the commander be instructed to cruize eastward, for intercepting such transports as may be laden with warlike stores and other supplies for our enemies, and for such other purposes as the Congress shall direct. That a Committee of three be appointed to prepare an estimate of the expence, and lay the same before the Congress, and to contract with proper persons to fit out the vessel.

Resolved, that another vessel be fitted out for the same purposes, and that the said committee report their opinion of a proper vessel, and also an estimate of the expence."

Navy marked a bold step toward independence. Ships flagged under the colonies were a step toward sovereignty. The Continental Navy signaled the start of an enormous undertaking, but the first frigates would not be completed until 1777. The vessels necessitated the printing of money and assumption of debt for their construction and would require infrastructure and bureaucracy for support. A navy contributed to American independence and the creation of a nation. Glover's men crewed the vessels and were the rudimentary processes and origins of the American navy. They challenged the Royal Navy's transports and other warships.

Despite the general's insistence on speed, one delay after another seemed to dog Washington's Navy. Fitting out the vessels proved to be a massive challenge; however, the core of many of the ships could only be described as rotting tubs. The most significant bottleneck was finding carpenters to complete the work. Moylan ranted about "the Jobbing of the Carpenters, who are sure the Idlest Scoundrels in nature."[10] Compounding the problem, the men refused to work on Sundays. Moylan scoffed at their piety and continued to bark orders: "Such religious rascalls are they, that we could not prevail on them to work the Sabbath. I have stuck very close to them since, & what by Scolding and Shame for their tory-like disposition in retarding the work, I think they mend something."[11] Washington demanded action and through his aide-de-camp Joseph Reed ordered, "You will immediately set every Hand to Work that can be procured & not a Moment in Time be lost in getting ready."[12] Despite the delays, Washington ordered two more vessels fitted out for war. Those would be followed by two more for a total of six ships. Reed needled Broughton, "Loose no Time—every Thing depends upon Expedition."[13] The prodding and pestering finally produced results.

On October 15, 1775, Glover notified Washington that the *Hancock* and *Franklin* stood ready at last for their crews drawn from Marblehead Regiment volunteers. "Would it not be best," Glover wrote Washington, "that every man be furnish with a Spear, or Cutlast, & a pare of Pistles, if to be had, as [muskets] is very unhandy in boarding."[14] The Marblehead-ers also brought on board a local weapon—the blunderbuss—equivalent to a shotgun and ideal for close-quarter, ship-to-ship combat. Glover also cautioned Washington that Captain Broughton had contracted what he hoped was just a cold from wading ashore when the *Hannah* beached in the mud in the fight against the *Nautilus*.

As the Marblehead crews coalesced in Beverly and prepared to sail, another stumbling block delayed launch: the lack of a surgeon. Storming enemy ships and engaging in hand-to-hand combat often resulted in widespread wounds, and the crews refused to sail without a doctor. Fortunately, Glover found a physician and the soldier-mariners prepared to sail.

To maintain secrecy, Washington issued Broughton and Selman orders that were to remain sealed until the ships went to sea, "not to be opened till out of site of land."[15] To ensure operational security, Moylan demanded to see the unbroken seals before the two captains sailed. Selman remembered handing over his envelope to the Irishman: "Horrors of death in all its forms would not have operated to have broke a seal or denyed a duty."[16] Satisfied, Moylan handed back the orders to each captain as they made final preparations for the voyage. Washing-ton put Broughton in command and before the voyage promoted the Marbleheader to commodore.

Shortly after Washington's cruisers left Beverly on October 22, Reed suggested a flag for the vessels. "What do you think of a Flag with a White Ground, a Tree in the Middle, the Motto 'Appeal to Heaven'?"[17] In authorizing armed warships, Congress and Washington were already taking an unprecedented step toward independence and sovereignty, but flying a separate flag would have been a monumental leap closer to that goal. Unfortunately, Glover received Reed's letter after the cruisers set sail, so Selman and Broughton flew their old commercial colors, a version of the Union Jack, but arranged a series of signals to recognize friend from foe.

The mid-autumn wind nipped at the hoisted sails of both ships as *Hancock* and *Franklin* navigated through the treacherous narrow channel at Beverly Harbor. The entrance remained unguarded, and fortuitously, British ship-hunters *Nautilus* and *Lively* lurked elsewhere. Each Yankee man-of-war sported four 4-pounder guns and numerous swivel guns. Passing Cape Anne, the ships sliced through the icy waters of the Atlantic toward Nova Scotia.

Once out of sight of land, Broughton and Selman opened their sealed envelopes. Inside Washington detailed their mission to capture the two powder-laden brigantines sailing from England to Quebec: "You are hereby directed to make all possible Dispatch for the River St. Lawrence, and there take such a Station as will best enable you to intercept the above vessels." The commander in chief stipulated, "Should you meet with any Vessel, the Property of the Inhabitants of Canada, not employed in any Respect in the Service of the ministerial army, you are to treat such Vessel with all Kindness and by no Means suffer them to be injured or molested."[18] Washington wisely considered the plight of the inhabitants of Canada and hoped to bring them over to the American cause or at least not push them even further into the arms of the British. Unfortunately, the lack of clarity and contradictory rules of engagement for seizing prizes would lead to great misunderstanding with the Marblehead captains on what was considered a legitimate prize.

Each cruiser measured between fifty and sixty feet long with a twenty-foot breadth. Seventy men crammed below deck in the slimy, damp hold that reeked of dead fish from their prior service as fishing vessels. One of those men was Marblehead private William Bean, who remembered the "secret expedition [and] was selected to go on board of . . . Selmans vessel."[19] Complications occurred when the ships entered the waters of Nova Scotia. When Selman's *Franklin* crossed Browns Bank, she sprang leaks. Fortunately, the two boats found shelter at the remote Country Harbor to make repairs. The pause forced the captains to reassess and reinterpret Washington's orders. Both men reasoned they had missed their opportunity to capture the powder ships on the St. Lawrence due to the downtime needed to mend the vessels, so they

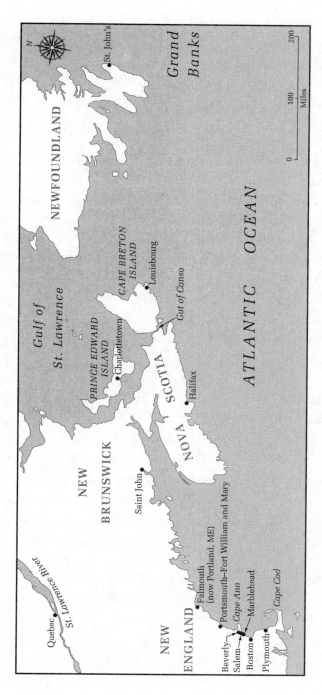

"Canada"

decided to stay and cruise the waters of Halifax for prizes. Ultimately, both Marblehead captains disobeyed Washington's orders but felt their results would exonerate them.

On October 29, the cruisers snared *Prince William* and the small schooner *Mary.* The boats contained fish and oil—Canadian boats conducting their normal affairs. Broughton, however, accused the captains of heading for Boston to trade with the British. Much as in his capture of the *Unity*, the Marblehead captain conveniently shoehorned the facts to fit his desired narrative.

After appropriating sundry equipment and provisions from the boats, *Hancock*'s second officer, Lieutenant John Devereux (also Broughton's son-in-law), and a skeleton crew sailed *Prince William* and her captured crew back toward Marblehead while Lieutenant Edward Homan sailed *Mary* to Beverly.

As Washington's cruisers worked the waters known as the Strait or Gut of Canso off Nova Scotia, two British brigs, the *Jacob* and *Elizabeth*, sailed through the Gulf of St. Lawrence toward Quebec. The boats brimmed with hundreds of barrels of powder, thousands of stands of arms, and enough clothing to equip an army. Contrary to American intelligence, the Crown considered the transports too valuable to sail alone, and the twenty-gun HMS *Lizard* escorted the tiny convoy. A fight with *Lizard* would have been formidable, but Broughton and Selman never had the opportunity. Remarkably, *Elizabeth* would never disgorge her cargo since the threat of American invasion precluded her stores from being offloaded, and Governor Guy Carlton ordered her to sail back to England. But the Marblehead men, busy with their questionable activities in the Gut of Canso, missed their best chance to capture the valued prize.

On the surface, hunting in the Gut of Canso seemed promising. The cruisers picked off several more dubious prizes, including a sloop, *Warren*, owned and captained by John Denny of New Haven, Connecticut. Selman and Broughton employed a bit of subterfuge to ascertain whether the *Warren* had allegiance to the American cause. "We at the conference, used the words 'Yankees' and 'Pumpkins' with apparent jeering, and asked after the Kings troops. They answered as men well-affected to the Ministry would. Upon being undeceived, they did not make such apologies as true sons of liberty, strongly attached to their interest, but had mistaken their company, might naturally be expected to do."[20] Broughton dispatched a prize crew to seize *Warren* and take her back to Beverly along with another ship, *Phoebe*. Washington's cruisers thus captured four prizes, none of them directly employed by the British government.

To snare more ships, the cruisers stationed themselves on the eastern side of the Gut of Canso and, on November 6, spotted another vessel. Broughton sent Selman to investigate, and in the process, *Franklin* lost her mainmast. Both ships anchored in a bay while the boat's small launch rowed ashore looking for a suitable tree to replace the mast. The Marbleheaders trudged through three-quarters of a mile of swamp and "morass" until they found a suitable forest. A work party of fifty men "cut down five trees before we could obtain one for a mast."[21] Using axes, adzes, and planes, they shaped the timber into *Franklin*'s new mast. Scores of men manhandled and dragged the massive log through the muck and floated it back to the ship.

With the *Franklin* once again operational, the Marblehead captains seized two more boats carrying lumber heading to the island of Jersey—dubious prizes that not even Selman and Broughton could construct a case for seizing. Still, they detained the pilots after one of the Canadians "acquainted with the Island of St. Johns [currently Prince Edward Island] a number of cannon was there in the fortress and recruiting was going on for Quebeck." The Marbleheaders had bumbled upon a new mission and called a council of war, "we with the advice of the officers, supposing we should do essential service by breaking up a nest of recruits."[22]

Selman warned the prisoners that if "they ran the ships ashore death to them would be inevitable." True to their word, the two captured pilots guided the American fleet through the treacherous waters around St. John's. The wind cut from the south as the "fall weather"[23] safely carried the two cruisers into the harbor. Selman and Broughton scrambled aboard the schooners' two small launches. Six men, their captain, and one pilot rowed ashore on each boat. Broughton headed to an old fort while Selman rowed toward the tiny village of Charlottetown. Spotting the two ships, the nervous inhabitants of Charlottetown shuffled to the dock to greet them. One of the pilots accompanied Selman and, according to a prearranged plan, identified the "Governor" with a "sign."[24] The governor of St. John's had traveled back to England, so the pilot fingered the Crown's representative in charge, Phillips Callbeck, who went by the lofty title of "commander and chief of the Island of St. Johns."[25] Callbeck civilly greeted the Americans, but Selman detained him and sent him back to the *Franklin*.

Broughton's skiff landed on the western side of the village near the fort. Encountering no opposition, his small crew rumbled through the main gate and found several large cannons. Determining the artillery pieces too heavy for transport back to the cruisers, his men spiked the guns.

Shortly after reaching the *Franklin*, Selman demanded Callbeck turn over the keys to his house and storehouse or they would break the doors down. Selman and Broughton and their men ransacked and plundered the island, but instead of breaking down doors, they opened them. Broughton called another council of war to determine what to do with commodities found in the storehouse: "The articles were for the recruiting service and were taken and sent on board Broughton's vessel."[26] Next, the Americans pillaged Callbeck's home, storming into the bedrooms, where they "broke open her [Callbeck's wife's] drawers, scattered her clothes about, read her letters from her mother and sisters."[27] The Marblehead mariners purloined everything, including the bed and window curtains, rings, and other jewelry. They guzzled Callbeck's casks of porter and rum.

Back on *Franklin*, Callbeck and another British official, Justice of the Peace Thomas Wright, seethed with outrage for their unlawful detention and demanded to visit their families. They "worked up the human pashions in the breast in their behalf they were allowed to go ashore that night and come on board the next morning." Selman warned both men they better show up. Remarkably, the two did. Livid about the detention and plundering, Wright ranted that if they encountered a British frigate, "I will have you hung to the yard arm."[28] One of the crew members, Marbleheader Private John Teshew, later recalled the voyage: "After crossing of some time we Sailed to the St. Lawrence and after cruising for some time we returned to Salem, having taken five or six brigs, the Governor, Commissary of Nova Scotia, brought them safe to Salem in December of the same year, but we did not succeed in capturing the British vessels which we went to the St. Lawrence to intercept."[29]

As the two captains of the *Franklin* and *Hancock* were failing to win Canadian* hearts and minds while marauding the coast of Nova Scotia, Washington was busy expanding his fleet and creating another naval base at Plymouth. With Glover recruiting more ships and crews, Washington's Navy doubled, adding two new captains hunting the seas for prizes, including John Manley.

---

* The inhabitants were not officially Canadian citizens. They were British subjects. Only two decades earlier, the inhabitants were French and did not have a strong allegiance to the Crown.

CHAPTER 22

"THIS INSTANCE OF DIVINE FAVOUR": CAPTAIN JOHN MANLEY AND THE CAPTURE OF THE *NANCY*

In the dim candlelight of his headquarters, on December 4, 1775, Washington drafted a letter to John Hancock and the Continental Congress that, once again, detailed the Continental Army's desperate need for gunpowder. The army required everything from foodstuffs to uniforms, but the dire lack of powder prevented the commader in chief from going on the offensive at Boston, and the dangerously low levels of ammunition potentially limited the army from defending themselves if the British launched an all-out assault on his siege lines.[1] The quest for and seizure of black powder remained the common thread among engagements at Fort William and Mary, Salem, Lexington and Concord, and Bunker Hill. Enlistments for the army reached a perilous state, as Elbridge Gerry noted to John Adams on the same day Washington wrote Hancock: "The Situation of the Army at this Time is critical, the Men declining to inlist on the Terms proposed by the General."[2] Washington broached a potential war-changing solution employing the navy, writing, "A fortunate Capture of an ordnance ship would give new Life to the Camp and an immediate turn to the Issue of this Campaign."[3]

Serendipitously, in the middle of November 1775, Washington's spy network obtained intelligence that a lightly armed British transport, loaded with ordnance, was missing. The report revealed that the British feared the ship had fallen into American hands. Stephen Moylan immediately notified prize agent William Bartlett and John Glover to send out every available cruiser: "his Excellency's express orders that [the vessels] be put to sea as soon as possible & keep a sharp Lookout for this Brigg which is without any force."[4]

The flag proclaiming "Appeal to Heaven" fluttered in the autumn wind, affixed to the schooner *Lee* as she churned through the blue-gray waters of Beverly Harbor toward Boston. Captain John Manley and his 72-ton ship immediately set out to intercept *Nancy*, a 250-ton brig bound for Boston.

Manley's biography is murky. Some sources identify his birthplace as Boston and others, England, but he spent his youth in Marblehead, during which he may have served in the Royal Navy, but later captained merchant ships. A fearless and aggressive natural leader, Manley would emerge as one of the finest captains of the Revolution. In 1764, he married Martha Hickman under the alias John Russell but, oddly enough, used the surname Manley everywhere outside Marblehead.[5]

Several miles off the east coast of Cape Anne, Manley spotted *Nancy* through his spyglass and directed his fifty-man crew from Marblehead to sail on a converging path. *Lee* had not been flying her colors. As the two ships approached each other, Robert Hunter, the captain of *Nancy*, called out for a pilot ship to sail the vessel into Boston. Manley gladly promised one. Meanwhile, several members of his crew lowered *Lee*'s small boat and rowed toward the unsuspecting brig. After the Americans boarded, they drew their pistols and cutlasses. Stunned, Hunter surrendered his ship.[6]

Once Manley ventured into *Nancy*'s hold, he found a floating arsenal: two thousand muskets, thirty-one tons of musket balls, thousands of bayonets, two thousand carriage boxes, kegs of flints, seven thousand 6-pound cannonballs, 150 carcass shells, and an enormous brass mortar with three hundred shells. The men christened the giant mortar "Congress." Washington's gregarious Irishman Stephen Moylan described the "glorious, truly ludicrous scene . . . with a bottle of rum in his hand, standing parson to christen, while godfather Mifflin gave it the name of Congress. Huzzas on the occasion I dare say were heard through all the territories."[7]

The ship's capture overjoyed Washington. Writing to Congress, he said, "I have a very singular pleasure in informing of you, that by Express last Night from Cape Ann, I received the glad tidings of the Capture of the *Nancy* Storeship from London, by Captn Manley, contents as pr the Inclosed Copy (taken by Mr Pierce to save me, you must know, the trouble of innumeration)—He, unluckily, miss'd the greatest prize in the World; their whole Ordnance; the Ship containing it [gunpowder], being just a head. But—he could not have got both; and we must be thankful, as I truly am, for this Instance of divine favour; for nothing, surely, ever came more Apropos."[8]

Fearing recapture by the British, Washington ordered Glover's Regiment and other militia groups to march to Gloucester to guard the ship: "That no part of it may slip threw my fingers (for I have no doubt, as this Capture was made in Sight of the other Vessell, of there being some bold push to recover it) I, instantly upon receiving the Acct, orderd four Companies down to protect the Stores—Teams to be Impress'd to remove them without delay—& Colo. Glover to Assemble the Minutemen in the Neighborhood of Cape Ann to secure the removal to places of safety."[9] Manley just captured one of the greatest prizes of the war, initially estimated by Captain Bartlett at £20,000.[10] Her cargo turned out to be worth far more: *Nancy*'s ordnance, once in the hands of Washington's army, would have an immediate impact on the Revolution at a crucial time.

The incident exasperated Admiral Samuel Graves, who fumed, "It is much to be lamented that a Cargo of such Consequence should be from England in a Vessel destitute of Arms even to protect her from a Row Boat. An Officer on board with a Man would have saved the Vessel."[11] Capture of *Nancy* made Manley not only a marked man with the British but also one of America's first heroes. A popular ballad immortalized his exploits:

> Brave Manley, he is stout, and his Men have proved true,
> by taking of those English ships, he makes their Jacks to rue;
> To our Ports he sends their Ships and Men, let's give
>   a hearty Cheer
> To Him and all those valiant Souls who go in Privateers.
> And a Privateering we will go, my Boys, my Boys,
> And a Privateering we will go.[12]

Manley went on a rampage. Shortly after seizing *Nancy*, the Marbleheader secured several more prizes: *Jenny*, *Betsey*, and *Little Hanna*, followed by *Happy Return* and *Norfolk*. With *Jenny* and *Little Hanna*, Manley employed subterfuge, appearing as Graves's decoy schooner, the very vessel hunting him. *Lee* initially embarked under the flag of Great Britain. When he closed in on his prey, Manley then swiftly raised "Appeal to Heaven," and his crew boarded the hapless vessels.

Despite numerous mishaps, foibles, and outright debacles, Washington's Navy increased in October and November 1775. John Glover managed the expansion with most of the crews coming from the Marblehead Regiment. But several ships captained and crewed by men outside Marblehead also joined the fleet. One of those commanders, a lawyer and sea captain dubbed "the Great Red Dragon,"[13] was Captain William Coit—a large, eccentric, jovial man typically adorned in a giant red cloak. Known for his sense of humor, Coit described his ship the *Harrison* to one of his friends, "If you were where you could see me and did not laugh, all your risible faculties must perish. To see me strutting on the quarterdeck of my schooner! . . . A pair of cohorns [mortars] that Noah had on the Ark, one that lacks a touch-hole . . . six swivels, the first that were landed at Plymouth, and never fired since. . . . I haven't time to give you her character in full but in short, she is the devil."[14]

Harrison's maiden voyage abruptly ended after she hit a sandbar outside the harbor, prompting Washington to label him the "blundering Captain Coit."[15] Moylan went further: "Coit I look upon as a mere blubber."[16] Fortunately, a speedy refit refloated the boat, but the vessel's troubles would not end there: the main mast had rotted at its base. Despite sailing on a ship that should have been condemned, the captain demonstrated great courage and captured two prizes loaded with livestock and foodstuffs right under the noses of the British warships near Boston's harbor lighthouse. "A humorous genius," Coit forced his prisoners to "land upon the same rock [Plymouth] our ancestors first trod when they landed in America where they gave three cheers, and wished success to the American arms."[17]

At sea, *Harrison* linked up with *Washington*, christened in the commander in chief's honor but without his consent, as Washington, renowned for his dignity, would never name anything after himself. Commanded by Rhode Islander Sion Martindale, a sea captain from a wealthy family in Rhode Island and cousin to Benedict Arnold, *Washington* would be one of the most expensive ships of Washington's Navy, with her outfitting costing over £1,000. She boasted six 6-pounder guns along with swivels, whereas most of Washington's cruisers carried only 4-pounders. Martindale had high hopes for the vessel. Joseph Reed, on the other hand, questioned Martindale's competence: "I cautioned him against an extravagant outset, but I fear his former Ideas upon the Subject are insuperable. There certainly can be no occasion for such a number of guns, unless he means to go without powder for them, as we cannot spare so much of that article."[18]

Washington, however, did not live up to her impressive armament. On her maiden voyage from Plymouth, she encountered several of Admiral Graves's warships and raced back to the safety of the harbor. On her next voyage, *Washington* was pummeled by a massive storm and strong gales, snow, and sleet ripped into the ship. Most of the men were not properly clothed, which led them to mutiny. The Rhode Islanders "inlisted to Serve in the Army and not as Marines,"[19] wrote the ship's surgeon, a Frenchman known as John Manvide who kept a journal on board the vessel. "As we were getting ready to go to Cape Ann, our entire crew revolted, 'We asked them what they wanted' To go to work again. But they were not willing to do anything. After a conference [with the officers] we decided to send a messenger to camp . . . to inform General Washington of this evil conduct."[20] Washington questioned Martindale's ability to command and even considered placing Coit in charge of the vessel instead.

A few days later, the ship again set sail from Plymouth with Martindale at the helm and headed toward Cape Ann, but her luck, as before, ran out. She encountered *Lively* and the *Fowey*. *Fowey* gave chase, her 6-pounders blasting away at the fleeing *Washington*. Eventually, the British warship caught the most heavily armed vessel of Washington's Navy, and Martindale anticlimactically surrendered without firing a single shot.

After the capture, the British hurled Martindale and the entire crew, including two Royal Navy deserters, into the hull of the ship and sailed toward Boston. Here Admiral Graves interrogated Martindale. Instead of refusing to talk, Martindale offered up valuable intelligence to save his own skin. First, the Rhode Islander revealed the missing *Nancy* had indeed been captured by Manley. Martindale detailed the scope of Washington's Navy and specifically gave Graves information on "the Red Dragon's" ship the *Harrison*, which he described as having "black Sides, Tallowed bottom, two Topsails and Oars on her Quarters" and as being "commanded by one Coit."[21] Martindale also willingly divulged the priceless protocol: a description of the colors, "Appeal to Heaven," and more important, how Washington's Navy employed them to distinguish friend from foe: "that the Signal to know each other was to hoist the Colours at the Fore topmast head, and lower the Main Sail half down."[22]

The admiral ordered an inspection of *Washington* for possible use in the Royal Navy. Admiral Graves believed that "putting a good Crew into her from the King's Ships and sending her to Sea directly we should lay hold of her Comrade or some other Rebel Cruizers."[23] But the plan to use the *Washington* as a decoy to draw in other American cruisers dissolved much the same way *Washington* was literally falling apart. Once in Boston, shipwrights returned with a negative report: the deck was disintegrating; the main beam, foremast beam, and deck decayed; the hull unseaworthy; and the bow spirit sprung. Vexed by the report, Graves had a look for himself and chimed in with a damning assessment of the rotting tub: "She exceeds their description of her badness."[24] Undeterred, the British would convert schooners into decoy ships to hunt Manley and Glover's other captains.

Graves then threw the seventy Rhode Island seamen along with Martindale in the hold of the HMS *Tartar*, which sailed toward England, where the British tried the men as pirates. Sailing to England on a separate ship at the same time was Ethan Allen, who had earlier helped seize Fort Ticonderoga and had been captured during an aborted attack on Montreal. Below deck of the *Tartar*, the men lived in miserable, stifling conditions, deprived of fresh air and starved of food. By the time *Tartar* reached Portsmouth, England, the crew had been ravished with smallpox and looked like walking skeletons. Once in England, the men became powerful symbols and pawns. The British placed the Americans in a show trial to maximize the propaganda value as they faced possible death sentences as pirates. Once again, Martindale betrayed his men. "Our captain petitioned to the court that his men were willing to serve his Majesty's [Royal Navy] voluntarily, which was false,"[25] remarked one of the men. The majority would never return to America; some would fight against their country impressed on his majesty's ships, and a few escaped British custody—including the cunning Captain Martindale.

Washington's other cruisers struggled to seize legitimate prizes. One of the commander in chief's new captains, Winborn Adams, a Durham, New Hampshire, native, had close ties to Congressman John Langdon. Adams captained the *Warren*, a schooner originally named *Hawk* but rechristened after the martyr of Bunker Hill, Joseph Warren. Adams and several members of his New Hampshire crew had participated in the attack on Fort William and Mary. The veteran mariners headed north in familiar waters while Manley and *Lee* headed south toward Boston. Adams sailed from Glover's Wharf in Beverly only to snare an illegitimate prize. On November 25, however, *Warren* captured *Rainbow*, a schooner loaded with potatoes and turnips bound for occupied Boston. Adams and his crew spent the bitter winter prowling north of Boston in search of British vessels. His crew lost many men from sickness, and two men died at sea. Their luck turned with *Sally*, an American ship captured by the British that contained over 120 casks of wine and a British crew who had seized the ship days earlier. A prize crew from *Warren* sailed *Sally* back to port, where Adams's men ultimately received an award of one-third of the prize from *Sally*'s original owners. She would be the last ship captured by Adams and his last cruise. Enlistments for the New Hampshire men expired, and Adams could not raise a new crew; the forty-five-year-old captain returned to Cambridge and rejoined his regiment and would ultimately die in battle.

Before Manley's capture of *Nancy*, many of the prizes seized by Washington's Navy had been illegitimate. An exasperated Washington exclaimed to Congress, "Our Rascally privateers men, go on at the old rate. Mutinying if they can not do as they please, those at Plymouth, Beverly, & Portsmouth, have done nothing worth mentioning in the Prize way & no Accts are yet recd from those further Eastward."[26] Washington's disgust reached its apogee with Captains John Selman and Nicholson Broughton. When their captures began entering Beverly and Marblehead, Washington discovered to his horror that almost none of the ships were valid prizes. The commander in chief dismissed the crews and sailed the ships back to their owners. Phillips Callbeck and Judge Thomas Wright were also released and returned to Canada. The number of prizes multiplied and cargo sat in a warehouse, leading John Hancock to implore, "Should not a Court be established by Authority of Congress, to take Cognizance of the Prizes made by Continental

Vessels?" Congress finally determined how to navigate the murky waters of prize captures by handing the issue off to admiralty courts in each colony, allowing them to rule on each vessel. Prizes in Marblehead and Beverly fell under the jurisdiction of Salem's Judge Timothy Pickering.

Shortly after Selman and Broughton returned to Marblehead, they were summoned to Washington's headquarters in Cambridge. Ardent patriots and fully committed to the cause, the two Marblehead captains thought they had served proudly and acted within Washington's guidelines.* Instead of inviting the two captains inside, Washington greeted them at the front door. As they described their voyages to Washington, the Marblehead captains attempted to justify their perspective. "[The general] appeared not pleased—he wanted not to hear anything about it," Selman later recalled to Gerry.

Furious, Washington dismissed their narrative and turned to Selman. "Sir, will you stand in Col. Glover's regiment?" Washington barked.

"I will not, sir," Selman responded.

Washington turned to Broughton. "You, sir, I understand you have said you will stand?"

"I will not stand," Broughton replied.[27]

John Adams would later write that America lost two great captains.[28]

---

* Washington's guidelines on prize vessels changed after the failed American operations to seize Canada. One could surmise that Washington no longer concerned himself with respecting Canadian property to win hearts and minds. Rather than avarice, one can conclude that the motivation behind the two Marblehead captains' captures was a zealous desire to carry out their duty.

John Glover, an influential and wealthy merchant from Marblehead, Massachusetts, guided some of the most critical operations of the Revolution, including forging the origins of an American Navy. The Marblehead Regiment's actions saved the Continental Army multiple times, altering the course of the Revolutionary War. (*Source: Wikimedia*)

John Glover's home in Marblehead, Massachusetts. Before the Revolution, Marblehead was one of the largest and most prosperous cities in New England, home to some of the wealthiest Americans in the colonies whose fortunes were derived from trade and cod fishing in the icy waters of the Grand Banks. Their trading relationships would prove to be indispensable to the Revolution. (*Source: Author photo*)

A genuinely unsung Founding Father and an intellectual mainspring of the Revolution, Elbridge Gerry of Marblehead became a signer of the Declaration of Independence, delegate to the Constitutional Convention, Massachusetts governor, and United States vice president. Although he was a man who despised the concept of political parties, he is forever remembered for the term "gerrymandering." (*Source: James Bogle after John Vanderlyn / Wikimedia*)

The atrocity known as the Boston Massacre played a key role in inciting the American Revolution. An African American, Crispus Attucks, was the first slain. (*Source: National Archives*)

Three New England doctors, all friends, played a crucial part in America's founding story. Dr. Benjamin Church's checkered character featured prominently. (*Source: US Army*)

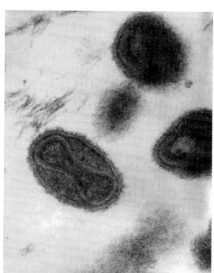

A year before the Revolution, the smallpox virus raged and divided the town of Marblehead along political fault lines, profoundly impacting the course of history. A Marblehead doctor also later saved the army from smallpox. (*Source: CDC*)

Samuel Adams, a driving force behind the Sons of Liberty, a secretive organization opposed to the Crown's policies, served as a mentor to Marblehead's Elbridge Gerry. (*Source: Wikimedia*)

THE DESTRUCTION OF TEA AT BOSTON HARBOR.

Several Marbleheaders played a key role in the Boston Tea Party, an event that propelled the American colonies into the Revolution. (*Source: Library of Congress*)

The TORY'S Day of JUDGMENT.

Mobs featured prominently in the pre-Revolutionary War period. "Peaceful protests" were manipulated by both Loyalists and Patriots to terrorize and intimidate. (*Source: Library of Congress*)

An African American Revolutionary War soldier. A more diverse collection of individuals than any other unit in the Continental Army, the Marblehead Regiment included free African Americans, Hispanics, and Native Americans within its ranks, making it one of America's first multiethnic units. This inclusiveness and unity, which tragically would not be seen again in America's armed forces for nearly two centuries, created a dynamic military unit that produced remarkable results. (*Source: National Guard*)

The author spent years reconstructing the Marblehead Regiment using original muster rolls and pension applications. These documents are the tremendous largely untapped oral histories of the Revolutionary War, giving voice to that generation of soldiers. (*Source: NARA*)

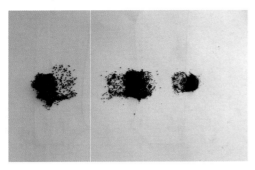

Gunpowder was the *unum necessarium* (one necessity). The organic production of powder (a combination of saltpeter, charcoal, and sulfur) was virtually non-existent in the colonies at the beginning of the Revolution. The Marbleheaders converted their trade contacts into crucial military supply lines. The quest for powder also led to Marblehead forging the origins of the Navy.
(*Source: Richard Azzaro*)

Marblehead merchants Lee and Gerry's most important contacts were with the mega-trading house owned by the Gardoqui family. Marbleheaders maintained friendships with the patriarch José Gardoqui and his three sons, including Diego, Spain's ambassador to what became the United States. American's first foreign aid came from Spain through the Marbleheaders.
(*Source: Wikimedia*)

British general Thomas Gage recognized how critical gunpowder was to the rebels, and he aimed to disarm the Americans by seizing it. Without powder and weapons, any revolution that turned into an armed conflict could be crushed by the empire's superior army. Gage's raid on the Somerville magazine was a tipping point tilting a political revolution toward armed rebellion.
(*Source: Wikimedia*)

Arguably the forgotten first shots and first blood of the Revolutionary War unfolded at Fort William and Mary as Americans seized crucial gunpowder from the fort in December 1774. (*Source: Author photo*)

The Marbleheaders supplied the bulk of the gunpowder and several cannons Gage was trying to seize at Concord. The raid to disarm Americans resulted in "the shot heard round the world" and the subsequent unfolding engagements. (*Source: National Army Museum*)

After failing to seize the majority of American munitions, the British had to run a gauntlet of thousands of armed Americans as the Redcoats desperately tried to retreat on "Battle Road" back to Boston. (*Source: Author photo*)

The Jason Russell House in Menotomy (now Arlington) was a focal point in the Battle of Lexington. The battle's bloodiest combat occurred there involving men from Marblehead and nearby Beverly, who would later join the Marblehead Regiment. (*Source: Author photo*)

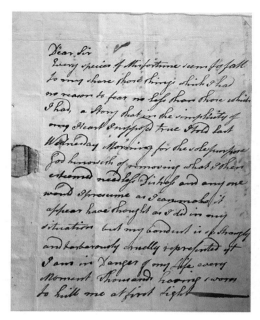

This extraordinary letter was written by a desperate Dr. Nathaniel Bond to Elbridge Gerry when he was wrongly accused of being a Loyalist. He sought protection from the angry mob who threatened to kill him because he tended to wounded British soldiers during the Battle of Lexington. Bond was later exonerated by his friend and fellow Resurrectionist, Dr. Joseph Warren. He would become a fighting surgeon and company commander in the Marblehead Regiment and later save the Continental Army by facilitating its vaccination against smallpox. Vaccination of the Continental Army was considered one of George Washington's greatest strategic decisions. (*Source: The author owns Bond's original letter*)

A Marblehead artillery company led by Samuel Trevett courageously battled on Bunker Hill, inflicting devastating losses on the British. The painting depicts the death of Dr. Joseph Warren, president pro tempore of the Massachusetts Provincial Congress, in that battle. Marblehead leaders such as Elbridge Gerry, Azor Orne, and Jeremiah Lee held some of the most important positions in the Massachusetts Provincial Congress and would play a vital role in shaping what would become the future United States. (*Source: Wikimedia*)

General George Washington had a special relationship with the Marbleheaders. As one of his most trusted units, they saved the army multiple times: first, at the "American Dunkirk" during the Battle of Brooklyn; next, their desperate rearguard action at the Battle of Pell's Point; and finally, at Trenton when, against all odds, they rowed the army across the Delaware. (*Source: Brooklyn Museum*)

Headquarters, Cambridge 1775.

Marbleheaders were some of the first troops to guard General Washington at his Cambridge headquarters, the Vassall House. (*Source: Homes of American Statesman*)

Son of Liberty, Dr. Benjamin Church, whose mistress resided in Marblehead, became one of America's first traitors, relaying priceless intelligence to the British. He used a cipher to send coded messages to British General Thomas Gage. (*Source: Library of Congress via DIA.mil*)

Marblehead major Caleb Gibbs formed and led the Commander in Chief's Guard, more commonly referred to as the Life Guard, an elite unit of hand-picked men tasked with protecting Washington. (*Source: Benson John Lossing,* The Pictorial Field-Book of the Revolution. *2 vols. New York: Harper, 1851–52*)

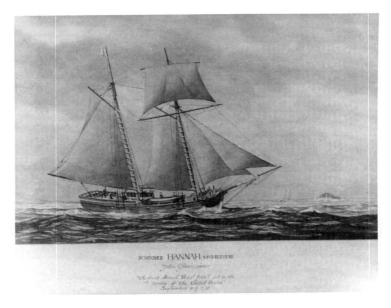

Men from the Marblehead Regiment crewed and led "Washington's Navy," forming the origins of America's Navy. Their first ship was John Glover's schooner, *Hannah*. Washington's Navy was a key step toward America's sovereignty and independence. (*Source: US Navy*)

Washington's Navy's birthplace was Glover's Wharf located in Beverly. *Hannah* and other cruisers launched from the wharf and seized British transport ships laden with gunpowder and ordinates that proved essential for the war effort. (*Source: Author Photo*)

In an unprecedented step toward American sovereignty and independence, Washington's cruisers flew a flag, the Appeal to Heaven. (*Source: US Navy via NARA*)

Marblehead captain James Mugford captured one of the most valuable prizes of the war, *Hope*, filled with enough gunpowder to supply the needs of the army for a month. Mugford was mortally wounded shortly after "with outstretched arms . . . righteously dealing death and destruction" to his enemy. (*Source: US Navy*)

Marbleheaders conducted several special operations-like missions during the Revolution, including a daring maneuver launching burning fireships into British warships. (*Source: Library of Congress*)

In an American Thermopylae-like stand at Brooklyn, the Marylanders, also known as "Washington's Immortals," formed the suicidal rearguard that allowed the army to retreat. Their actions were one of the most important small-unit engagements in America's Revolutionary War that bought "an hour, more precious to American liberty than any other in its history." (*Source: Wikimedia*)

The Marblehead Regiment operated the boats that evacuated the Continental Army from Brooklyn to Manhattan, executing an "American Dunkirk" as a "providential" fog screened their movements across the East River. (*Source: Library of Congress*)

Glover's Rock is an iconic land-mark at the Battle of Pell's Point. (*Source: Author Photo*)

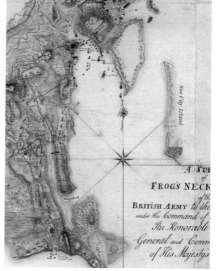

Period map of the British landings at Throgs Neck and Pell's Point. (*Source: Library of Congress*)

Through their initiative, without orders, the Marbleheaders captured a crucial bridge at Trenton that sealed a decisive American victory that changed the course of the war. (*Source: Wikimedia*)

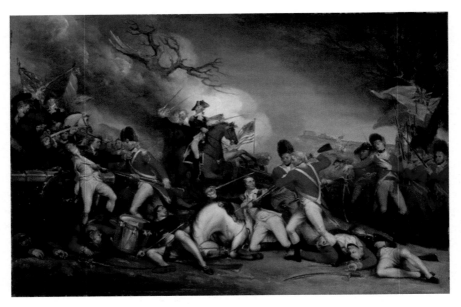

Marbleheaders also fought at the Battle of Princeton. (*Source: Wikimedia*)

The cemeteries in Marblehead and Beverly are the final resting places for many of the members of the Regiment. Marblehead and Beverly paid an enormous price in blood and treasure for American independence. By the end of the war, Marblehead had 378 widows, 35 percent of the town's female population, and 652 children never saw their fathers again. (*Source: Author Photo*)

CHAPTER 23

SNOWBALL FIGHT AND
A DIVERSE REGIMENT

Two groups of men eyed each other uneasily from either side of Harvard Yard in Cambridge. On one side stood a regiment of Daniel Morgan's Virginia riflemen, backwoods frontiersmen with a reputation for brawling and lack of discipline. Their rustic dress included "white linen frocks ruffled and fringed."[1] The knee-length hunting shirts seemed "half-Indian" and highly unusual to some observers, who sometimes referred to the Virginians as "shirt men."[2] Facing them were the Marbleheaders, proudly sporting "round jackets and fisher's trousers."[3] Adding to the tension, a few of the Virginians owned slaves, while the Marblehead Regiment contained several free African Americans.[4] Some of the outsiders, however, may have taken issue with the easy mixing of the races. One officer echoed the racism of the time and wrote that in the Marblehead Regiment, "there were a number of negroes, which, to persons unaccustomed to such associations had a disagreeable, degrading effect."[5]

After the Marblehead Regiment had departed Washington's headquarters at the Vassall House, their duties included manning the siege line around Boston. They bivouacked around a local tavern called the Ship, where the thirsty sailors drank their fill and released steam in their off-duty hours. One observer called them "extravagantly excentric and sportful," adding, "The men were . . . all the time in motion, inventing and contriving amusements and tricks."[6]

One of those diversions was to mock the newly arrived Virginians' attire. Israel Trask, a young Massachusetts boy who had gone to war with his father and was present that day, later wrote that "the riflemen bore [the jokes] with more patience than their wont" at first.[7] But the Marbleheaders soon grew tired of merely hurling insults and started pelting the Virginians with snowballs, as well. The riflemen naturally reciprocated.

Hurling snowballs rapidly devolved into exchanging punches. Soon "both sides were reinforced, and in a little while at least a thousand were at fisticuffs, and there was a tumult in camp worthy of the days of Homer."[8] In their anger, the rioting mass resorted to "biting and gouging" as the situation escalated.

To everyone's shock, General Washington appeared on the scene at the height of the tumult, accompanied by his African American servant, William Lee. For two decades, Lee stood by Washington. The body servant did everything from laying out Washington's clothes to organizing his papers to fighting by his side in battle, and he became something of a minor celebrity in colonial America. Without hesitation, the two men rode their horses into the mob as far as they could. Then, "with the spring of a deer, [Washington] leaped from his saddle, threw the reins of his bridle into the hands of his servant, and rushed into the thickest of the melees, with an iron grip seized two tall, brawny, athletic, savage-looking riflemen by the throat, keeping them at arm's length, alternately shaking and talking to them."[9]

Within seconds, the throng stopped fighting. A hush descended upon the scene as the men turned to watch the general reprimand the two Virginians he had singled out. "In this position the eye of the belligerents caught sight of the general," Trask wrote. "Its effect on them was instantaneous flight at the top of their speed in all directions from the scene of the conflict. Less than fifteen minutes time had elapsed from the commencement of the row before the general and his two criminals were the only occupants of the field of action." So great was their respect for their general that the "hostile feelings between two of its best regiments . . . [were] extinguished by one man."[10] In the words of another observer, "Here, bloodshed, imprisonments, trials by court-martial, revengeful feelings between the different corps of the army, were happily prevented by the physical and mental energies of a single person, and the only damage resulting from the fierce encounter was a few torn hunting frocks and round jackets."[11]

The presence of black soldiers within the Marblehead Regiment, which the Southern riflemen were not accustomed to, likely contributed to sparking the melee. The paradox of liberty and freedom coupled with enslavement was an issue the Founders would continue to grapple with throughout the war and for decades to come. Glover's Regiment served as a microcosm of the integration that occurred in some Revolutionary War units, where African Americans fought for freedom alongside their fellow American brothers in arms.

Congress had qualms about black men serving in the Continental Army with the view that it could divide an already divided nation and play into the hands of the British. Mostly white, the army had within its ranks free blacks and enslaved Americans serving in place of their masters. Native Americans also served, ultimately including members of the Stockbridge Indians from western Massachusetts and other tribes.[12] Pressures for more able-bodied men mounted, and fear escalated that free blacks might flock to the British Army, as many would: some twenty thousand African Americans served in the British military, mostly in support roles such as teamsters, tradesman, and laborers. However, Washington effectively blocked Congress's order that African Americans could not serve in December 1775: "As the General is informed that the numbers of free negroes are desirous of enlisting, he gives leave to the recruiting officers to entertain them, and promises to lay the matter before the Congress, who, he doubts not will approve it."[13] Massachusetts militias, however, clearly had free men serving much earlier. Congress cited them in their decision in January 1776 "that the free negroes who have served faithfully in the army at Cambridge may be reenlisted therein, but no Others."[14] Unwilling to tackle the thorny issue of slavery directly for fear it might affect the unity of the colonies, Congress gradually ceased opposition to African American enrollment.

Many of those men were serving in the Marblehead Regiment. The fragmented muster rolls record some, but not all, of their names.

Tragically, many of the African Americans would die before pension applications were instituted in the nineteenth century, and their names and heroic service would be lost to history.

Black men, such as Crispus Attucks, from Massachusetts also played a role in activities leading up to the Revolution and its earliest battles. For instance, before the Boston Massacre, "according to common Custom, when a Riot was to be brought on, the Factioneers would employ Boys & Negroes to assemble & make Bonfires in the Streets. . . . Those Boys and negroes assembled before the Customs House, and abused ye Centinel; he called for Aid. . . . Rioters pelted the Soldiers with Brickbats, Ice, Oystershells & broken Glass Bottles . . . calling out 'Damn You fire, fire if you dare!'"[15] An anonymous Loyalist pamphleteer sarcastically described the diverse nature of protesting mobs: "People of all sizes and all hues! red-skins, yellow-skins, green-skins, grey-skins, bay-skins, black-skins, blue-skins! Glorious prospect! Enchanting variety!"[16] The critic then described the defending British troops: "The sons of loyalty and order were approaching. Hateful sight! no variety in their appearance; all of one colour—white as the unsullied snow! Their conduct uniform throughout—firm, steady, peaceable and decent."[17]

Caesar Glover, a freeman with ties to the Glover family, joined his Marblehead Regiment as a private at its inception at age thirty-three and ultimately would fight through three years of war. A rare African American obituary reveals that he was brought from Africa as a child before he obtained his freedom.[18]

The Marblehead regimental muster rolls list several black soldiers,[19] including Manuel Soto. In Captain Francis Symonds's company was Frentharo Manwell, who had a string of aliases and was also known as Entharo or Intharo and Manwil or Manuel. He enlisted in August 1775.[20]

Other diverse nationalities populated the unit, including Spaniards Francis Grater and Joseph Story, and Guernsey native of the Channel Islands, twenty-one-year-old Peter Dural.[21] Grater, a sixteen-year-old immigrant from Barcelona, a fisherman before the war, volunteered and, in his own words, "enlisted and was never drafted."[22]

One black soldier on the muster rolls, Romeo, was a private[23] in Glover's Marblehead Regiment and served in Captain John Glover Jr.'s company; he worked for Gabriel Johonnot prior to the Revolution. Romeo initially enlisted on May 1, 1775, and records indicate that he received a bounty coat (a bonus) for reenlistment.[24]

As America's sea power expanded, many African Americans, such as twin brothers William and Thomas Habins, also served as privateers or on navy vessels throughout the war. Nineteen years old and from Salem, William was five feet four, while Thomas was four feet eleven; they served aboard the brigantine *Addition*.[25]

African Americans served in a variety of roles on American fighting vessels. Many men hailed from Essex: tall, twenty-three-year-old sailor Fortin Pruther on board the ship *Pilgrim*,[26] and Cuff Wood and nineteen-year-old Cuff Blew[27] from Marblehead, listed as "negro," aboard the ships *Boston* and *Franklin*. Roles ranged from those of marines like Cuff Wood to those of cooks like Prince Woodbury[28] and Caesar Thistle. Thistle met his demise when he fell overboard.[29] Also lost at sea was Marbleheader Samuel Parsons, a black man who served on the frigate *Boston*, commanded by James Tucker.[30]

As the war progressed, more African Americans joined the cause, including Marblehead freemen who enlisted in the Continental Army, such as Cato Prince, and nineteen-year-old Boston Black,[31] who later served as an attendant to John Glover.[32] Many African Americans had only a single name or had been bestowed with the names of ancient Greek or Roman figures. The soldiers of the Revolution often ended their years in destitution. Prince's pension application years later stated that he had "no personal [items] nor real estate; he is sixty-two years of age; has no family; is infirmed and unable to do any kind of work and before his pension lived on charity."[33]

Several Native Americans served in the regiment as well. During the Revolution, most Indian nations aligned with the British. However, some tribes fought with the Americans, among them the

Oneidas. In Massachusetts, the Stockbridge Indians, also known as the Stockbridge Mohicans, who settled in a bucolic meadow in the Berkshire Mountains in Stockbridge and converted to Christianity, also battled on the side of the Americans. Some Marbleheaders had Native American ancestry, such as Philip Mohegh."[34] "Light"-complexioned Marbleheader Sarragoshah, a nineteen-year-old seaman on board the *Franklin*, may have also been Native American.[35]

The snowball fight in Harvard Yard typified one of Washington's most significant challenges, which was to weld together disparate Americans from different parts of the colonies who had their own traditions and ideas about freedom. Marblehead fishermen, the backwoodsmen of Virginia, and the silk-stockinged gentlemen from Maryland all had to be melded into a unified army to fight one of the best-trained fighting forces in the world at the time, the British Army. The incident demonstrated Washington's leadership, the respect the men afforded him, and also the diverse nature of the Marblehead Regiment, nearly two centuries ahead of its time.

CHAPTER 24

BEVERLY

Beverly had the look and feel of a pirate base. Warehouses filled with captured goods surrounded the wharves, where a dozen prize ships sat rotting while menacing black-painted cruisers covertly sailed in and out of port. Under John Manley's command, Washington's fleet mushroomed to five schooners based out of the harbor. With so much American naval power concentrated in one area, Beverly became a prime target for a crippling British raid aimed at destroying the fleet, recapturing the prizes, and burning the warehouses and wharves. Sensing an impending attack, the Beverly Committee of Correspondence begged Washington on December 11, 1775, to strengthen the harbor's defenses: "Beverly is much Exposed to their most unnatural Savage Like Creuelty. the Town Lying more then four miles on the Sea coast and a grate part of that way Conveiniant for Landing, the Inhabitents of this Town withe the assistance of Some of the Neighbouring Towns have thrown up Brestworks in Several of the most advantagious places within the Same and have no Cannon or Ammunition Or next a kin to none to Support them with, and what renders us more obnoxtious to their most unnatural Creuelty and Vengence is that the Contenental Privaters and others make this Harbour their Place of randevoze and have of Late Brought into this Harbour a Number of very Valluable Prizes, which we think are very much Exposed to the Enemy as also the Town in General."[1] Washington's prize agent in Beverly, Captain William Bartlett, concurred with the committee and added, "Those Valuable Prizes brought in here are much Exposed as we have nothing to Defend them with."[2]

Washington assigned John Glover the task of hardening and manning the town's defenses. Glover's Regiment left their damp trenches outside Cambridge and marched to Marblehead in mid-December. Then, on the road north to Beverly, the men saw firsthand how the Revolution had economically decimated the town. One outsider, a soldier and traveler, recalled,

> We pass'd over a stony road to Marblehead which is a dirty disagreeable Place at present they are here in great Distress as the Town is built among Rocks & Stones, where is no land to cultivate.
>
> Marblehead and the people in general are Fisherman or concern'd in that Way, which Source of Support is now at an end many of the men are in the army & the Rest are out of Employ and almost every house swarms with Children of these hardy, temporate Men.
>
> Their situation is miserable the Streets & Roads are fill'd the poor little Boys and Girls who are forc'd beg of all they see the Women are lazy & of Consequence dirty Creatures—there are about 400 houses here & 4 or 5 of them large neat house—they have a small Battery in a Point near to try to keep of the men of War.
>
> One remarkable object of Charity here was a little Boy whose left arm was shriveled up & dead and his Legs were contracted and folded up like a Taylor's, and of no strength this emaciated creature would move in an odd manner with the assistance of his Right hand into the middle of the Road before your horse and would beg in a most moving manner and you must give him something or drive over him—I do not want ever to see such another Place.[3]

Captain Moses Brown's company from Beverly joined the regiment. A Harvard graduate and attorney before the war, Brown fought at Menotomy near the Russell House in a firefight that killed Beverly's

Reuben Kennison and wounded Nathaniel Cleves, who "had his finger and ramrod cut away with a shot from the enemy."[4] Twenty-eight years old, Brown ran a successful mercantile business with his brother-in-law Israel Thorndike. Eventually, Brown's company formed the 7th Company within the Marblehead Regiment.[5]

Brown's company had a number of African American soldiers within its ranks. Based on a list of privates outlined in his orderly book, which includes their age, height, hometown, and complexion, as well as who supplied their firearm, the company was composed of one-third dark-complexioned privates, among them Aesop Hale and Caesar Raymond, free black men of Beverly,[6] likely joined by Scipio Dodge, Nathaniel Small, and Hannibal.[7] The average age was twenty-four, and 20 percent of the men in company were only sixteen years old. Most furnished their own firearms. All were from Beverly except one man from Marblehead. Also within their ranks was a diminutive five-foot, one-inch Irishman.[8]

Together the black and white brothers in arms built a barracks to house the regiment that would man the fortifications and gun positions in Beverly to protect the harbor. Glover posted a detail of men at the outer fort at Woodbury's Point and at Bartlett's Wharf to guard the prize ships. At Tuck's Point, near the mouth of the harbor, Glover constructed a fort and posted a guard of one officer, one corporal, and ten privates with orders to hail and challenge all ships entering and leaving the harbor. He further commanded, "If it appears that the Boats or Vessels so hailed were coming from or going to the Man of War now at Anchor before this harbor, he is to order her to bring too & come on Shore; and should any Boat or Vessel so hailed refuse to answer or come on shore after hailing three times, the Centry is to fire a Gun over her, if she persists he will fire a second Gun before her fore foot; if she does not then bring too, he will then endeavor to fire into her & alarm the main Guard, the Officer of which will immediately send an Express to the Commanding Officer of the Regt. The same orders are to be given to the Sergeant commanding the Outer post."[9]

Marblehead private John Rhodes Russell and his fellow enlisted men learned the "art Military," the tactics of the day, as Glover used this downtime to train and forge his men into a fighting unit. The regiment drilled and paraded to hone their skills for battle, as Captain Brown described in his orderly book: "Ordered that the Regt be paraded hours of Nine o'clock in the Morning and at 4 o'clock in the afternoon, at which time the roles will be called and if any soldiers are absent without giving Reasons to the satisfaction of his Commanding Officer; he or they so offending shall be delt with agreeable to the Rules & Regulations of the Continental Army, and punished accordingly."[10]

Glover employed a carrot-and-stick approach to discipline. He incentivized proper drill and garrison duty and disciplined those who were careless. "And in Order to encourage the Men to learn the Art Military and to be good Soldiers, there will be given out to the Captains or Commanding Officers twenty-five New Guns, with bayonets, pouches, & twelve rounds to Each which are to be lent to those men of this Company who will take the best Care & are likely to make good use of them—and should any Guns, bayonets, pouches or Ammunition so given out be damaged wasted or lost, thro Carelessness or neglect, the persons Chargd & Convicted thereof shall make good all such damages & suffer such other Punishment, agreeable to the nature of his Offence. Good Soldiers will be noticed by his Officers & may Expect to Receive every Reasonable indulgence they can wish."[11]

With the new year, some of the men's enlistments expired, and the regiment went from being designated as the 21st Continental Regiment to the 14th Continental Regiment. The regimental commander threatened to punish soldiers who stepped out of line: "On the Contrary all idle refractory, mutinous fellows will be punished with severity but it is hoped that none of this Character will be found in the 14th Regt."[12]

One humorous disciplinary incident involved Captain William Bartlett's dog and a bayonet-wielding Marbleheader. The prize agent's canine bit Private Andrew Smith. Hours later, Smith returned to the scene of the crime and lunged at the dog with his bayonet and said some "ill"[13] words to Bartlett. Hauled in front of a court-martial, the overzealous private stood awaiting judgment from a court composed of Glover's son, Captain John Glover Jr.; Captain William Raymond Lee;

and Lieutenant Joshua Orne, son of Colonel Azor Orne and initially an ensign, the man who traditionally carried the regiment's flag. The officers rendered an opinion: "Prisoner had received some Injury from the Dog a few hours before he attempted to stab him, in some measure alleviates the Crime, but for the ill Treatment of Capt. Bartlett, the Court thinks Proper he should ask Capt. Bartlett's Pardon at the head of the Regt., John Glover, President." The next day Andrew Smith addressed Bartlett and apologized in front of the entire regiment.

Notable figures in the regiment were assigned to these duties in turn as officers of the day as well as officers of the main guard. On March 7, 1776, Ensign Robert Wormstead, who had recovered from his wounds at Bunker Hill, assumed that position.

Regimental surgeon Doctor Nathaniel Bond attended to the medical needs of the troops and at times received medical supplies and instruments, as these April 1776 orders attest: "Before You leave Cambridge it will be Necessary to see a proper Regimental Medicine Chest provided, and Deliver'd, to each of the Surgeons of the Four Regiments. . . . Also a Chest for Colonel Glover's Regiment, on Command at Beverly."[14] The badly needed chest contained a wicked-looking assortment of probes and ball extractors.

Bond had years of surgery experience, including taking care of the wounded after the Battle of Bunker Hill. Musket balls were quite large, .50–.69 caliber, causing devastating wounds. If an injury from a musket ball was not too deep, the surgeon attempted to remove the ball and then stop the bleeding, leaving the wound open to drain. If the ball had fractured bones in multiple places, the only real option for treatment was amputation.

Doctors used sharp lancets and saws to hack off limbs, while tourniquets, when they were available, choked off the bleeding artery. Surgery of the day involved plying the patient with a strong dose of liquor and then offering him a stick to bite. Orderlies held the patient down while the surgeon sawed through the bone as quickly as possible, tied off the arteries, and sewed the wound shut over the remaining stump. Unsurprisingly, only a little over a third of the men who had an amputation survived.[15]

The chest also contained a witch's brew of herbal remedies, state-of-the-art medicine for the period, such as Peruvian or Jesuit's bark, potassium nitrate, camphor, laudanum (opium), jalap, castor oil, Epsom salts, ipecac, red mercuric oxide, and sulfur in hog's lard. Despite the best efforts of the surgeons, the greatest invisible killers were the microscopic organisms, bacteria, and viruses that led to gangrene and other fatal diseases.

During the fall of 1775, Marblehead and Beverly lived under the specter of attack and destruction, but the Royal Navy never challenged Glover's defenses; Falmouth (now Portland, Maine), on the other hand, received the full wrath of the British. A squadron of warships anchored off the Falmouth shore and issued a letter claiming the inhabitants of the town were "guilty of the most unpardonable Rebellion." The British gave the townspeople two hours to "remove without delay the human species out of the town," at which time they would "execute a just punishment."[16] At 9:00 a.m. on October 18, 1775, the bombardment commenced, burning most of the wooden houses to the ground. Reverend Thomas Smith recalled, "A horrible shower of balls from three to nine pounds weight, bombs, carcasses [shells filled with incendiaries designed to burn wooden structures], live shells, grape shot and musket balls. The firing lasted without cession [all day] during which time several parties came ashore and set buildings on fire by hand."[17] Many British officers favored a strategy of extreme violence and terror to break a population, raiding and burning port towns until the Americans capitulated. The British had employed harsh tactics against civilians in Scotland and Ireland to suppress rebellions. Admiral Samuel Graves favored such policies, but William Howe forbade the use of these brutal tactics against civilians, as they were anathema to his principles and sensibilities. Nevertheless, the British unevenly applied the approach in a limited manner. Contrary to their intent to suppress the rebellion, the burning of Falmouth and later Norfolk, Virginia, steeled American resolve and emboldened the Americans on their path to independence.

*   *   *

The New Year brought significant change to Washington's Navy. Of the original six captains, only John Manley continued to command. Sion Martindale and his crew were imprisoned and en route to England, Nicholson Broughton and John Selman were dismissed, William Coit left, and Winborn Adams returned to his regiment, since all of his crew's enlistments had expired with the new year. Washington appointed Manley to a new position—captain and commander. Eventually, Washington promoted the Marbleheader to commodore.

In one engagement at sea, Manley battled the eight-gun *General Gage* with only sixteen men. One contemporary source described the melee: "Taken the prizes, & had put his people on board them some time before the Tender came to Their assistance, that there were two other Vessels from Nova Scotia with stock, in company with these ships, & that the whole fleet with the Tender, wod have been taken, had it not been for the cowardice of one of our Continental armed Vessels, who was very near them, but dared not engage, & who made the best of his way off—Commodore Manley fought in very disadvantageous circumstances not having more than sixteen of his own people on board; but then, he receivd considerable assistance from his prisoners, more particularly from the Captains, who did as much as they dared do in such circumstances."[18] Washington wrote Manley on January 28, "Your Conduct in engageing the eight Gun Schooner, with So few hands as you went out with, your attention in Secureing Your prizes, & your general good behavior since you first engaged in the Service, merits mine & your Countrys thanks."[19] Manley's reputation for success attracted the attention of the British.

A cannonball crashed through the hull of *Hancock*, missing John Manley's head by a mere six inches as he lay ill in his captain's quarters. The ball came from a new threat: *Hope*.

To hunt Manley and his swift cruiser, the British had fitted out their schooner the *Sea Nymph* with eight 4-pounder guns and several swivels. The crew of fifty men received a complement of nine marines, and the British rechristened the ship *Hope*. The Royal Navy hoped to lure the Americans into a trap using the nimble craft. Severe winter froze many New England harbors. On January 30, 1775, Manley freed *Hancock* from the ice-choked Plymouth Harbor and sailed north, where she encountered the British ship. Manley initially tried to outrun the *Hope* as both ships headed toward Boston. Hoping to evade the British and, if necessary, reach American lines, Manley turned the ship into the North River. *Hancock* soon ran aground near Scituate. The Marbleheaders worked feverishly to get the boat moving.

Hope peppered the stranded craft with an astonishing four hundred cannonballs,[20] remarkably failing to injure any of Manley's crew. Water flooded the ship, and *Hancock* sank deeper into the muck. In a repeat of the engagement that pitted the *Nautilus* against the *Hannah*, Manley ordered the vessel scuttled, abandoned ship, and rowed ashore, where he contacted the local militia. They sent out artillery and musket fire to engage the *Hope*, which now had its own problems avoiding sandbars in the river.

At dawn the next morning, Lieutenant George Dawson, the captain of the *Hope*, attempted to finish off his quarry. He sent two small boats to row out to the *Hancock* and burn it to its waterline. Once they had braved musket and artillery fire from Manley's men and the militia onshore, Dawson's crew found the waterlogged vessel impossible to torch. After removing a swivel gun and a flag, they abandoned the *Hancock*, confident she would never sail again. Miraculously, despite damage to its hull, the following day, on February 1, Manley's crew refitted the *Hancock*, making her nearly seaworthy.[21]

To deal with the *Hope* and other prowling British vessels, Manley changed tactics in February 1776. Instead of sending a single cruiser to patrol a lane to pick off British ships, Manley's warships operated in a group of four or five vessels. At the time, Manley had a fleet of five cruisers operating out of Beverly: *Lee*, *Warren*, *Hancock*, *Franklin*, and a new boat, the *Lynch*.

Manley had an opportunity to try out his new tactics on his nemesis, the *Hope*. Battle scarred but refitted and refloated, the *Hancock* was back in action with three other vessels in the fleet.

Destitute and barely able to feed his family, Loyalist Ashley Bowen recorded not only life in Marblehead but the action at sea. Bowen often found himself caught between the Loyalist and Patriot camps of the town. "Between two stools, the tail comes to the ground," as Bowen described his situation. Merchants refused to sell him their goods, and work became a constant challenge. Bowen nonetheless recorded the battle between the two British warships, *Hope* and *Tryal*, and Manley's fleet. "This evening I saw a brig and a schooner engage four of Continental schooners."[22] The American ships "shot in the hull" the *Hope*, and Manley's blasting cannons also shredded the ship's rigging and wounded several crew members "before night came on and they parted."[23]

The winter brought despair to the Marblehead sailors in Washington's Navy. Fueling the melancholy, most of the men had not received any pay for months. Prizes continued to rot on wharves, and cases remained backlogged in the courts. Washington tasked Glover with finding crews for the navy, which became increasingly difficult, as Glover explained to Washington on January 3, 1776: "I am now indeavouring to man the Armd Vesels, which at present is Very Difficult, on Acct of the mens not being paid off for their past Services, which is the only Objection they have."[24]

CHAPTER 25

WASHINGTON'S LIFE GUARD AND LIFTING THE SIEGE OF BOSTON

Washington's headquarters, Cambridge, March 12, 1776

The soldiers stood at attention as the commander in chief inspected each man. Snow gathered on their coats, and cold wind bit their faces. The men assembled, ramrod-straight, in parade formation next to Washington's headquarters at the Vassall House in Cambridge. Washington walked slowly among the rows of men, scrutinizing each soldier. The grouping represented a microcosm of the colonies—mariners, tradesmen, farmers, backwoodsmen; Washington somehow had to weld their regiments into an army. But on this cold day in March, the general searched for a specific type and look of men he required for a small, handpicked, elite unit. The commander in chief had excellent instincts for selecting the right men for positions, and ideally, he wanted men from each of the colonies. A day before, on March 11, 1776, Washington's general order outlining his expectations reached the officers:

> The General is desirous of selecting a particular number of men as a guard for himself and baggage. The Colonel or Commanding Officer of each of the established regiments, the artillery and riflemen excepted, will furnish him with four, that the number of wanted may be chosen out of them. His Excellency depends upon the Colonels for good men, such as they can recommend for their sobriety, honesty and good behavior. He

wishes them to be from five feet eight inches to five feet ten inches, handsomely and well made, and as there is nothing in his eyes more desirable than cleanliness in a soldier, he desires that particular attention be made in the choice of such men as are clean and spruce. They are to be at headquarters tomorrow precisely at 12 o'clock at noon, when the number wanted will be fixed upon. The General neither wants them with uniforms nor arms, nor does he desire any man to be sent to him that is not perfectly willing or desirous of being in this Guard. They should be drilled men.[1]

"Drilled men" meant Washington wanted troops familiar with the field drills of the day, combat veterans preferred—men who had endured the stress and hardship of battle. A Marbleheader was chosen to forge the men into an elite unit. Captain Caleb Gibbs, Glover's adjutant, had made an indelible impression on Washington after the two men met during the period when Glover's troops bivouacked at the Vassall House. The next day, Washington appointed Gibbs to command the unit. Lieutenant George Lewis, Washington's nephew, became Gibbs's second-in-command.

Washington granted Gibbs authority, stating in general orders, "Any orders delivered by Caleb Gibbs and George Lewis, Esquires—officers of the General's Guard, are to be attended to in the same manner as if sent by an aide-de-camp."[2] In other words, the commanders of the guard could issue orders on Washington's behalf. Washington also pressed both Gibbs and Lewis into writing letters on his behalf, and Gibbs's name appears frequently in Washington's official correspondence in March 1776.

Gibbs was responsible for shaping and creating a unique unit in American history. Officially titled the Commander-in-Chief's Guard, the group sometimes is also dubbed His Excellency's Guard, Generals Guard, or often the Life Guards. Initially, it consisted of about fifty men. Later, in 1777, it included "Four serjeants, Four corporals, a fife and drum, and fifty rank and file."[3] Eventually, the unit ballooned to over two hundred men—a sight to behold: "The battalion of the General's guards encamped within the precincts of his house; nine wagons destined to carry his baggage, ranged the yard . . . a great number of grooms holding fine horses belonging to the general officers and their aides-de-camp."[4]

Despite the Guard's size and military prowess, Washington tended to ride with only a few of his aides-de-camp and Billy Lee, who accompanied Washington everywhere. Washington trusted Lee with his life and developed a deep rapport with him, later freeing him from enslavement. Muscular and athletic, an excellent horseman who could keep up with Washington, Lee was later described by Thomas Jefferson "as the best horseman of his age, and the most graceful figure that could be seen on horseback."[5] Lee was an integral member of Washington's military household. As Washington's valet, he assisted Washington in countless tasks, including organizing his personal papers, and acting as a messenger.

Among the enlisted members of the Life Guard standing on the frozen field of the Vassall House was Private Carswell Gardner. Only weeks earlier, he had been rotting in the bowels of a British prison ship. Gardner enlisted on New Year's Day 1776, and while on Dorchester Neck, the British had taken him prisoner, confining him for six weeks, "the later part on board *The Empress of Russia*, a transport ship belonging to the enemy." British prison ships were floating concentration camps; few Americans survived the starvation and disease that raged below their decks. Living within the filth generated from human excrement, sweat, and bilge water, Gardner plotted a daring breakout. "Watching his opportunity," he made his escape, accompanied by one of the *Empress*'s crew members on one of the ship's small boats, named *The Agents Cutter*. The two men rowed across the harbor to American lines. Gardner sold the cutter for "eighty dollars, which he received in one dollar each, all bearing the head of John Hancock," and made it back to his unit. He was then "drafted from his company for the purpose of forming a guard for General Washington in which he was appointed a sergeant of the command given to Captain Gibbs."[6]

Marblehead private James Knox joined Gardner as an enlisted member of the Guard. The twenty-one-year-old enlisted in Marblehead on April 1775 and found himself in the vortex of the Battle of Bunker Hill with Samuel Trevett's artillery company. Knox gained experience as a guard for General Charles Lee "stationed outside of Bunker Hill . . . and eventually obtained permission to go to headquarters and enlist in General Washington's Guard."[7]

The newly minted Life Guard members also included Thomas Hickey, an Irishman who only a few years earlier had deserted the British Army. "Dark complexioned" and well built, the former enemy soldier lived in Wethersfield, Connecticut, and "bore a good character." Washington selected Hickey from Knowlton's Rangers, who fought alongside Trevett on Bunker Hill. Over the coming months, Hickey "gained the confidence of the commander-in-chief." Washington considered the foreigner "a favorite."[8]

Musicians played a surprisingly important role, and the unit had its own musicians. Fifers and drummers signaled the unit's movements on the field, but the Guard's musicians more often announced formal presentations and parade ground activities. Drummer William Green, drawn from Loammi Baldwin's 26th Massachusetts Continental Regiment, joined the guard on its founding on March 12.[9] Like Hickey, Green had prior service in his majesty's army—a loyalty he never entirely relinquished.

Donning flashy blue-and-buff jackets and single-breasted red vests with twelve gilt buttons, the members of the Guard cut an impressive figure. They sported buckskin breeches, black shoes, and white bayonet holders and belts. They festooned black hats with white tape, and later wore bearskin or leather headgear.[10] Officers wore a similar uniform but dressed in black knee-high boots, exhibited epaulets on their uniforms and cockades in their hats, and fastened rapiers or short swords to their left sides.

The unit carried the distinctive commander in chief's flag. Allegedly designed by Washington himself, the square, silk flag contained thirteen six-point stars on a blue background. The stars matched the six-point stars adorning Washington's epaulet.

The Life Guard also carried its own banner. Across the top of the flag ran a scroll with the motto "Conquer or Die," underneath which stood a guard wearing a bearskin hat and holding the bridle of a horse next to Lady Liberty, who carried a smaller flag and a shield with an eagle perched next to her.

Seven months had passed since Washington's arrival in Boston, and during that time, the general amassed a trove of letters, orderly books, and maps. Washington also traveled with a war chest to cover everything from mundane personal finance to spies on the payroll. He charged Gibbs with managing his expenses and receipt book. One sentinel from the Life Guard always monitored the war chest. This personal baggage was of great concern to Washington, and he entrusted Gibbs and the Life Guard with securing these crucial effects. When the army moved, the baggage traveled with the Guard in a series of wagons.

The Life Guard trained for threats on the commander in chief's life and provided security for the general's headquarters. Two guards always stood at attention at the entrance of Washington's offices, and two guards posted in its rear. The guard also patrolled the perimeter of the camp, drilled, and had contingency plans in place for an attack by the enemy. Gibbs was the architect, manager, and officer in charge of this elite group.

While in Cambridge, Washington headquartered on the Vassall estate and, later, in commandeered mansions or, when in the field, his tents. When the Continental Army marched, erecting the headquarters tent and setting up camp equipage fell on the shoulders of the Guard. Three impressive two-layer, canvas marquees enabled the gentleman planter to camp in grand style. One marquee acted as a two-room sleeping quarters, a second as baggage storage, and the third as an office and dining room.

The Guard adapted to Washington's daily routine. Washington rose as early as 4:00 a.m. and worked until 7:00 a.m., when staff served him a small breakfast. He performed a myriad of tasks and worked on administrative issues until 3:00 p.m., when dinner was served. Washington's management style placed a great deal of emphasis on dining and personal engagement. His table could include twelve or more officers, their wives, congressional delegates, and, as the war progressed, foreign observers. Dinner could last several hours, depending on the circumstance.

One of the wives of the officers, Martha Daingerfield Bland, provided a rare view into one of the dinners:

> Now let me speak of our Noble and Agreable Commander (for he commands both Sexes) one by his Excellent Skill in Military Matters the other by his ability politeness and attention we visit them twice or three times a week by particular invitation—Ev'ry day frequently from inclination—he is generally busy in the forenoon—but from dinner till night he is free for all company his Worthy Lady seems to be in perfect felicity while she is by the side of her Old Man as she calls him, we often make partys on Horse Back the Genl his lady Miss Livingstone & his Aid de Camps who are Colo Fitz Gerald and agreable broad shouldered Irishman—Colo Johnson Brother of Mrs Malone who is exceedingly witty at everybody's expense but cant allow other people to be so at his own, tho they often take the liberty. Colo Hamilton a sensable Genteel polite young fellow a West Indian.[11]

Gibbs managed the housekeeper and cooks, who served succulent chicken, beef, goose, peas, bread, and other provisions procured from locals. While in Cambridge, Washington's table may have also included more exotic cuisine such as sea turtles when Marbleheaders seized a British flagged vessel. The Patriots devoured the delicacy: "The Lovers of Turtle in the Camp are like to be indulg'd with a feast of it, by the Marbleheadmen this Week taking a Schooner."[12]

Mrs. Bland vividly remembered Gibbs as the life of the party: "Capt Gibbs of the Genls Guard a good-natured Yankee [known for his singing] who makes a thousand Blunders in the Yankee stile and keeps the Dinner table in constant Laugh."[13] The meal, served on fine china with silver, was washed down with Madeira, tea, cider, and rum.

If time permitted, the event included an after-dinner meal consisting of leftovers and small dishes served around 7:30 p.m.[14]

Washington handpicked Gibbs and his aides-de-camp; all were intelligent men and strong writers and were skilled in social graces. Assisted by his aides, Washington took advantage of dinner to talk business and probe for information. A typical example of Washington's dinner invitation reads, "His Excellency requests the favor of your company at dinner tomorrow if you are not engaged. At any rate he wishes to see you sometime tomorrow without fail, and that you will bring with you an accurate state of the troops under your command, and also of Major Porter's command."[15]

In time, the Commander-in-Chief's Guard would undertake the crucial task of imbuing the Continental Army with standardized tactics and discipline missing in the ragtag American force. For now, the guard had the sacred duty of protecting Washington as the siege of Boston took a dramatic turn.

Six feet tall, rotund, with a booming voice, twenty-five-year-old Colonel Henry Knox had presence. Previously a street-gang thug and then a Boston bookseller, the portly and affable Knox became proficient in martial affairs from studying military tomes in his shop. In an army staffed by twentysomethings brimming with ideas, Knox came up with one of immense importance: bringing the guns captured by Ethan Allen and Benedict Arnold at Fort Ticonderoga and Crown Point back to Boston. Dragging sixty tons of artillery over three hundred miles of mountains and forest and across major rivers appeared impossible. But Knox made it happen, employing forty-two largely horse-drawn sleds for the herculean task of towing the guns. "Snow detain'd us some days & now a cruel thaw, hinders from Crossing the Hudson River which we are oblig'd to do four times from Lake George to this Town—the first severe night will make the Ice on the river sufficiently strong 'till that happens the Cannon & mortars must remain where they are most of them at the different crossing places & some few here—these inevitable

delays pain Me exceedingly as my mind is fully sensible of the importance of the greatest expedition in this Case—In eight or nine days after
the first severe frost they will be at Springfield from which place we can
get them easily transported Altho there should be no snow—but to that
the roads are So excessively bad Snow will be necessary,"[16] wrote Knox
on January 5, 1776. The ice-covered Hudson River claimed one of the
most massive cannons when it broke through the ice, but with the help
of locals, Knox recovered the artillery piece.

Two months after his initial departure from Ticonderoga, on January 25, Knox delivered the guns to Cambridge. With the artillery in
hand, Washington renewed his plans for an attack on Boston. But lack
of powder and the eight-thousand-or-more-strong British garrison made
the attack very iffy. During a council of war, forty-nine-year-old Major
General Artemas Ward presented another plan: "The attack must be
made with the view of bringing on an engagement, or of driving the
enemy out of Boston and either end will be answered much better by
possessing Dorchester Heights."[17] The heights were less than a mile
from Boston, and cannon fire could easily sail over the harbor and hit
the city—whoever controlled the heights controlled Boston.

The challenge: how to build a fort atop the heights in the middle
of winter before the British stormed the redoubt prior to its completion.
Washington would find his answer at one of his dinners. A guest that
day was thirty-old-year-old Rufus Putnam, who, as a teenager during
the French and Indian War, gained just enough knowledge of fieldworks to make him dangerous. During the meal, Washington asked the
Braintree native how to build a fortification on frozen ground quickly.
Confessing, "I never read a word on the subject . . . but was imployed
in Some under British Engineers," he told Washington he'd get back to
him since "no excuse would do." Pondering the question while walking back to his bed, "now mark thoft Singular circumstances I call
providence," Putnam visited General William Heath's quarters and
noticed a book on his table entitled *The Attack and Defense of Fortified
Places*, by John Muller, and asked to borrow it. "He refused me." "I again
repeated my request . . . he again refused and told me he never Lent

his books."[18] Eventually, Heath relented, and Putnam went back to his quarters and fell asleep with the book on his chest. The next morning Putnam found the answer on page 4 in a fortification term he had never heard of, "chandeliers."*[19] Putnam told Washington the solution lay in building a series of prefabricated wooden frames five feet high filled with tree branches bundled together that could be quickly transported atop Dorchester Heights and assembled into walls. The walls could later be topped off with earth, and embrasures could be formed in the fortification to protect the artillery from Ticonderoga.

To the horror of the British, shells started exploding on their positions on March 4, 1776. Knox's artillerists fired on the city as a diversion for the real attack from Dorchester Heights. Washington wanted the noise created by artillery to cover the construction of the fieldworks on Dorchester. Thanks to Manley, Knox's guns now had shot and shells from the capture of *Nancy*. Even the massive mortar renamed Congress went into action and hurled its enormous shells into Boston until it blew up, likely from being mishandled by the neophyte American artillerists. Powder had to be employed sparingly and, as usual, remained in critical supply. As Thomas Cushing wrote to Gerry, "I wish we had a larger quantity here [near Dorchester Heights]."[20] The Marbleheaders' supplies from their trade routes also bore fruit, as Cushing indicated: "[I] am glad to here you have more Powder arrived at the southward."[21] One ship alone, trading with José Gardoqui and Sons, carried "four hundred & thirty barrels Powder or in other words twenty one tons and half."[22]

On the night of March 4, the Americans converged on Dorchester Heights. A full moon illuminated their movements as they quickly seized the high ground with no resistance from the British. American innovation and ingenuity were on full display as three hundred teams of wagons loaded with entrenching tools and prefabricated "chandeliers," gabions, and fascines (bundles of sticks) formed the bulwark of three

---

* Muller described "Chandeliers, are wooden frames. made of two pieces fixed crossways" two pieces, at about four set asunder and upon their intersections are erected two vertical pieces of five feet high, each supported by three buttresses; the interval of these two pieces is filled up fascines, to cover the troops upon occasion."

fortifications on top of the mount. Hundreds of men bit into the frozen ground with pickaxes and shovels as they put the chandeliers into place and shoveled dirt and rock into the cylindrical gabions. Working like a colony of bees, the men remarkably completed the bulk of the work in about an hour. From Dorchester Heights, the Americans could shell the British positions inside Boston with impunity. As dawn broke over Boston, the horrified British saw the three forts that seemingly materialized out of thin air overnight: "It was discovered on the fifth in the morning that the enemy had thrown three very extensive structures with strong abattis round them on the commanding hills on Dorchester Neck, which must have been the employment of at least 12,000 men."[23]

William Howe immediately responded to the crisis and ordered 2,400 of his men into boats to launch an amphibious assault and storm the heights. This is exactly what Washington hoped for—a frontal assault directly into the teeth of his defenses where the defenders would outnumber the attackers. It would have been a bloodbath. Washington even positioned heavy barrels loaded with dirt and rock the Americans could roll down on the advancing Redcoats. However, as would occur many times during the Revolution, weather would alter history. An enormous storm set in, blowing the boats in the harbor, making it impossible to launch the assault. Howe postponed the attack, but the storm raged until March 6, creating two priceless days for Washington to move in more troops and further strengthen the defenses. Washington also had a nasty surprise waiting for Howe. If the British attacked Dorchester Heights, four thousand men under the command of Israel Putnam would attack the British lines in Boston simultaneously.

General Howe realized his situation was no longer tenable and decided to evacuate Boston. Terrified to fall into the hands of their fellow Americans, thousands of Loyalists crammed aboard Howe's ships, including scores of Loyal Marbleheaders. They sailed to Halifax, from which they would regroup and receive reinforcements, and Howe would invade New York. But from that day forward, St. Patrick's Day, March 17, would become known as "Evacuation Day."

CHAPTER 26

DARK DAYS AND *HOPE*

A dense, heavy fog set over the Atlantic. Wraith-like, the twelve-ship British convoy churned through the thick mist. Mysteriously, the transport *Hope* had separated from HMS *Greyhound*, which had kept a watchful eye on the most valuable vessel in the flotilla, on May 10, 1776. *Hope* had left Cork, Ireland, five weeks earlier carrying a priceless cargo of 1,500 barrels of powder. Bound for Boston, the convoy had not known that William Howe had evacuated the city on March 17. After the debacle with *Nancy*, Vice Admiral Moylneux Shuldham replaced Admiral Samuel Graves. One of Shuldham's first changes included mandating that British warships now escorted the transports loaded with troops and supplies. Unlike most journeys, this one involved drama from the start. Before leaving Cork, the commander of the flotilla received an anonymous letter that insinuated that the master of *Hope*, Captain Alexander Lumsdale, "was disaffectedly inclined." A petty officer and two enlisted crew members were placed on board with directions "to attend very particularly to the conduct of the Master and if he suspected him of any design to separate from the convoy or to put the ship in the way of being taken by the Rebel Privateers to confine him and take command of [the *Hope*]."[1] The suspicious circumstances of the letter, combined with *Hope*'s disappearance, deepened the mystery.

In Beverly, Captain James Mugford Jr., a twenty-six-year-old Marbleheader with a ship master's warrant, dealt with his own crisis. Men wouldn't sail because they had not been paid. The newly established prize courts held up prize money and wages. Ardently dedicated to the cause, on his own initiative, Mugford secured a month's wages for a core group of a dozen men. Encouraged by this payment of owed wages, more crew members joined from John Glover's Marblehead Regiment, along with two officers, Thomas Russell and Jeremiah Hibbert. As one of Washington's prize agents, William Bartlett observed that Beverly had the "great advantage arising from having this most Valiant Regiment here being Always Ready to man the vessels when called for, which is very often."[2] Bartlett cautioned, however, "There will be a Sufficiency when the Prizes are sold, that does not Satisfy the Hungry belly at the Present."[3] In less than twelve hours, Mugford had the *Franklin* ready and sailed with a skeleton crew of twenty-one men from Glover's Wharf on May 15. Mugford's and Lumsdale's paths would soon cross.

On May 17, through his spyglass, Mugford spotted a lone vessel creeping toward Boston burdened with its massive 282-ton heft. The heavily armed ship carried several 4- and 6-pounder guns along with swivels. Putting sails to the wind, the *Franklin* caught up to the *Hope*. The Marblehead crew flooded the ship. Marblehead private Moses Stacey "was one of the number who volunteered from the ranks to join the gallant Capt. James Mugford."[4] Despite being potentially outgunned, the Marblehead captain and his men courageously boarded the *Hope* to find the crews evenly matched. Mugford had twenty-one to the *Hope*'s eighteen. He demanded that Lumsdale surrender and hand over the *Hope*'s manifest under a threat of death. What Mugford found on its pages astounded him: one thousand carbines, stacks of bayonets, five gun carriages, piles of cartridge boxes, ten thousand sandbags (probably to even out the weight of the ship), and the stupendous 1,500 barrels of gunpowder. The *Hope* carried enough powder to supply either army's needs for a month, one of the most valuable prizes of the war.

Coincidentally, two months earlier, Congress had urged Americans to enter into a day of prayer on May 17. As the *Franklin* escorted the *Hope* to Boston, the captured ship grounded at Pulling Point Gut, northwest of the city near Deer Island, before reaching the harbor. On shore, "the inhabitants, on leaving their respective places of worship after forenoon's service (it being the day of Continental fast) had the pleasure of seeing the most valuable prize, taken since the commencement of the war, just outside the harbor," as if in direct answer to their prayers. They deemed *Hope*'s cargo of such "inestimable value" that they "thought prudent to bring up to town the greatest part of it in boats; and a large number being immediately dispatched, the same was soon safely landed and properly deposited."[5]

Later that day, tides freed the ship, and she moored in Boston Harbor. Mugford then returned to sea to hunt more British transports, leaving four men to guard the *Hope*. *Lady Washington*, captained by Joseph Cunningham, joined the *Franklin* for the hunt. Sailing out of Boston Harbor, *Franklin* grounded near the same spot as had the *Hope*. Despite evacuating Boston a month earlier, several ships of the British fleet remained, lurking as a threat anchored off Nantasket Road on a peninsula only a few miles south and west of Boston Harbor.

Two British warships saw Mugford's stranded vessel and, not knowing it was the same captain and crew who had captured *Hope*, the British captain ordered a boarding party from the HMS *Renown* and *Experiment* under the command of Lieutenant Joshua Harris to attack the disabled vessel that night. Carrying a silver-hilted sword, Harris and his men, in at least five boats, rowed silently toward the *Franklin* and the *Lady Washington*. Between nine and ten o'clock, Mugford discovered the threat slithering over the black water toward his vessel. He hailed the boats, and "they responded they were from Boston." Mugford commanded his men to ready the swivels, blunderbusses, and cannons to repel the boarding party. "Keep off or I will fire upon [you]." They begged him, "for God sakes, not to fire."[6] Mugford ordered his anchor cable cut, which maneuvered the *Franklin* into a broadside so her guns faced the oncoming rowboats. Mugford fired his musket, and the crews of *Lady Washington* and *Franklin* followed suit, discharging everything they had. Musket balls, cannon, and the shotgun effect of the blunderbuss sailed across the water and tore into the small boats and the flesh and bone of the men aboard them. Before the *Franklin*'s cannon could discharge another deadly blast, some of Lieutenant Harris's men were upon the ship. In the melee, Mugford and his men sank two of the small boats and peppered the boarders with "small arms and [harpoon] spears with such intrepidity, activity, and success."[7]

Blood flowed on the deck from the wounded and dead members of the boarding party as Mugford and his crew repelled them. "They cut off the hands of several of the crews [of the boarding party] as they laid them on the gun-wale."[8] A contemporary source described "Mugford, with outstretched arms . . . righteously dealing death and destruction."[9] Eventually, he received a mortal wound to his chest and cried out to Lieutenant Russell, "I am a dead man, don't give up the vessel, you will be able to beat them off."[10] Seaman Moses Stacey later recalled that "they succeeded in sinking & [indecipherable] a number of the boats and beat them all off although at the sacrifice of the life of their gallant commander who fell by a pistol ball in the breast, while reaching over the side and having hold of one of the masts of a launch endeavoring to sink her."[11]

Eventually, Russell vanquished the final boarding party. What was left of Lieutenant Harris's troops limped back toward their ships. Initial American accounts credited the crews of *Franklin* and *Lady Washington* with killing scores of British boarders. Officially the British acknowledged eight men killed.[12] Obviously, scores of men were wounded, several missing their hands.

The next morning *Franklin* broke free of the mud, and her crew mournfully sailed back to Marblehead with their captain's body, the first captain in Washington's Navy to die in combat. News of Mugford's heroics reached Marblehead, and thousands thronged to the wharf to greet the ship. Ashley Bowen recounted the reception: "This day fair [and] pleasant. . . . The corpse of James Mugford is brought to town to be buried. . . . Seventy of Colonel Glover's regiment came and attended the funeral." On the day of the burial, flags at the fort and on the ships in the harbor flew at half-mast. "Church bells tolled, muffled drums beat a dead march," and guns aboard the *Franklin* fired as a "grand procession" of officers, Glover's Regiment, and Mugford's family and "the citizenry of Marblehead"[13] accompanied Mugford's body from the New Meeting House to the Old Burial Hill, where the other heroes of the town lay at rest.

Several days later, an American fifer found Lieutenant Harris's body washed ashore on Deer Island, "in his pocket, five guineas and four dollars, a gold watch, and by his side a silver-hilted sword."[14]

Despite the ongoing process of adjudication within the prize courts, most of the captured vessels and their cargos continued to rot away on wharves and in warehouses in Beverly and Marblehead. Unpaid prize money and even wages created widespread discontent and made it difficult to find crews to man Washington's cruisers. A few months earlier, Massachusetts legalized the process for privateering, creating even more competition for crews.

In April 1776, Washington left Boston for New York. Command of the fleet passed to General Artemas Ward. Leadership challenges existed at the fleet level as well. Commodore John Manley refused to sail. Washington's finest captain demanded a larger ship. Eventually, the Marblehead captain would join the Continental Navy. The navy assigned him one of the new frigates under construction, the *Boston*, and Manley's crew included several African Americans, including marine Cuff Wood.[15] The gap created by Manley's decision to captain the *Boston* led to more crews and captains departing.

Within this dark and lean period, twenty-eight-year-old Marblehead captain Samuel Tucker would emerge as commodore of the fleet. Born into privilege in Marblehead as the son of a shipmaster, resolute, square-jawed, and thin-lipped Tucker could not resist the siren call of the sea and rebelled against his father's collegiate aspirations for him. "For such was his repugnance to the still life of literature, that his feelings became violent, and at eleven years of age he formed a desperate plan."[16] He ran away, spending the next ten years learning the ways of the sea, fighting pirates, and battling storms until, as the master of a merchantman, he married Mary Gatchell of Marblehead in 1768 at age twenty-one.[17] Once back in Marblehead, the young captain put past differences behind him. A loyal son, he cared for his ailing father in their family home and later provided for his mother until her death at age ninety-one as she had "no other to look up to for either succor or aid in the least, during more than thirty years."[18]

"Orders were given to beat up for volunteers from the Regiment to man the Schooner Samuel Tucker Esq. Commander, a Continental armed vessel: when the Drum beat round the Regiment . . . I with others stepped forward and volunteered," recalled one soldier mariner.[19] Lieutenant Marston Watson from Plymouth, an officer in the 14th Continental Regiment, also joined the crew and is recorded as "going on a cruise at sea, as lieutenant under the command of Samuel Tucker."[20] Not long after the cruise, Watson rejoined his brothers in arms in Beverly to continue the fight on land.

At the beginning of the Revolution, Tucker was in London and allegedly was offered a command with the Royal Navy. To the offer, the outspoken captain responded, "Damn his most gracious majesty; do you think I would fight against my native country?"[21] The retort immediately made the Patriot a fugitive from the authorities. On the run, he found a friendly ship owned in part by Founding Father and financier of the Revolution Robert Morris. According to legend, when in transit across the Atlantic, the vessel encountered a severe storm. "They began to despair of life, when Tucker stepped up, cheered all hands, advised them to make an effort, and, taking the helm, guided the vessel through the tempest. . . . Grateful for the rescue of his property from destruction, [Morris] introduced [Tucker] to General Washington."[22] Tucker briefly served in the Marblehead Regiment, but after Manley chose to captain the *Boston*, Washington tapped Tucker to command the *Franklin*.

The American captain described one of his earliest encounters in Washington's Navy in a letter to a member of Congress written in his own hand:

> I will give a sketch of our proceedings and doings at the commencement of the Revolution. The first cruise I made was performed in January, 1776; and I had to purchase the small arms to encounter the enemy with money from my own pocket, or

go without them; and the consort above mentioned [his wife, Mary] made the banner I fought under; the field which was white, and the union was green, made therein in the figure of a pine tree, made a cloth of her own purchasing and at her own expense. Those colors I wore in honor of the country—which has so nobly rewarded me for my past service—and the love of their maker, until I fell in with Colonel Archibald Campbell, in the ship *George*, and brig *Annabella*, transports with about two hundred and eighty Highland troops on board, of General Frazer's corps. About ten P.M. a severe conflict ensued, which held about two hours and twenty minutes. I conquered them with great carnage on their side, it being in the night, and my small barque, about seventy tons burden, being very low in the water, I received no damage in loss of men, but lost a complete set of new sails by the passing of their balls; then the white field and pine tree union were riddled to atoms. I was then immediately supplied with a new suit of sails and a new suit of colors, made of canvas and bunting, of my own prize goods. I then went on duty again. I quit here, fearing any further detail would be too tedious, as I could fill a dozen sheets from memory.[23]

Under Tucker's command, the crew of *Franklin* seized *Henry and Esther*, which carried a large cargo of wood and military blankets. Next, they captured the 60-ton sloop *Rainbow*, containing wood and provisions. The triumphant mariner sailed the seized vessel back to Gloucester, where the captain of *Rainbow* duped the prize agent into releasing the ship.

Over the coming months, Tucker captured many more ships, and after Manley's departure from Washington's Navy and entry into the Continental Navy, Washington appointed the young captain commodore of his fleet. Even while in New York City, Washington attempted to manage his navy remotely. However, the pressing needs of the army overwhelmed his ability to exercise control over the navy, which Congress ultimately placed under the auspices of its Marine Committee.

The last of Washington's cruisers was decommissioned in the fall of 1777. Many of the Marblehead captains transferred to the Continental Navy, bringing their inestimable experience with them.

Washington's Navy captured fifty-five vessels in total.[24] Some of the cargos were priceless and came at precisely the right time to have a profound impact on the war effort, including the captures of the *Nancy* and its valuable ordnance and thousands of small arms and the *Hope* with her godsend of 1,500 barrels of precious gunpowder. Washington's Navy also kept a large amount of foodstuffs out of the stomachs of the British Army and fed his own soldiers' growling bellies. The Marbleheaders' naval success sparked a boom in privateering by various ships within the colonies, which proved to have an enormous impact on the war. British transports had to be escorted, creating a significant opportunity cost for the British, whose ships could have been used in other operations against the Americans. The asymmetric warfare of the cruisers and privateers hampered and delayed the supply chain for the entire British expeditionary force, which started in London, three thousand miles away. Writing to the secretary of state for the colonies, Lord Dartmouth, Howe summed up Washington's Navy: "[They] will hurt us more effectually [at sea] than anything they can do on Land during our Stay at this Place."[25]

Marblehead ships also answered the call by smuggling crucial powder and supplies by running the gauntlet of British ships blockading American ports. Ships transported sixty-nine thousand pounds of gunpowder alone from the Caribbean.[26] Jeremiah Lee and Elbridge Gerry's relationship with the Gardoquis blossomed into Spain's primary path to supplying America with scores of cannon, tons of powder, thousands of muskets, and military supplies,[27] and ultimately into an alliance.

Washington and Glover created the process for buying, fitting out, arming, and crewing vessels and the protocols for signals, flags, and later prize courts to determine the validity of captures. Most important, they nurtured some of Marblehead's greatest captains, among them Manley and Tucker, who would later become legends in the Continental Navy. The pathbreaking, pioneering efforts of the Marbleheaders proved indispensable. The extraordinary efforts of Washington, Glover, Marblehead, and Beverly formed the origins of the US Navy.

After withdrawing from Boston, Howe waited for reinforcements in Halifax and trained his army in light infantry tactics to adapt to the American style of warfare. Eventually, a large portion of the British Army, along with Hessian allies, some thirty-two thousand troops, and nearly half of the Royal Navy, over seventy warships and more than five hundred transports, would take part in the largest invasion of North America in history. With the loss of Boston, the British did not have a friendly port on the East Coast from Halifax to Florida, so Howe planned to capture New York. Few ports were broad enough or deep enough to support the massive invasion fleet. The city also possessed an enormous Loyalist population. New York had tremendous strategic significance, as John Adams wrote: "[New York is the] nexus of the Northern and Southern Colonies, as a Kind of Key to the whole Continent, as it is a Passage to Canada to the Great Lakes and all the Indians Nations. No Effort to secure it ought to be omitted."[28] In April, Washington's army marched south.

CHAPTER 27

KILLING WASHINGTON
AND THE INVASION

Caleb Gibbs and the Guard rode near the commander in chief. Departing on April 4, 1776, the cavalcade traveled through Providence, Norwich, and New London and arrived in Manhattan on the thirteenth of the month. A mixed reception greeted Washington upon reaching the city, as many of its twenty-thousand-plus residents remained ardent Loyalists. Shortly after arriving, Gibbs set up Washington's headquarters in a sprawling brick mansion on Pearl Street.

With New York, Washington had a significant problem on his hands—how to defend the indefensible. The Royal Navy could potentially attack the island of Manhattan at almost any point. Evacuating the incredibly vulnerable city would have been the most practical solution, but local and national leaders resisted that idea, pressuring Washington to hold New York. Washington erected forts and defensive works throughout the city and island in preparation for the anticipated invasion.

On the one hand anticipating external danger such as the Royal Navy, Washington also had to guard against internal threats like the hatred festering among the Loyalists and a group of confederates led by Royal governor William Tryon, who had fled the city and now lived on the massive seventy-four-gun HMS *Duchess-of-Gordon*, anchored in New York Harbor. Safely behind the guns of his floating waterborne lair, Tryon entertained a slew of Loyalist patrons and hatched "a barbarous and infernal plot."[1] Upon the arrival of the planned British invasion,

Tryon plotted to raise Loyalist troops to blow up powder magazines, spike cannon, seize crucial ground, and, in "the greatest and vilest attempt ever made against our country,"[2] carry out the assassination of George Washington by members of his own Guard.

As the defense of New York lurched forward, Washington departed for Philadelphia to address Congress and ordered Gibbs to move his sleeping quarters to Richmond Hill,* a twenty-six-acre mansion surrounded by meadows and gardens located in what is now the heart of the West Village on Varick and Charlton Street. Washington and the Guard often traveled the route to and from the headquarters through dirty, ramshackle houses and a mushrooming bordello district known as the Holy Ground, which catered to the carnal needs of the soldiers. "The whores (by information) continue their employ, which is become very, very lucrative," recalled Massachusetts colonel Loammi Baldwin. "Their unparalleled conduct is sufficient antidote against any desires that a person can have that has one spark of modesty or virtue left in him to blast atum [sic] must certainly be lost before he can associate with those bitchfoxy jades, jills, hags, strums, prostitutes, and these multiplied into one another."[3] Shockingly, a New York City survey taken shortly after the war estimated that 20 percent of women of childbearing age engaged in prostitution.[4] The filth, drinking, and debauchery of his men never sat well with the gentleman planter from Virginia, but Washington found them impossible to squelch.

Numerous taverns lined the route from Washington's headquarters to Richmond Hill, each happy to ply the Guards and Washington's soldiers with alcohol for their hard-earned pay. On a spring night in one of these drinking establishments, a member of Washington's Guard, Drummer William Green, "fell into a conversation on politicks" with Loyalist gunsmith Gilbert Forbes. Green found that "Forbes's pulse beat high in the Tory scheme." Raising a glass, Green boldly toasted to the king's health. Not just any Loyalist, Forbes had direct links to

* Years later, future vice president Aaron Barr bought the mansion.

Governor Tryon and was actively recruiting men to join a Loyalist legion to facilitate the "barbarous plot."[5]

Sensing a kindred spirit, Green sought Forbes out a few days later and, remarkably, "he [Green] supposed I was a friend, and immediately proposed to inlist some men [the Guard] into the King's service, and told me he could procure considerable numbers to join him," remembered Forbes.[6]

Careful to cloak his involvement in the conspiracy, Forbes demurred and blew off Green's advances. He denied having a hand in the recruitment of deserters. But Green persisted and kept returning to see Forbes, and "at last I fell into the scheme,"[7] recalled the Loyalist gunsmith-spy.

The conspiracy expanded when Green brought fellow Life Guard Sergeant Thomas Hickey into the fold. The dark-complexioned, muscular Irishman met Forbes and demanded money—the miserly gunsmith parted with half a dollar. The Loyalist sensed an opportunity, and opened his wallet to Green. Forbes gave Green eighteen dollars to be utilized to recruit more members of the Guard. Eight members of Washington's elite unit allegedly turned coat.[8]

Not satisfied with just his fellow soldiers, and perhaps in a drunken haze, Hickey went outside the Guard and recruited recent immigrant William Welch. After asking Welch to go to a "grog shop,"[9] the burly Irishman exclaimed he had something of great importance to tell him, but before revealing the secret, Hickey made him swear on a bible. Welch did so, and Hickey rambled, "This country was sold, that the enemy would soon arrive, and that it was best for us Old Countrymen to make our peace before they came, or they would kill us all."[10] The Life Guard member then went on to say he would use a particular secret mark to identify those on the side of the king and would bring him to a "man who let have a dollar by way of encouragement."[11]

The conspirators further widened their operation to include a person in the general's inner circle with intimate access to his daily activities: Washington's housekeeper.[12] Years later, a legend formed regarding the attempted poisoning of Washington's green peas. Through the closeness of the housekeeper to the commander in chief and the Life

Guards as his personal bodyguards, Hickey and other members of the Guard would assassinate Washington, spike cannons, and destroy magazines.[13] Seemingly paragons of duty and honor, treasonous members of the elite unit would diabolically execute the plot upon the arrival of the British fleet.

Invasion loomed within days.

With nefarious plots swirling since the arrival of Patriot troops in Manhattan, Washington implored the New York Provincial Congress to establish a "Secret Committee to confer with him on the dangers to which this Colony is exposed from its intestine enemies."[14] To counter the threat, New York formed the Committee of Intestine Enemies, later known as the Committee of Conspiracies. The small group consisted of august American Patriots and brilliant legal minds, including John Jay, future chief justice of the Supreme Court. Centuries later, the Central Intelligence Agency would credit Jay as the father of American counterintelligence.[15]

Jay and his secret committee went to work.

Tryon's plot proceeded according to plan—the arrival of the British invasion fleet was only days away—until the second week of June, when authorities arrested two of Washington's Guards, Hickey and Michael Lynch, for passing counterfeit currency in the city. Fake paper money was a massive problem in the colonies and led to soaring inflation. The Patriot government vainly tried to staunch the flow of counterfeit bills by arresting anyone caught with the bogus money. Authorities apprehended the two men red-handed and threw them into the dark and damp jail in New York City. Both men shared a dirty cell with Isaac Ketcham, also jailed for an unrelated counterfeiting scheme.

The cellmates talked. They had something in common: all were charged with counterfeiting and all shared Loyalist sympathies. Hickey, in his Irish brogue ranting about his loyalty to the king, shockingly revealed elements of the plot. He believed the British fleet would be arriving soon and wanted to let Ketcham know whose side he was on. Sensing an opportunity to save his own skin, Ketcham wrote a note from his cell on June 16 that changed the course of events: "Sir: I . . .

have something to observe to the honorable House if I could be admitted. It is nothing concerning my own affair but entirely on another subject."[16]

Ketcham appeared in front of Jay and the committee and revealed what he had learned. Thunderstruck that members of Washington's Guard could be involved in such treachery, Jay ordered Ketcham to cull more from the Guards and report back.

Back in their cell, Ketcham drew more details out of Hickey about the plot and his contacts. Pulling on these threads, the committee arrested the mayor of New York, David Mathews, and other members of the cabal and Gilbert Forbes. The Loyalist gunsmith was clapped in irons and initially refused to talk, but a pastor sent to his cell to inform him "his time was very short, not having above three days to live, advised him to prepare himself"[17] and loosened his tongue. The committee's expert questioning uncovered that the dramatic scope of the plot to kill Washington even involved his housekeeper. Jay immediately informed the commander in chief.

Washington ordered Gibbs to assemble a group of handpicked men to arrest Green and other treasonous members of the Guard. Gibbs rolled up more conspirators, including "the General's housekeeper . . . ; it was said she is concerned."[18]

With the plot exposed and many of its principals detained, Washington curiously selected only one man for a court-martial: Thomas Hickey. The other members of the Guard, including the conspiracy's apparent ringleader, William Green, did not have a court-martial. Perhaps Washington selected Hickey since he was a former British soldier. A board of officers swiftly convicted him of "sedition and Mutiny, and also of holding a treacherous correspondence with the enemy for the most horrid and detestable purposes."[19] Details of precisely how Washington and the other officers were to be killed, the magazines destroyed, and the attack on Knight's Bridge carried out are not located in any of the trial documents. The proposed activities of the plot may have deliberately been covered up because news of the scheme would have been a powerful propaganda victory for the British and emboldened Loyalists.

By sending Hickey to the gallows, Washington made a statement. Hickey would be the first American soldier executed by the Continental Army during the Revolution. Under a tree located in a field east of what is now the Bowery, eighty soldiers with "bayonets fixed took up the march from the brick guard house . . . to the place of execution."[20] Over ten thousand of Washington's troops assembled in formation, along with nearly the entire city. Tens of thousands witnessed the execution. Against an overcast sky, soldiers escorted Hickey to the hangman's tree.

"He appeared unaffected and obstinate to the last." As Hickey approached the tree, a chaplain took him by the hand "and bade him adieu."[21]

"A torrent of tears flowed over his face. . . . But with an indignant scornful air he wiped 'em with his hand from face, and assumed the confident look,"[22] recalled one witness to the event.

Marbleheader and commander of the Guard, Caleb Gibbs, watched as the noose tightened around one of his men's necks: a man he trusted and trained for the sacred duty of protecting their commander in chief. Hickey cryptically uttered these last words:

"Unless Green was very cautious, the Design would as yet be executed on him."[23]

The witness who heard Hickey recorded that he referred to General Nathanael Greene, but Hickey had nothing to do with Greene, who was stationed in Long Island and was not involved in the court-martial. Hickey most likely referred to Drummer William Green, who he knew had betrayed him.

The following day, June 28, in Washington's general orders addressed to the entire army, he warned, "The unhappy fate of Thomas Hickey, executed this day for Mutiny, Sedition, and Treachery; the General hopes will be a warning to every soldier in the army, to avoid those crimes, and all others, so disgraceful to the character of a soldier, and pernicious to his country. And in order to avoid these crimes, the most certain method is to keep out of the temptation of them and particularly to avoid lewd women, who, by the dying confession of this poor criminal, first led him into practices which ended in untimely and ignominious death."[24] One wonders whether Washington's enigmatic reference is to the lewd women of the red-light district or his housekeeper.

A brilliant young artillery captain, Alexander Hamilton, also witnessed the execution and wrote, "It is hoped the remainder of those miscreants now in our possession will meet with a punishment adequate to their crimes."[25] Hamilton's hope did not come to fruition. Green cheated the hangman's noose; he was dismissed from the army and disappeared. Likewise, not much is known about the fates of the other plotters, and their names seem to have mysteriously disappeared from history.

On June 29, 1776, New Yorkers witnessed a jarring sight. Instead of the picturesque emerald waters of New York Harbor, the bay appeared to resemble "a wood of pine tree trimmed." Over half of the mighty Royal Navy surrounded New York. Hundreds of ships with their naked masts had dropped sail and anchored. "All London was afloat,"[26] remembered one of Washington's soldiers. The British invasion force had arrived.

Twenty-three thousand British regulars and ten thousand of their Hessian allies descended on American shores over the next six weeks via New York's harbors, carried by more than five hundred transports and seventy British warships. Some vessels invaded Staten Island, which served as an ideal staging area for the invasion of Long Island and Manhattan while the British ships bided their time until reinforcements arrived, led by General Howe's brother, Admiral Richard "Black Dick" Howe.

Those reinforcements included the ten thousand Hessian troops who fought beside the British. At the time, the Hesse region of Germany was "the largest suppliers of troops in the world, [and] also the most expensive."[27] Unlike the idealistic, volunteer, poorly supplied American army, the Hessians were professional soldiers who had trained for battle since early childhood. To them, the idea that the Americans could meaningfully oppose them in battle seemed almost laughable.

Hessian boys registered with the military at the age of seven. When they became teenagers, they went before officials who decided whether they would join the army or become "indispensable personnel" like farmers, merchants, or craftsmen. It was a choice without a choice. Some voluntarily joined for the money, but even those who wanted to refuse were forced into service. Once they were part of the army, they faced strict discipline.

While the Americans fought for their freedom, the Hessians were primarily in it for the money. And the money was good. As one Hessian captain noted, "Never in this world was an army as well paid as this one during the civil war in America. One could call them rich."[28] They augmented that pay with rampant looting, which undermined the British Howe brothers' efforts to maintain good relations with the Loyalist population. Neither orders nor strict punishments could get them to stop.

Later, in early September, the Howe brothers would try negotiation one last time. They met with the Americans for a peace summit at Staten Island. Ultimately, the effort was unsuccessful because the Americans understood that the Howes had no leverage to negotiate an overarching treaty. Ambrose Serle, William Howe's private secretary, succinctly summed up the meeting: "They met, they talked, they parted."[29]

On July 4, 1776, the United States declared independence from Great Britain. In Beverly, in what is now fittingly known as Independence Park, overlooking the scenic, lush, blue-green, bay-like channel, John Glover assembled the Marblehead Regiment and read Jefferson's iconic words to the men. The declaration's signers committed treason in the eyes of the Crown. Benjamin Rush, one of the signers, recalled the moment when Elbridge Gerry signed: "Do you recollect the pensive and awful silence which pervaded the house when we were called up, one after another, to the table of the President of Congress, to subscribe what was believed by many at that time to be our own death warrants? The Silence & the gloom of the morning were interrupted I well recollect only for a moment by Col: Harrison of Virginia who said to Mr Gerry at the table, 'I shall have a great advantage over you Mr: Gerry when we are all hung for what we are now doing. From the size and weight of my body I shall die in a few minutes, but from the lightness of your body you will dance in the air an hour or two before you are dead.' This Speech procured a transient smile, but it was soon succeeded by the Solemnity with which the whole business was conducted."[30] Despite the death sentence hanging over his head, the Marbleheader considered the act of signing the greatest moment of his life. Recently, the British had put down an insurrection in Ireland, and a judge leveled a barbaric sentence on captured revolutionaries: "You are to be drawn on hurdles to the place of execution, where you are to be hanged by the neck, but not until you are dead, for while you are still living your bodies are to be taken down, your bowels torn out and burned before your faces, your heads then cut off, and your bodies are to be divided into four quarters."[31]

Despite the threat to their lives if they failed, the regiment believed in their cause. Their time guarding Beverly had come to an end; within days, the unit prepared to make the long march to New York City to join Washington. The 14th's collective actions would ensure the declaration's words remained a reality.

CHAPTER 28

"WE WISH TO GIVE THEM ANOTHER DRUBBING": FIRE SHIPS AND INVASION

In the warm air of the summer night of August 19, two American ships glided silently toward their prey: the twenty-gun *Rose* and the forty-four-gun *Phoenix*. These two British warships lay anchored, unsuspecting, in the Hudson River north of New York City. "The night was dark and favorable to our design, and the enemy did not perceive our vessels until they were near aboard them,"[1] recalled one Patriot.

The American crew, led by Marbleheader Thomas Fosdick, knew that this could be their last mission. As the designated crew members lit the two ships on fire, the floating forests of kindling suddenly erupted into a mass of heat and light. The British sailors aboard the *Rose* and *Phoenix*, roused from their sleepy stupor, immediately grasped the danger in front of them. While Fosdick and his men tossed grappling hooks onto the British vessels, the Americans abandoned the fire ship. "This gallant enterprise struck so great a panick upon the enemy that they thought it prudent to quit their station."[2]

The British ships' captains remained cool enough in the face of the approaching fire to cut the ropes drawing them closer to the fire ships. However, the captain of the *Phoenix* was not fast enough to avoid being boarded by the Americans. And the *Rose*, despite its captain's desperate maneuverings, could not escape from the conflagration. The captain of the *Rose* recorded in his journal that the Americans "set the Tender

Instantly in a Blaze. . . . We veer'd away but finding we could not get clear of her cut the [anchor] Cable."[3]

The Americans who had not managed to scramble aboard the enemy vessels now faced the very real danger of being burned alive. They bolted for the holes they had previously cut in the sterns of the fire ships and clambered aboard small whaleboats fastened there.

Not all of them made it out alive. Perhaps the last man to leave was Captain Thomas, who was with another unit at the helm of one of the fire vessels. Washington himself commended the valiant officer: "One of the Captains—Thomas—it is to be feared perished in the attempt, or in making his escape by swimming, as he has not been heard of—His bravery entitled him to a better fate."[4]

Fosdick survived, but the operation was not quite as successful as the Americans would have wished. They did not destroy the warships entirely, but they did inflict damage—to the vessels and to the enemy's morale. Washington wrote, "Though this enterprise did not succeed to our wishes, I incline to think it alarmed the Enemy greatly—For this morning, the *Phoenix* and *Rose* with their two remaining Tenders taking the advantage of a brisk and prosperous gale with a favorable tide, quitted their stations and have returned and joined the rest of the Fleet."[5]

Moses Brown chronicled the Marblehead Regiment's contribution to the operation in his orderly book the next day: "The General thanks the Officers & men for the spirit & Resolution—which they showed on grappling the Vessels before they quitted the Fire Ships—and as a Reward of the Merit present each of those who stayed last on board and are somewhat burnt Fifty Dollars . . . the General would have been generous in proportion to the Service."[6]

The incident was a highlight in the career of Thomas Fosdick, who experienced a meteoric rise from the rank of fifer to ensign to some of the highest levels in the fledgling navy. He had assumed the role of regimental adjutant when Caleb Gibbs joined Washington's Guard.[7] Fosdick and Glover would later be joined as family when Glover married Fosdick's sister.

Days earlier, Patriot galleys rowed by crews of up to sixty men had attacked the heavily armed British warships. "We engaged them an hour and a half, and then we thought to retreat to Dobb's Ferry, about four miles below the ships. The damages we sustained are as follows, viz: *Washington*, four slightly wounded, sail and rigging much damaged, thirteen shot in her hull. *Lady Washington* cracked her 32-pounder; no other damage. *Spitfire*, one killed, two badly wounded, hull and rigging much damaged. *Shark*, none killed or wounded, hulled four times. The *Whiting*, one man lost both legs, and four more wounded, rigging much damaged, two men wounded, one of them mortally. . . . We wish to give them another drubbing. We saw many splinters drifting down."[8]

The fire ships were the last act in this series of waterborne engagements in the summer of 1776 that forced the British vessels to retreat back to New York harbor and Staten Island, accomplishing the primary goal of preventing them from cutting off the American supply lines from the Hudson Valley to New York City.

Within days, the British would invade Long Island, where the Marblehead men would again play an indispensable role.

The morning of August 22 broke clear with a bright blue sky. *Phoenix* and *Rose*, still bearing scars from their encounter with the fire ships, prepared for the British invasion of Long Island. Thousands of oars dipped into the blue-green waters of Gravesend Bay as four thousand troops made their way toward the beaches of Long Island. Except for skirmishing and rifle fire from the Americans, in the coming days, thousands more would land unopposed to bring the total up to approximately twenty thousand British troops. The bulk of the American defenses lay in a series of forts in Brooklyn along with fieldworks on a stony spur known as the Heights of Gowanus. British and Hessian allies coiled like a snake, eventually striking on the night of August 26.

The largest battle of the Revolution, up until that point, began in the most unlikely of locations: a watermelon patch. Around 11:00 p.m. on August 26, 1776, a group of British scouts stumbled upon the rare and highly prized bulbous fruit and immediately began consuming it. Planted by a savvy owner of the Red Lion Inn, the watermelons were meant to attract tourists, but they proved equally attractive to soldiers.

The Redcoats' late-night feast did not go unnoticed. Lookouts stationed by former British officer and Pennsylvania physician Colonel Edward Hand soon heard the sounds of the Redcoats gorging themselves. The riflemen fired a few shots at the British intruders, igniting an epic battle.

General Henry Clinton's grand plan took the form of a large-scale hammer-and-anvil maneuver. General James Grant's forces, the anvil, attacked the right side of the American line deployed along the shore on Gowanus Road. Fighting alongside them, General Leopold von Heister's column of Hessians would attack the center, located near today's Prospect Park, in an area now known as Battle Pass. They hoped to engage the Patriots and keep them in place—neither advancing nor retreating—while the main body of the British forces executed a long, sweeping flanking maneuver. This larger body, led by Clinton and William Howe, would head through the Jamaica Pass around the American defenses on the Heights of Gowanus, serving as the hammer to pound the Americans from behind and prevent their escape.

Around 9:00 p.m. on Monday, August 26, Clinton set his plan into motion. The hammer force of ten thousand men led by Clinton and Howe, who were to encircle the Americans' left flank, were the first to leave. As a deception, the British left their tents pitched and their fires burning in the field where they had been camped. With Lexington and Bunker Hill veteran Captain William Glanville Evelyn of the light infantry leading the British advance, they slipped through the countryside as silently as possible, meeting virtually no opposition in the Jamaica Pass.

An hour or two later, it was time for Grant's forces to march. Because his scouts had warned him about the sentries near the inn, Grant waited for nearly three hours before launching the attack. When untested militia replaced the riflemen as lookouts around two o'clock in the morning, Grant seized his opportunity. With three hundred Redcoats rapidly closing in, the militia ran in terror. However, they were not all fast enough to escape. Grant's men captured their leader, Major James Bond, and several others. However, enough escaped to get word of the British movement to General Israel Putnam, the veteran of the Battle of Bunker Hill. Unfortunately, Old Put fell for the British ruse and failed to anticipate the flanking maneuver that was about to strike. He rode down to the American camp, located next to the Vechte-Cortelyou farmhouse near the present-day junction of Fifth Avenue and Third Street, and woke Lord Stirling, who was the commander of the forces in the area.

Roused from his slumber by the sound of signal guns, as the drummers beat a call to arms, thirty-three-year-old Major Mordecai Gist of Smallwood's Maryland Regiment instantly awoke. Gist, over six feet tall, was described as possessing a "frank and genial manner" and was one of Maryland's first agitators for independence; he later emerged as one of America's most powerful Freemasons. He was also one of Baltimore's wealthiest residents. In December 1774, the merchant founded Maryland's first military company during the Revolution, the Baltimore Independent Cadets. Their charter called for sixty men—a "company composed of gentlemen of Honour, Family, and Fortune, and tho' of different countries animated by a zeal and reverence for rights of humanity" to join voluntarily and unite "by all the Sacred ties of Honour and the Love and Justice due to ourselves and Country."[9] The men outfitted themselves with the best equipment and weapons money could buy and had spent the previous year training for war. Within moments, Gist had organized his men, and under Lord Stirling's command, they marched toward the Red Lion Inn to confront Grant.

Stirling's real name was William Alexander, but he was known as Lord Stirling because he claimed to be a Scottish earl (a claim the House of Lords did not recognize). Described as an "overweight, rheumatic, vain, pompous, gluttonous inebriate,"[10] Stirling was chronically in debt before the war, as were many of the leading voices of the Revolution. Like Putnam, Stirling fell for Grant's feint. He later wrote, "I fully expected, as did most of my officers, that the strength of the British army was advancing in this quarter to our lines."[11]

Believing Grant's men were the main thrust of the British assault, Old Put sent over a thousand men to confront them. Gist recalled, "We began our march to the right at three o'clock in the morning, with about thirteen hundred men, and about sunrise, on our near approach to the ground, discovered the enemy making up to it, and in a few minutes our advanced parties began the attack."[12] As the first light of dawn broke "with a Red and angry Glare," Gist positioned his men to face the Redcoats, and they "immediately advanced and took possession of the ground and formed a line of battle. In the meantime, [the British] began warm fire with their artillery and light infantry, from their left, while the main body was forming in columns to attack us in the front."[13] So far, everything was unfolding according to Clinton's plan.

The Americans took up their positions and "immediately drew up in a line, and offered them battle in the true English taste." They withstood the British artillery fire—exactly as Grant had hoped. The Redcoats advanced to within three hundred yards, while the Royal Navy trained their guns on Stirling's lines. As one participant noted, "Both the balls and shells flew very fast, now and then taking off a head." He added, "Our men stood it amazingly well, not even one showed a disposition to shrink. Our orders were not to fire till the enemy came within 50 yards of us: but when they perceived we stood their fire so coolly and resolutely, they declined coming any nearer, though treble our number."[14]

To shore up the morale of his men, who were now vastly outnumbered, Stirling delivered a rousing speech. He reminded them that Grant had little respect for the American troops facing him and had once boasted before the House of Commons that with five thousand men he could march from one end of the American continent to the other. Stirling railed, "[Grant] may have 5,000 men with him now—we are not so many—but I think we are enough to prevent his advancing further on his march over the continent than that mill pond."[15]

As Grant had intended, the two lines of men remained stationary from sunrise until late in the morning. Then, for no apparent reason, the British retreated two hundred yards and ceased fire.

The Americans soon realized the horror of their predicament. "We soon heard the fire on our left, and in a short time discovered part of our enemy in our rear," Gist recalled. "Surrounded, and [with] no probability of reinforcement, his Lordship [Stirling] ordered me to retreat with the remaining part of our men, and force our way through our camp."[16]

The battle was going entirely according to Clinton's plan. Howe and Clinton had penetrated deep behind American lines, successfully traversing the Jamaica Pass to flank the Americans. In the silence, two heavy cannon fired, and the shock wave echoed across the fields. It was the signal that Grant and the Hessians designated to renew their attack on the American right flank (Stirling) and the center (John Sullivan).

General Leopold von Heister's Hessians marched steadily toward the American lines on the Gowanus Heights and assembled in an open field in front of the pass. With three whole brigades in the column, the line of highly trained Hessians stretched nearly a mile long. "With colors flying, to the music of drums and hautboys as if they were marching across Friedrich's Platz at Cassel. . . . They did not fire a shot, but pressed steadily forward until they could employ their bayonets."[17] The Hessians settled into their butchery, ruthlessly killing the far less experienced American soldiers. They showed no mercy to groups of stragglers, instead often surrounding them, lowering their bayonets, and then slowly tightening the circle, killing all those inside.

Although groups of Americans still fought desperately here and there, the Hessians and Grant had broken the main force. Stirling and the Marylanders retreated. Heavy flanking fire peppered the Marylanders from both sides until they "came to the marsh [and a stone house], where [the main force] were obliged to break their order, and escape as quick as they could to the edge of the creek, under a brisk fire."[18]

Stirling ordered the main body of his men to jump into the marsh at the present-day site of the Gowanus Canal and swim eighty yards across the swift current of Gowanus Creek to reach the relative safety of the American defenses on Brooklyn Heights. The swim was necessary because the Americans had destroyed the bridge across the creek earlier in the day, leaving themselves no other way to retreat. Making matters worse, on the right flank of the marsh stood a stone house and its grounds, currently occupied by hundreds of British troops and one of Britain's most vaunted commanders, Charles Edward Cornwallis (Earl, later Marquess, Cornwallis).

The son of an earl, Cornwallis was born in London and had a very aristocratic upbringing, including schooling at Eton and Cambridge. When he was eighteen, he became a member of the prestigious foot guards and found that he loved the army. While still a young man, he also became a member of the House of Lords, through which he gained connections that furthered his military career. His physical appearance was considered fairly unattractive. Thanks to a sports injury, one of his eyes looked unusual, and he was, by his own description, "rather corpulent"[19] with a double chin. By contrast, his wife, whom he loved dearly, was known for her beauty. Eager for battle, he volunteered in the Seven Years' War, in which he served with distinction and was noted for his gallantry in battle. He also volunteered for service in putting down the American uprising, even though he was one of only six lords in Parliament who voted against the Stamp Act. A soldier's soldier, Cornwallis led from the front and on several occasions had his horse shot out from under him. Almost recklessly brave, the earl was the perfect embodiment of his regiment's motto, "Virtutis fortuna comes" (Fortune is the companion of virtue). Yet he saw to his men's needs, often generously paying for their equipment and provisions out of his own pocket. After the American Revolution, he led British forces in India to defeat Tipu Sultan. As a reward, he received a staggering fortune of tens of thousands of pounds sterling, which he gave to his men.

Howe had placed Cornwallis in command of the light infantry that had spearheaded the flanking maneuver. Desperate to allow the rest of the army to escape, Stirling ordered a suicidal preemptive strike on the earl's position. "I found it absolutely necessary to attack a body of troops commanded by Lord Cornwallis, posted at the [Vechte-Cortelyou] house near the Upper Mills," Stirling recounted to Washington. "This I instantly did, with about half of Smallwood's [Battalion], first ordering all the other

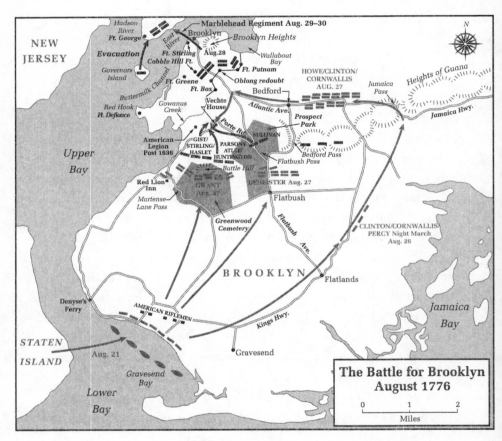

NEW
JERSEY

Hudson
River
Ft. George

Evacuation

Governors
Island

Red Hook
R. Defiance

Upper
Bay

Buttermilk Channel

Gowanus
Creek

American
Legion
Post 1636

Red Lion
Inn

Martense-
Lane Pass

Denyse's
Ferry

STATEN
ISLAND

Aug. 21

Gravesend
Bay

Lower
Bay

East
River

Marblehead Regiment Aug. 29–30

Brooklyn

Aug.28

Ft. Stirling
Cobble Hill Ft.

Ft. Greene

Ft. Box

Vechte
House

Porte Rd.

GIST/
STIRLING/
HASLET

PARSONS/
ATLEE/
HUNTINGTON

Battle Hill

GRANT
Aug. 27

Greenwood
Cemetery

AMERICAN RIFLEMEN

Brooklyn Heights

Wallabout
Bay

Ft. Putnam

Oblong redoubt

Bedford

Atlantic Ave.

SULLIVAN

Prospect
Park

Bedford Pass

Flatbush Pass

DE HEESTER Aug. 27

Flatbush

Flatbush Ave.

BROOKLYN

Flatlands

Kings Hwy.

Gravesend

HOWE/CLINTON/
CORNWALLIS
AUG. 27

Jamaica
Pass

Heights of Guana

Jamaica Hwy.

CLINTON/CORNWALLIS/
PERCY Night March
Aug. 26

Jamaica
Bay

N

**The Battle for Brooklyn
August 1776**

0   1   2
Miles

"The Battle for Brooklyn"

troops to make the best of their way through the creek."[20] Gist recalled, "We were then left with only five companies of our battalion."[21]

Cornwallis's crack troops separated the right wing of the American army from the safety of Brooklyn Heights.

Cornwallis's men, including Captain William Glanville Evelyn, trained their muskets and a light cannon on the advancing Americans.

"Fire!"

As they surged forward, men dropped.

But despite the carnage, the Americans were not yet through. "Close up! Close up!"[22] Over the din of battle, the Marylanders advanced again, charging into the hail of fire coming from the Redcoats in and around the Vechte-Cortelyou house.

The British continued "pouring the canister and grape upon the Americans like a shower of hail." In the melee, "the flower of some of the finest families of the South [were] cut to atoms."[23]

Yet the Marylanders still refused to give up. Gist's men "closed their ranks over the bodies of their dead comrades, and still turned their faces to the foe."[24]

Over and over, the Marylanders renewed their attack on Cornwallis's position, giving the rest of Stirling's men time to escape. "We continued the attack a considerable time," recalled Stirling, "the men having been rallied and the attack renewed . . . several times."[25]

One Marylander noted, "Our men fought with more than Roman valor."[26]

During the battle, Stirling brazenly "encouraged and animated our young soldiers with almost invincible resolution,"[27] recalled Gist. The commander even began to believe his men could drive the British from their position, but then the Hessians arrived.

Having broken through Sullivan's defenses, the professional soldiers attacked the Marylanders from the rear, while Grant's forces fired from the flank.

"Surrounded on all sides by at least 20,000 men, we were drove with precipitation and confusion," Gist dramatically recalled.[28]

The British showed no mercy in victory, taking few prisoners. One Redcoat officer noted, "The Hessians and our brave Highlanders gave no quarters; and it was a fine sight to see with what alacrity they dispatched the rebels with their bayonets, after we had surrounded them so they could not resist. We took care to tell the Hessians that the rebels had resolved to give no quarter—to them in particular—which made them fight desperately, and to put to death all that came into their hands." Another of the Redcoats added, "We were greatly shocked at the massacre made by the Hessians and Highlanders after victory was decided."[29]

One Marylander later wrote, "My captain was killed, first lieutenant was killed, second lieutenant shot through [the] hand." The Hessians also killed two corporals and two sergeants in the company, "one in front of me [at the] same time my bayonet was shot off my gun."[30]

Few would survive. Cornwallis cut off the remaining Americans from their retreat, and Gowanus Creek remained the only way out for those who had somehow managed to avoid being slaughtered or captured. With the waters of the bay at high tide, the men had to wade and swim through waist-deep and often neck-deep water while evading the British fire.

Peering through his spyglass from a nearby hill located behind fortifications in the American lines, George Washington was visibly moved by the Marylanders' courage and great sacrifice. According to one account, "Gen. Washington wrung his hands, and cried out, 'Good God! What brave fellows I must this day lose!'"[31]

As the Marylanders swam for their lives, those on Brooklyn Heights brought up two small cannon to cover them. Still, many died. Some fell to bullets, while others did not know how to swim. One officer remembered, "Most of those who swam over, and others who attempted to cross before the covering party got down, lost their arms and accoutrements in the mud and creek, and some fellows their lives."[32] In an effort to prevent more drowning, Captain Samuel Smith, in command of the 8th Company in Smallwood's Battalion, made the swim not just once but several times. "He and a sergeant swam over and got two slabs into the water on the ends of which they ferried over all who could not swim."[33]

One soldier recounted the grisly sight of cannonballs taking off the top of a comrade's head. Despite the bloody carnage, some survived. Gist recalled, "A party retreated to the right through the woods, and Captain Ford and myself, with 20 others, to the left, through a marsh; nine only of us got safe in."[34]

Many others did not make the crossing and were killed or captured—which was also a virtual death sentence. Smith summed up the depth and breadth of their sacrifice: "The men were surrounded, and almost all killed, for the Hessians gave no quarter on that day. The loss of the regiment was about 250; the residue got off, as best they could."[35]

The Marylanders' audacious, suicidal charge near the stone house allowed the right wing of the American army to survive. It tied up Grant's and Cornwallis's forces, which not only bought priceless time, but also prevented the British and Hessians from assaulting the American defenses on Brooklyn Heights. In this American Thermopylae, with their blood, the Immortals bought "an hour, more precious to American liberty than any other in its history."*[36]

Had Howe pressed the attack on the forts that afternoon, all the circumstances would have been aligned for a crushing American defeat. The British might have captured much of the American army, maybe even Washington and his top commanders. That could have snuffed out the Revolution, turning it into little more than a footnote in the history of the British Empire. For their actions, the Marylanders would later be eternalized as "Washington's Immortals," the "Maryland 400," and the "Bayonets of the Revolution."[37]

---

* The assault of Washington's Immortals on Cornwallis's troops arguably remains one of the most important elite small-unit engagements in American history. "Gentlemen of Honour, Family and Fortune" bought crucial time for the Patriot cause, allowing hundreds of colonial troops to retreat through a gap in British lines. Somewhere beneath the surface, perhaps under a garage or below a paved street, are the Marylanders' undiscovered bodies. Their remains lie intermingled in what should be hallowed ground, buried in a mass grave or multiple graves that tragically have yet to be found. The Marylanders' entire eight-year story is told for the first time in *Washington's Immortals: The Untold Story of an Elite Regiment Who Changed the Course of the Revolution* by Patrick K. O'Donnell.

CHAPTER 29

THE DECISION

August 29, 1776, Brooklyn, New York

Lightning arced overhead and cold rain, interspersed with occasional hail, drenched Redcoats and rebels alike. The nor'easter pelted the combatants and ultimately would change the course of history. Hungry, exhausted, and covered in mud, the Marbleheaders hunkered down in the mile-long maze of trenches that connected the five American forts on Brooklyn Heights. The mariners huddled together for warmth as the dirty, soupy water slowly rose to ankle depth and then began creeping up their legs.

Two days earlier, the Americans had lost several significant engagements in Brooklyn. Now, the British and Hessians had Washington's army trapped with their backs to the East River, and it looked like the Revolution might end just weeks after the signing of the Declaration of Independence. The Marblehead Regiment rowed from Manhattan on August 28 to reinforce Washington's troops on Long Island. "It was evident that this small reinforcement, inspired no inconsiderable degree of confidence. The faces that had been saddened by the disasters of yesterday, assumed the gleam of animation, on our approach; accompanied with a murmur of approbation in the spectators occasionally greeting each other with the remark, that *'these were the lads that might do something.'*"[1]

After arriving at the water-filled trenches, the Marbleheaders engaged in several intense skirmishes with the British. Volunteer teenage drummer Philip Follet "had to run for his life with his drum upon his back; until he finally was overtaken by the enemy and made a prisoner."*² The Marbleheaders spent the day fighting the Redcoats and the miserable weather. Before the night was over, Washington would call upon their skills to save his army from destruction.

For many of the Americans, the fighting in Brooklyn had been their first real battle, and it had been demoralizing. Benjamin Tallmadge, an officer who would later become Washington's spymaster, captured the experience of many when he wrote, "This was the first time in my life that I had witnessed the awful scene of a battle, when man was engaged to destroy his fellow man. I well remember my sensations on the occasion, for they were solemn beyond description, and very hardly could I bring my mind to be willing to attempt [to take] the life of a fellow creature."³

Though the British had soundly defeated the rebel forces arrayed on a rocky outcropping known as the Heights of Gowanus, forcing them to retreat to their fortifications in Brooklyn Heights, rather than mount an immediate assault on the forts and potentially end the war by destroying or capturing a large portion of the Continental Army, General William Howe decided instead to lay siege and sail the Royal Navy up the East River to cut off the Patriots' retreat. He ordered his troops to dig zigzagging approach trenches toward the American lines and advance as closely as possible with minimal loss of life. He had learned the bloody lesson of the Battle of Bunker Hill: the British had won, but only at tremendous cost, and he was determined not to make the same mistake again. He later explained to Parliament, "The most essential duty I had to observe was not wantonly to commit his majesty's troops, where the object was inadequate. I knew well that any considerable loss sustained by the army could not speedily, nor easily, be repaired. . . . The loss of 1,000, or perhaps 1,500 British troops, in

---

* According to Philip Follet's pension file, he was "confined and suffered much in his imprisonment but was finally released in December of the same year [1776]" and "arrived safe home to Marblehead in January 1777." Afterward, he joined the navy on Samuel Tucker's frigate *Boston* and later died of smallpox. The British confined many of the Americans on prison ships in New York Harbor. Thousands died upon these floating concentration camps, which were rampant with disease and filled with starving men.

carrying those lines, would have been but ill repaid by double that number of the enemy, could it have been supposed they would have suffered in that proportion."[4]

To the Redcoats, the Patriot fortifications appeared too strong to take by a direct assault. Another British officer noted, "We had no fascines to fill ditches, no axes to cut abatis, and no scaling ladder to assault so respectable a work. Lines were a mile and a half [in] extent including angles, cannon-proof, with a chain of fine redoubts, or rather fortresses with ditches, as half a line the intervals; the whole surmount with a most formidable abatis finished in every part."[5]

The Americans, by contrast, took a very different view of their chances. "Our intrenchment was so weak, that it is most wonderful the British General did not attempt to storm it soon after the battle, in which his troops had been victorious," wrote Tallmadge. "Gen. Washington was so fully aware of the perilous situation of this division of his army, that he immediately convened a council of war."[6]

In Washington's headquarters, a mansion known as Four Chimneys that sat atop the heights, the general called on his nine general officers for advice on the afternoon of the twenty-ninth. Outside, the downpour from the raging storm pelted both armies. Some believed retreating across the river was their best option, but several of the generals, including Israel Putnam, thought an amphibious evacuation impossible. Unaware that the storm had prevented the British from sailing up the river, he predicted the Royal Navy would surely attack during the crossing. A single British ship on the East River had the potential to sever the means of retreat. Also, the portion of the East River nearest to Washington's army was a mile wide and known for its treacherous currents. Even under the best of circumstances, such a crossing would be fraught with difficulty. Attempting such a feat in the midst of a raging storm, hemmed in by enemies on both sides, seemed suicidal.

Ultimately, Washington sided with those of his officers who argued in favor of evacuation. He knew that his men had reached their breaking point. In the words of one of the officers on the scene, the army had sustained "incessant fatigue and constant watchfulness for two days and nights, attended by heavy rain, exposed every moment to an attack from a vastly superior force."[7] By retreating, Washington hoped to salvage his remaining forces and live to fight another day.

But escaping from Long Island would be grueling and treacherous. Tallmadge observed, "To move so large a body of troops, with all their necessary appendages across a river a full mile wide, with a rapid current in the face of a victorious well-disciplined army, nearly three times as numerous as his own, and a fleet capable of stopping the navigation, so that not one boat could have passed over, seemed to present most formidable obstacles."[8]

One of the gravest challenges Washington faced was a lack of vessels to transport his men. He had requisitioned ten flat-bottomed boats, not nearly enough to move his nine-thousand-strong Long Island force and its weapons across the East River over the course of a single night. The gargantuan task of rounding up the necessary vessels in the span of about eight hours would fall to Brigadier General William Heath and Assistant Quartermaster Hugh Hughes. Hughes received orders "to impress every kind of watercraft from Hell Gate on the Sound to Spuyten Duyvil Creek that could be kept afloat and that had either sails or oars, and have them all in the east harbor of the City by dark."[9] A particular emphasis was placed on commandeering flat-bottomed boats, which could carry horses and cannons.

Washington strove to maintain airtight secrecy to prevent word of the intended retreat from reaching the ears of the British. To that end, he deceived even his own officers about the night's plans. Washington told John Glover that he expected reinforcements to arrive and that the Marbleheaders should pack up their equipment and be ready to move immediately upon their arrival. Glover would not learn the truth until late that evening when it was time for the Marblehead Regiment to man the vessels carrying the army back to New York. The entire plan could be blown sky-high by a single traitor. Loyalist civilians, some of whose homes were near the fortifications at Brooklyn Heights, posed a threat, or a defecting soldier could betray the operation and jeopardize the fate of the Continental Army, potentially dooming the weeks-old United States.

CHAPTER 30

AMERICAN DUNKIRK

The fate of the army—in fact, the fate of the entire Revolution—now lay on the muscled shoulders of the fishermen and sailors of the Marblehead Regiment.[1] The Americans not only faced tens of thousands of British regulars and Hessian troops arrayed in front of them, but in addition, they would pit their skills and strength against three extremely potent natural enemies: time, wind, and tide.

It was the middle of summer; therefore, the night would be short. The Marbleheaders faced the monumental task of transporting Washington's men and materiel under the cover of darkness to screen their movement from watchful eyes. Amphibious operations and disengagement under pressure are some of the most complex and dangerous in warfare. Even with a rearguard, the Americans rendered themselves vulnerable as they departed their defenses and boarded the boats. A British night attack might prove unstoppable.

"Colonel Glover, who belonged to Marblehead, was called upon with the whole of his regiment fit for duty, to take the command of the vessels and flat-bottomed boats. Most of the men were formerly employed in the fishery, and so peculiarly well qualified for the service,"[2] wrote contemporary historian William Gordon.[3]

The Marbleheaders had worked together as a team for over a year. Many had also served together in the Grand Banks. These men, their leadership, their grit, and their priceless experience sailing the most treacherous waters in the world would be indispensable in accomplishing the near-impossible that night. Captains William R. Lee, Moses Brown, Thomas Grant, Thomas Fosdick, and John Glover Jr. provided superb leadership; Lieutenant William Hawks, Robert Wormstead, and a core group of experienced corporals, sergeants, and privates had forged strong bonds evident even to outsiders. "The colonel [Glover] went over . . . to give directions; and about seven o'clock at night, officers and men went to work with a spirit and resolution peculiar to that corps."[4]

Underpinning the close-knit relationships, multiple family ties ran throughout the regiment, creating bonds of steel, including those of several father-and-son teams like Captain William Courtis and his son Private William Courtis Jr. Captain Thomas Grant was joined by his fifer son, Thomas Grant Jr. Twelve-year-old Grant recalled that they "took part by water to New York City and landed by the east river a little bit above."[5]

The first boats manned by the Marbleheaders to make the crossing did not carry troops. Instead, Brigadier General Alexander McDougall, a former merchant mariner who was in charge of the evacuation, ordered the horses, ammunition, cannons, and baggage transferred to the other side of the river. As "the heavy rains[,] which [had] fallen two days and nights, with but little intermission,"[6] continued to fall, they spiked the largest guns—which were too heavy to move and would have sunk in the oozing, brown mud on the shore if the men had tried to load them into the boats. The decision to transport the equipment, guns, and ammunition first had two significant consequences. First, it postponed the notification of the men about the planned retreat for as long as possible, decreasing the likelihood that word of the covert plan would reach the British. Second, it left the army without the ammunition and guns they would need to continue to hold out against the enemy, making retreat the only option.

William Heath and Hugh Hughes assembled a motley collection of sailing and rowed vessels. "Having been brought up to the Seas," as Marbleheader William Hawks phrased it,[7] the mariners of the Marblehead Regiment—likely including African Americans such as Manuel Soto, Romeo, Aesop Hale of Beverly, Sciaipo Dodge, Nathaniel Small, Hannibal,[8] and Spaniard Francis Grater—quickly had to acquaint themselves with the unfamiliar boats to navigate successfully the swirling currents of the East River. Completing the entire trip in utter darkness added an additional layer of complexity. Even the minimal light from a shuttered lantern might tip off the British about the operation underway. The sailors would have to trust their instincts and nautical knowledge to guide them successfully to the other side of the mile-wide river. The mariners took extraordinary measures to ensure secrecy and prevent the discovery of their clandestine mission, including wrapping their oars in cloth to minimize the sound they made dipping into the water.

At approximately 10:00 p.m., McDougall gave the order to begin transporting the troops. Glover and his men moved the sick and injured to the boats first. After making the crossing and returning, they transported the militia, which remained in reserve.[9] To maintain secrecy as long as possible, no one told the men on the front lines that they were leaving Brooklyn until right before they boarded. Joseph Plumb Martin, a Connecticut teenager who kept a diary of his experiences in the war, wrote,

> We were strictly enjoined not to speak, or even cough, while on the march. All orders were given from officer to officer, and communicated to the men in whispers. What such secrecy could mean we could not divine. We marched off in the same way that we had come on to the island, forming various conjectures among ourselves as to our destination. Some were of opinion that we were to endeavor to get on the flank, or in the rear of the enemy. Others, that we were going up the East River, to attack them in that quarter; but none, it seems, knew the right of the matter. We marched on, however, until we arrived at the ferry, where we immediately embarked on board the bateaux, and were conveyed safely to New-York, where we were landed about three o'clock in the morning, nothing against our inclinations.[10]

Another American recalled, "The brigades were ordered to be in readiness with bag and baggage to march, but knew not where or for what; the 2d did not know where the 1st had gone; nor the 3d, the 2d."[11]

While the soldiers could not ascertain where they were going or why, some of the Loyalists who lived in Brooklyn knew exactly what was afoot. According to legend, Catrina Rapalje, the wife of a wealthy local, John Rapalje, sent her enslaved black servant to warn the British soldiers that Washington's army was escaping. The Rapaljes* were one of the first Dutch families to settle in New York in the 1600s, when it was known as New Netherlands. Staunch Loyalists, the family, and Catrina in particular, were vocal about their support for the king. Catrina publicly drank tea in defiance of the revolutionaries. One Brooklyn historian noted, "Her conduct caused much discussion, and drew down upon her the umbrage of the Whig militia, who fired a cannon ball into her home while she was drinking her favorite beverage. The ball passed close to her head and lodged in the wall. This action not only seriously annoyed the lady, but served to stir within her bosom the spirit of revenge, and she eagerly awaited an opportunity to gratify her spit." In addition, earlier in August, Washington had ordered her husband, John, arrested and sent to Connecticut, giving his wife additional reason to "mete out punishment to her enemies."[12] If her message had gotten through the chain of command, and the British had attacked, the course of the Revolution would have been altered at that moment, but a language barrier prevented the slave from delivering the communications in time. The man had the misfortune of first encountering a group of Hessians who did not speak English. The servant, who primarily spoke Dutch and broken English, could not make them understand him. The Germans did not take him to a British officer until late the next morning, and by then, it was too late.

In the early hours of the crossing, fortune appeared to favor the Americans. Carefully, the Marbleheaders dipped their cloth-coated oars into the murky, cold waters of the East River. The tide and the

---

* In October 1779, the New York Act of Attainder declared that John Rapalje and fifty-eight other people were, "*Ipso Facto*, convicted and attainted" of being enemies of the state. It further reported that the state had the right to seize their property and execute Rapalje and the others named in the act. Rapalje fled to England, taking with him the town records, much to the chagrin of Brooklyn's residents. He lived in England until his death.

winds collaborated to push the boats swiftly across the waterway, and over the next two hours, Glover and his men made multiple crossings.

Then the tide shifted, and their luck turned.

With every stroke of their oars, the Marbleheaders now fought against Mother Nature, who seemed hell-bent on sending the Americans downriver and into the clutches of the Royal Navy. "About nine, the tide of ebb made, and the wind blew strong at north-east, which adding to the rapidity of the tide, rendered it impossible to effect the retreat in the course of the night, with only that number of row boats which they could command, and the state of the wind and tide put it out of the power of Colonel Glover's men to make any use of the sail boats."[13] For the wind-powered sloops, the combination of wind and tide proved insurmountable. Despite the best efforts of the expert seamen, the Marbleheaders nearly lost control of their vessels on their return trip across the river.

The weather and swirling river placed the evacuation in immediate peril. Glover's men could not possibly deliver everyone across before morning using only the rowed boats. General McDougall sent Colonel William Grayson, one of Washington's aides-de-camp, to find the commander in chief and apprise him of "their embarrassed situation." McDougall "gave it as his opinion that a retreat was impracticable that night."[14]

Fortuitously, Grayson could not find Washington, so McDougall proceeded with the retreat. Before midnight, the fickle winds shifted again, making it possible to return the sloops to service. "But about eleven the wind died away, and soon after sprung up at south-west, and blew fresh, which rendered the sail boats of use, and at the same time made the passage from the island to the city, direct, easy and expeditious."[15] Once again, a series of the smallest details tipped favorably toward the Americans. Had Rapalje's servant spoken clear English or encountered British soldiers rather than the German-speaking Hessians first, had Grayson found Washington, or had the wind not shifted a second time, history could have turned out far differently.

Despite the miraculous wind shift, however, the Americans had lost precious time. Dawn was coming and with it the British Army.

At the embarkation point, chaos ensued. The troops understood the necessity of returning to New York if they wanted to survive, and they rushed to get into the boats when their turns came. The Americans loaded the boats so full that "many were but about 3 inches out of the water."[16] One of the men who made the crossing shortly after midnight later said that he did not know whether "his whole Regiment went over together or his whole company, for such was the hurry, paddling, and confusion that every man threw himself on board the boats at every chance he could get."[17]

The sight of the men fighting for a place on the boats enraged Washington. Displaying his enormous strength, the commander in chief picked up the biggest rock he could find, stood near one of the vessels, and threatened to "sink it to hell"[18] unless the men who had pushed others aside got out of the boat. The show of force immediately restored order.

The Marblehead soldier-mariners worked through the night and accomplished an ostensibly impossible task, transporting most of the Continental Army—thousands of men—across the East River in just nine hours. One Marbleheader recalled making a breathtaking total of eleven trips across the mile-wide river. However, even this was not enough. When the first rays of dawn crept over the entrenchments, Americans were still manning fortifications. For those who remained in the trenches, including the Marylanders, the approach of daylight brought the chance of a renewed attack from the British—and certain death. But then a thick fog miraculously appeared and cloaked the rest of the escape. "As the dawn of the next day approached," Benjamin Tallmadge, one of the officers in the rearguard, later wrote, "those of us who remained in the trenches became very anxious for our own safety, and when the dawn appeared there were several regiments still on duty. At this time a very dense fog began to rise, and it seemed to settle in a peculiar manner over both encampments. I recollect this peculiar providential occurrence perfectly well; and so very dense was the atmosphere that I could scarcely discern a man a six yards' distance."[19]

One of the soldiers who made the crossing in the early morning recalled that the water, which had been so turbulent the night before, was smooth as the fog rose with the dawn. The deus ex machina fog at exactly the right time and place proved crucial to saving the United States. Gordon recounted, "Providence further interposed in favor of the retreating army, by sending a thick fog about two o'clock in the 'morning which hung over Long-Island, while on New-York side it was clear. . . . The fog and wind continued to favor the retreat, till the whole army, [more than] 9,000 in number, with all the field artillery, such heavy ordnance as was of most value, ammunition, provision, cattle, horses, cars &c., were safe over."[20]

Among the last to cross the river was the commander in chief himself. Washington's Guard, led by Marbleheader Major Caleb Gibbs, remained behind with the commander in chief as he managed the embarkation. Washington's leadership proved as vital to the operation as the miraculous fog, the shift in the wind, the skill of the Marbleheader soldier-mariners, and all the other variables that combined to save the American army that day. Disregarding the concern of his officers for his own personal safety, the general stayed behind until the first rays of dawn at 6:00 a.m. to oversee the retreat and encourage the men. Major Benjamin Tallmadge recalled, "It was one of the most anxious, busy nights that I ever recollect, and being the third in which hardly any of us have closed our eyes to sleep, we were all greatly fatigued."[21]

British troops did not discover the evacuation until nearly everyone was safely away. "In about half an hour after the lines were finally abandoned, the fog cleared off and the British were seen taking possession of the American works. Four boats were on the river, three half way over, full of troops; the fourth, within reach of the enemy's fire upon the shore, was compelled to return; she had only three men in her who had tarried behind to plunder. . . . The retreat was effected in less than thirteen hours, a great part of which time it rained hard."[22]

Many Americans of the time saw the hand of God in the perfect timing and execution of the retreat. "Had it not been for the providential shifting of the wind, not more than half the army could possibly have crossed, and the remainder, with a number of general officers, and all the heavy ordnance at least, must inevitably have fallen into the enemy's hand. Had it not been also for that heavenly messenger, the fog, to cover the first desertion of the lines, and the several proceedings of the Americans after day-break, they must have sustained considerable losses. The fog resembled a thick snarled mist, so that you could see but a little way before you. It was very unusual also to have a fog at that time of the year. My informer, a citizen of New-York, could not recollect his having known any at that season, within the space of twenty or thirty years. Governor's-Island, on which were two regiments, is evacuated likewise, with the loss of only one man's arm, by a cannon shot from the ships."[23]

They could have added to that list of remarkable circumstances that made the famous crossing possible the indispensable Marblehead men. As one historian later observed, "This event, one of the most remarkable in the war, did much toward establishing the fame of Washington and confidence in his ability as a military leader. It would, however, have been impossible but for the skill and activity of Glover and his Marblehead Regiment."[24]

Glover's waterborne retreat revealed the added flexibility that his amphibious capabilities contributed to Washington's army. In this case, it saved them from destruction or annihilation, but on later occasions, it would allow them to put an enormous force in a key place using waterways as avenues of approach. Washington's muster-master general, the plucky Irishman, and participant in the evacuation, Stephen Moylan, summed up the crossing: "Perhaps there does not occur in History a Sadder retreat, so well Concerted, so well-executed, then was made from that Island."[25]

CHAPTER 31

KIPS BAY

September 1776, Washington's headquarters, Manhattan

A ghost walked through the door of Washington's headquarters: Captain Sion Martindale. After a trial in London where he betrayed his crew and offered them into service with the Royal Navy, he and the officers were returned to America with the promise of freedom. In June 1776, the British brought back the captain along with many of the officers from his captured ship, *Washington*, which had been seized without a shot fired in December 1775. However, upon arrival at Halifax, Martindale and his fellow officers were incarcerated and "treated in the most rascally manner"[1] for five weeks before they joined an escape effort. Six of the fourteen escapees were recaptured, but Martindale and four officers from *Washington* made it safely to Maine. From there, the oily captain moved down the Eastern Seaboard on foot, gathering endorsements and spinning phony tales of his exploits that were printed in local newspapers and recounted in pulpits along the way.

After surviving the Battle of Brooklyn and retreating across the East River, he was finally admitted into General Washington's headquarters, where Martindale's appeal for his back pay met its appropriate end. "Only God or the Continental Congress could do that,"[2] the general informed Martindale, elegantly sidestepping the wayward captain's incorrigible behavior.*

---

* Martindale was later recaptured by the British while in Rhode Island around May 1778. He escaped and later captained a privateer in 1780 and eventually left the war.

*   *   *

After the Americans successfully evacuated Brooklyn, both sides paused to consider their options. Washington ordered the withdrawal of the army from lower Manhattan to stronger positions near Harlem. He also made a temporary leadership change. On September 4, Washington ordered, "Col. Glover is to be considered as Commandant of his Brigade, and to be obeyed accordingly."[3] That put John Glover in charge of the 14th as well as the 3rd, 13th, and 26th Continental Regiments, with the 26th being commanded by Loammi Baldwin, whom the Marbleheaders had fought side by side with at Lexington and Menotomy.

Washington reconsidered his strategy. British naval superiority provided the enemy with the ability to surround Manhattan and cut off the Americans' communications and supply lines with the mainland. That made evacuation—and perhaps burning the city—a possibility, and perhaps even the best option, but political considerations made that unpalatable. Washington knew that withdrawal would make the recapture of Manhattan without a massive naval force that could defeat the Royal Navy practically impossible.

Allowing the buildings to remain intact would have left housing and wharves for the British to employ in their war efforts. But New York was the second-largest city in the colonies at the time, and leaving thousands of Americans without homes would not bolster support for the Patriot cause. Abandoning New York, with its high Loyalist population, would have a high political cost. In a time when hearts and minds influenced political will, evacuating New York would push its inhabitants into the arms of the British and create a pool of recruits for Loyalist provincial units. Washington was inclined to side with those who favored setting New York on fire and leaving. "Had I been left to the dictates of my own judgment, New York should have been laid in ashes," he wrote a month later.[4] However, the majority overruled him. They would remain in New York for the time being.

General William Howe and his brother, Admiral "Black Dick" Howe, again sent the Continental Congress an invitation to meet and discuss the cessation of hostilities. Both Howe brothers had some sympathy for the colonists' position and had argued against the Intolerable Acts in Parliament. Despite being in charge of the military operations aimed at quelling the Revolution, they hoped to solve the problem diplomatically and bring the American colony back into the fold of the British Empire. As a gesture of good faith, the British released Major General John Sullivan, one of the ringleaders of the raid at Fort William and Mary, whom they had captured during the Battle of Brooklyn, to carry the message to Congress. However, a diplomatic solution could only be effected with an overwhelmingly decisive defeat of the bulk of Washington's army, a principle that General Henry Clinton understood but the Howe brothers did not appreciate. Members of the Continental Congress were far less inclined to make peace and considered Sullivan's release insulting. In a letter, John Adams noted that the British had nearly caught the Americans like birds in a net. "But the most insolent thing of all is, sending one of those very pigeons as a flutterer to Philadelphia, in order to decoy the great flock of all."[5] While many of the Founding Fathers would have preferred not to accept the invitation, the body eventually voted to send Adams, Benjamin Franklin, and Edward Rutledge to see what the Howes had to offer.

The resulting peace conference took place on September 11 in a Staten Island mansion that the British had been using as a barracks and left in a deplorable condition. The two sides met for three hours. By Adams's account, Lord Howe told the Patriot delegates "he had requested this Interview that he might satisfy himself, whether there was any probability that America would return to her Allegiance [to the Crown]."[6] The Howes very much wanted a diplomatic solution that would convince the Patriots to end their rebellion. But they had minimal authority with which to negotiate. The American delegation assured the brothers that Americans would never again consent to be ruled by the British. In Franklin's words, "Therefore, it was the Duty of every good Man, on both sides of the water, to promote Peace, and an Acknowledgment of American Independency, and Treaty of Friendship and Alliance, between the two Countries."[7]

Of course, the Howes could not approve independence for the colonies, so the entire conference accomplished nothing. Adams wrote, "The whole Affair of the Commission appears to me, as it ever did, to be a bubble, an Ambuscade, a mere insidious Maneuvre, calculated only to decoy and deceive:—And it is so gross, that they must have a wretched Opinion of our Generalship, to suppose that We can fall into it."[8]

Even before the conference, the Howe brothers had begun positioning their ships for the invasion, suggesting that they, too, probably had little hope that the meeting would result in a meaningful agreement. Two significant obstacles plagued the British as they tried to use military force on the Americans. First, they faced a chronic shortage of troops. Second, clearing and holding American territory proved problematic, which, in turn, hindered them from protecting the population and building political support for the Crown. They could have addressed both by seizing the opportunity to nurture loyal colonists by forming American Loyalist units and staffing them with Loyalist officers, a process the Crown was slow to roll out. Moreover, they generally did not treat the Loyalists on an equal footing with British regulars, which hampered morale. Instead, the radical American principles of liberty and freedom drew more colonists to the Patriot side. These novel, world-changing ideas and ideals, while radical at the time, fueled one of the greatest revolutions in history and would inspire and influence generations.

Washington girded for battle and urged his men to prepare for invasion. "The state of Ammunition and Arms should be a subject of constant attention to every officer and soldier. The General hopes the justice of the great Cause in which they are engaged, . . . the importance of defending their country, preserving the liberties and warding off the destruction . . . will inspire every man with firmness and resolution in Time of Action, which is now approaching."[9]

Four days after the peace conference, the British launched an assault on Manhattan via Kips Bay and the East River. Henry Clinton had implored the Howes to land near King's Bridge at the top of Manhattan. The navy considered a landing there risky because of the unpredictable tides near Hell Gate. However, if a landing at King's Bridge had been successful, the British would have severed the Americans' line of retreat from Manhattan, effectively trapping Washington's army. As had happened at Bunker Hill, the Howes overruled Clinton, possibly eliminating yet another way to end the war or at least effecting the withdrawal of the Americans from their strong defenses in Harlem. The unsuccessful Staten Island Peace Conference compelled Washington to change his strategy yet again. Upon receiving orders from Congress to stay in New York no longer than necessary, Washington began drawing up plans to retreat from the city. Washington assured Congress, "We are now taking every method in our power to remove the stores, in which we find almost insuperable difficulties. They are so great and so numerous, that I fear we shall not effect the whole before we meet with some interruption. . . . Our sick are extremely numerous, and we find their removal attended with the greatest difficulty. . . . However, nothing on my part, that humanity or policy can require, shall be wanting to make them comfortable, so far as the state of things will admit."[10]

Plans for that part of the evacuation again relied heavily on the skills of the Marbleheaders. Washington wanted the 14th Regiment to ferry the many ill and injured soldiers, as well as the military supplies, to Orangetown, New York, about twenty miles up the Hudson, where they would presumably be safe from the British. This was no small undertaking because as much as a quarter of the army may have been incapacitated, and they were once again having difficulty finding sufficient vessels for the operation.[11]

The mission did not go according to plan.* A contemporary historian related that the Marbleheaders successfully transported five hundred men to New Jersey on the night of September 13–14: "It was thought necessary to evacuate the city as fast as possible, and to remove the sick, the ordnance, stores, and provisions. Colonel Glover was employed in this service; he began upon it about nine at night. By sun rise the next morning, his brigade had got safe over the Jerseys, the sick in and about

---

* Some historians dispute whether the wounded were actually moved; the author believes they were.

the city amounting to five hundred."[12] But before they could move the baggage, Glover received orders to march at once to King's Bridge above Harlem at the top of Manhattan. Though tired from the nighttime operation, they obeyed, making the fifteen-mile trek and arriving on the morning of September 15. "The poor lads had just unslung their packs, when up drives an express with an account that the enemy were landing: on which they marched back without any kind of refreshment, joined five other brigades, about seven thousand, and formed on Harlem plains."[13]

Before noon on September 15, British ships announced their arrival in Kips Bay with tremendous broadsides from their cannons, providing cover for the Redcoats and Hessians arriving in the flat-bottomed boats that served as the landing craft of the day. Admiral Howe's secretary, Ambrose Serle, wrote in his diary, "So terrible and so incessant a roar of guns few even in the army and navy had ever heard before."[14] On the receiving end of the thunderous bombardment, one Connecticut soldier, Joseph Plumb Martin, later wrote that he "made a frog's leap for the ditch and lay as still as I possibly could, and began to consider which part of my carcass would go first."[15]

Hearing the thundering cannon fire, Washington rushed back to the front lines, but what he found horrified him. "To my great surprize and Mortification I found the Troops that had been posted in the Lines retreating with the utmost precipitation and those ordered to support them, Parson's & Fellows's Brigades, flying in every direction and in the greatest confusion, notwithstanding the exertions of their Generals to form them. I used every means in my power to rally and get them into some order but my attempts were fruitless and ineffectual, and on the appearance of a small party of the Enemy, not more than Sixty or Seventy, their disorder increased and they ran away in the greatest confusion without firing a Single Shot,"[16] Washington wrote John Hancock the next day. Many Americans had abandoned all pretense of military discipline and run for their lives. In retrospect, it was probably foolhardy for Washington to make a stand under the mighty shore bombardment of the Royal Navy.

"Take the walls!" General Washington cried. "Take the cornfield!"[17]

The commander in chief's shouts fell on deaf ears as the Connecticut militia fled en masse from the onslaught of British and Hessian troops heading their way. Cannons on the Royal Navy ships fired grapeshot and "langrige" (a collection of rods, bolts, and other shrapnel, an antipersonnel munition designed to kill and maim) with such force that they seemed to go "quite across the island."[18] Desperate to encourage their men to fight, the officers resorted to physical violence. "Wretches, who, however strange it may appear, from the Brigadier General down to the Private Sentinel, were caned and whip'd by the Generals Washington Putnam & Miflin," recalled one officer, "but even this Indignity had no Weight as they could not be brought to stand one Shot."[19]

"Are these the men with whom I am to defend America?!" Washington shouted in exasperation.[20]

With enemy troops a mere eighty yards away, Washington froze as the American troops ran headlong from the battle. As Nathanael Greene vividly remembered, Washington became "so vexed at the infamous conduct of his troops that he sought death rather than life."[21] Terrified that the catatonic general would fall to the torrent of lead aimed directly at him, an aide pulled Washington off the field.

The militia continued to flee from the battle until they met a group of men who filled them with confidence: Colonel Glover and the Marblehead soldier-mariners. Donning a Scottish broadsword and a brace of silver pistols, Glover led his men in battle and stemmed the flood of retreating troops. "The Americans that had fled upon the approach of the enemy, stopped not till they were met by Col. Glover's and the five other [units]. The forces being joined, the whole marched forward and took post on some heights where they remained,"[22] one historian explained. Fortuitously, it was at this moment that Glover's Brigade arrived on the scene. Another witness recorded, "The officers of Colonel Glover's regiment, one of the best corps in the service, and who were indeed gentlemen, immediately obliged the fugitive officers and soldiers, equally, to turn

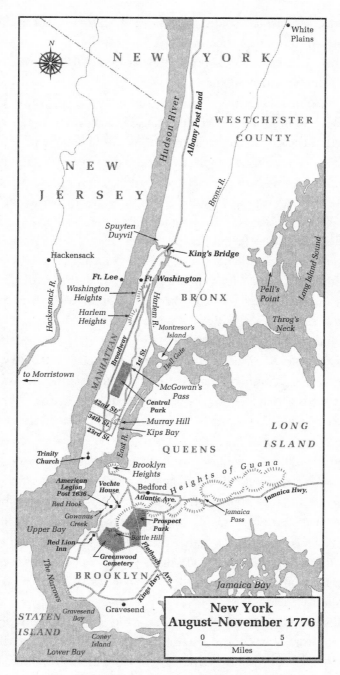

"HudVal—New York August–November 1776"

into the ranks with the soldiers of Glover's regiment, and obliged the trembling wretches to march back to the ground they had quitted."[23]

With most of them clad in their distinctive fishers' trousers, the multiethnic Marblehead men charged into the vortex of battle. In his letter to John Hancock, he expressed his diminishing faith in his soldiers. "I should hope the Enemy would meet with a defeat in case of an Attack, If the Generality of our Troops would behave with tolerable bravery," he wrote. "But experience to my extreme affliction has convinced me that this is rather to be wished for than expected; However I trust, that there are many who will act like men, and show themselves worthy of the blessings of Freedom."[24] The conduct of some soldiers off the field of battle left much to be desired as well. New York sergeant Peter Richards of the general's own Life Guard was court-martialed shortly after the battle for "abusing and striking Captain Gibbs and sentenced to be reduced to the ranks and whipped thirty-nine lashes."[25]

Glover echoed Washington's frustration with the lack of seasoned officers and soldiers in the Continental Army in a letter to his brother: "We have few old Regi[ments] if detach by themselves I believe would do Honour to there Country, but we are Oblige[d] to intermix them with the raw troops which is by far the Gratest part of the army. Consiquintly Confuse the whole."[26] Glover used the retreat from Manhattan as a prime example: "This we saw verefide on the 15th, the day we evacuated New York and happy for us we began the retreat so timely as we did otherwise the whole that were in the City must have been cut off the enemy having landed 18,000 men on that day on the East Side about four miles from the City Coverd by ten Sail of men of war & opesitt to them on the North river Came up three Large Ships the whole kept up a constant cannonading with grape shot & langrige quite a crost the island. I lost two men in the retreat, Wormsted Trefrey of Marblehead and Benjamin Rawden of Lynn."[27]

Glover departed from this talk of the retreat to advise his brother to solicit help from now-congressman Elbridge Gerry regarding the familiar story of lack of powder. "Mr. Gerry has it in his power to do more for you than any one Else,"[28] he wrote to Jonathan. Glover expected Gerry to use his position in Congress to help the Marbleheaders. Elected to Congress, Gerry served two terms from February 1776 to 1780 and also sat on the powerful Marine Committee, where he continued to foster his ideas on America's navy.

At the same time as the British invaded Manhattan, the American army attempted to attack strategically located Montresor's Island, now known as Randall's Island, sandwiched between the East River and the Harlem River east of Manhattan. Based on intelligence from two defecting sailors who swam away from the British ship *Bruno* toward American lines, the island was sparsely defended but housed many British officers and much baggage and supplies. Glover detailed the combat on the island when the British greeted the attacking boats with withering fire as they landed at dawn on September 16: "They were met by the enemy at the water's edge before they landed with the party in his [Jackson's] boat, gave them battle and compelled them to retreat, called to the other boats to push and land, but the scoundrels, coward-like, retreated back and left him and his party to fall a sacrifice. The enemy seeing this, 150 of them rushed out of the woods and attacked them at thirty yards distance. Jackson with his little party nobly defended the ground until every man but eight was killed on the spot, and himself wounded, before he ordered a retreat. Major Hendly carrying off Col. Jackson was shot dead as he was putting him into a boat, and not a single man of the eight but what was wounded."[29] The other officers involved in the raid were later tried for their cowardice, but the sentencing wasn't severe enough to satisfy Washington or Glover.

Glover vented his frustration in a letter to his family: "In Short if Some example is not made of such Raskely Conduct, there will be no incouragement for men of Spirit to Exert themselves. As the Case now is they will all ways fall a Sacrifice wile Such Low Lives Scoundrils that have Neither Honour nor the Good of their Country at heart, will Sculk behind and Get off Clear."[30]

Knowing that the central part of Manhattan was lost, Washington ordered his men to retreat, but they were far from out of danger.

At that point, General Howe could have badly damaged Washington's army if he had pursued the Americans relentlessly. But in one of the stranger episodes of the Revolution, he decided to stop for tea and cake at a mansion then called Iclenberg and later rechristened Murray Hill. According to one historian, "The British Generals [were] wasting their time at the house of Mr. Robert Murray, a Quaker, (where Mrs. Murray, a good and true friend to the American cause, entertained them civilly with cakes and wine) and their army being consequently inactive."[31] Some have suggested that Howe had a romantic interest in Mrs. Murray, which seems far-fetched, given that she was a mother of twelve in her fifties. Far more likely is the possibility that Howe was still hesitant to risk his men unnecessarily and wanted to wait for the rest of his troops to disembark before pressing forward.

In any event, the delay gave the bulk of Washington's troops the time they needed to evacuate and regroup on the high ground of Harlem Heights. The following day, Washington turned once again to Knowlton's Rangers, whose commander had performed so well alongside the Marbleheaders at the Battle of Bunker Hill. Knowlton and about 150 of his men infiltrated the British lines, fired on the pickets, and then retreated behind a stone wall. The British followed in hot pursuit, trailing behind the Rangers by only about five minutes.

Certain of victory against the men who had fled so cravenly just a day before, the British light infantry blew bugle horns as if they were taking part in a fox chase and charged straight into the teeth of the American defenses. Sensing an opportunity, Washington sent Knowlton's Rangers and a group of riflemen down through a gully to circle behind the light infantry. The attack didn't go quite as planned. The Rangers fired too early, hitting the British in the flank instead of the rear. As the melee evolved, the Redcoats managed to kill Knowlton. Anticipating an easy victory, the light infantry charged the Americans; however, they advanced too quickly and found themselves nearly enveloped. The Americans were victorious at the Battle of Harlem Heights, forcing the British to retreat. "[From] the appearance of blood in every place where they made their Stand and on the fences they passed, we have reason to believe they had a good many killed and wounded," Washington wrote in a letter.[32] While the battle was small, it had an important psychological effect on both the Americans and the British after the recent string of defeats. It was one of the first decisive defeats of British regulars by Continental forces.

Washington's army pursued the enemy for a few hours, but then the general ordered them to retreat behind their defenses. On September 20, muster rolls for the 14th Continental revealed 279 effective men for duty, with 126 men still being back in Beverly in Washington's Navy. The regiment had eight companies, and regimental surgeon Nathaniel Bond now led the 4th Company.[33]

For several days, the Americans worked to improve the fortifications atop the high ground while the British concocted battle plans and enjoyed the delights of the many fine houses in New York City. That all came to an end the night of September 20–21. Just before midnight, a fire broke out in a tavern called Fighting Cocks on the southern tip of Manhattan. The inferno soon raged out of control. Terrified residents fled for their lives. "It is almost impossible to conceive a scene of more horror and distress," wrote one eyewitness. "The sick, the aged, the women, and children, half-naked, were seen going they knew not where, and taking refuge in houses which were at a distance from the fire, but from whence they were in several instances driven a second and even a third time."[34] The night erupted in a cacophony of sounds: the boom of houses falling, the ratting of army wagons sent in to fight the fire, the terrified screams of women and children, and throughout it all, the ceaseless crackle of the flames.

When the hellish night was over, one-quarter of the houses in the city had been destroyed. Loyalists and the British blamed the fire on the rebels. Still, they never found enough evidence of arson to bring anyone to trial, despite capturing many men they suspected of arson. Washington called the fire an accident, but noted that it had helped his cause, writing to his brother, "Providence, or some good honest fellow, has done more for us than we were disposed to do for ourselves."[35]

* * *

September 21, 1776, was also notable for another reason besides the fire: it was the day the Patriots lost one of their most famous—yet unsuccessful—intelligence agents. While the job of spying for one's country seems fairly glamorous today, in the eighteenth century, most men of honor considered it ignoble and not worthy of a gentleman. Before the Battle of Harlem Heights, Lieutenant Colonel Thomas Knowlton asked his men for volunteers for a clandestine mission, and one man replied, "I'm willing to fight the British and, if need be, die a soldier's death in battle, but as for going among them in disguise and being taken and hung up like a dog, I'll not do it."[36] However, Knowlton found a willing volunteer in Nathan Hale. The twenty-one-year-old captain with blond hair and blue eyes was a Yale graduate who thirsted for action. He would pose as a Loyalist schoolmaster and attempt to infiltrate the British forces. The goal was to obtain warning of any impending attack.

While he was enthusiastic about his mission and a fervent Patriot, Hale seems to have been ill prepared for intelligence duty. He had no real training, no codebook, no contacts, and possibly not even any money for travel. His sole preparation seems to have been a few personal meetings with Washington, during which he received instructions to travel first to Connecticut and then to Brooklyn, where the British forces were stationed. Unfortunately, Hale did not arrive in Connecticut until September 15, the very day that Howe's men were landing in Kips Bay. Unaware of the situation, Hale continued with his now-pointless mission, traveling on to Brooklyn. On September 21, the British captured him.

No one knows for sure how he was captured, but a manuscript that surfaced, written by a Loyalist Connecticut shopkeeper named Consider Tiffany, seems to reveal what happened to Hale. According to Tiffany's account, Colonel Robert Rogers began to suspect Hale was a spy almost immediately. Born in Massachusetts to Irish parents, Rogers served in the British Army and led Rogers's Rangers during the French and Indian War, developing "Rules of Ranging." A notorious debtor with a checkered past, Rogers would lead one of the most successful ranging forces, a Loyalist unit called the Queen's Rangers, during the Revolutionary War. Rogers posed as a Patriot, telling Hale that he himself was a spy for the Continental Army. "This intrigue, not being suspected by the Capt, made him believe that he had found a good friend, and one that could be trusted with the secrecy of the business he was engaged in; and after the Colonel's drinking a health to the Congress: informs Rogers of the business and intent," wrote Tiffany. Rogers invited Hale to dinner, where British soldiers seized him. "But before he was carried far, several persons knew him and called him by name; upon this he was hanged as a spy, some say, without being brought before a court-martial."[37] It was at that point that the hapless spy might have uttered the words that have made him famous: "I only regret that I have but one life to lose for my country."[38]

CHAPTER 32

THE FORGOTTEN BATTLES THAT SAVED WASHINGTON'S ARMY

October 12, 1776, Throgs Neck, New York

Crouching behind a woodpile, Colonel Edward Hand gazed in astonishment at the sea of Redcoats in front of him. The Irish immigrant was a physician and a former surgeon's mate in the British Army, but he had resigned his appointment in 1774, immediately before the commencement of the Revolution. Married to an American, Hand lived in a part of Pennsylvania that was a hotbed of political unrest, and like many of the principal Patriots, he was a Freemason. Even though he and the twenty-five men with him were facing what would eventually amount to more than four thousand of the enemy, Hand maintained his composure, steadying his expert riflemen crowded around him. Methodically, they went through the tedious process of loading and firing their rifles, timing their shots so that someone was always ready to fire on the British troops as they attempted to cross the narrow causeway spanning the marsh in front of them. Small puffs of smoke rose in the air, and the acrid smell of gunpowder infiltrated his nostrils while rifles cracked on either side of him.

Taking a scrap of parchment from his pocket, Hand dashed off a note requesting reinforcements and tasked a messenger with delivering it to Washington. He then picked up his own weapon and joined his men in their ceaseless efforts to fend off the enemy.

In the hopes of trapping the Continental Army in Manhattan, Lord William Howe had transported a portion of his troops by sea to

Throgs Point, also known as Throgs Neck, Frog's Point, and Throck's Point, located in the Bronx, under the cover of dense morning fog. After the Battle of Harlem Heights, Washington and Howe carefully deliberated their next moves. The Americans remained in their fortified position on the plateau, where Fort Washington provided cover to the west. Believing that Howe might attempt to flank his army rather than undertake another frontal assault on the high ground, Washington sent small groups of men to defend potential landing sites on Long Island Sound. He also detached thousands of men to King's Bridge, an essential crossing point over the Harlem River for any flanking force, and Washington sent another portion of the army across the Hudson River to New Jersey. That left him with roughly ten thousand men in and around Fort Washington.

Still loath to expose his forces to any unnecessary risk, Howe had decided that the flanking move was the far better option. He chose to take advantage of his naval superiority by loading his army onto ships and transporting them up the Long Island Sound by sea. From there, they could swing around to King's Bridge and potentially bottle up the Americans. To that end, he attempted the landing at Throgs Neck.

Relying on what proved to be faulty intelligence, Howe believed the point to be a peninsula, but in actuality, high tide made it more like an island. Swampy marshland surrounded the narrowest part of the neck. To step foot on the mainland, his troops had to cross either a single bridge or a narrow strip of land wide enough for only one or two men at a time.

One British officer recalled the landing: "This morning before day break our Troops from New York Island embark'd on board flat Boats and other Craft in the East River opposite the South End of Black-well's Island and lay at an Anchor till daybreak went. We went with a very strong tide and thick fog through Hell gates towards the Sound (An Artillery Boat with Guns and men overset some [distance], a very horrid place to pass). We continued to row Eastward and Landed on Frog's Neck in West Chester about 10 o'clock without any Opposition (One Frigate covered the Landing)."[1]

The British landed near the estate of James and Charity Ferris, who owned a mansion at the tip of the peninsula. James had fought for the Patriots, and the British captured him and sent him to the Sugar House Prison in New York, where he would spend the next five years. His wife, Charity, also strongly supported the cause of the Revolution, and this intrepid, unsung heroine would play a minor role in the battle.

Before invading, the British ships commenced naval gunfire support against Throgs Neck. According to legend, Mrs. Ferris bravely walked back and forth on her veranda during the attack until the Royal Navy, perhaps not wanting to kill a civilian woman, ceased fire. More than likely, the Royal Navy stopped because they had completed their preparatory cannonade. After disembarking, the Redcoat officers occupied the Ferris mansion,* and although she secretly spirited her daughters out of harm's way by sending them with an enslaved servant who rowed them across the sound by night, she remained behind to cook for the men—and, according to legend, gather intelligence. She instructed her young servant to memorize every word he heard the officers utter as he waited on their table or ran into town on errands for them. He faithfully repeated all he heard to Mrs. Ferris, who then immediately sent the information on to Washington.

After scrambling out of their eighteenth-century versions of landing craft, the British moved inland. "We march'd immediately forward for about three miles until we came to a small Bridge and Mill dam over West Chester Creek where a small party of Rebels appeared to oppose us and we halted," a British officer recorded in his diary.[2]

---

* According to Charles E. Crowell's *Partial Genealogy of the Ferris Family*, "The family (James Ferris and family) happened to be at breakfast on the morning of the 12th of October, 1776, when a gun from the British flagship announced the disembarkation of the British troops on Throckmorton's or Throg's Neck. . . . On the next day General Lord Howe, supposing that he had been deceived by his guides and landed upon an island, summoned them before a board of officers. As they entered, he struck the table violently with his sword and demanded in a threatening manner how they could dare to deceive him. After a proper explanation had been made, he declared he would hang every one of them unless he was given safe passage."

Colonel Hand and his small detachment of Pennsylvania riflemen had been stationed on the point to guard against such an attempt by the British, but they never imagined that the two dozen of them would need to hold off an army. As soon as the Continentals realized British intentions, they quickly tore up the wooden planks on the bridge, leaving only the causeway to connect the point to the Bronx. A woodpile near the far end of the causeway was ideally positioned to provide cover, and Hand and his men took full advantage of it. The marksmen picked off the British soldiers one by one as they attempted to cross. Officers, in particular, remained in the riflemen's sights.

Miraculously, Hand and his crack riflemen managed to check Henry Clinton's forces long enough for reinforcements. Later that day, 1,800 Massachusetts and New York Continentals arrived, bringing with them two cannon. Those additional Americans included the Marbleheaders, as several accounts relate.

Marching with the 14th Regiment was Plymouth native Marston Watson, who had earlier sailed in Washington's Navy with Samuel Tucker. He had been in the thick of the fighting since the Battle of Brooklyn and was "engaged . . . [at] Frogs Neck."[3] Teen soldier Jabez Tarr also faced "the enemy [who] landed at Frog's Neck . . . a skirmish there."[4]

On October 12, 1776, the 14th Regiment consisted of eight companies led by Captains William Courtis, James Grant, John Glover Jr., Nathaniel Bond, Joseph Swasey, William R. Lee, Moses Brown, and Gilbert Warner Speakman. Of the 419 men on the muster rolls for that day, records show that, remarkably, only one soldier had deserted.[5] Desertions plagued the Continental Army, and many units remained understrength. The Marblehead Regiment had one of the lowest rates of desertion of any regiment in the Continental Army due to the number of familial ties and the close-knit nature of the Marblehead community.[6]

According to a British account, the Americans hastily constructed breastworks on the spot. "They continued to Extend these Works, also began a new line about one mile to their left opposite to a place where the Creek and Marsh were, sometimes fordable. They fired several

Cannon Shot and wounded some of our men."[7] Over the next six days, Clinton made several attempts to traverse the bottleneck; however, the Patriots stymied him every time. The Americans halted an amphibious landing—an exceptionally rare occurrence in history. On October 12, another American brigade arrived, and Howe decided to try a different tack. Despite his failure at Throgs Neck, he did not give up on his plan. Howe loaded his men back onto their vessels and headed roughly five miles up Long Island Sound to Pell's Point, from where he could travel down the Eastchester Road to King's Bridge and trap Washington's army. Yet, once again, they would encounter John Glover's brigade.

As dawn broke on October 18, Colonel John Glover climbed a small rise. Upon reaching the summit, he lifted his spyglass to his eye to scan the horizon; what he saw exceeded his worst nightmares. By his own account, he "discovered a number of ships in the Sound underway; in a short time saw the boats, upwards of two hundred sail, all manned and formed in four grand divisions."[8] They were landing at Pell's Point, a peninsula on the Long Island Sound.

Skirmishers, including militiaman Abel De Veau, engaged the British shortly after they disembarked. According to family history, De Veau "lay behind the large rock standing on the City Island road and fired upon the British Army. The British followed them up and they retreated, keeping up the fire along Pelham Lane, and lost two men before they got to Prospect Hill."*[9]

Meanwhile, Glover immediately sent a message to General Lee telling him about the ships he had seen. Then, without waiting for orders, he formed up his brigade to march toward the point and oppose

---

* Historians have debated the location of the start of the Battle of Pelham Bay for decades. While early accounts place the beginning of the battle near the large boulder known as Glover's Rock, some modern researchers believe that the fight could not possibly have started there. The De Veau family history offers a plausible explanation for the discrepancy—a party of militia engaged the British near the rock before falling back and joining with Glover's men.

the British and Hessians. The brigade included the 3rd, 13th, 14th, and 26th Continental Regiments from Massachusetts. By the time Glover arrived, the British had marched a mile and a half inland and seized the high ground. "The enemy had the advantage of us," Glover wrote, "being posted on an eminence which commanded the ground we had to march over."[10]

At this point, Glover likely joined up with Captain De Veau's militia, as the family history says that De Veau fell in with another unit and "made a gallant defense" until the Redcoats' superior numbers forced them to retreat.[11] By his own account, Glover detailed forty men to hold off an advance party of British soldiers while he quickly arranged his four regiments. He placed the 14th, under the command of Captain William Courtis[12] (Gabriel Johonnot had been sick, and Major William R. Lee was the brigade major), in the rear with their three field pieces, which could not traverse the rocky ground, and he positioned the other three regiments in successive lines. He then rode forward to lead his men in battle. As he neared the front lines, his mind churned with second guesses and thoughts of what might go wrong. He later recounted,

> Oh! the anxiety of mind I was then in for the fate of the day,—
> the lives of seven hundred and fifty men immediately at hazard,
> and under God their preservation entirely depended on their
> being well disposed of; besides this, my country, my honour,
> my own life, and every thing that was dear, appeared at that
> critical moment to be at stake—I would have given a thousand
> worlds to have had General Lee, or some other experienced
> officer present, to direct, or at least approve of what I had done—
> looked around, but could see none, they all being three miles
> from me, and the action came on so sudden it was out of their
> power to be with me.[13]

Despite his anxiety and the haste demanded by the situation, Glover hatched an ingenious battle plan. Stone fences interspersed with boulders and rocky outcroppings lined Split Rock Road, which would force the roughly four thousand enemy soldiers, three-quarters of them battle-hardened Hessian allies, to stick to the roadway and advance in a column.* By placing his men behind the stone fences, he set up a defense in depth to inflict as many casualties as possible despite being outnumbered approximately five to one. This was a novel form of warfare for the time and demonstrated the evolving nature of the American way of war.

The American advance guard approached within fifty yards of the enemy. They exchanged five rounds with the Redcoats and Hessians and then fell back on Glover's orders, having inflicted four casualties. A British officer recalled, "After moving on about a mile towards East Chester, I was ordered by the General to the top of a rising ground in front with the Advance Guard of the light infantry to reconnoitre, but we were immediately fired upon from behind trees and heaps of Stones where the Rebels lay concealed, and from which they were very soon forced to retire."[14]

"Huzzah!" Believing they had the Americans on the run, the British "gave a shout and advanced."[15] Checking their advance, Glover had positioned Colonel Joseph Read's 13th Continental Regiment, from Cambridge, Massachusetts, behind a stone wall. When the Redcoats were within thirty yards, the Americans suddenly rose up as one, rested their weapons on the stout wall, and fired on the enemy with their motley assortment of muskets. With the enemy so near and with the fence providing a convenient resting place for their weapons, many of the American bullets found their mark, and dozens of Redcoats and Hessians dropped. At the vanguard of the British attack, the Americans faced the elite light infantry. In the thick haze of smoke, Read's men likely expected an order for a bayonet charge, but none came.[16] Astonished, the remaining British troops turned tail and ran, choosing to wait for the main body of the force to approach. In a letter home, one of the Americans recounted, "The enemy came very near the wall, and

* Today, a portion of the battlefield runs through the early holes of the Split Rock Golf Course. You can still see the remains of the stone fences and the rocks on the course.

received a general fire from our troops, which broke their advanced party entirely, so that they ran back to the main body, formed, and came on again in large numbers, keeping up a heavy fire with field-pieces on the walls and men. They advanced now very near, and received a second fire, which entirely routed them again, and then retreated in a narrow lane by a wall, in a confused, huddled manner, near which were posted a large body of Riflemen and some companies of Musketmen, who at this favourite moment poured in upon them a most heavy fire once or twice before they could get out of the way; and they were seen to fall in great numbers."[17]

When the bulk of the force arrived, the British charged the American position, and again, Read's regiment rose from their hiding places and fired as one. This time the disciplined Redcoats and Hessians returned fire. For about twenty minutes the two groups of men continued "firing at will" while British artillery lobbed cannonballs at the Americans sheltered by the stone wall.[18] After exchanging seven rounds, Read's regiment retreated. Partially sheltered by the fences, they were able to withdraw behind the point, where more of their comrades lay in wait on the other side of the road.

Repeating their earlier performance, the British shouted and pressed forward, but the 3rd Continental Regiment, a Massachusetts Bay unit led by Colonel William Shepard, was waiting behind another stone wall on the opposite side of the road. Shepard, a veteran of the French and Indian War, had his men stagger their fire so that they could keep a constant stream of lead turned on the enemy. "He rose up and fired by grand divisions by which he kept by a constant fire, and maintained his post until he exchanged seventeen rounds with them, and caused them to retreat several times."[19] One of the mortally wounded was British captain and light infantry officer William Glanville Evelyn. Prepared for death, he wrote in his will, "As all Men who have taken upon them the profession of Arms, hold their Lives by a more precarious tenure than any other Body of People; and as the fatal experience of this Day shews us how particularly it is the case of those who are engaged in war, even with the most despicable Enemy."[20]

In the fierce fighting, the British retreated several times, once "so far that a soldier of Colonel Shepard's leaped over the wall and took a hat and canteen off of a Captain that lay dead on the ground they retreated from."[21]

Shepard himself was wounded in the encounter, taking a bullet to the neck. According to nineteenth-century historian John Lockwood, "While the surgeons were probing for the ball his consciousness returned. 'Bring me a canteen,' he said. Finding that he could drink, and that the organs of his throat were not severed, he said to the surgeon: 'It is all right, doctor, stick on a plaster and tie on my cravat, for I am out again.'"[22]

Eventually, the enemy's overwhelming numbers forced Glover's men to retreat. Again, the Continentals repeated the same maneuver with the forward troops retreating behind Colonel Loammi Baldwin's 26th Continental Regiment, which was once again hiding behind a stone fence and boulders that lined the sides of the road. But this time, the maneuver was not as successful, and the British forced the Patriots to give up ground much more quickly. Glover noted that with "the ground being much in their favour, and their heavy train of artillery, we could do but little before we retreated to the bottom of the hill."[23]

The Marbleheader then led his men through a small creek and up a hill to where he had left the 14th Regiment with the artillery. Having learned the lesson that it was unwise to pursue the retreating Americans, the British halted their advance. A cannonade ensued as the two sides took turns firing until nightfall, but the artillery battle resulted in very little damage.

Under the cover of darkness, Glover retreated another three miles and reflected, "After fighting all day without victuals or drink, laying as a picket all night, the heavens over us and the earth under us, which was all we had."[24] He had seen another body of troops approaching on his flank and needed to avoid being cut off. The men of the brigade, feeling emboldened by the success of Glover's tactics, left "with the greatest reluctance Imaginable though with as much good order and Regularity as ever they marched off a Publick Parade."[25]

Howe declined to pursue the Americans, who had done so much damage to his forces. The total number of British casualties is unknown, but they must have been substantial because Howe grossly overestimated the number of Continentals he had faced, believing them to be over ten times their actual number. In hindsight, it is easy to understand how Howe and Clinton could have estimated so poorly. One historian noted, "It is difficult to believe that four hundred Americans, familiar with the use of firearms, sheltered by ample defenses from which they could fire deliberately and with their guns rested on the tops, could have fired volley after volley into a large body of men, massed in a compacted column in a narrow roadway, without inflicted as extended damage as this."[26] The Americans lost only six men dead and thirteen wounded, including Shepard, whom Glover described as "a brave officer."[27]

Far more critical than the casualties they inflicted was the strategic advantage and time that Glover's men bought for Washington. While the Massachusetts men held off the enemy, Washington began moving the bulk of his forces north toward White Plains. Some historians have noted that Howe might have been able to stop the retreating Americans if he had pressed forward after the battle at Pell's Point. However, his fear of Glover's men kept him in place while the Americans escaped once again.

Major William Raymond Lee recorded General Lee's orders in his orderly book: "All the wounded to be immediately carried to Valentine's Hill, at the second Liberty Pole where Surgeons should repair to dress them—They are afterwards to be forwarded to Fort Washington."[28] Bond, with his training, would have tended to the wounded, but those transported to Fort Washington would ultimately be doomed.

The Patriot commanders understood the value of what Glover's Brigade had done for their cause. "The efficient manner in which Col. Glover executed the orders he had received was honorably noticed by General Lee and the Commander in Chief in the following General Orders."[29] Lee sent a message saying, "General Lee returns his warmest thanks to Colonel Glover and the brigade under his command, not only for their gallant behavior yesterday, but for their prudent, cool, orderly and soldier-like conduct in all respects. He assures these brave men that he shall omit no opportunity of showing his gratitude."[30] William Raymond Lee in his orderly book captured General Washington's additional words of praise: "The hurried Situation of the Gen. the two last days having prevented him from paying that attention Col. Glover and the Officers and Soldiers who were with him in the Skirmish on Friday last, their merit and good behavior deserved. He flatters himself that his thanks, though delayed be acceptable to them, as they are offerd with great Sincerity & Cordiality—at the same time he hopes that every other part of the Army will do their duty with equal Bravery & Zeal whenever calld upon, & neither danger nor difficulties nor Hardships will discourage Soldiers engaged in the cause of Liberty, & while we are contending for all that free men hold dear and Valuable."[31]

As the war progressed, the Marbleheaders were at the forefront of pioneering a new American way of war, and Pell's Point provided an example of this evolving style of combat. The reflex to adapt flourished from the beginning of the Revolution and remains evident to the present day. Tactically, the Americans tended to concentrate their firepower on a specific point on the battlefield where it had the greatest impact. They fought forward and developed defensive maneuvers, a defense in depth that wore down the enemy. They took advantage of the terrain and made the best possible use of the troops at their disposal. At the strategic level, the Americans used intelligence as a force multiplier, helping them position their units to the best advantage. In addition, the Marbleheaders and the rest of the Americans relied on speed and flexibility, combined with judicious risk-taking; they avoided needlessly sacrificing men's lives for operations that did not produce results.

The British Army had already mastered its style of combat when the war began. It had established rules for its soldiers to follow in battle—a European style of fighting. As the war progressed, it began to realize the need to revise those rules, and it also adapted. Both the Continental Army and the British Army were readjusting their forces, tactics, and strategy to fight the Revolution. A race ensued. The winner would be the army that could reshape itself faster.

Over the last two months, Glover and his brigade of indispensable men had saved Washington's army from what could have been certain defeat. They would have more opportunities to prove their worth in the coming days in the looming battle at White Plains. A letter home from a soldier in East Chester noted, "The main Body of our Army lay . . . waiting for the Enemy to attack us; it is my opinion if they should not do it soon, we shall attack them; we have gained the Advantage of them, the two last Engagements, there is no Dispute but what a general Attack will commence very soon. I think the Salvation of America depend upon our Conduct in the next Engagement; it will either be the Destruction of the British Army, or ours; the two Armies are so near together, that they must be both engaged at one Time."[32]

CHAPTER 33

WHITE PLAINS

October 20, 1776, East Chester, New York

The sound of music and conversation wafted through the night, causing Glover and his men to pause just a moment. Without a doubt, a few of them clutched more tightly to their weapons in preparation for an anticipated attack. When it became apparent the enemy had not discovered them, they pressed on again, praying that the creak of the wagons and the clattering of the horses' hooves would not give them away.

The day before, Glover's Brigade had marched all the way from their position near Pell's Point to General Charles Lee's camp. The Continental Army was making its way to White Plains, and Lee led the rearguard. Almost immediately, Lee summoned Glover. "General Lee sent for and informed me there were two hundred barrels of pork and flour at East Chester, if the enemy had not taken it: would be glad I would think of some way to bring it off," John Glover recalled.[1]

The resourceful Marbleheader commandeered fifteen wagons and led his entire brigade on a daring night raid. By Glover's account, they "went down so nigh to the enemy we heard their musick and talk very plain." They managed to evade the watching eyes of the British and Hessian patrols and "brought off the whole."[2]

On Wednesday, October 23, the Marbleheaders again proved their worth in a skirmish with the enemy. Glover dispatched a small group of men from the 14th on a scouting mission. When the Marbleheaders encountered a Hessian patrol, they immediately attacked and "killed twelve and took three prisoners; one of the slain was an officer of rank, on horseback."[3] The scouts led the horse and the prisoners back to camp in triumph, having lost only one man from their own regiment.

But Marbleheaders were not out of danger yet. The bulk of Washington's forces had arrived in White Plains on Tuesday, October 22, but Lee's rearguard was still en route. William Howe had pressed so close to the Americans that the British were plainly visible to Glover. He watched as Howe's men divided into two columns that marched straight for Lee's forces.

Recognizing the danger, Lee tried to outrun the enemy. "General Lee immediately gave orders for his division, which consisted of eight thousand men, to march for North-Castle to take the ground to the eastward and north of them, about fourteen miles distance," recalled Glover. But that decision nearly proved disastrous. "We had not marched more than three miles before we saw the right column advancing in a cross road to cut us off, not more than three quarters of a mile distance."[4]

The Marbleheaders, a trusted and elite regiment, were specifically positioned to act as the rearguard of the army as it marched toward White Plains. Lee gave specific orders on how to execute the maneuver:

A Captain & 60 form the Rear guard—The Rifles under Col. Hand form a Right flank Column, from which small Detached parties Commanded by Serjeants must be detachd further to the Right in Indian file and Flankers to the Right Column. The Baggage of the whole is to march in the front of Glovers Brigade till the Army arrives to the Fork of the Road leaving to White—plains & Dobb's Ferry, where it is to file off to the Latter, under the Escort of . . . Regt.—A few men with proper Tools to proceed the Rifles, to remove any Obstructions which may impede their March.

The greatest care to be taken that if Soldiers dont Straggle out of the Road, neither for Water or any thing else, without permission of their Commanding Officer, nor more than two at a time, & not more than five minutes—Any Captain or Commanding

Officer who dont put this order in Execution strictly will be put in Arrests immediately.

The most profound Silence to be observed on the March.[5]

The rearguard was in a precarious position. A column of eight thousand men, 150 wagons, and assorted baggage and artillery occupied a full four miles of road, and Howe's troops were about to attack. Thinking fast, Lee ordered his men to turn to the west, away from the advancing column. He left one brigade, led by Alexander McDougall,* stationed on a hill to cover the division's retreat.

Howe unleashed his artillery on McDougall and his men, inflicting heavy casualties. They held the hill as long as they could, but the British cannons killed twenty men and injured forty more. Unable to remain any longer, McDougall ordered a retreat, but the covering force had done its job—barely. By marching through the night, Lee's force, including Glover's Brigade, made it to the perceived safety of White Plains—which was about to become the scene of yet another battle.

While Lee, Glover, and the rest of the rearguard were racing away from Howe, Washington was arranging his battle lines on the low hills of White Plains. He took over the Elijah Miller House as his headquarters and placed most of his forces in two defensive lines concentrated around Purdy Hill. It was a strong position: the Americans held the high ground and were behind the Bronx River. Gangs of soldiers worked like beavers to construct field fortifications.

Washington also belatedly sent McDougall's Brigade, composed of regular and militia regiments from Delaware, Maryland, and New York, to reinforce Chatterton Hill, a 180-foot-high crag on the Patriots' right flank. The British chose to attack there first, led by assault troops commanded by Hessian colonel Johann Rall. The son of a soldier, Rall was no stranger to war. His service began as a child cadet in his father's regiment and now spanned nearly four decades. The German had pre-

---

* Like many of the Marblehead men, McDougall had experience as a seagoing merchant and privateer. MacDougal Street in New York City is named for him.

viously fought in the War of the Austrian Succession, the French and Indian War, and the Fourth Russo-Turkish War, as well as the Battle of Brooklyn.

Glover and the other Marbleheaders watched from a nearby hill as thirteen thousand British, in their full military splendor, assembled near the forces on Chatterton Hill. "The sun shone bright, their arms glittered, and perhaps troops never were shown to more advantage," recalled one participant.[6]

The sight was too much for the militia. Hundreds of them fled as the British approached or shortly after the fighting began. Young drummer boy Thomas Grant Jr. recalled fighting "at White Plains when they had a battle with the enemy."[7] He was joined by fellow child soldier, sixteen-year-old Jabez Tarr, who recollected, "[We] moved to White Plains, where the army made a stand and was in the battle fought there."[8] McDougall was left with approximately six hundred men with which to defend his position against the thousands of British and Hessian troops and their twelve cannons. However, the troops were some of the best warriors in Washington's army, including Washington's Life Guard, commanded by Marbleheader Caleb Gibbs.[9] The attack began on October 28, 1776, and the Americans were forced to withdraw from the hill. Fifty-year-old Johann Rall was the hero of the battle after leading the breakthrough.

The British soon turned their attention to the high ground defended by Glover's Brigade. The colonel had wisely deployed his six cannons on the mount, where they could fire down into the valley below, which the enemy would need to traverse in order to assault Glover's position. The Americans waited tensely as the British approached, marching in columns.

Glover ordered his men to fire as soon as the British came into range.[10] An intense artillery cannonade rained down on the heads of the British and Hessian troops. Now it was their turn to break, and some fled the battlefield.

Meanwhile, the British troops who had taken possession of Chatterton Hill had busily added to its fortifications. Washington and his generals understood that when the British completed the new breast-works, the enemy would have a superior field position, which would allow them to tear into the American lines. The commander in chief took the only viable option and ordered another retreat to the north.

Once again, Charles Lee's force included Glover's Brigade with the Marblehead Regiment serving as the rearguard. The general ordered Glover's Brigade to guard another key hill near an intersection of two main roads—a hill the British would almost certainly attack if they planned to pursue the retreating Patriots. As he had previously, Glover positioned his cannon on the high ground, where they would have maximum range. He dispatched teams to provide a clear field of fire for the Americans. Glover welcomed another engagement, writing, "I am posted on a mountain, commanding the roads to Albany and New England; the enemy on one opposite, about one mile distance. We expect an attack every moment; I don't care how soon, as I am very certain, with the blessing of God, we shall give them a drubbing."[11] The Marbleheaders and others then stationed themselves in defensive fortifications about halfway up the hill and waited.

They did not wait long. A sizable group of British troops rushed toward the hill on November 1. The effect was the same as it had been previously. "Our Cannon from the top of the Hill began to play briskly upon them, which soon made them run and scamper in the greatest confusion I ever saw," wrote Colonel Loammi Baldwin.[12] Several Marbleheaders were in the melee. Private John Savage fought in the Battle of White Plains and rearguard that followed,[13] as did Lieutenant Joshua Orne, John Rhodes Russell, John Teshew,[14] Marston Watson,[15] Romeo, Aesop Hale, and Moses Stacey, who was "doing his duty."[16] Some Marbleheaders were wounded while battling in New York, among them Lieutenant William Hawks: "I was wounded in the right Arm and also in the left Breast, the effects of which speak loudly for themselves at this day," wrote Hawks later. "I also received a Bayonet Wound."[17] The regiment's wounded were treated by the skilled hands of Doctor Nathaniel Bond, who doubled as company commander and fighting surgeon.

The British regrouped on another nearby hill, where they set up their cannons in opposition to Glover's. The skirmish became an artillery duel as each side attempted to use its guns to destroy the other side's cannons. "The shot from our hill flew so thick and well directed that the enemy were soon silenced and have annoyed us very little since," Baldwin remembered.[18]

With the success of Glover's rearguard, Washington retreated most of his troops across the Hudson River to New Jersey. However, he left Glover and the Marbleheaders, an elite and dependable unit, behind in North Castle, on the border of Connecticut. There they would remain until November 26, when Lee began moving them south to link up with Washington's forces in New Jersey. The Marbleheaders would not rejoin the main body of the army until shortly before the dramatic attack at Trenton in late December.

The British turned their attention to the last large American force in New York: Fort Washington.

CHAPTER 34

THE DARKEST DAYS

After their victory at White Plains, the British forces controlled most of New York City and the surrounding area. The lone exception was Fort Washington in Manhattan, located near the eastern base of the present-day George Washington Bridge. Perched 230 feet above the Hudson River, its citadels, earthen walls, and redoubts sprawled for over a mile and contained 140 brass and iron cannon. General Washington had wanted to abandon the fort, but Nathanael Greene considered the position impregnable and persuaded him to leave a garrison there. Washington acquiesced against his better judgment, and on November 16, eight thousand British and Hessian troops attacked, surrounding the fort on three sides. A week earlier, Fort Washington's adjutant, William Demont, had fled the bastion and handed the order of battle and the plans for the citadel's defensive works to the British. Thanks to this largely forgotten American traitor, the British knew the fort's weak points and precisely where to focus the three prongs of the British attack.

"All that are my grenadiers, march forwards!" Hessian colonel Johann Rall barked to his assault troops.

"Hurrah!" the Germans shouted.[1]

For hours, Virginia and Maryland riflemen had desperately been holding Mount Washington, a key pass near a hill. They fired so many rounds that some of their rifles failed them. Under this hail of musket and cannon fire, Rall's men pressed forward, mopping up resistance on the slopes leading up to the main star-shaped bastion of Fort Washington. The last of the defenders retreated inside the fort's walls. Rall had his quarry—hundreds of American soldiers—trapped.

Because the Americans lacked a well or other water source inside the fortification, Rall knew they could not hold out for long. He sent a message to the fort's inhabitants, requesting their immediate surrender. They had thirty minutes to decide. Once again, Johann Rall made history.

One of the fort's defenders was Massachusetts native Athelston Andrews, who recollected, "The next morning the British attacked our picket guard between the city and the fort, and between the fort and Kings Bridge, both these positions had works thrown up and mounted with Cannon. He was posted at the picket near Kings Bridge, which was attacked by the Hessians and carried, we retreated to the Fort, and the Fort surrendered. We were all taken and put in close confinement."[2] Andrews was joined by the injured from White Plains, who had been moved to the perceived safety of the walls of Fort Washington. Most would never return home alive.

It was all over before nightfall. Washington, witnessing the action from Fort Lee in New Jersey, urged Colonel Robert Magaw, the fort's commander, to hold out as long as possible, hoping to pull off another daring nighttime escape.

But it was not to be.

Only a handful of men managed to flee across the river to Fort Lee, where one man saw "Gen George Washington in tears walking the porch,"[3] as Washington watched the fall of Fort Washington through his spyglass. The rest, more than 2,800 men, surrendered.

Disregarding all the rules of war, the Hessians who accepted the surrender stormed the fort and began slaughtering those inside Washington's walls. In the chaos of the ensuing melee, American Richard Thomas Atkinson furtively lowered the fort's flag, which bore the inscription "Don't Tread on Me." He then handed the colors to another soldier, who "put them within his breeches," risking life and limb.[4] He covertly carried the flag in captivity until he was able to escape and deliver the colors to Washington months later.

Next, the enemy forced the 2,838 prisoners to run through a gauntlet of British and Hessians who punched and kicked them and stole their belongings before shipping them to the filthy, disease-filled prison ships in New York Harbor. For most of the men, it was a death sentence; the British furnished these floating concentration camps with little food. Thousands of Americans would perish on the vessels before the war's end.[5]

For Washington, the fall of the fort that bore his name was the lowest point of the Revolution up to that moment. Observers said that he "wept with the tenderness of a child."[6]

Then, merely three days after the surrender at Fort Washington, the British landed in New Jersey, boldly climbed a tiny trail on a steep cliff, and forced the Patriots to abandon Fort Lee. In their haste, the Americans had to leave behind much of their artillery, equipment, and food, which fell into the hands of the enemy. In the Continental Congress, representatives began to wonder whether they had made the right choice for commander.

When the Congress appointed George Washington to lead their armies in the fight against Great Britain, the Virginian was not the only candidate for the job. His chief rival was General Charles Lee— the man under whom John Glover and the 14th Continental now served.

In fact, many people, including Lee himself, arrogantly believed Lee to be the superior candidate for the position. Born in England in 1732, Lee was the son of a general and had served with distinction in the French and Indian War. While he was in America, he built strong ties with the Mohawks, marrying a chief's daughter. The tribe actually adopted the mercurial Englishman and gave him the nickname Ounewaterika, or Boiling Water, in reference to his volatile temper.

Lee fought in Portugal under General John Burgoyne and saw action in Poland, where he acted as an aide-de-camp to King Stanislaus II and participated in the Russo-Turkish War. In 1773, he resigned his commission and moved to the colonies, purchasing an estate near that of his friend and Patriot general Horatio Gates.

Given his military experience, Lee assumed he would lead the Patriot armies as a matter of course. But Lee was undeniably odd. Often described as slovenly and coarse, he was a sloppy dresser who cursed incessantly. William R. Lee recalls a bizarre interaction with the haughty Lee:

> On one occasion, happening to call just as the General was sitting down to dinner, he observed, "Major Lee, why the devil do you never dine, breakfast, or sup with me; you are frequently at my quarters, either in the morning, at the dinner hour, or in evening." The major replied, "General, you have never invited me to take a seat at your table." "That is just like all you damned Yankees; never stand on ceremony, but in the future, whenever you come into my quarters at the time I am taking my meals, sit down and call on the servant for a plate." "Very well, sir," said the major, "I am very much obliged to you and will avail myself of your politeness now," and placing a chair at the table, requested that a plate might be brought to him. The General was astonished, looked unutterable things, and never again hinted that Major Lee's company would be agreeable. This the major well understood, and therefore was glad of an opportunity to try the character of an officer who had at times the appearance of being hospitable and generous, but still never wished the sincerity of his proffered kindness tested.[7]

But General Lee's selfishness became evident at White Plains, where he lodged in a small house near a road that General Washington was obliged to pass when on reconnoitering excursions, and one day returning with his staff, they called and took dinner. They had no sooner gone than General Lee observed to his aide, "'You must look me out another place, for I shall have Washington and all his puppies continually calling on me, and they will eat me up.' The next day General Lee, seeing Washington out upon like duty, and supposing that he should have another visit, ordered his servant to write with chalk upon the door,

'No victuals dressed here today.' When the company approached and saw this notice, they laughed heartily, and pushed off with much good humor for their own table, without a thought of resenting the habitual oddity of the man."[8]

John Adams wrote of him, "He is a queer Creature—But you must love his Dogs if you love him, and forgive a Thousand Whims for the Sake of the Soldier and the Scholar."[9] By all accounts, Lee loved his dogs, particularly his Pomeranian, Spado, much more than he liked most humans. When Lee heard about Adams's description, he simply laughed. "I am called whimsical and a lover of Dogs," he wrote to Doctor Benjamin Rush. "As to the former charge, I am heartily glad that it is my character, for untill the common routine of mankind is somewhat mended I shall wish to remain and be thought eccentric—and when my honest quadruped Friends are equal'd by the bipeds in fidelity, gratitude, or even good sense, I will promise to become as warm a philanthropist as Mr. Addison himself affected to be—to say the truth I think the strongest proof of a good heart is to love Dogs and dislike Mankind."[10]

In addition, Lee wanted to be paid for leading America's troops. By joining the Patriot cause, he was giving up his estates in England. By contrast, Washington was willing to work for free, only being reimbursed for his sizable expenses, and he possessed none of Lee's peculiarities. Appointing a Southerner to lead the armies, the bulk of whom came from New England, was a good political move as it tied the fledgling country more closely together. Politically savvy Washington was also able to forge coalitions and alliances—a skill the peculiar Lee lacked. With all those points in Washington's favor, perhaps Lee should not have been surprised that the Continental Congress named Washington commander in chief.

Even though Washington was a lover of dogs as well, the two men did not get along. Washington relied on Lee for advice; however, Lee resented the Virginian and did not hold a high opinion of his abilities. He reportedly said that Washington was "not fit enough to command a Sergeant's Guard."[11] In many of his orders to Lee, Washington adopted a less-than-forceful tone, perhaps to mollify Lee's pride. "Upon the whole therefore I am of Opinion & the Gentlemen about me concur in it that the publick Interest requires your coming over to this Side with the Continental Troops," Washington wrote to Lee after the Battle of White Plains. He spelled out his reasons and added, "Unless therefore some new Event should occur, or some more cogent Reason present itself I would have you move over by the easiest & best Passage."[12] Lee's reply demonstrated that he was inclined to do whatever he wanted. "I have received your Orders and shall endeavour to put 'em in execution," he wrote before explaining that he had just received some intelligence about the Queen's Rangers and was planning to pursue them before joining Washington. The next few weeks revealed that while he and his troops, which included the Marblehead Regiment, planned to join Washington, he also planned to take his own sweet time.

What remained of the main element of Washington's battered army retreated through New Jersey. Most of the men had joined the army in the summer, expecting the fighting to last only a few months. Few had brought clothing suitable for the cold winds of November, and what clothing they did have was falling apart from hard wear. On November 20, they crossed into Hackensack. A local minister recalled, "It was about dusk when the head of the troops entered Hackensack. The night was dark, cold, and rainy, but I had a fair view of them from the light of the windows as they passed on our side of the street. They marched two abreast, looked ragged, some without a shoe to their feet, and most of them wrapped in their blankets."[13] The Continental Army was in dire need of supply. Elbridge Gerry attacked the issue from his position in Congress, using his contacts in the Iberian Peninsula to help furnish Washington's army with essentials. Honest and ethical, Gerry was sensitive of being accused of profiteering. "I prefer any Loss to the least Misunderstanding," he wrote in a letter to James Warren.[14]

British forces led by General Charles Edward Cornwallis were not far behind. Over the coming weeks, they would push the Americans deeper into the countryside, constantly sending out scouting parties to skirmish with the Patriots' rearguard. With the British nipping at their heels, the Americans marched, first to Newark, then New Brunswick, Princeton, and Trenton before crossing into Pennsylvania. For several days, the remains of Washington's force crossed the Delaware illuminated by huge pyres near the river. Renowned artist Charles Wilson Peale, who was a member of the Pennsylvania militia, described the hellish scene: "All the shores were lighted up with large fires, boats continually passing and repassing, full of men, horses, artillery, and camp equipage." Scores of exhausted soldiers filed past Peale. "A man staggered out of line and came toward me. He had lost all his clothes. He was in an old, dirty blanket jacket. His beard long and his face full of sores . . . had so disfigured him that he was not known to me at first sight. Only when he spoke did I recognize my brother James."[15]

Not just the men's clothing and bodies were battered and worn—their spirits had been bruised just as badly. With each military defeat, political will within the new nation shifted closer to despair. An officer from Delaware wrote that in November 1776, "a thick cloud of darkness and gloom covered the land, and despair was seen on almost every countenance."[16]

On November 30, the Howe brothers issued an amnesty proclamation that offered pardon and protection to rebels who signed an oath of loyalty to the king within sixty days. Thousands of Americans, including several members of Congress, flocked to sign the oath. One disgusted Patriot recalled, "To the disgrace of the country and human nature, great numbers flocked to confess their political sins to the representative of Majesty, and to obtain pardon. It was observed, that these consisted of the very rich and the very poor, while the middling class held their constancy."[17]

Hard currency was scarce, and the young nation had begun printing its own money. However, during the harsh winter of 1776, some shopkeepers stopped accepting the Continental bills. Mobs and the shifting political tides of their neighbors struck fear in the hearts of some citizens. A clergyman in New Jersey noted that "there was constant alarm," and that people had ceased showing up to church. Some even hid out in the woods or refused to leave their homes. While people had "been eager" to agitate for revolution, "as the first [of the New Year] came closer, many drew away, and there was much dissension among the people."[18]

On December 8, another hammer fell. General Henry Clinton led an expedition to seize Newport and take control of Rhode Island. The British now had an additional deepwater port for the Royal Navy and effectively knocked another state out of the war. Everything was going according to plan—the Howes' plan.

During this time, even Washington fell prey to despair. In a letter to his cousin Lund, who was overseeing the estate at Mount Vernon in his absence, Washington described himself as "distressed by a number of perplexing circumstances." He added, "I wish to Heaven it was in my power to give you a more favourable Acct. of our situation than it is." Defeats, sickness, and desertion had dwindled the size of his army, and many of the enlistments were due to expire on January 1. That would leave the general with mostly militia, which had already proved unreliable in battle. He concluded that unless more men enlisted, "I think the game will be pretty well up, as from disaffection, and want of spirit & fortitude, the Inhabitants instead of resistance, are offering Submission, & taking protections from Genl Howe in Jersey." He even went so far as to have Lund get ready for defeat. "Matters to my view . . . wear so unfavourable an aspect . . . that I would look forward to unfavorable Events, & prepare Accordingly in such a manner however as to give no alarm or suspicion to any one," he wrote. "As one step towards it, have my Papers in such a Situation as to remove at a short notice in case an Enemy's Fleet should come up the River— When they are removd let them go immediately to my Brothers in Berkeley."[19]

Another eyewitness felt the gloom that was infecting the country and decided it was his responsibility to do something to counter it. Thomas Paine, who had previously written the pamphlet *Common Sense*, which stirred up Patriotic fervor in the colonies, was traveling with the army and experiencing all the same hardships and despair as the soldiers. In November and December 1776, he wrote the first of a series of articles that he would publish under the title "The American Crisis."

"These are the times that try men's souls," Paine wrote. "The summer soldier and the sunshine patriot will, in this crisis, shrink from the service of their country; but he that stands by it now, deserves the love and thanks of man and woman. Tyranny, like hell, is not easily conquered; yet we have this consolation with us, that the harder the conflict, the more glorious the triumph."[20]

He spoke in glowing terms of the character of the men who fought, including their leader. "I shall not now attempt to give all the particulars of our retreat to the Delaware," he wrote. "Suffice it for the present to say, that both officers and men, though greatly harassed and fatigued, frequently without rest, covering, or provision, the inevitable consequences of a long retreat, bore it with a manly and martial spirit. All their wishes centered in one, which was, that the country would turn out and help them to drive the enemy back. Voltaire has remarked that King William never appeared to full advantage but in difficulties and in action; the same remark may be made on General Washington, for the character fits him. There is a natural firmness in some minds which cannot be unlocked by trifles, but which, when unlocked, discovers a cabinet of fortitude; and I reckon it among those kind of public blessings, which we do not immediately see, that God hath blessed him with uninterrupted health, and given him a mind that can even flourish upon care."[21]

The pamphlet had an almost immediate effect on the morale of both the military and civilians. The looming prospect of disaster seemed to spur Americans into action, and some even believed that such a crisis was necessary to give people the proper motivation to fight. "Our republic cannot exist long in prosperity," Doctor Benjamin Rush later wrote in a letter to John Adams. "We require adversity and appear to possess most of the republican spirit when most depressed."[22]

Congress and Elbridge Gerry seemed to be reinvigorated by the likelihood of a catastrophe. After they decided to flee from Philadelphia to Baltimore to escape the approaching British troops, Samuel Adams wrote, "We have done more important business in three weeks than we had done, and I believe should have done, at Philadelphia, in six months."[23]

The Marblehead Regiment and Glover's Brigade continued to march with Lee. As the army retreated into New Jersey, General Lee made specific orders as to how the march should proceed. Major William R. Lee recorded, "The different Divisions to advance Picquets, at least half a mile in—Front of their respective Posts—The advancd Sentries are on no account to make fires. The Corps or Picquets to throw up little Works, or slight Redoubt, to secure them against Surprises—Upon Return of their Scouts, immediate reports are to be made to Head Quarters of what they discover'd—A fifth part of every Division, whatever may be its Force to mount as a Reserve Picquet, ready to turn out at a Moment's Warning, they are always to have two days provision ready cook'd—their Blankets ready pack'd up & their Arms in good Order, they are to be compos'd of Quick marchers, no convalescents among them, they are to do no other duty nor put on no Fatigue."[24]

Without the main body of British troops pursuing them, they had time to conduct court-martial trials, including for the incident at Montressor Island. "The Court Martial whereof Gen Bell was president having found Capt. Waisner guilty of Misbehaviour before the Enemy in the attack on Montresurer Island, order him to be Cashierd with Infamy."[25] Not all Continental officers always conducted themselves as gentlemen: "Major Austin . . . Charged by the Gen. with Wanton Cruel barbarous treatment, of . . . Women & Children not only Unworthy the Character of an Officer but of a Human Creature, the Court having consider the care Of the Prisoner are of [the] Opinion that he is guilty of a Breach of the 21st Article in the Section of the Rules of the Government of the forces of the United States of America. Therefore sentence him to be discharge[d] from the Service."[26]

Desertion was rare with the Marblehead Regiment, because of the tight-knit nature of the community, and the fact that the men were bound together by friendship, family, and community bonds. When it occurred, though, it was dealt with in the most severe manner: an excerpt shortly after the Battle of White Plains in Lee's orderly book related that an individual from another regiment was "convicted by a General Court Martial of which Col. Hitchcock was president, of Deserting from the Camp, & found near the Enemy's Sentries is Sentenced to Suffer Death."[27]

Another incident that seemed at first to be a tragedy may have also helped the Patriot cause. In late November and early December, Washington repeatedly ordered General Lee to move his forces, including Glover's Brigade, to Pennsylvania, where they could augment his dwindling troops. On November 27, he wrote, "My former Letters were so full and explicit as to the necessity of your marching as early as possible, that it is unnecessary to add more on that Head. I confess I expected you would have been sooner in motion."[28] On December 1, he added, "I must entreat you to hasten your march as much as possible or your arrival may be too late to answer any valuable purpose."[29] Again, on December 10, he said, "I cannot but request and entreat you & this too by the advice of all the Genl Officers with me, to march and join me with your whole force with all possible expedition."[30]

But rather than rushing to join the rest of the army, Lee chose to take a slow, meandering route. On the evening of December 12–13, he took a room at a tavern in Basking Ridge, New Jersey, accompanied only by about a dozen guards. He started drafting a letter to General Horatio Gates that expressed his dislike for Washington. "Entre nous, a certain great man is damnable deficient," he complained. "He has thrown me into a situation where I have my choice of difficulties: if I stay in this province, I risk myself and army; and if I do not stay, the province is lost forever. . . . In short, unless something which I do not expect turns up, we are lost."[31]

Lee was correct on at least one account—he himself was about to be lost. Early in the morning on December 13, Cornet Banastre Tarleton,[32] a ruthless officer in the British 16th Light Dragoons, showed up at the tavern door. Having been tipped off to Lee's whereabouts by a Loyalist informant, Tarleton had his cavalrymen surround the build-ing. "I ordered my men to fire into the house through every window and door, and cut up as many as they could," Tarleton later recalled.[33]

Frightened for her life, the tavern owner ran to the door and called out that General Lee was inside. Living up to his reputation for mer-cilessness, Tarleton replied, "If the general does not surrender in five minutes, I will set fire to the house." Within moments, Lee appeared, still wearing his dressing gown. Tarleton immediately took him prisoner.

Although Washington lamented the loss of his experienced adviser, in hindsight, Lee's capture was actually a blessing in disguise for the Patriot cause. Lee would spend sixteen months in captivity, where he betrayed his country by writing detailed letters to William Howe, enu-merating how the British could swiftly defeat the Americans. Without Lee slowing their progress, that portion of the army, including the Marbleheaders, soon began arriving on the banks of the Delaware. It also meant that Washington no longer had a rival for leadership of the Continental Army. He found himself more solidly in control of the American forces.

The enlistments for many of the Continental soldiers, including the Marblehead Regiment, were set to expire at the end of the year. Unless these soldiers could be persuaded to reenlist or more recruits were found to take their place, the Americans would soon find themselves with nearly no men. The corps of hardened, resilient winter soldiers, men who believed in the cause, were all that kept the Continental Army together. However, given the recent string of defeats, recruitment of new troops waned, and enthusiasm and political will to continue the Revolution sagged. Washington needed a victory—badly.

His adjutant general, Colonel Joseph Reed, a native of Trenton, saw that the mood in the countryside was turning against the Patriots. "[The officers] are all of opinion, my dear General, that something must be attempted to revive our expiring credit, give our cause some degree of reputation, and prevent a total depreciation of the Continental money, which is coming on very fast." He added, "In short, some enterprise must be undertaken in our present circumstances, or we must give up the cause. . . . I will not disguise my own Sentiments that our Cause is desperate & hopeless if we do not take the Collection of Troops at present to strike some Stroke."[34]

Troops from the opposing sides were skirmishing as they came into contact with each other, but Washington needed a large-scale offensive to achieve the kind of victory that might sway public opinion. He also needed to make sure any plans for that assault didn't reach the ears of the enemy commanders—a task that was growing more difficult by the day as more colonists aligned themselves with the Loyalists. And he had only a few days to accomplish that attack before much of his army would dissolve.

CHAPTER 35

COUNTERATTACK

December 24, 1776, Patriot camp on the Pennsylvania side of the Delaware River

After spending the night at a nearby farmhouse, Benjamin Rush rode into camp for a meeting with General Washington. Rush, a Pennsylvania physician who had signed the Declaration of Independence with Elbridge Gerry and later served as surgeon general of the Continental Army, wrote that Washington "appeared much depressed and lamented the ragged and dissolving state of his army in affecting terms."[1] Rush did his best to reassure the Virginian, but while they were speaking, the general was distracted by another task. "I observed him to play with his pen and ink upon several small pieces of paper." Washington was writing the passphrase that soldiers would need to know to enter the camp over the next few days. As the two men were talking, one of the slips fell to the floor, and the physician retrieved it. "I was struck by the inscription upon it. It was 'victory or death.'"

Two days earlier, General Washington had gathered his officers, including John Glover, at Brigadier General Lord Stirling's headquarters to discuss a possible attack on the British forces. Hessian troops were garrisoned in various towns and winter quarters in southern New Jersey, including Trenton, which was just across the Delaware River. Several of those towns lay within striking distance, and Washington expressed the hope of attacking at least some of them before the year came to a close. The men debated for several hours the wisdom of various plans of attack, but they failed to reach any conclusions. The council of war ended, having accomplished almost nothing.

Immediately after its conclusion, Loyalist spies informed the British about the meeting. They knew that the Americans were planning a counterattack—and that they had not yet solidified any plans. The fact that spies lurked among the Pennsylvanians who lived along the Delaware—and possibly among his own men—was no surprise to Washington. A week earlier, he had written to Lord Stirling, "I do not doubt but [the enemy] are well informed of every thing we do."[2] He urged Stirling to recruit spies of his own and gather intelligence about the Hessians in Trenton before closing his letter, "We are in a neighbourhood of very disaffected people. Equal care therefore should be taken that one of these persons does not undertake the business in order to betray us."[3]

With that thought in mind, Washington wisely called the first council of war as a ruse. The real planning session took place later that night and focused on Glover and a smaller, more trusted group of officers. They began hatching a complicated plot to assault Trenton on the night of December 25–26.

Trenton was the westernmost British outpost in New Jersey and closest to Washington's army, making it arguably the most vulnerable. Trenton straddled the oldest road in America, the King's Highway, between Philadelphia and New York. Comprising a hundred homes, a church, and a few mills and iron furnaces, Trenton boasted a two-story stone barracks built during the French and Indian War that stood near the center of town. The difficult task of defending the city fell upon the shoulders of Colonel Johann Gottlieb Rall.

One of the great Hessian commanders of Revolution, Rall had distinguished himself at the Battle of White Plains, leading the breakthrough at Chatterton Hill, and then the assault at Fort Washington, miraculously dodging musket balls and cannon as he led from the front once again. One of his fellow officers remarked, "Colonel Rall was truly born to be a soldier, but not a general. This man, who by capturing Fort Washington has earned the greatest honor . . . considered as a private individual, he merited the highest respect. He was generous, magnanimous, hospitable, and polite to everyone; never groveling before his superiors but indulgent with his subordinates. To his servants he was more a friend than master. He was an exceptional friend of music and a pleasant companion."[4] Considered "the Hessian Lion,"[5] Rall terrified his American foes with his courageous and distinguished acts on the battlefield. The regiments in his brigade were arguably some of the toughest and most battle-hardened of the Hessian forces in North America. Men under his command had iron discipline, and in the heat of battle would draw upon that discipline in the most arduous combat situations. In the two weeks before Christmas, the Americans relentlessly harassed the Hessians with raids. Rall pleaded for more reinforcements and more ammunition, but his superiors denied his requests.

Three Hessian regiments—the Rall, Lossberg, and Knyphausen—consisting of about 1,500 men, defended Trenton along with a complement of twenty British dragoons detached to Rall for scouting and reconnaissance. To secure Trenton, Rall organized a ring of outposts that guarded every land approach to the village. The Hessian also positioned one regiment of the three, the "Regiment Du Jour," to be on constant alert. Near the barracks and in "alarm" houses nearby, "the regiment of the day"[6] remained alert and ready for the Americans.

The Hessian Lion dreaded his troops' precarious position. With the rebel forces just a few miles away, small groups of his men skirmished with American units on an almost daily basis. Having been warned by a British network of spies and informants that an attack was imminent, Rall kept his soldiers fully dressed to be ready at a moment's notice to ward off American attacks.

Rall rigorously drilled the men and put them out on patrol, and the Hessian commander favored a quick reaction force that could deal with American incursions. He knew the weakness of his position and told Colonel Carl Emilius von Donop, who commanded the Hessian troops in Bordentown and Burlington, "I have not made redoubts or any kind of fortifications because I have the enemy in all directions."[7] He turned down the advice of his engineers to build defensive redoubts and fortifications—a fatal mistake. Even worse, far from sending reinforcements, Colonel Donop asked that Rall send some of his men to reinforce Donop's position. "I am liable to be attacked at any moment," an exasperated Rall exclaimed. "I have the enemy before me, behind me and at my right flank. . . . It is then, my brother, absolutely impossible."[8] Constant American incursions forced the exhausted troops to remain on high alert. Frustrated, Rall glowered at one of his officers, exclaiming, "Scheiszer bey Scheisz [shit on shit]! Let them come. . . . We will go at them with the bayonet."[9]

Comfortably ensconced in his opulent New York headquarters nearly seventy miles from Trenton, General William Howe was feeling far more confident than his American counterpart and the harried Rall. Following the string of victories in New York, Rhode Island, and New Jersey, he had every reason to think that the war would soon be over with the rebellious American colonies restored to their rightful place in the British Empire. Howe believed it was only a matter of time before the Patriots' political will collapsed.

This mind-set led General Howe to make several fateful decisions in December. First, he chose to pursue the war in a gentlemanly manner. Rather than wiping out Washington's army when he had the opportunity, he pursued the Continentals at a leisurely pace, never taking a risk that might endanger his men. That gave the far more desperate Americans openings through which they escaped time and time again. Rather than concentrate his troops and launch a final offensive to destroy Washington's army once and for all, he dispersed them throughout several population centers in New Jersey, and through these posts he attempted to maintain control of most of the state. Eighteenth-century armies generally did not fight during the coldest months in the European style of warfare. Supplying an army during the winter proved challenging. The preferred method of moving supplies, by water, could be hampered by ice. Ground transportation was at the mercy of mud-clogged or snow-covered roads. An army, dependent upon horses and oxen to move its materiel, required sufficient forage which was scarce during the winter. Instead, they rested and waited for spring to resume their campaigning.

Howe further divided his army by sending a sizable force to seize Newport, Rhode Island. General Henry Clinton argued forcefully in favor of cutting off and ultimately destroying the Continental Army rather than capturing Newport. With Washington's army on the ropes, Clinton advised "relentless chase, notwithstanding efforts at concili-ation, the lateness of the season or anything else that might damage the chance to crush the retreating Americans."[10] Howe overruled him. Clinton also warned Howe of the vulnerability of Trenton and the other outposts. But Howe dismissed his concerns.

Washington hoped to raid Trenton quickly before Rall could call in reinforcements from Princeton or Bordentown. To that end, the com-mander in chief planned for the Continental Army to surround the town and envelop Rall's men. He would lead the main body of the troops across the Delaware River at McConkey's Ferry, some nine miles north of Trenton. Washington's force, including the Marblehead Regiment, would then march south, dividing into two divisions along the way, allowing them to approach the town from two directions. A smaller group, led by Brigadier General James Ewing, would cross at Beatty Ferry, much closer to Trenton. They would secure the bridge over Assunpink Creek, cutting off a potential Hessian retreat to Bordentown. At the same time, Colonel John Cadwalader would lead a sizable group of militia and Continentals across the river at the Neshaminy Ferry near Burlington. Their goal was to keep the British and Hessians in the Burlington-Bordentown area occupied so that they could not reinforce the troops at Trenton.

Washington's desperate gamble involved some of the riskiest mili-tary maneuvers an eighteenth-century army could perform: a night attack, an assault river crossing, and several unique columns that had to closely coordinate to surround Trenton. Moreover, nearly all of these complicated actions would have to work with precision timing for the plan to succeed.

To achieve a quick, decisive victory, Washington relied heavily on his light artillery. Influenced by the youthful yet rotund Henry Knox, he planned to use eighteen artillery pieces to support the assault; the usual tactics of the time would have recommended bringing no more than six to eight.[11] Washington wanted to overwhelm Rall's troops with the shock and awe of highly mobile and flexible firepower. After witnessing the Boston Massacre, Knox immersed himself in the military sciences and became convinced that artillery would prove the key to success on the battlefield. "In the modern mode of carrying on a war," he wrote, "there is nothing which contributes more to make an army victorious than a well regulated and well disciplined artillery provided with a sufficiency of cannon and stores."[12] Several New Englanders and Marblehead men would prove vital to the execution of the plan.

Since Knox had already proved himself so adept at moving artillery from Fort Ticonderoga and Crown Point, Washington naturally tasked him with the logistics of getting the army—and its all-important artillery—across the Delaware. Knox, in turn, called upon the most experienced mariners in Washington's army, John Glover and the Marblehead Regiment, to conduct arguably one of the most crucial operations of the war.

CHAPTER 36

THE CROSSING

"You need not be troubled about that, General, my boys can handle that."[1] John Glover laconically assured Washington that the Marblehead Regiment could do the near impossible. Considering all the variables and complexities involved in transporting thousands of soldiers and their cannon across the Delaware to attack Trenton, the commander in chief had asked Glover whether it was even imaginable that the plan would succeed.

Assured by Glover, Washington and Henry Knox were relying on the Marblehead Regiment to do something even more challenging than their previous feats: cross a nearly one-thousand-foot-wide, ice-choked river at night and, unbeknownst to them at the time of the planning, during a raging nor'easter. Atlantic tidewaters created swift currents that made the river even more treacherous. If any boats crossing at McConkey's Ferry accidentally swept downstream, they would tumble over an eight-foot waterfall, capsizing the vessels and endangering the men inside. Very few men in the army could swim, and drowning—not to mention frostbite and hypothermia—posed a deadly threat for anyone who went overboard. Facing a task as daunting as this, most experienced sailors would recommend postponing the operation until a time with more favorable weather conditions. However, based on the Marbleheaders' experience forging a navy, their miraculous evacuation of the army across the East River, and the brilliant delaying action at Pell's Point that saved Washington's army, Glover had complete confidence in his men.

As dusk fell on Christmas afternoon, portions of the Continental Army arrived at the assembly area at McConkey's Ferry. Glover's men directed them toward the boats. To transport the troops, they used Durham boats, so named because they typically carried iron and coal to and from the Durham Ironworks via the Delaware River. The craft measured between forty and sixty feet long, but only about three and a half feet deep. Ominously painted black, the vessels had flat bottoms and two pointed ends like a canoe. Around the outside edge was a narrow strip of decking to be used by the sailors when the vessel was full of cargo or, in this case, passengers. Sailors would plant their poles in the bottom of the river and then precariously walk the planking along the length of the boat, propelling it forward as they went.

As the sun slowly dipped below the horizon, the temperature grew colder. "If I recollect aright the sun was about half an hour high and shining brightly, but it had no sooner set than it began to drizzle or grow wet, and when we came to the river it rained," remembered John Greenwood, a Massachusetts fifer.[2] A howling wind lashed the men's faces. "Some of them have tied old rags around their feet; others are barefoot, but I have not heard a man complain. They are ready to suffer any hardship and die rather than give up their liberty,"[3] recalled one officer. They shivered, blew on their hands, and stomped their feet to stay warm. Wearing threadbare, tattered uniforms and other bits of clothing, some of them swaddled in lice-infested blankets, the army clambered into the boats.

Officers affixed white pieces of paper to their hats to designate their status and to distinguish friend from foe.* Earlier, officers had been ordered to carry their muskets and had been given additional ammunition; however, "none but the first officers knew where we were going or what we were going about, for it was a secret expedition," recalled Greenwood.[4]

A few feet away, the river raged. The Delaware was running higher than usual, and large chunks of ice, tossed about by the surging currents, smashed into the boats by the bank. The vessels themselves bobbed this

* The tradition of affixing a white piece of paper on one's hat before combat operations continued into America's modern wars. During World War II, soldiers painted a vertical white stripe on the rear of many American officers' helmets. Noncommissioned officers' helmets had a horizontal white stripe on the rear.

way and that, entirely at the mercy of the wind and waves. No doubt the Marbleheaders eyed the water apprehensively. As experienced mariners, they had the best understanding of the enormity of the task that lay before them.

General Washington led the column of approximately 2,400 men. As they neared McConkey's Ferry, he ordered a halt, rode a few more feet in front of them, wheeled his horse, and stood up in his stirrups. The commander in chief then "made us such an animating speech that we forgot the cold, the hunger and the toil under which we were ready to sink and each man seemed only to be anxious for the onset," recalled one Continental soldier.[5]

The 14th Continental, commanded by Major William Raymond Lee, climbed into the various boats and took up the eighteen-foot oars and poles they would use to navigate the crossing. The Marblehead officer also had direct command of the vessels transporting the army. With muscles straining, the Marbleheaders began the laborious process of transporting the small groups of men across the hazardous river.* No one knows exactly how many vessels the Patriots had at their disposal, but the best estimates are that the group at McConkey's Ferry used four ferry boats and between sixteen and twenty-five Durhams.[6]

Under the best circumstances, moving such a large force to the other side of the Delaware with so few boats would require many hours, and these were far from the best circumstances. As the water grew more frigid, larger chunks of ice began to form in the river. Initially, the Durham boats' pointed prows had helped the soldier-mariners slice through the thin sheets of ice. The Marbleheaders now needed their poles to break up the ice and push aside the largest floes to clear the path and prevent damage to the boats. "The floating ice in the river made the labor almost incredible,"[7] recalled Knox. Some boats drifted off course, but the Marbleheaders regained control of their crafts and propelled them toward the New Jersey bank of the Delaware.

---

* The Marbleheaders were assisted by sailors from the other Massachusetts regiments and men from Pennsylvania familiar with the Delaware.

Conditions grew much worse around 10:00 p.m., when a severe storm descended upon the crossing, and high winds carrying sleet and snow whipped the boats and the men. The weather made an indelible mark on the memories of most of the mariners. Decades later, 14th Continental lieutenant Marston Watson often regaled his son with stories "of the severity of the weather on the night of the 25th of December 1776 when the army crossed the Delaware River to make their attack on the Hessians."[8]

With his trademark booming voice, Knox yelled loudly enough to be heard above the roaring wind, encouraging the men to press on. "The force of the current, the sharpness of the frost, the darkness of the night, the ice . . . and a high wind, rendered the passage of the river extremely difficult; and but for the stentorian lungs and extraordinary exertions of Colonel Knox, it could not have been effected in season to favour the enterprise," recalled one officer.[9] Some of the Marbleheaders he encouraged included the father-and-son pair Captain Thomas Grant and his fifer son, Thomas Grant Jr. The young fifer was only fifteen at the time.[10] One teen soldier not joining Grant was Jabez Tarr, who had "taken sick with a fever about 10th or 15 Dec. 1776; [and] was confined"[11] to camp.

The Marbleheaders put their bodies, hardened by years of experience at sea, to the test. Their training and mastery of some of the most dangerous and fertile fishing grounds, the Grand Banks, paid dividends. Having served together as fishermen and later in Washington's Navy, the soldier-mariners from Marblehead and Beverly were highly disciplined and worked as a team as they propelled the boats across the Delaware. "Perseverance accomplished what at first seemed impossible,"[12] remembered Knox.

The other elements of the army not guided by the Marbleheaders all failed that night to cross the Delaware. The assault on Trenton would have to rely on only one prong of attack instead of three. The Marbleheaders had once again proved indispensable.

Experienced officers led the indefatigable Marblehead mariners. "There was an appearance of discipline in this corps; the officers seemed to have mixed with the world, and to understand what belonged to their stations,"[13] recalled one participant. Captains William Courtis, Nathaniel Bond, John Glover Jr., and Thomas Fosdick and Lieutenants William Hawks and Edward Archibald, Joshua Orne, and expert swordsman Robert Wormstead[14] captained the boats that fought through the treacherous waters. These men had known each other for years before the war and were tied together by bonds of brotherhood and family. Orne, who had left Harvard a year and a half earlier, had impeccable character. One Marbleheader noted, "The best man . . . he is one of the few men, within my knowledge, who wou'd execute the duties of such an office with faithfulness toward the Public and to himself."[15] Glover raved about Fosdick's leadership to Washington, calling him "a diligent, active young man & a good disciplinarian."[16]

War had forged their leadership and honed their skills for a crucial inflection point where success or failure rested on brawny sea-scarred shoulders. These were the right men at the right time in history.

The crossing of the Delaware was made possible by the skilled hands of veterans like Marbleheader Private John Savage,[17] who rounded out the companies filled with privates, corporals, and sergeants that these captains led. Among the first groups that Savage and other Marbleheaders brought across the raging Delaware that night were Virginia and New Jersey Continentals led by Captain William Washington and Captain John Flahaven. For transporting horses and artillery, the 14th Continental would rely on ferryboats, or "flats," as they were known. Like the Durhams, these boats also measured about the length of a school bus, but they were rectangular in shape, lacking the Durhams' ice-breaking pointed prows. Thin slats of wood crossed the flat floors, allowing the horses to maintain their footing during transport. A gangplank at either end could be lowered against the riverbank for loading and unloading. The crews also carried the same long poles used on the Durham boats.

Captain William Washington was the commander in chief's second cousin. Hulking but carrying a paunch, he had a zeal for combat, as one fellow officer described: "War was his game, and he was good at it."[18] General Washington later relied on his kinsman heavily as a commander of light cavalry. The advance group he led included future president James Monroe—then still a teenager. William Washington and Flahaven played a crucial role in the night's operation. General Washington ordered his second cousin* and Flahaven to take forty men each and "post on the road about three miles from Trenton and make prisoners of all going in or coming out of town."[19] Secrecy was essential to success, and it was up to these men to ensure that word of the operation did not reach Johann Rall's men.

Much time was spent waiting and freezing that night, on both the Pennsylvania and then the New Jersey side of the river. Fifer John Greenwood wrote, "I was with the first that crossed, we had to wait for the rest and so began to pull down the fences and to make fires to warm ourselves, for the storm was increasing rapidly." Before midnight, the storm became much worse, and the men began to fear the very real possibility that they could freeze. "After a while it rained, hailed, snowed, and froze, and at the same time blew a perfect hurricane; so much so that I perfectly recollect, after putting the rails on to burn, the wind and the fire would cut them in two in a moment, and when I turned my face toward the fire my back would be freezing," Greenwood recalled. "By turning round and round I kept myself from perishing before the large bonfire."[20]

If the storm made waiting on the banks uncomfortable, it made crossing the river hazardous in the extreme. With their pointed prows, the Durham boats had been designed to ferry goods up and down the river, taking advantage of the current whenever possible. That shape made them a far worse choice for crossing the river, especially when the current was swift. In the throes of a full-blown nor'easter, keeping the boats on course took all the strength that the men at the oars and poles could muster. In a testament to the Marblehead mariners' skill, not one man died in the crossing.

* William Washington was the son of Bailey and Catherine Washington and was George Washington's second cousin once removed.

Several African American members of the Marblehead Regiment, such as Aesop Hale, Romeo, and Caesar Glover, the last of whom "enlisted in 1775 in the company commanded by Captain Glover,"[21] helped navigate the crossing alongside some Native American members of the regiment, performing brilliantly and courageously. "Though deficient, perhaps in polish, it possessed an apparent aptitude for the purpose of its institution, and gave a confidence . . . to inspire," recalled one officer who witnessed the regiment in action.[22] One black soldier, Oliver Cromwell, recalled that night on his one-hundredth birthday, and "his eyes brightened at the name of Washington."[23]

At some point during the night—no one knows exactly when— Washington himself made the dangerous trip across the river. Rowing Washington's boat was twenty-one-year-old Marbleheader Private John Rhodes Russell, who had fought in all the regiment's major engagements. Once on the other side of the river, wrapped in his cloak, Washington superintended the landing of his troops. "I have never seen Washington so determined as he is now. . . . He is calm and collected, but very determined. . . . The storm cuts like a knife,"[24] another officer recalled. Washington knew that no matter how furious the storm became, there could be no turning back on his desperate gamble to save the Revolution. In his report of the battle for John Hancock, Washington wrote, "As I was certain there was no making a retreat without being discovered, and harassed on repassing the River, I determined to push on at all events."[25]

Initially, Washington had planned for all the men to be across the Delaware and marching on Trenton by midnight, arriving in town by 5:00 a.m. "But the quantity of Ice, made that Night, impeded the passage of Boats so much, that it was three OClock before the Artillery could all be got over, and near four, before the Troops took up their line of march," Washington wrote Hancock. "This made me despair of surprizing the Town, as I well knew we could not reach it before the day was fairly broke."[26]

With the storm continuing to rage, the nine-mile march to Trenton was nearly as hazardous as the crossing had been. "Many of our poor soldiers are quite barefoot and ill-clad," wrote one of the officers. "Their route was easily traced, as there was a little snow on the ground, which was tinged here and there with blood from the feet of the men who wore broken shoes."[27] Greenwood remembered, "During the whole night it alternately hailed, rained, snowed, and blew tremendously. I recollect very well that at one time, when we halted on the road, I sat down on the stump of a tree and was so benumbed with cold that I wanted to go to sleep; had I been passed unnoticed I should have frozen to death without knowing it; but as good luck always attended me, [a sergeant] came and, rousing me up, made me walk about."[28]

Even with the suffering, Greenwood found the march memorable: "The noise of the soldiers coming over and clearing away the ice, the rattling of the cannon wheels on the frozen ground, and the cheerfulness of my fellow-comrades encouraged me beyond expression, and the big coward as I acknowledge myself to be, I felt great pleasure."[29]

CHAPTER 37

TRENTON: THE TIDE TURNS

Through snow and sleet driven nearly horizontal by the punishing winds, the men and horses trudged and slid across the icy road. One private recalled, "Our Army was destitute of shoes and clothing. . . . It was snowing at this time and the night was unusually stormy. Several of our men froze to death."[1] One of those near casualties was Marblehead lieutenant Joshua Orne, who became so numb from the piercing cold that he passed out along the side of the road. Fresh snow blanketed Orne's body, and he would have "perished had he not been accidentally discovered, when nearly covered in snow, by someone in the rear of the regiment."[2]

Pushing forward on the nine-mile journey to Trenton through the pelting snow, the army navigated deep, treacherous ravines and manhandled the horses and artillery down and up several steep grades. The artillerists unharnessed the cannon from the horses to accomplish the difficult task, and the column of men moved slowly through the vortex of the storm as they fastened heavy drag ropes around trees and lowered the guns down the slopes.

Washington rode near the vanguard of the army and spoke in a "deep and solemn voice," encouraging his men forward: "Soldiers, keep by your officers. For God's sake, keep by your officers."[3] At one point, Washington's "horse['s] hind feet both slip'd from under him," down the slick gradient. One of the great riders in North America, Washington "seiz'd his horse's Mane & the horse recovered"[4] and rode forward. The intense labor expended maneuvering the guns cost precious time in an operation already behind schedule.

As they trundled forward, Captain John Glover Jr. realized their cartridge boxes and "even the best secured weapons" were "wet and not in firing condition."[5] Word of the problem reached Washington, and he responded, "Tell General [John] Sullivan to use the bayonet. I am resolved to take Trenton." Throughout the night, the commander in chief remained determined and resolute; adversity brought forth his best qualities. "Press on! Press on, boys!"[6] Washington shouted as he rode up and down the line encouraging his men.

In the biting wind and falling snow, the Americans suddenly heard a shout. Washington put spurs to his horse and, to his utter amazement, encountered sixty ghost-like American soldiers emerging from the blizzard. They approached from Trenton. Washington had not ordered an advance party to cross the river. Captain George Wallis led the American company. He told Washington that he was ordered by regimental commander Adam Stephen to cross the river and avenge the loss of one of Stephen's men who was killed by the Hessians days earlier. Acting on his own initiative, before Washington's army crossed the Delaware, Stephen ordered the raid. Washington immediately summoned Stephen to the front of the column to confirm the story, which he did. In a tower of rage, Washington accosted Stephen: "You, Sir, may have ruined all of my plans by having put them on their guard."[7] Turning his back on Stephen, Washington calmed down and invited Wallis's company to join his column. Instead of destroying the element of surprise, the rogue raid had unintended consequences. It is highly likely the attack inadvertently led Johann Rall to lower his guard by causing him to believe that Wallis's strike was the American offensive about which British intelligence had forewarned. The course of the battle and history likely changed because of Stephen's unauthorized assault.

Wallis's men were not the only people wandering on the nine-mile stretch of roads to Trenton on the night of December 25–26. Civilians milled around their homes or traveled the road. In the divided country, one could not ascertain friend from foe or Patriot from Loyalist, especially amid a raging nor'easter. Washington ordered anyone outside his home detained or forced to march with the army. One of those Americans was Doctor John Riker, who left his house to determine why his dogs were barking. "He came out in the dark to learn the cause and encountered my command," recalled Virginia lieutenant James Monroe. "And supposed we were from the British camp ordered us off. He was violent, and determined in his manner, and very profane, and wanted to know what we were doing on a stormy night." Monroe ordered the man inside his home or he would detain him. Realizing Monroe was with Washington's army, Riker eagerly stammered, "I know something is to be done, and I am going with you. I am a doctor and may be of help to some poor fellow."[8]

About five miles from Trenton, Washington's plan called for the Americans to split into two divisions and attack both sides of the town simultaneously. Glover's Brigade marched in the vanguard of Sullivan's First Division, the right wing of the attack, which tramped down the River Road that ran parallel to the Delaware. Washington and Nathanael Greene, who composed the left wing of the attack, advanced down the Pennington Road that ran through northern Trenton with the Second Division. Glover's Brigade consisted of several veteran regiments, including the 14th Continental, along with an attached battery of artillery led by Harvard graduate and Gloucester native Winthrop Sargent.

Johann Rall spent Christmas Day next to a warm hearth playing checkers with a local Loyalist, Stacy Potts. Multiple sources had ominously warned the Hessian commander that the Americans would attack Trenton. General James Grant, who had a spy in Washington's camp, relayed information to Rall that the Americans might attack. "I don't believe he will attempt it, but be assured that my information is undoubtedly true, so I need not advise you to be on your guard against an unexpected attack at Trenton."[9]

Not entirely dismissing the warnings, Rall put his men through the paces, sending out patrols looking for the Americans. The colonel strengthened outposts and ordered all three of the regiments in his command to sleep in their uniforms with their cartridge boxes and weapons nearby. But his men were exhausted from the unrelenting American raids, and that night the force of Americans led by Virginian captain George Wallis hit one of Rall's outer outposts and wounded six of his men. Rall rode out to the incursion and chased the Americans as they fled into the woods. Could this be the attack he had been warned of by General Grant? His men were neither idle nor drunk but exhausted.

The storm seemed like a welcome respite. Perhaps Wallis's raid, which the Hessians disrupted, put him at ease. The Americans could never attack in a nor'easter. After the raid, a weary Rall spent the evening in the home of a Loyalist and played checkers. Later that night, Rall switched from checkers to playing cards, and when one of his officers suggested sending away the garrison's baggage, Rall acidly retorted, "Fiddlesticks! These clodhoppers will not attack us, and should they do so, we will simply fall on them and rout them."[10] Rall's disdain for the Americans' fighting ability would come to bear in his strategy, to his detriment. As the evening wore on, a servant sent by a Bucks County Tory named Hunt delivered a note to Rall. The messenger attempted several times to see Rall in person. The latter finally granted an audience. Annoyed by the disruption, the Hessian commander thrust the note into his pocket without reading it before retiring to his quarters for the evening. But unlike the other warnings, this message warned the Hessian of Washington's army crossing the Delaware. Surprise, the most crucial element of Washington's attack, hung by the slimmest of threads.

An hour after the gray streaks of dawn, the nor'easter continued to rage, screening the Americans' movements as they approached Hessian outposts nearly a mile from Trenton. John Greenwood remembered, "[The morning was] dark and stormy so that we could not see very far ahead."[11] Thanks to the reduced visibility, the Americans surged forward in a fast trot and approached within two hundred yards before the sentries sounded the cry, "Der Feind! Heraus! Heraus!" (The enemy! Turn out! Turn out!).[12]

From intelligence furnished by his scouts, Washington knew the location of the Hessian outposts. Washington and the Life Guard remained on Trenton's high ground, affording them a commanding view of the town. The commander of the guard, Caleb Gibbs, accompanied Washington. A member of the guard who also made the crossing but remained "with the baggage" was Marblehead Private James Knox.[13] As Washington's Second Division, led by Greene, entered the town, he shouted to his onrushing troops, "There my brave fellows, are the enemy of your country. Remember now what you are about to fight for!"[14] The troops moved down a hill along the west side of the town, entering the village through the house lots and alleys. Rall's troops poured out of Trenton's homes as the Americans discharged their weapons and charged. Small groups clashed throughout the city, wielding bayonets, pistols, rifles, and fists in the bitter house-to-house fighting. Soon smoke from the cannons and muskets filled the streets and combined with the continuing storm, adding to the murk and confusion.

Rall's adjutant, Lieutenant Jakob Piel, woke his commander from his slumber by banging on the door and, when there was no response, shouting up to the room. The German commander opened the window of his quarters, wearing his nightclothes, and asked, "What's the matter?"

"Do you not hear the firing?" Piel retorted.

The Hessian commander responded, "I will be there immediately."[15] Rall jumped on a horse and rode to the position of Lieutenant Andreas Wiederholt, whose men had manned the outer outposts but had fallen back into Trenton. Wiederholt was a seasoned soldier who had risen from private to sergeant major before his promotion to officer. He, alongside Rall, led the attack on Fort Washington and seemed to be immune to the thousands of balls fired by the defenders of the fort as he led the near-suicidal charge. Wiederholt reported to Rall, "The enemy was strong, that they were not only above the city but they were already in it on the left and right sides so that he should not consider this to be only a minor thing." Rall then asked about the strength of the American attack. Wiederholt responded, "[He] could not say with certainty. But that he had seen four or five battalions moving out of the woods and had received fire from three of them before I [Wiederholdt] had to retire from my post."[16]

Wiederholt's report was flawed. The Americans had not enveloped the town but only attacked from the north and west. The all-important bridge over the Assunpink and link to Bordentown and other Hessian forces at this moment was held by Rall's men and lay open. On the southern side of the bridge lay excellent ground to wage a pitched battle. Based on his experience routing Americans in every previous conflict and Wiederholt's report, Rall followed his instincts and the iron German doctrine of many wars: he rallied his men and counterattacked.

"Artillery Forward!"[17] Rall barked.

The Hessians rolled their guns down King Street, a principal thoroughfare that ran through the heart of Trenton. After unlimbering the artillery, the Hessians fired about a dozen times at Washington's men. One ball hit American horse-drawn artillery, striking a horse "in its belly and knock[ing] over on its back. While it lay there kicking."[18] In the swirling storm, Americans infiltrated the town, fired upon the Hessians from the houses, and approached the guns. Washington's men charged and captured several Hessian artillery pieces.

"All who are my grenadiers forward!"[19] Rall shouted, and the Hessian drums sounded.

Always in the thick of the fighting, Rall ordered his men to retake the guns because he considered their loss a dishonor to the regiment. The control and operation of the artillery would turn out to be an inflection point of the battle. By this time, the Americans had permeated large portions of the town. Marksmen took up secure positions in houses and behind fences and picked off the Hessians.

American artillery commanded by Colonel Henry Knox belched flame and iron into the Hessian positions. The Germans reclaimed their guns—but at great cost. Knox then rode up to several Americans, including Captain William Washington and Lieutenant James Monroe, extorting them, "My brave lads, go up and take those two pieces. There is a party going on and you must join them."[20]

The small band of Americans surged forward, long knives, toma-hawks, and muskets in hand. Freezing sleet pelted their faces. In the ensu-ing hand-to-hand melee, Captain William Washington went down with serious wounds in both hands. Monroe took over and led the mixed corps of Virginians and New Englanders, retaking the guns. In the fracas, a musket ball pierced Monroe's chest and ruptured an artery. Doctor Riker, the stranger whom Monroe had encountered only hours earlier on the road to Trenton, saved the life of the future fifth president of the United States by clamping the artery as crimson blood fountained from his chest. The engagement left a trail of carnage. "Here succeeded a scene of war, of which I had often conceived but never saw before,"[21] Knox later wrote. Another participant captured the macabre melee: "My blood chill'd to see such horror and distress, blood mingling together, the dying groans, and 'Garments' rolled in 'blood' the sight was too much to bear."[22]

"My friends, in a few minutes we shall be in presence of the enemy, and I hope you will behave like the men I take you to be," Captain Moses Brown solemnly addressed his men as they approached the Hessian posi-tions. Brown's men had a high opinion of his "courage and conduct."[23] With the battle raging in the heart of Trenton, Glover's Brigade and the Marblehead and Beverly men, near the vanguard of Sullivan's division, marched down River Road on the western side of the town.[24] Led by Brown and the other officers, the regiment emerged along Front Street and burst through the Hessian pickets in southern Trenton. Some of the men shouted, "These are the times that try men's souls!"[25] repeating Thomas Paine's famous words as their battle cry. The division pushed in the direction of the Knyphausen Regiment. One participant noted that the Americans, including John Stark from New Hampshire, whom the Marbleheaders had fought alongside on Bunker Hill, "dealt death wher-ever [they] found resistance, and broke down all opposition."[26] Uniquely armed with the blunderbuss, a favorite weapon of the Marbleheaders that they had brought from their homes, they pelted the Hessians they encountered. Acting similar to a shotgun, the weapon was deadly at close quarters.[27]

Recognizing that the crucial bridge spanning Assunpink Creek (a tributary of the Delaware River that flows through Trenton) was guarded by a small number of Hessians, without orders, Glover directed his men to attack the guard. They stormed the stone bridge, scattering the eighteen men commanded by Hessian lieutenant Johannes Müller. The bridge was the crucial line of communication to the Hessian garrison at Bordentown and the principal means of escape for Rall's troops, connecting him to Colonel Carl Emilius von Donop's forces in Bordentown, six miles away. The British had positioned the Hessians to be mutually supporting each other in the event of an American attack. However, a series of events would prevent the two Hessian forces from ever reuniting, thereby changing the course of history.

On December 23, a force of several hundred Continentals and militia under the command of Colonel Samuel Griffin, recently arrived from Virginia, attacked Donop's troops in a set of skirmishes and deliberate retreats, luring them to Mount Holly, New Jersey, over twenty miles away from Trenton. Donop was slightly wounded in the engagement and, by the time of the attack on Trenton, was comfortably ensconced and under the tender care of a beautiful widow in Mount Holly. While it is hotly debated who that person was, according to one legend, it may have been none other than renowned flag-maker and Patriot Betsy Ross.

Donop's subordinate, Captain Johann Ewald, summed up the matter sardonically in his diary: "This great misfortune, which surely caused the utter loss of the thirteen splendid provinces of the Crown of England, was due partly to the extension of the cordon, partly to the fault of Colonel Donop, who was led by the nose to Mount Holly by Colonel Griffin and detained there by love. . . . Thus the fate of entire kingdoms often depends upon a few blockheads and irresolute men."[28]

After crossing the bridge, Glover turned east and took up positions on the crucial high ground on the southern bank of the Assunpink. Had

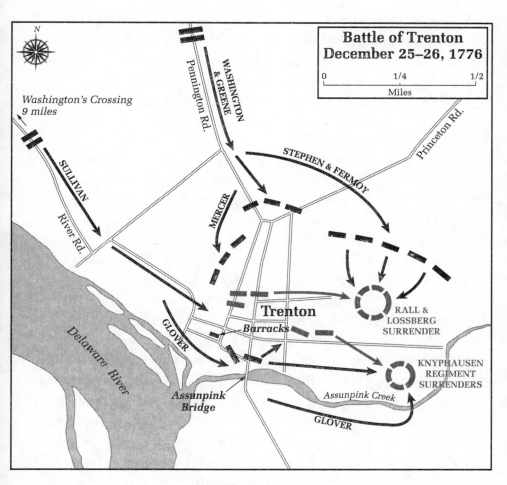

"Battle of Trenton"

Rall withdrawn his troops to this high ground at the start of the battle, the outcome would likely have been different. Glover and his Indispensables, on their own initiative, had just seized some of the most valuable real estate in the entire battle. Rall might have been able to hold the ground or inflict losses on the Americans and effectively withdraw the bulk of his men to a neighboring British outpost—instead of a crushing victory for Washington, the battle could have been indecisive. Capture of the bridge and positioning of the cannon by Glover's men doomed Rall's regiments. From this elevated position, Captain Winthrop Sargent's two 6-pounder cannons blasted the Knyphausen Regiment.

Elements of Rall's and Lossberg's regiments vainly tried to make a stand in Trenton, but the Hessian commander eventually ordered them to retreat to an apple orchard to the southeast. Rall rallied his men and assessed the situation. He sent his adjutant, Lieutenant Jakob Piel, to see whether the bridge across Assunpink Creek had been blocked by the Americans. Piel ran toward the bridge and discovered a large group of men. In the storm, he mistook the men for those in the Knyphausen Regiment; he got within thirty paces before realizing the mistake.

After assembling his regiments, the Hessian Lion decided on a desperate plan to turn the tide. He would attack directly into the heart of Trenton with all three of his units. In the cacophony of musket fire, smoke, and haze, confusion reigned. Rall attempted to align all three of his regiments for the forlorn attack. The Knyphausen Regiment's commander, Major Friedrich von Dechow, requested orders as to whether they should march south or "about left." Rall responded with a single word. Dechow misunderstood. Rall wanted the unit to march in unison into Trenton rather than attack the bridge. Instead of about-facing and marching toward Trenton, they marched toward the bridge and Glover's men. Had all three regiments attacked at once, the assault had a small probability of success. It was Rall's only hope.

The Americans aimed for the Hessian officers—anyone wearing epaulets or carrying a sword. At that moment, two bullets struck the

Hessian commander in the side, mortally wounding him. On horseback, Washington led the attack, urging his troops forward, shouting, "March on, my brave fellows, after me!"[29]

Hit from three sides, the two Hessian regiments, now practically leaderless, lowered their guns and their flags around 9:00 a.m. in a sign of surrender. Washington had just ordered his men to load canister in their guns when the officer in charge of the field pieces informed him, "Sir, they have struck."[30]

"Struck!" replied Washington.

"Yes, their colours are down."

"So they are,"[31] the general responded, spurring his horse forward to meet with the enemy. The two groups greeted each other, and "after satisfying their curiosity a little, they began to converse familiarly in broken English and German."[32]

Following the misunderstood order, near the Assunpink, detached from Rall, the Knyphausen Regiment battled to find an opening in the American encirclement. The American fusillade of deadly musket and artillery fire from the high ground wounded and killed scores of Hessians, bombarding them in the rear and flanks. Blocked from crossing at the stone bridge, the three-hundred-man regiment frantically combed the side of the creek for a place to ford. Sargent's two cannon rained deadly shot into the Hessians, slaying the Germans from the commanding high ground the Marbleheaders had seized earlier.

In desperation, some of the Hessians plunged into the ice-filled Assunpink; several drowned in the swift-running waters of the river. The New Englanders relentlessly pursued them, as one Continental recalled: "Our regiment [waded into the water] which proved about mid-thigh, in order to cut off the enemy's retreat; we marched back to the ferry wet . . . the next morning two of our men perished in the cold and wet, and one Hessian."[33] In a test of human endurance, one group led by Captain Joachim Baum successfully crossed and fled twelve miles to the British garrison in Princeton the next morning nearly dead from exposure to the frigid water and cold air. But the greater part of the regiment was trapped and cut down by musket and cannon. Soon, the Knyphausen's commander, Major Friedrich von Dechow, who had been suffering from two wounds received at Fort Washington, was mortally wounded with a ball to the hip. One of his officers looked for guidance and pleaded, "We cannot give ourselves up like this." Dechow responded, "My dear sir, do as you like. I am wounded."[34] Several of Dechow's men moved the doomed commander off the field, carrying a musket with a white handkerchief fastened to it. The rest of the regiment lay down their arms and capitulated.

To deliver the news of the Knyphausen Regiment's surrender, Major James Wilkinson rode to Washington, who was perched on his horse and surrounded by Marbleheader Caleb Gibbs's Life Guard. With presence and bearing but also displaying his renowned brevity, Washington took Wilkinson's hand and responded, "Major Wilkinson, this is a glorious day for our country."[35]

The Americans captured the bulk of Rall's garrison. Glover's men not only transported the army across the river, they sealed the fate of the Trenton garrison by closing their main egress of escape.

The Hessian Lion lay mortally wounded on a bench in the Methodist church on Queen Street. When the commander was disrobed, "the note of Wall, the Bucks County Tory [whose servant tried to deliver a note to Rall on Christmas Day], came to light."[36] When Rall understood its contents, he simply remarked,

"If I had read this at Mr. Hunt's I would not be here."[37]

After the surrender, Washington visited Rall. His men carried the Hessian leader back to his quarters, and through an interpreter Washington spoke to the commander on his deathbed. Rall asked for kind treatment of his men. Washington later made certain of the Hessian prisoners' humane treatment, stating, "[Prisoners] should have no reason to complain of our copying the brutal example of the British army in their treatment of our unfortunate brethren."[38] Through

Washington's leadership, the Continental strategy and tactics generally aligned with the principles of the Revolution. This democratic army of amateur citizen-soldiers followed a code of conduct that John Adams called a "policy of humanity."[39] This policy governed everything from the way soldiers were supposed to treat civilians to giving quarter to enemy combatants who had surrendered—treating them with respect and not just executing them, as the British often did.

Word of the surrender soon spread to the men still positioned throughout Trenton. A tremendous shout shook the town as the triumphant Americans threw their hats into the air and cheered the victory. To their absolute delight, they found forty hogsheads of rum and cracked them open. One observer noted the drunken rabble: "With [Hessian] brass caps on it was laughable to see how our soldiers would strut, fellows with their elbows out, and some without a collar to their half-a-shirt, no shoes, etc." By the time Washington found out about the alcohol and ordered the casks destroyed, "the soldiers drank too freely to admit of Discipline or Defense in Case of Attack."[40]

Washington had intended to continue his push forward and attack Princeton and New Brunswick after Trenton. He had to scotch those plans for a further offensive, however, owing to the state of the army and the inevitable British counterattack, as Washington explained in his report to Congress: "But the numbers I had with me being inferior to theirs below me and a strong battalion of light infantry being at Princeton above me, I thought it most prudent to return with the prisoners* and artillery we had taken."[41] The victorious yet drunken men rowed back across the icy Delaware. The blizzard continued to rage, and this crossing was even more treacherous than the first, costing the lives of three men. The freezing temperatures threatened all those poorly

---

* Estimates vary, but according to Washington when he wrote to Hancock on December 27, 1776, he had captured 886 men and twenty-three officers. He estimated twenty to thirty men were killed and stated that Rall and seven officers were wounded (the number, according to Stryker, was over twenty), while Washington's army suffered few losses of their own. Washington also captured Hessian artillery pieces and hundreds of muskets, cartridge boxes, and equipment.

clothed from both sides. Lieutenant Marston Watson "composed part of the guard, who had charge of the Hessian prisoners, and the extreme difficulty of keeping them from freezing."[42] It was noon the next day before all the Americans got back to their camp, some having been awake and fighting against the elements and the enemy for fifty hours.

CHAPTER 38

THE EPIC STAND AT ASSUNPINK CREEK

Hundreds of Americans were not able to cross the Delaware River on Christmas Day because they lacked the skill of the Marbleheaders guiding their boats across the treacherous river. One of those groups included the volunteer militia force started by Benjamin Franklin prior to the Revolution, the Philadelphia Associators, led by thirty-four-year-old Colonel John Cadwalader. At the urging of his men on December 27, Cadwalader led the Associators across the Delaware, unknowingly instigating one of the most important but nearly forgotten battles of the Revolution. Believing Washington remained in Trenton, Cadwalader was determined to join him there. One of those Associators was elderly Presbyterian minister John Rosbrugh, their chaplain. Before crossing, the man of God wrote to his wife, "You would think it strange to see your Husband, an old man, riding with a French fusee slung at his back." Carrying his musket, he scribbled a prophetic prediction in the letter: "This may be ye last letter ye shall receive from your Husband."[1]

Washington's troops had won a victory but were exhausted. They had been marching and fighting without rest for more than two days. The commander in chief had not intended to fight again so soon, but the actions taken by Cadwalader and his Philadelphia Associators contributed to forcing his hand. The Americans now had over 1,500 troops, mostly volunteer militia, stranded on the New Jersey side of the river, vulnerable to the enemy.

The general called a council of war, which led to the decision to reinforce Cadwalader and also support elements of the New Jersey militia that had further risen up against the British in December. Once again, Washington ordered his troops to load up on boats and cross the icy river on December 29. Once again, the Marbleheaders facilitated the crossing of the river in several places, but this treacherous crossing took place in daylight, so it proved easier.

The enlistment period for the bulk of Washington's men assembled in Trenton expired on New Year's Day. Some of the army's best units would evaporate, and men would travel back to their homes.

Washington assembled and addressed the army. He alluded to the victory at Trenton and urged the men to stay a month longer.

Drums beat for volunteers.

No soldiers stepped forward.

Wearing rags, shoeless, freezing, and bone-tired, one man recalled, "The soldier fixed on home and the comforts of the domestic circle, and it was hard to forgo the anticipated pleasures of the society of our dearest friends."[2]

The "general wheeled his horse about" and rode in front of his men. Washington mustered his oratorical prowess and once again addressed the troops. "My brave fellows, you have done all I asked you to do and more than could be reasonably expected,"[3] he began.

"But your country is at stake, your wives, your houses, and all that you hold dear. . . . If you will consent to stay one month longer, you will render that service to the cause of liberty and to your country which you probably can never do under any other circumstances. The present is emphatically the crisis, which will decide our destiny."[4]

Drums beat a second time for volunteers.

Many men felt the force of Washington's words. One soldier whispered to the man next to him, "I will remain if you will." Others muttered, "We cannot go home under these circumstances."[5] A few slowly stepped forward, followed by hundreds more, including Marblehead officers William Courtis; Doctor Nathaniel Bond; Marston Watson;

Edward Archbald, who later served as an officer in Colonel John Lamb's 2nd Continental Artillery; and others.[6]

Private William Thompson, an original member of the Marblehead Regiment from its inception, recalled, "We were paraded and solicited to enlist again for a short term . . . that myself and 8 of my fellow townsman who belonged to Captain Swasey's Company accordingly enlisted for an additional six weeks."[7]

Likely William Raymond Lee, William Hawks, and Joshua Orne joined Washington before returning to Marblehead to raise what became known as Lee's Additional Continental Regiment. Marblehead Loyalist Ashley Bowen remarked several weeks later, "This evening came to town Colonel John Glover and some of his regiment."[8] Many men stayed to fight with Washington. Lee was able to recruit nine of the original officers of the regiment. Other Marblehead officers and enlisted men would also serve in different regiments.[9] Marbleheader Caleb Gibbs and the Life Guard remained by Washington's side.

Tragically, half the men who stepped forward that wintry day and volunteered to stay with the army were slain in the subsequent two battles. Many soldiers would perish at the hands of the silent killer, all too familiar to Marblehead, and now raging through the Continental ranks: smallpox.[10] One of those men fighting the pox was Doctor Nathaniel Bond. The Marblehead physician eventually retired from the role of company commander and reverted to the role of healer, as he had on Cat Island. In the coming months, he supervised the inoculation of Washington's army.[11] But in the coming weeks, Bond still continued to lead his company.

Despite his most impassioned pleas, Washington had his doubts about how many of Glover's men he could retain: "I shall know today," he wrote to the Executive Committee of the Continental Congress, "how many of Colo Glover's Regt. are willing to continue the land service. I don't expect many will be prevailed upon to stay, and I will endeavor to procure the rest for the purpose of fitting out the Frigates upon the best terms I can."[12]

Congress hoped that the victory would spur more reenlistments but advised Washington that if sailors from the New England regiments "obstinately persist in being discharged from your service on New Year's Day we think it advisable to prevail upon them to come down here [to Philadelphia] & assist in getting the frigates out."[13] Glover's men did not crew the new frigates in Philadelphia. Instead, some of the Marbleheaders remained with Glover. The allure of privateering, with crews keeping a portion of prizes captured at sea, was tempting. Some of the men could not ignore the distress of their impoverished, hungry families back in economically depressed Marblehead and Beverly. Additionally, Glover's wife suffered from poor health. Always the reluctant soldier, Glover longed to return home and be by her side.

The Marbleheaders and most of Brown's Beverly Company, who remained with John Glover, began the long march north to Marblehead. John Glover Jr. remained by his father's side and journeyed with an infirm Gabriel Johonnot, who, "in consequence of great bodily inability, the result of a violent fever . . . brought on by severe duty was compelled to decline the command of the regiment."[14] Together the sick, wounded, and healthy members of the 14th Continental Regiment, including Johonnot and Romeo, trekked on foot back to Marblehead and Beverly. Hungry, poorly clothed, and often barefoot, the men made the three-hundred-mile trudge in the dead of winter.[15] An unknown number of Marblehead Regiment men volunteered to reenlist and fight with Washington in battles that would unfold in the coming days.

Teenage fifer John Greenwood also left the army, determined to return to his parents in Boston. When Greenwood told an officer in his unit he was leaving, the lieutenant responded, "My God! You are not, I hope, going to leave us, for you are the heart and soul of us and are to be promoted to ensign." The miserable Greenwood responded, "I would not stay to be colonel." Vermin covered Greenwood's body. "I had the itch so bad that my breeches stuck to my thighs, all the skin being off, and there were hundreds of vermin upon, owing to a whole month's march and having been obliged, for the sake of keeping warm, to lie down at night among soldiers who were huddled close together like hogs."[16] Upon returning to New England, Greenwood joined Marblehead commodore John Manley at sea.

As the news of Washington's victory spread, the mood in both camps shifted dramatically. Emboldened by the victory, Congressman Elbridge Gerry exclaimed in a New Year's Day letter, "The middle States are roused from their late supine state, & are exerting themselves to reinforce the army; I hope a proper spirit will be exercised on this occasion & the enemy be driven from the Jersies."[17] Only a week earlier, the rebellion seemed over. But the disaster at Trenton unraveled William Howe's carefully laid plans. Militia attacks in New Jersey intensified, and faulty intelligence led the British to believe, incorrectly, that Washington's forces numbered sixteen thousand. Rumors spread of looming attacks on the Crown's outposts in New Jersey. Hessian captain Johann Ewald summed up how the war's momentum had shifted: "Thus the times changed! The Americans had constantly run before us. For weeks we expected to end the war with the capture of Philadelphia,[18] and now we had to render Washington the honor of thinking about our defense. Due to this affair at Trenton, such a fright came over the army that if Washington had used this opportunity we would have flown to our ships and let him have all of America."[19]

One man who would not be returning to England was Charles Edward Cornwallis. The British general was aboard a vessel bound for England to tend to his wife, who was in failing health. As the ship prepared to leave port, an express messenger brought news of the debacle at Trenton. Howe canceled Cornwallis's leave and assigned his best general to lead the counterattack against Washington.

On New Year's Day, his thirty-eighth birthday, the earl assembled the cream of the British Army in North America. At his disposal stood the elite and seasoned light infantry, Highlanders, grenadiers, guards, and Hessians, most with over a decade of experience. Cornwallis placed the light infantry, in the front of his eight-thousand-man army, creating a slow-moving scarlet line that stretched for over a mile. Through muck and mud from New York to Princeton, the column trudged toward their enemy.

Upon reaching the crucial post at New Brunswick, Cornwallis left six hundred troops to guard the British Army's massive £70,000 sterling war chest along with military supplies. Cornwallis continued his march accompanied by several regiments of Hessians spoiling to avenge the losses at Trenton. Hessian officers ordered their men not to take prisoners: "They were to kill all the Rebels they could without mercy."[20]

Unlike Johann Rall in his military stand made in the center of Trenton, Washington wisely decided to defend the high ground across the Assunpink, which Glover had captured only days earlier. In the general orders from Trenton dated December 30, 1776, Washington revealed his plan: "All the artillery to be Draw up on the high Ground over the Bridge two pieces to be posted to Command the pass at the Bridge. Upon an alarm, the Troops are to form on the Ground in the rear of the artillery to form in three Lines. Stevens & Mercers Brigades in the front Line, Lord Sterling & Formoys Brigades form the Second Line there to be under Command of General Green, Sergeants, Glovers & St. Clairs Brigades to form the third line, to be under the command of Major General Sullivan. . . . A distance of two hundred & fifty yards to be left between each Line. Colonel Glovers is Desired to post the Guards." Washington added, "The General expects to march very Soon he Desires that the officers and soldiers to hold themselves in complete readiness to advance at a moments warning."[21]

By January 2, 1777, the American army had girded for Cornwallis's counterattack heading straight for them. Washington sent French general Matthias de Roche-Fermoy and a brigade of Americans, including Edward Hand's Pennsylvania riflemen, to slow down Cornwallis's advance. Roche-Fermoy had appeared in Washington's camp in November and presented dubious credentials. Washington had given him the benefit of the doubt and handed him command of a brigade.

James Wilkinson called him a "worthless drunkard,"[22] and as the British juggernaut bore down on his command, Roche-Fermoy turned tail and galloped off to Trenton.*

Outnumbered nearly ten to one and no stranger to a desperate situation, Colonel Edward Hand calmly took command. His men set up opposite a dismantled wooden bridge across Big Shabakunk Creek. Armed with lethal long rifles accurate up to three hundred yards, his riflemen crouched behind boulders and logs, waiting for the vanguard of Cornwallis's army to approach so they could ambush them. The British had to cross the creek and then pass along the Post Road that snaked through woods a mile deep intersected with ravines and gullies. Hand's rifle fire cut down the elite British troops, forcing them to retreat in confusion. Skilled hunters since their childhood and crack shots, Hand's men cut through the British ranks. To deal with the snipers, the British brought up artillery and lined up in formation to mass the fire of their muskets. British fire "scoured the wood for a half an hour before they entered it,"[23] remembered James Wilkinson. Hand and other troops made a series of stands that continued to slow the British advance on Trenton. At about 3:00 p.m., Hand ordered his men back to a ravine called Stockton Hollow, where they made their final stand before retreating sometime around 4:00 p.m. The Americans burned a staggering seven hours of daylight, allowing the rest of Washington's army and those Marbleheaders who stayed with it to dig in on the eastern side on the high ground of the Assunpink. Darkness swiftly approached, and night attacks, even by the most experienced army, were very difficult to execute.

Civilians fled Trenton before Cornwallis's advancing army, and Washington's forces retreated across the stone bridge on the Assunpink. One man trapped in Trenton was Chaplain John Rosbrugh. Hessians surrounded the elderly pastor, who sank to the ground on his knees

---

* Roche-Fermoy was assigned to another command near Fort Ticonderoga, bizarrely setting fire to his own quarters before the evacuation of the post. After not receiving a promotion, he left the army.

and begged for mercy for the sake of his wife and children. Hessians taunted him, stole the watch Rosbrugh offered for his life, stripped him naked, and ruthlessly bayoneted him seventeen times, leaving the last bayonet standing in his body. They also inflicted multiple saber slashes to his head before leaving him where he lay, the first US chaplain killed in battle.[24]

After moving into Trenton, Cornwallis's massive army set up in formation. Cannons boomed, and the two armies' artilleries dueled for twenty-five minutes. Wilkinson recounted his vivid memories of the onslaught: "I recollect perfectly the sun had set. . . . I could distinguish the flame from the muzzles of our muskets."[25] The British elite troops coiled for an assault.

The stone bridge crossing the Assunpink stood between the two camps.

"Defend the bridge to the last extremity!" Washington ordered. Colonel Charles Scott of the Virginia Regiment uttered a "tremendous oath" before agreeing, "To the last man, excellency."[26]

Beside the Americans, the nearly frozen Delaware River cut off any hope of retreat—and they had no boats for crossing even if it had been possible. In front of them, a much larger force of British and Hessian troops was inexorably approaching.

Holding the bridge became a crucial inflection point—a make-or-break point in the Revolution. If the British broke through, the Continental Army would face destruction.

Though it had won a decisive victory in the very same place just a few days before, the American army now found itself in the grip of despair. "This was the most awful crisis," wrote one of the officers present, "no possible chance of crossing the River; ice as large as houses floating down, and no retreat to the mountains, the British between us and them." Another echoed the same sentiment, recalling, "If there ever was a crisis in the affairs of the Revolution, this was the moment; thirty minutes would have sufficed to bring the two armies into contact, and thirty more would have decided the combat; and, covered with woe, Columbia might have wept the loss of her beloved chief and most valorous sons."[27]

The Virginians, Marylanders, the men of the Marblehead Regiment who reenlisted, and other men in Washington's army waited on the banks of the creek. One private summed up the situation: "On one hour, yes, on forty minutes, commencing at the moment when the British troops first saw the bridge and creek before them, depended the all-important, the all-absorbing question whether we should be independent States, or conquered rebels!"[28]

Along the Assunpink, Washington arranged his troops with the skill of a chess master. His most trusted veteran Continentals, along with the invaluable artillery pieces, guarded the likeliest crossings. He posted men and artillery on the coveted high ground. Near the all-important stone bridge stood the New Englanders, Marbleheaders, and the Life Guard, along with Colonel Charles Scott and his Virginians. Washington interspersed the less reliable militia among the regulars to bolster their courage and prevent gaps in the line. Scott extolled his men before the melee and gave them instructions: "Well, boys, you know the old boss has put us here to defend this bridge; and by God it must be done, let what will come. . . . Whenever you see them fellows first begin to put their feet upon this bridge do you shin 'em. Take care now and fire low. Bring down your pieces, fire at their legs, one man Wounded in the leg is better [than] a dead one for it takes two more to carry him off and there is three gone. Leg them dam 'em I say leg them."[29]

Leading by example, Washington remained next to the bridge. Described by one of his officers in battle as "born with iron nerves and an unending dignity of port which distinguished all his actions, and struck the most presumptuous with awe,"[30] the general exhibited a calm composure that steeled his men as dense, solid masses of Americans crossed the narrow stone bridge. One private remembered how Washington led from the front: "The noble horse of Gen. Washington stood with his breast pressed close against the end of the west rail of the bridge, and the firm, composed, and majestic countenance of the

General inspired confidence and assurance in a moment so important and critical. . . . The horse stood as firm as the rider, and seemed to understand that he was not to quit his post and station."[31]

As Hand's troops streamed over the bridge to take up positions along the miles-long defensive line, Washington directed Daniel Hitchcock's Regiment to "March to that field and form immediately." The commander in chief extended his arm and pointed to the field near the bridge. As the men passed several cannon posted in front of the bridge, the guns were "drawn aside." After the Americans crossed, the artillery were "once again placed at the end of the bridge and discharged into the front of the enemy column which was advancing towards it."[32]

The New Englanders had barely crossed when Hessian grenadiers made their first attempt to storm the bridge and traversed halfway across before American fire stopped them. "They continued to advance, though their speed was diminished. And as the column reached the bridge it moved slower and slower until the head of it was gradually pressed nearly over, when our fire became so destructive that they broke their ranks and fled,"[33] one American witnessed.

The setback did not halt the enemy's elite troops in front of a column "nearly a mile long." Again, "officers reformed the ranks and again they rushed the bridge."

The British shouted and repeated, "Huzzah!"

"And again was the shower of bullets poured upon them with redoubled fury."[34]

Deadly fire broke the British assault near the center of the bridge. Elated in their triumph, the Americans raised a cheer at the sight of the British retreat. "It was then that our army raised a shout," recalled one man, "and such a shout I never since heard; by what signal or word of command, I know not. The line was more than a mile in length, and from the nature of the ground the extremes were not in sight of each other, yet they shouted as one man."[35] Still, the Redcoats remained undaunted. They reformed and charged a third time. "We loaded with canister shot and let them come nearer. We fired all together again, and such destruction it made, you cannot conceive," noted one American artillerist.[36] A tremendous series of shouts echoed along the American line as the British withdrew into Trenton.

Three attempted assaults left the bridge coated in blood and limbs, devastation unleashed from nearly point-blank cannon and musket fire. "The bridge looked red as blood, with their killed and wounded and their red coats,"[37] wrote one soldier. Corpses carpeted the bridge.

Assunpink turned into a brilliant defensive stand against the Crown's best troops. However, the army still faced encirclement and destruction by Cornwallis's larger force and British units about to march down from Princeton. That evening Cornwallis gathered his senior officers. The British general considered that Washington might launch a night attack and prepared his army, but he remained convinced he had Washington trapped. During the council, Sir William Erskine opined, "My Lord, if you trust those people you will see nothing of them in the morning."[38] Erskine warned that Washington would run to fight another day, as much of the last six months had borne out. According to legend, Cornwallis retorted, "We've got the old fox safe now. We'll go over and bag him in the morning."[39]

CHAPTER 39

PRINCETON

On the cold evening of January 2, Washington also called his own council of war. Unlike Charles Edward Cornwallis in the autocratic meeting he convened, Washington sought the advice of his subordinates. The army once again found itself in a desperate situation. The Delaware flanked one side of their position. If they attempted to retreat across the river with the few boats they had available (and without the services of the bulk of the Marblehead men), it was likely that the British would pounce before the army crossed, potentially destroying or capturing a large portion of Washington's force. Retreating into southern New Jersey was unviable since it was primarily populated by Loyalists and within striking range of the British posts and Cornwallis's army. If they stayed where they were, Cornwallis would certainly attack again in the morning. Although Washington held a solid position defending the bridge at Assunpink Creek, the enemy might use one of the fords upstream to flank the Continental Army, potentially encircling and annihilating it. Washington chillingly reminded the council the loss of the corps he commanded "might be fatal to the country,"[1]

During the meeting, General Arthur St. Clair, a tough Scot who served in the British Army during the French and Indian War, suggested "the idea of turning the left flank of the enemy in the night: gaining a march upon him, and proceeding with all possible expedition to Brunswick."[2] While St. Clair took credit for introducing the idea to the council, it is more likely that Washington knew exactly what he wanted to do but did not want to appear overbearing. A man who did not know he had only hours left to live seconded the proposal:

"General Mercer immediately fell in with it, and forcibly pointed out both its practicability, and the advantages that would necessarily result from it."[3] Capture of the massive British war chest at New Brunswick, Washington reasoned, might very well end the war. The depot also contained a windfall of much-needed supplies. Washington's operation was perilous: delays or loss of the element of surprise could lead to the destruction of the army by placing it between two British forces (the troops at Trenton and those stationed at Princeton), where it could be trapped and obliterated. But first, the Continental Army had to defeat the smaller British garrison at Princeton. Once that occurred, Washington determined to retreat to the formidable high ground around Morristown for winter quarters that also contained numerous Patriot farms to feed the army. By positioning himself in Morristown, Washington hoped it would force the British to contract their perimeter closer to New York, allow the Whigs to regain control of the countryside, and intimidate and control the Loyalists. The commander in chief also wanted to foster the local New Jersey militias and combine with them to drive the British out of New Jersey.

On the other hand, remaining in New Jersey exposed the army to the full weight of the British. They would be far away from the relative safety of the natural barrier of the Delaware River and Pennsylvania. The absence of the bulk of the 14th Continental Regiment and boats indirectly forced a Cortés-like strategy of burning the ships and moving inland to achieve victory. Since an amphibious retreat would be nearly impossible, and an exit into southern New Jersey unsustainable, attacking Princeton became the most viable option. The Continental Army would once again conquer or die.

The desperate gamble could work only if the enemy remained utterly unaware of Washington's intended destination. A single deserter, as nearly occurred in Long Island or at Trenton, could destroy the entire enterprise. Washington employed stealth and stratagem to enable the bold plan. The Americans torched fence rails to keep their campfires flaming brightly. Clanging shovels and pickaxes created the illusion of digging entrenchments for battle the next day. A tiny fragment remained to maintain the ruse as the army began the long, cold march. "Orders were given in a whisper; muskets were gingerly handled and footfalls lightly planted."[4] They even went so far as to wrap the wheels of their cannons in pieces of cloth to prevent any noise from reaching the ears of the sleeping enemy.

Despite the army's best efforts to mask its intentions, the British detected hazy movements through the flickering flames of the American campfires. British sentries reported the movement to Cornwallis, who remained convinced the intelligence indicated Washington maneuvered to attack his left flank rather than a march to Princeton.

Temperatures plummeted to twenty degrees, and an inky black sky dappled with a few stars canopied the Marbleheaders and their fellow Americans as they pondered their predicament. One soldier recalled, "[We were in] the most desperate situation I had ever known it; we had no boats to cross the Delaware, and if he had, so powerful an enemy would certainly destroy the better half before we embarked. To cross the enemy's line of march, between this and Princeton, seemed impracticable; and when we thought about retreating into the south part of New Jersey, where there was no support for an army, that was discouraging." Despite the dire nature of their situation, the same soldier approached his officer and inquired about their lot and the state of the Revolution, receiving the reply, "I don't know; the Lord must help us." Remarkably, he then recorded, "The men and officers seemed cheerful and in great spirits."[5] Sleep deprived, hungry, barefoot, and freezing, the men somehow reached deep within themselves and tapped a reservoir of hope and resilience as they slogged toward Princeton. Marblehead lieutenant Marston Watson vividly remembered the bone-chilling "severity of the forced march from Trenton to Princeton on the night of 2–3 January 1777."[6] All through the night, the exhausted Continental Army and the remaining Marbleheaders silently marched, leaving a trail of bloody footprints in their wake, until they approached a creek two miles outside Princeton around dawn. By the light of the rising sun, they saw a landscape transformed by a coating of tiny, stunning spears of ice on every branch, fence, and blade of grass. "The morning was bright, serene, and extremely cold, with a hoar frost that bespangled every object."[7] Here, Washington split his force, as he had done at Trenton to surround Princeton from two sides and envelop the British, as well as hold the crossing at the creek to block Cornwallis's pursuit.

Marbleheaders were likely scattered among units marching in column toward Princeton.

Leading one column were John Mercer's Brigade with John Cadwalader's Philadelphia Associators just behind. But as they marched, something unexpected caught Mercer's attention. The glint of sunlight on steel gave the men the first warning that the battle would begin sooner than expected.

Coincidentally, the British were also on the move that morning. Most of the three regiments and several troops of dragoons stationed in Princeton were headed to Trenton, where the rest of Cornwallis's troops were waiting. Lieutenant Colonel Charles Mawhood, a competent veteran commander with a reputation for eccentricity, was equally surprised to see Mercer's men emerging from the woods approaching Princeton. As his two small spaniels playfully yipped and barked around his brown pony's feet, Mawhood ordered a halt and contemplated while the Americans did the same. "We drew up on a woody eminence and looked at them for a considerable time," recalled one of the British soldiers. "Colonel Mawhood had two choices, either to retire back to Princeton, where . . . we might have defended the works about it, or push on to Maidenhead where the 2d Brigade lay."[8] Eventually he reached a decision. The British commander ordered his approximately seven hundred men to drop packs, fix bayonets, and form a line of attack.

Mercer and his men "rushed without reconnoitering into a thick planted orchard and were soon surprised to find themselves in the presence of a well [drawn] up line of infantry, with flanking [picket] and two pieces of cannon."[9]

"Huzzah! Huzzah!" the Redcoats shouted as they executed a vicious bayonet charge. Surging forward, they bore down on the Americans. Almost immediately, Mercer's horse collapsed under him as a well-aimed bullet struck the beast. First surprised by the enemy, now seeing their leader fall, Mercer's terrified men scattered despite his protests. Mercer bravely drew his sword and continued to fight on foot; but forsaken by his men, he took seven bayonet wounds to the belly. Mortally wounded, he would die several days later.

Now leaderless, the panicked men ran for their lives with the British just steps behind. All would have been lost then had not Cadwalader, with his much larger force of 1,200 Philadelphia Associators along with three companies of Continental Marines, arrived and joined the battle. Leading from the front of his men, Cadwalader ordered his Associators to halt and fire at the oncoming British troops. Taking courage from the example of their brothers in arms, some of Mercer's men stopped running and headed back to the battle. This gave the Patriots numerical superiority, but Mawhood's superior tactics soon overcame that advantage. Mawhood had positioned his troops "so that every man could load and fire incessantly."[10] While the Patriots reloaded, the enemy pounded them. Overcome by the artillery fire, Cadwalader's front lines broke and "threw the whole in confusion."[11]

Witnessing the flight, General Washington galloped toward his routed men. Each time he passed a group of soldiers, he urged them to find their courage and hold their ground, waving his hat to them before proceeding. Despite Washington's valor, many of his men continued to run, leading one British officer to remark, "I am convinced that had the other [British] brigade been with us we might have defeated the whole American army.[12] Risking imminent death, Washington rode to within thirty paces of the British lines, presenting an irresistible target to the Redcoats. A tremendous volley rang out as the enemy aimed for the general. Miraculously, Washington seemed invulnerable to bullets and remained on his horse, calling on his men to join him in facing the enemy. "His Greatness is far beyond description. I shall never forget what I felt at Princeton on his account, when I saw him brave all the dangers of the field and his important life hanging as it were by a single hair with a thousand deaths flying around him. . . . He is surely America's better Genius and Heaven's peculiar care,"[13] wrote James Reed to his wife. Marblehead lieutenant Marston Watson participated in the "attack on the British regiments and [witnessed firsthand] General Washington's intrepid bearing on that occasion."[14]

"Parade with us, my brave fellows!" Washington shouted. "There is but a handful of the enemy and we will have them directly."[15]

The Americans rallied, and with the commander in chief now directing the battle, the British line buckled and eventually broke. But the iron discipline and mental toughness of many of the British troops showed as they fought on in smaller groups while other Crown troops ran for their lives.

Washington, urging his men to pursue Mawhood's men, repeated the humiliating battle cry that the Crown's forces had shouted when his troops fled the field at Harlem Heights:

"It is a fine fox chase, my boys!"[16]

As they advanced, they were horrified to see that the formerly glistening white landscape had turned scarlet. The frozen ground could not soak up the gore, so "all the blood which was shed remained on the surface."[17]

Scores of British troops girded for battle in Nassau Hall of the institution formerly known as the College of New Jersey, now Princeton University. The Americans, under the command of Alexander Hamilton, brought a cannon to bear and fired into the building, forcing the bulk of the Redcoats to surrender. St. Clair's Brigade attacked through Frog Hollow, a steep ravine that led into the back gate of the college. The American advance was followed up by General John Sullivan, whose attack enveloped the British, forcing many to surrender.

British resistance in the college and several redoubts allowed Mawhood and part of his force to escape. Washington gave chase to Mawhood's routed men. As he did many times during the Revolution, Washington called a council of war from the back of his saddle. After several miles, Washington relented and gave up all hope of claiming the prize in New Brunswick: a war chest containing one of the most enormous fortunes in North America along with priceless military supplies. Henry Knox wrote in a letter to his wife, Lucy, "We at first intended to have made a forced march to Brunswick; but our men having been without either rest, rum, or provisions for two nights and days, were unequal to the task of marching seventeen miles further. If we could have secured one thousand fresh men at Princeton to have pushed for Brunswick, we should have struck one of the most brilliant strokes in all history."[18] Arthur St. Clair later detailed his regrets: "The design of proceeding to Brunswick was necessarily abandoned; it was eighteen miles distant, and the troops were very much fatigued, and as the principal deposit of the enemy's military stores was at that place, they had certainly not been left unguarded; resistance was therefore to be expected, which would require some time to overcome, and a superior army was close upon us."[19] Listening to the advice of his generals, Washington lamented to John Hancock on January 5, "In my Judgment Six or Eight hundred fresh Troops upon a forced march would have destroyed all their Stores and Magazines—taken as we have since learnt their Military Chest containing 70,000£ and put an end to the War."[20] But the men were exhausted.

Mawhood and his troops had taken on Washington's entire force, inspiring awe with their desperate and bold actions. They also disrupted the primary focus of Washington's plan: New Brunswick and the capture of supplies and the war chest.

So much of the timing of the operation miraculously worked in Washington's favor. What if Mawhood had been only a few hundred yards down the road to Trenton and not seen Washington's force? What if Princeton took longer to subdue, or what if Washington captured the war chest only to be in the jaws of Cornwallis's superior forces in New Brunswick and never escaped to Morristown? Choices made by Washington and his general officers, as well as timing outside their control, blended perfectly to secure the American victory and preserve the Continental Army.

Washington prudently decided to march toward the safety of the steep hills around Morristown, New Jersey. The Marbleheaders who remained with Washington in the army did not get very far. On the afternoon of January 3, the men limped into Rocky Hill, New Jersey, about a three-hour march from Princeton. Exhausted, sleep deprived, starving, and low on ammunition and supplies, they arrived at the Somerset Court House, but the army could not march a step farther. As one of the few trained surgeons present, battle-worn Doctor Nathaniel Bond tended to the walking wounded.

Abandoning New Brunswick was a prudent decision: Cornwallis had assumed that Washington was heading toward New Brunswick, and that is where he prepared to battle, missing a golden opportunity. Had Cornwallis accurately determined the nearly defenseless Continental Army's location only a few hours' march from Princeton, he could have destroyed it.

Trenton and Princeton had changed the course of the war; now Washington seized the initiative. Instead of pursuing a defeated American army, the Redcoats heard rumors of new threats: an army of American troops (the corps formerly led by the recently captured Charles Lee) advanced from Morristown, and New Jersey militiamen harassed supply lines among the few fortified garrisons. Misinformation planted by Washington led the British to believe the American armies were bigger than their own. Cornwallis abandoned many of the posts in New Jersey. Instead of attacking, the British turned to the defensive. William Howe's plan of offering pardons to Americans to attempt to win over the population of New Jersey was also severely damaged. Had the triple victories at Trenton and Princeton not taken place, the war might well have ended in 1777. For the British, the debacles at Trenton and Princeton vanquished the notion that the rebellion was near broken.

After three days of grueling marching, Stephen Moylan wrote about the victories from the army's new encampment in Morristown: "It was glorious . . . America will—by God, it must—be free."[21] Word of the victories spread worldwide and ended the assumption that amateur citizen-soldiers who just months earlier had been farmers, bakers, and blacksmiths could not defeat the most highly trained and experienced regulars in the world. Even Prussian king Frederick the Great sent his praise: "The achievements of Washington and his little band of compatriots between the 25th of December and the 4th of January, were the most brilliant of any record in the annals of military achievements."[22] The Marbleheaders, Washington's indispensable men, were essential to making these victories possible.

CHAPTER 40

HOME AND BACK

On the cold, snowy evening of January 20, 1777, the tattered remains of the regiment limped back into Marblehead. Many of them were sick. Many were wounded. The men had marched for weeks, traversing more than three hundred miles on the journey from Trenton, enduring the brutal, wintry elements. With their muscles spent and bones weary, only willpower propelled them forward the final steps home.

But upon arriving in Marblehead, they found a festering economic disaster instead of a joyous homecoming.[1] With Marblehead's fishing industry shuttered while most of its inhabitants fought in the Revolution, those left behind were starving. A twentysomething Marblehead woman explained, "We cannot now get meat nor bread, we see the world is naught but cheat. . . . Some say they an't victuals nor drink. Others say they are ready to sink." Financially, both Marblehead and Beverly experienced a soul-crushing depression and, with the men off to war, women had to survive on their own. As Molly Gutridge revealed, "It's hard and cruel times to live. . . . Money is not worth a pin."[2]

The women of the area did not acquiesce. When the merchants began refusing to accept the rapidly depreciating paper money, about sixty of the women of Beverly donned their lambskin cloaks with riding hoods and marched in formation down to the docks. Led by one of their number who was carrying a musket, they headed first to a distillery whose owner had recently died. When the foreman saw such a fearsome group approaching, he locked the gates, but the undaunted women simply asked some men who supported their cause to break them down with axes. Once inside, they grabbed the foreman by the hair and might have scalped him, except that—fortunately for him—he was wearing a wig. The now-bald foreman fled in terror, locking himself in the counting room. The women took possession of two barrels of sugar, which they loaded onto carts they had brought for that purpose. The incident convinced the rest of the merchants that it was in their best interest to negotiate with the feisty throng.

Most of the returning men were not in much better shape than the town. Exhausted physically, mentally, and monetarily from years of conflict, the citizen-soldiers had no reserves left on which to draw. John Glover, physically drained, infirm, nearly ruined financially, and with his wife sick, decided to part ways with the army. He considered the absence permanent, but in February 1777, Congress promoted him to brigadier general. Glover initially declined the commission, writing to George Washington on April 1, 1777, "I Cannot think myself in any Degree Capable of doing the duty, necessary to be done, by an officer of that Rank."[3]

Washington responded first by conveying understanding of Glover's situation and then praising the Marbleheader: "After the conversations, I had with you, before you left the army, last Winter, I was not a little surprised at the contents of yours of the first instant. . . . I know of no man better qualified than you to conduct a Brigade. You have activity and industry, and as you very well know the duty of a colonel, you know how to exact that duty from others."[4] A master motivator, Washington then laid on the guilt:

> I have with great concern observed the almost universal list-lessness, that prevails throughout the continent; and I believe, that nothing has contributed to it more, than the resignation of officers, who stepped early forward and led the people into the great cause, in which we are too deeply embarked to look back, or to hope for any other terms, than those we can gain by the sword. Can any resistance be expected from the people when deserted by their leaders? Our enemies count upon the resignation of every officer of rank at this time, as a distrust of,

and desertion from the cause, and rejoice accordingly. When you consider these matters I hope you will think no more of private inconveniences, but that you will, with all expedition, come forward, and take that command which has been assigned you. As I fully depend upon seeing you, I shall not mention anything, that has passed between us, upon this subject, to the Congress.[5]

Glover relented and returned to the service. In short order he found himself, once again, in command of a brigade of New Englanders who would serve decisively in the Revolution.

During the summer of 1777, Glover and his new unit moved north once again. Assigned to General Horatio Gates, they would soon face off against British forces commanded by General John Burgoyne, who invaded New York from Canada. Throughout September and October, the two armies fought a series of pitched battles, now known collectively as the Battles of Saratoga. And while Glover and his men frequently distinguished themselves, they also suffered casualties. On September 19, at Freeman's Farm, Glover's men fought nonstop for more than six hours in the heaviest combat. Glover explained, "Both armies seemed determined to conquer or die. One continual blaze, without intermission till dark. . . . During which time we several times drove them, took the ground, passing over great numbers of their dead and wounded. We took one field piece . . . and obliged to give up the prize. They were bold, intrepid and fought like heroes, and I do assure you Sirs, our men were equally bold and courageous & fought like men."[6]

Just weeks later, the armies faced off again. On October 7, a portion of Glover's Brigade, under the command of Benedict Arnold, launched a furious counterattack on the British. This time the outcome was more decisive. Glover's men and those with them forced Burgoyne to retreat back north toward Canada.

However, all was not as it seemed. Three days later, Burgoyne appeared to be retreating hastily to Fort Edward. Gates sent Glover's brigade and other elements of the army to destroy what he thought was Burgoyne's rearguard. Fortunately, a British deserter warned Glover that Burgoyne had actually set up a massive ambush. Glover notified Gates and the other commanders, avoiding a potential debacle.

His plans foiled, Burgoyne and his army of more than 5,700 troops surrendered on October 17. The decisive victory at Saratoga, made possible by important contributions from Glover's men, including many Marbleheaders from the original regiment, had a seismic impact on the Revolution; the victory contributed to the Franco-American alliance and mushroomed the Revolution from a North American conflict into a global war. Tremendously appreciative of Glover's actions, Gates granted Glover's men the honor of escorting the British prisoners back to Massachusetts. But for Glover, the victory was overshadowed by the loss of his son John Glover Jr. and his daughter-in-law. After returning from Trenton, John Jr. likely went back to sea as privateer, and was lost at sea. His beloved wife, Hannah, after whom he had named the first armed vessel of the United States, died of disease soon thereafter.

The following summer, France sent a fleet of twelve ships of the line under the command of Admiral comte d'Estaing to North America. D'Estaing decided to sail for Newport, Rhode Island, which was then occupied by the British. The Americans also began preparing for an assault, stockpiling supplies and raising additional troops for a combined and joint operation on Newport. As news of the French involvement spread, volunteers streamed in from Massachusetts and New Hampshire and, together with the Rhode Island militia and Continentals, prepared to attack. If all had gone according to plan, it could have been a potentially decisive Yorktown-like victory three years before 1781.

But it was not to be. A storm pummeled the ships, wreaking havoc. Shortly after, the British and French navies engaged in several skirmishes, which damaged vessels from both fleets. Neglecting to coordinate with the Americans, d'Estaing decided to send his fleet to Boston for repairs—effectively killing the Newport operation. As a direct result of the loss of French support, militia members abandoned their duties in droves just as quickly as they had assumed them. John Sullivan and Nathanael Greene, the Patriot commanders in charge of the American forces, became incensed.

Facing seemingly insurmountable difficulties, the Americans abandoned their plans for a siege, instead setting up defensive positions around two key high points near Newport. When the inevitable fight arrived, Glover's Brigade again played an important role. In command of the troops that held the crucial hill, Glover had orders to hold at all cost to allow John Sullivan's men to escape. In an epic stand, Glover's men held the mount, driving back the attack.

With casualties mounting on both sides, the Patriots retreated from the hill and the island in an orderly manner, leaving the British in control of Newport. But with their stand, John Glover and his brigade had once again helped save a portion of the army.

By the summer of 1782, Glover had had enough of the war. He wrote to Washington, "When I enter'd the service in 1775 I had as good a Constitution as any Man of my Age, but it's now broken & shatter'd to pieces, good for nothing, & quite worn out; However [I] shall make the best of it."[7] In addition, outfitting Washington's Navy and his men had ruined him financially. "The expense of my little fortune, earned by hard labor and industry; to sacrifice . . . and total ruin of a family of young children." Able to eke out only two hours of sleep every night, Glover likely suffered from post-traumatic stress disorder. "So far as my State of health will permit; which at present, is Very much impaird, and exceedingly precarious, (God, alone, knows how long it may Continue So) as my want of Sleep, night Sweats . . ."[8]

Glover officially retired from the Continental Army in July 1782, having succeeded at all the tasks Washington assigned him, but at nearly unbearable personal cost.

Marblehead's and Beverly's sacrifice to the Revolution was enormous. Scores of Marbleheaders expired from sickness, from battlefield wounds, or in captivity. Despite the hardships they endured—lack of adequate pay, food, and clothing—most of the Marblehead Regiment went back to war. Some, like teen soldiers John Rhodes Russell and Manuel Soto, continued to battle on land with new units.

Fittingly, a bronze statue of Russell, located in Trenton, memorializes his service and the valor of the regiment.

This sort of recognition was far from the norm, however. Much more commonly, the Marbleheaders' decisions to stand up against their oppressors continued to cost them until their dying days. For example, Caesar Glover fought for three more years of the Revolution. After leaving Washington's Army, he worked as a laborer the rest of his life. When he died, he owned only a paltry few earthly possessions, including six spoons, a shovel, and some crockery.[9]

Some met a more tragic fate. Joshua Orne went on serving as an officer in Lee's Regiment. After surviving many years of hard fighting, he tragically died from a fall that resulted in a "blow to the head"[10] while descending the steps from the American consul's door in Bordeaux, France.

Lieutenant William Hawks continued the fight in Major William Raymond Lee's newly formed regiment[11] with several of the other officers, such as Marston Watson. According to one source, the Continental Army mysteriously cashiered Hawks out of its ranks.[12]

And still others earned accolades and advancement for serving with distinction. After Princeton, Caleb Gibbs and the Life Guard, along with the remnants of the Continental Army, encamped at winter quarters in Morristown.

At Morristown, Nathaniel Bond reverted to physician and his smallpox expertise. In February 1777, the variola virus ravaged the Continental Army. Washington wrote, "Necessity not only authorizes but seems to require the measure, for should the disorder infect the Army in the natural way and rage with its usual virulence, we should have more to dread from it than from the Sword of the Enemy."[13] The risk was enormous; nearly a fifth of the Continental Army had contracted the disease; a real possibility existed the army could be incapacitated from smallpox. In America's first national public health declaration, the commander in chief boldly ordered Doctor Bond to inoculate the army. "Under these circumstances I have directed Doctr Bond to prepare immediately for inoculating in this Quarter, keeping the matter as secret as possible, and request that you will without delay inoculate

All the Continental Troops."[14] Leaning on his experience at Cat Island, Bond organized the development of new hospitals, and he facilitated thousands of troops' inoculations. Washington chose to conduct inoculations during the winter when both sides went into quarters, and fighting slowed—time for men to recover from a procedure that either killed or cured. The doctor who had been wrongly accused of being a traitor at the beginning of Revolution by an enraged mob, helped save the army. Bond's personal sacrifice would cost him his life; he died treating the soldiers he saved. Historian Joseph Ellis later claimed, "When historians debate Washington's most consequential decisions as commander in chief, they are almost always arguing about specific battles. A compelling case can be made that his swift response to the smallpox epidemic and to a policy of inoculation was the most important strategic decision of his military career."[15] Once again, a Marbleheader proved indispensable.

The Guard and Gibbs continued protecting Washington and fighting as an elite unit of light infantry on special missions and in battle. While wintering in Valley Forge, in the spring of 1778, Washington designated the Guard to demonstrate Baron Von Steuben's drills and utilized the elite unit to move around and train other regiments. Steuben taught the army military drills, tactics, and proper camp life, as encapsulated in his manual *Regulations for the Order and Discipline of the Troops of the United States*, the standard for decades. In 1779, Gibbs received a promotion and transferred to a regiment where he served for the remainder of the war.

Elbridge Gerry, the overlooked Founding Father and a political mainspring of the Revolution, continued to play a paramount role in shaping the nascent United States, serving in Congress and as governor and vice president. Early on, he was one of the first leaders to advocate the importance of foreign alliances.

Gerry's republicanism continued to shape his life of service. Many of his principles revolved around mitigating the centralization and concentration of power. For instance, the Marbleheader would play a key role in the formation of the electoral college. He despised factions and political parties, considering them "self-seeking and divisive, obstacles in the way of unanimity and national purpose, and dangerous to the stability of the American society."[16] He feared standing armies and believed in the wisdom, virtue, and valor of the American people as a whole. He also concerned himself with public service as a source of happiness. Gerry and many Founders were driven by what one historian called "the spur of fame," and strove to achieve immortality in the role of founder of a new nation. In that vein, Gerry's greatest interest was preventing his inchoate country from disintegrating or being controlled by a foreign power. The lesson he learned from the smallpox war and the loss of the hospital remained seared in his mind: the fury of an ungoverned mob could be just as tyrannical as a dictator. Mobs and anarchy once again revealed themselves in Shays's Rebellion in 1786 and 1787. An armed uprising in western Massachusetts of about four thousand rebels led by Revolutionary War veteran Daniel Shays over debt, foreclosure issues, and taxes threatened the United States. Fearful of demagogues, aristocratic government institutions, and the rise of a despot, Gerry used his political influence to protect the country. Gerry, reluctantly, against the core of his republican principles, understood the importance of employing force, if necessary, to suppress the insurrection. As he wrote, "Nothing more nor less than this, whether republicanism or aristocracy should prevail."[17] Revolutionary firebrand Samuel Adams, then president of the Massachusetts Senate and later governor, took an even harder position. Adams had no sympathy for an insurrection against a republic governed by the people, and found Shays's Rebellion bore no comparison to fighting the tyranny of the Crown. Adams wrote, "In monarchies the crime of treason and rebellion may admit of being pardoned or lightly punished, but the man who dares rebel against the laws of a republic ought to suffer death."[18]

Near the end of his life, Gerry became more partisan to protect the America he so carefully helped forge. He took what he believed to be steps to preserve it, such as the approval of gerrymandering, during his term as governor. James Madison, who bravely fought in Trenton, chose Gerry as his vice president in 1812, but Gerry died in office on November 23, 1814. The Marbleheader is the only signer of the Declaration of Independence buried in Washington, DC.

On the other side of the political spectrum, Loyalist Ashley Bowen, who also stayed true to his principles, suffered in a different manner: somehow, he avoided being drafted into the service of the United States, either paying the penalty or finding a substitute to serve in his place, and scraped out enough of a living to feed his family. The traitor Doctor Benjamin Church, after his trial and conviction, was confined to jail and remained imprisoned until 1778 when he was banished from the colonies. He sailed for Martinique, but the vessel was lost at sea, and he was never heard from again.

Other Marbleheaders went back to war in a different way—joining the expanding Continental Navy.

Captaining the frigate *Boston*, Samuel Tucker transported John Adams and John Quincy Adams to France in 1778. The two future presidents embarked upon this mission to acquire vital loans for the advancement of the Revolution, and they eventually crafted the peace treaty that would end the war. The voyage itself was eventful: a lightning storm struck one of Tucker's sailors in the head and nearly demasted the ship. According to John Adams, the lightning burned a hole in the top of the man's skull, and he soon died raving mad. Following the delivery of the precious father-and-son cargo, within days, several Royal Navy warships began pursuing the *Boston*. A desperate race ensued, culminating in a ship-to-ship battle, with the American craft leveling a broadside on the enemy, enabling a forceful boarding to capture the prize. Later, Tucker was captured but escaped from prison on Prince Edward Island, which the Marblehead men had raided earlier in the war.

Another Marbleheader, John Manley, embarked on several voyages also filled with swashbuckling adventure, broadsides, captures, and daring escapes. One of Manley's battles involved the British frigate *Jason*. A Marblehead crew member recalled the dramatic ship-to-ship action: "They ordered us to heave to, or they would fire upon us. We replied, 'Fire away and be damned, we have as many guns as you.' They then gave us a broadside—Our captain would not let us fire until they got abreast of us. They gave us another broadside, which cut away some of our running rigging, and drove some of our men from the tops. We gave them a broadside which silenced their bow guns. The next we gave her, cut away her main topsail, and drove her maintop-men out of it."[19]

The battle continued for hours, but eventually Manley was forced to surrender. Initially, the British imprisoned the marauders on Prince Edward Island; they later sailed to England, where the Americans were held in Britain's notorious Mill Prison. Escaping three times and apprehended after each attempt, Manley eventually obtained his freedom in a prisoner exchange. Rejoining the Revolution in command of the frigate *Hague*, Manley captained one of the Continental Navy's final voyages of the war, capturing a prize ship and later engaging in a thirty-six-hour chase against a fifty-gun British warship. Eventually, *Hague* ran aground, and both ships pummeled each other. Extricating his vessel, Manley sailed from the Caribbean back to Boston when the Revolution ended.

The British also chased Sion Martindale. In May 1778, the British captured Martindale on a raid on Bristol, Rhode Island. The scoundrel captain spent months rotting in a British prison ship until his release in November. Undaunted, Martindale again tried his hand at privateering, outfitting what amounted to a rowboat with a swivel gun. Remarkably, he still snared several prizes.

Washington allowed the enlistment of William Coit, the Red Dragon, in Washington's Navy to expire. Despite Coit's successful track record, Washington considered him too "blundering." But Connecticut had a fast ship, the *Cromwell*, and they needed a captain. Only a month after Coit took the boat, she was struck by lightning and sent back to port for repair. Coit once again lost command and became a privateer.

Washington's last cruiser, the *Lee*, departed port on March 20, 1777. Six months later, Washington's Navy disbanded. While this first Continental Navy was short-lived, it sowed the seeds that would eventually become the US Navy and grow into one of the most effective military forces in the world.

The Marblehead Regiment saved the Continental Army multiple times, and in so doing, they enabled the birth of a new country. They created

the first American navy, which would serve as the origins of the US
Navy. Washington's Navy was created at a time when Americans still
considered themselves English; it was an enormous step in sovereignty
and independence. The Marbleheaders flew the first flag, created the
infrastructure and methodology for a navy, transported the ideas of the
Revolution around the world, and helped forge alliances. The creation
of a navy corresponded with the creation of a nation. The Marblehead
men stood against the greatest naval power on Earth and secured vital
powder and supplies at the most critical time. Laborers, riggers, sailmakers, and fishermen came together in the darkest days of the American
struggle and surmounted the treacherous East River, carrying out the
miraculous American Dunkirk. They later maneuvered the impassable
ice-choked Delaware at Trenton and played a decisive role in one of the
most significant battles in the history of the United States. The soldier-
mariners' indispensable actions made the crossing a reality. Their envelopment and seizure of the bridge at Assunpink Creek transformed the
battle from a minor victory into a crushing triumph that changed the
course of the war. They spearheaded a novel, American style of war,
and their collective actions altered the trajectory of history.

Over 150 years before their time, this group of men of various
races and socioeconomic conditions came together to defeat one of
the greatest armies on the globe and confront the most powerful navy
in the world. They developed a brotherhood while enduring exigent
circumstances that bred adaptability and resilience. They were one
of the first and most diverse units of their kind in the army, and they
determined how Americans should fight—intermingled, not segregated,
amalgamating a unity of purpose. An integrated regiment would not
fight in another American war for nearly two centuries. Through their
extraordinary accomplishments during the war, the Marbleheaders had
just begun to address race relations. The evil institution of slavery would
persist in the United States for decades. But the Revolution galvanized
and strengthened values regarding race within Massachusetts. Many
Marbleheaders, such as Elbridge Gerry, were ardent abolitionists and
powerful voices in the movement that abolished slavery in Massachu-

setts in 1783 and later during the framing of the Constitution, which Gerry forcefully argued should "not give any sanction" to slavery.[20]

The mariners had initiated an exceptional standard; however, the regiment's exceptionalism, their unity, transcended their diversity. Inexorable bonds of blood, family, friendship, and honor melded them. The members banded together in their beliefs and purpose. They sacrificed for their common cause and struggled for liberty, freedom, and a nascent country barely six months old. Through their sacrifice and extraordinary actions, they fostered and forged a country.

They warred in a divided country. They not only fought one of the toughest adversaries in the world—the mighty armed forces of Great Britain—but also some of the most tenacious, the Loyalist Americans who were their neighbors. The greatest foes Americans have ever fought, throughout time, have been their fellow Americans. Had the British stoked this internal division more—through race and the divisiveness of the institution of slavery—and formed more Loyalist American units earlier in the war, and given them equal footing with their British counterparts, the Revolution might have collapsed from its internal division. The British would have divided and conquered. And while years of grueling work lay ahead on race, the diverse men of the Marblehead Regiment broke new ground with a more egalitarian view of race in society that was centuries ahead of their time.

The members of the Marblehead Regiment often fought for no monetary gain and became broken men—physically, economically, and mentally. Some paid the ultimate price, surrendering their very lives. They served honorably, against tremendous hardship, and did not desert their brothers in arms.[21] The price to Marblehead was enormous in blood and treasure. By the end of the war, the town had 378 widows, 35 percent of the female population in the town, and 652 children would never see their fathers again.[22]

Their generation—America's greatest—fought for a higher purpose and sparked a Revolution with groundbreaking ideals and principles, creating a constitution that changed the world. Some journalists have tried to define America by highlighting America's darker moments, but as L. P. Hartley said, "The past is a foreign country, they do things differently there."[23] America's history is a strange and foreign land filled with good and rife with bad and ugly moments, but the achievements of the Marblehead Regiment serve as a shining example for future generations.

British historian George Trevelyan summed up their effort: "It may be doubted whether so small a number of men ever employed so short a space of time with greater or more lasting results upon the history of the world."[24]

The indomitable Henry Knox recalled that freezing Christmas night on the Delaware to the Massachusetts legislature:

> I wish the members of this body knew the people of Marblehead as well as I do—I could wish that they had stood on the banks of the Delaware River in 1776 in that bitter night when the Commander in Chief had drawn up his little army to cross it, and had seen the powerful current bearing onward the floating masses of ice, which threatened destruction to whomever should venture upon its bosom. I wish that when this occurrence threatened to defeat the enterprise, they could have heard that distinguished warrior demand, "Who will lead us on?" and seen the men of Marblehead, and Marblehead alone, stand forward to lead the army along the perilous path to unfading glories and honors in the achievements of Trenton. There, Sir, went the fishermen of Marblehead, alike at home upon land or water, alike ardent, patriotic, and unflinching, whenever they unfurled the flag of the country.[25]

Dramatis Personae

Principal Characters

John Glover: Short, scrappy, and tenacious commander of the Marblehead Regiment; instrumental in the formation of the navy; saved Washington's army through multiple amphibious operations

Doctor Nathaniel Bond: Body snatcher/resurrectionist, fighting surgeon, and company commander in the Marblehead Regiment

Elbridge Gerry: Born with birdlike physical features; intellectual mainspring behind Marblehead's revolutionary movement; a man who did not believe in political parties; "grumbletonian" who was instrumental in shaping the navy and the nascent United States; future vice president of the United States; forever associated with the term *gerrymandering*

George Washington: His excellency, the commander in chief

William Raymond Lee: Aristocratic merchant with natural talent for military tactics; eventual commander of the Marblehead Regiment

Caleb Gibbs: Marbleheader and commander of Washington's Guard, also known as the Life Guard or Guard, the precursor to the Secret Service

Samuel Trevett: "Finished gentleman of the old school" and daring Marblehead officer

Robert Wormstead: Swashbuckling Marbleheader and expert fencer

John Glover Jr.: John Glover's son and company commander

Joshua Orne: Left Harvard to join the Revolution; an officer who fought through all the regiment's battles

Ashley Bowen: Ardent Loyalist, rigger, prolific diarist of Marblehead

Gabriel Johonnot: Member of the Boston Tea Party and staff officer in the regiment

William Hawks: Ensign and resilient soldier-mariner in the Marblehead Regiment

Jeremiah Lee: Rotund scion of Marblehead who used his fortune and influence to affect the early stages of the Revolution

Robert "King" Hooper: Dark-haired, triple-chinned Marblehead shipping magnate; Lee's archrival and an ardent Loyalist with close ties to General Gage

Romeo: Intrepid African American soldier-mariner and veteran of almost all the Marblehead Regiment's campaigns

John Rhodes Russell: Teenage soldier-mariner who fought through all the Marbleheaders' campaigns and rowed Washington across the Delaware

Manuel Soto: African American; early and resilient member of the Marblehead Regiment

THE REGIMENT

Private Caesar Glover: African American soldier-mariner with ties to the Glover family and veteran of many of the Marblehead Regiment's battles

Lieutenant Marston Watson: Resilient officer with the Marblehead Regiment

Captain William Courtis: Sailmaker turned company commander

Captain Moses Brown: Beverly lawyer turned company commander

Captain Thomas Fosdick: Daring captain and company commander

Private Jabez Tarr: Boy soldier and veteran of nearly all the Marblehead Regiment's campaigns

Private Thomas Grant Jr.: Eleven-year-old fifer and part of a father-son pair in the Marblehead Regiment

THE NAVY

Nicholson Broughton: Zealous Patriot from a long line of sea captains who "seemed like descendants of the ancient sea-kings" and captain of the first ship in Washington's Navy

John Selman: Close associate of Nicholson Broughton; Marblehead sea captain

John Manley: Marblehead sea captain who captured one of the great prize ships of the Revolution

Samuel Tucker: One of the US Navy's pioneering and most successful sea captains

Sion Martindale: Rogue sea captain who sold out his crew

"The Blundering" William Coit: Colorful, jovial lawyer turned sea captain

Winborn Adams: New Hampshire native; participant in the raid on Fort William and Mary; captain in Washington's Navy

SUPPORTING WITNESSES

Michael Corbett: Marblehead sailor who threw a harpoon that struck and killed a British naval officer attempting to impress him in one of the first acts of deadly defiance against the Crown before the Revolution

John Adams: Future president and member of Congress who defended Corbett and obtained his acquittal; close friend of Elbridge Gerry; was instrumental in the rise of an American navy

Doctor Benjamin Church: Nefarious physician within the inner circle of American leadership whose mistress resided in Marblehead

Azor Orne: Scion of Marblehead; prominent Patriot leader

John Langdon: Shipowner; revolutionary mainspring behind raid on Fort William and Mary; closely aligned with Elbridge Gerry in the rise of the American navy

Samuel Adams: Firebrand revolutionary, Son of Liberty, and mentor to Elbridge Gerry

Paul Revere: The one and only, Son of Liberty, with close ties to the Marbleheaders

Colonel Henry Knox: Washington's rotund artillery commander

The Earl Cornwallis: One of the great British battlefield commanders of the Revolution, beloved by his men, and nemesis of the Marblehead Regiment

General William Howe, 5th Viscount: Commander of British forces in North America in the early part of the Revolution

General Thomas Gage: Governor of Massachusetts and military commander

Doctor Joseph Warren: Charismatic and brilliant orator and eventual president of the Revolutionary Massachusetts Provincial Congress with ties to Elbridge Gerry and Nathaniel Bond

General John Sullivan: One of the leaders of the attack on Fort William and Mary, later had Marbleheaders under his command

Captain W. Glanville Evelyn: British officer within the light infantry who battled the Marbleheaders in multiple engagements

Colonel Johann Rall: Hessian commander, courageous hero of the Revolution, who crossed paths with the Marbleheaders on the battlefield

Lieutenant James Madison: Future president of the United States and war hero

Margaret Kemble Gage: Beautiful American-born wife of British general Thomas Gage with suspected Patriot sympathies

Life Guard sergeant Thomas Hickey: A member of Washington's Guard involved in a plot to kill Washington

Life Guard drummer William Green: A man with loyalty to the Crown and himself

John Jay: New York Committee of Plots and Secrets; future chief justice of the United States Supreme Court; father of American counterintelligence

Stephen Moylan: Washington's muster-master general, aide-de-camp, and man who coined the term "the United States of America"

Betsy Ross: Renowned flag-maker and potential seductress

Sarah Cochran: America's first female Loyalist combatant

ACKNOWLEDGMENTS

Every book is a journey. Each has found me. I savor the research, the writing, the places, and the people I have met throughout my odysseys. History is my passion. For nearly thirty years, I have amassed oral histories, collaborated on films and documentaries, and written books to preserve and share history. We must save our priceless history, especially the story of America's founding. Much like an archaeologist, I strive to unearth shards from the past and meld them together to bring to light a complete, meaningful, and often previously untold story. Creating *The Indispensables* propelled me on an astonishing sojourn that spanned more than half a decade. During that time, I combed through letters, diaries, memoirs, and pension files, meshing them in a pointillistic manner to open a window into the past with the aim to breathe life into the Revolution. In my research, I not only uncovered the documents from America's War of Independence, but I also walked the grounds where these extraordinary Americans fought and lived.

The Indispensables would not have been possible without the assistance of invaluable repositories of historical information. I want to thank the Mount Vernon Ladies' Association. As a fellow at the Fred W. Smith Library at Mount Vernon, I had the remarkable opportunity to live on the estate while researching and writing this book. I am grateful to my colleagues at Mount Vernon: Dr. Douglas Bradburn, president, and CEO; and Dr. Kevin Butterfield, executive director of the Fred W. Smith Library.

New York Public Library, the Library of Congress, the National Archives, The Society of the Cincinnati, and other historical societies and libraries that I visited furnished essential research for *The Indispensables*. At the Boston Public Library, Joe Moschella left no stone unturned to locate several lost books and rare manuscripts that eluded researchers. I appreciate the outstanding staff at the Beverly Historical Society and Phillips Library. I am very grateful for the help I received from Ann Clutterbuck at the Massachusetts Historical Society and Dr. Louis Mirror and Alexander Kassl from the New-York Historical Society, my favorite research and speaking venue.

At the Marblehead Museum, Lauren McCormack made the Marblehead Archives available to me. Robin Silva took extraordinary efforts to locate an eighteenth-century letter buried in microfilm at the Portsmouth Athenaeum. The staffs at the New Hampshire Historical Society and the New Hampshire State Archives, including Brian Burford, were truly helpful, as was the staff at Washington Crossing State Park. I would be remiss if I neglected to mention the esteemed David Library, which I regret has closed its doors.

Every author has friends on whom he leans for advice and early readings of the manuscript. I am grateful for their time and thoughtful comments. Special thanks to Micah Leydorf and Cyndy Harvey for all their wisdom and cogent comments that strengthened the manuscript. Justin Oldham and John Resto provided invaluable feedback. A special thank-you to my dear friend Ben Ibach, who always has brilliant advice on just about any topic. I am thankful for the outstanding maps created by one of the best mapmakers in the business, my friend for over twenty years, Chris Robinson. I am also grateful to my friend Roger Williams, who has always unconditionally lent a hand.

I am grateful to Revolutionary War historians Don Hagist and Todd Braisted for their encouragement and comments on the manuscript's early drafts. I am indebted to Dr. Glenn Williams, historian at the US Army Center of Military History, for reading the manuscript line by line and providing expert and sage comments.

An author's life can be a solitary one, and I am eternally grateful for my family's support. I am deeply in debt to my gorgeous and brilliant fiancée, ophthalmologist Dr. Lori Snyder. She spent countless hours employing her eagle eye and acumen to strengthen the manuscript with numerous insightful and salient comments.

I also appreciate my agents' diligent work, specifically my literary agent, Eve Attermann and my film and television agents, Flora Hackett and Elizabeth Wachtel, at William Morris Endeavor (WME). I am profoundly grateful for the thoughtful comments and outstanding guidance provided by my exceptional editor, George Gibson, the best editor with whom I have ever had the privilege to work. And this book would never have become a reality without the vision and support of my publisher, the legendary Morgan Entrekin.

NOTES

PROLOGUE

1 George Washington to Lund Washington, December 10–17, 1776, in *The Papers of George Washington: Revolutionary War Series*, vol. 7, *October 1776–January 1777*, ed. Philander Chase (Charlottesville: University of Virginia Press, 1987), 289 (hereafter *PGW: RW*).

CHAPTER 1: SEEDS OF REBELLION

1 John Adams to Jedidiah Morse, January 20, 1816, Adams Papers, National Archives (hereafter NARA). Also, the following is referenced in this narrative: "Adams' Minutes of the Trial: Special Court of Admiralty, Boston, June 1769," *The Adams Papers*, Legal Papers of John Adams, vol. 2, *Cases 31–62*, ed. L. Kinvin Wroth and Hiller B. Zobel (Cambridge, MA: Harvard University Press, 1965), 293–322.

2 John Adams to Jedidiah Morse, January 20, 1816, Adams Papers, NARA. Also, the following is referenced in this narrative: "Adams' Minutes of the Trial: Special Court of Admiralty, Boston, June 1769," 293–322.

3 John Adams to John Quincy Adams, January 8, 1808, Adams Papers, NARA.

4 Ibid.

5 Ibid.

6 Ibid.

7 John Adams to Jedidiah Morse, January 20, 1816, Adams Papers, NARA.

8 Ibid.

9 John Adams to John Quincy Adams, January 8, 1808, Adams Papers, NARA.

10 Alexander Hamilton, a Scottish doctor, traveled the East Coast and recorded that Marblehead had about five thousand inhabitants. By the 1760s the number was higher. Alexander Hamilton, *Gentleman's Progress: The Itinerarium of Dr. Alexander Hamilton*, 1744, ed. Carl Bridenbaugh (Chapel Hill, NC: University of North Carolina Press, 1948), 118.

11 Doctor Robert Honyman in *The Journals of Ashley Bowen (1728–1813) of Marblehead*, ed. Philip Chadwick Smith, 2 vols. (Salem, MA: Peabody Museum of Salem and Colonial Society of Massachusetts, 1973), 2:422 (hereafter *Journals of Ashley Bowen*)

12 Roads, *History and Traditions of Marblehead*, 77.

13 *Journals of Ashley Bowen*, 423.

14 James Trecothick Austin, *The Life of Elbridge Gerry: With Contemporary Letters to the Close of the American Revolution* (Boston: Wells and Lily, 1828), 1:4.

15 Eric G. Grundset, *Forgotten Patriots, African American and American Indian Patriots in the Revolutionary War* (Washington, DC: National Society of the Daughters of the American Revolution, 2013), 79. Many blacks in colonial America were African or West Indian.

16 Lorenzo Greene, *The Negro in Colonel New England, 1620–1776* (New York: Columbia University Press, 1942), appendix A, 337.

CHAPTER 2 : MARBLEHEAD'S LEADING FAMILIES

1 John Glover to Jonathan Glover and Azor Orne, September 5, 1777, John Glover Letterbook, Peabody Essex Museum, Salem, MA. The author carefully examined the entire collection of Glover's papers and in some cases transcribed portions.

2 Carin Gordon, "The Ornes," Marblehead Magazine, https://www.legendinc .com/Pages/MarbleheadNet/MM/FirstFamilyFolder/Ornes.html. "A Sermon, Preached to the First Congregational Society in Marblehead, on Lord's Day, June 12, 1796, Occasioned by the Death of the Hon. Azor Orne, Esq," https://www .legendinc.com/Pages/MarbleheadNet/MM/FirstFamilyFolder/Ornes.html.

3 George Billias, *Elbridge Gerry, Founding Father and Republican Statesman* (New York: McGraw Hill, 1976), xiii.

4 James Moody, *Narrative of the Exertions and Sufferings of Lieut. James Moody*, ed. Charles Bushnell (New York: privately printed, 1865), 13. Moody happened to be from New Jersey, but he is a fine example of an American who initially chose neither side.

5 Billias, *Elbridge Gerry*, 7.

6 Thomas Jefferson, *The Papers of Thomas Jefferson* (Princeton, NJ: Princeton University Press, 2018), 12:229.

7 Billias, *Elbridge Gerry*, xiii.

8 Thomas Amory Lee, *Colonel William Raymond Lee of the Revolution*, Essex Institute Historical Collections (Salem, MA: Essex Institute, 1917), 10.

9 George Norbury MacKenzie, *Colonial Families of the United States* (Baltimore: Grafton Press, 1917), 351.

10 *Journals of Ashley Bowen*, 660.

11 Ibid., 661.

12 Samuel Roads Jr., *The History and Traditions of Marblehead* (Boston: Houghton, Osgood, 1880), 67.

13 Writ of assistance, manuscript signed by John Temple, surveyor general of His Majesty's Customs in the Northern District of America, Boston, January 4, 1762, original document sold by Sotheby's, December 2005, https://www .sothebys.com/en/auctions/ecatalogue/2005/william-guthman-collection-of -manuscript-printed-and-graphic-americana-n08174/lot.1.html.

14 J. L. Bell, "You Won't Believe How Samuel Adams Recruited Sons of Liberty," *Journal of the American Revolution*, February 5, 2014, https://allthingsliberty .com/2014/02/you-wont-believe-how-samuel-adams-recruited-sons-of-liberty/. The claims in the 1936 biography *Sam Adams: Pioneer in Propaganda* that Adams was a barroom troll, propagandist, and mob puppeteer have been largely disproven.

CHAPTER 3: MASSACRE AND TEA

1 *Boston Gazette and County Journal*, March 12, 1770, 1–3.
2 *A Short Narrative of the Horrid Massacre in Boston: The Fifth Day of March, 1770, by Soldiers of the 29th Regiment . . . with Some Observations on the State of Things Prior to That Catastrophe* (Boston: Edes and Gill, and T. and J. Fleet, 1770), 96–97.
3 *Massachusetts Spy*, June 10, 1773.
4 Benjamin Church, "The Choice: A Poem," written 1752, published 1757, National Humanities Center, http://nationalhumanitiescenter.org/pds /becomingamer/ideas/text4/churchchoice.pdf.
5 Franklin Bowditch Dexter, *The Literary Diary of Ezra Stiles* (New York: C. Scribner's Sons, 1901), 619.
6 *Pennsylvania Chronicle*, March 26–April 2, 1770, 38.
7 Samuel Roads Jr., *The History and Traditions of Marblehead* (Boston: Houghton, Osgood, 1880), 85–86.
8 Ibid., 86.
9 "Elbridge Gerry, Gentleman Democrat," *New England Quarterly* 2, no. 1 (1929): 10.
10 James Trecothick Austin, *The Life of Elbridge Gerry: With Contemporary Letters to the Close of the American Revolution* (Boston: Wells and Lily, 1828), 1:16.
11 Ibid.
12 Roads, *History and Traditions of Marblehead*, 89.
13 Ibid., 91.
14 *Essex Gazette*, December 15–22, 1773.
15 Austin, *Life of Elbridge Gerry*, 1:25–26.
16 Francis Samuel Drake, *Tea Leaves: Being a Collection of Letters and Documents Relating to the Shipment of Tea to the American Colonies in the Year 1773, by the East India Tea Company* (Boston: A. O. Crane, 1884), clxvi.
17 "Reminiscence of Caucuses in 1772," *American Magazine of Useful and Entertaining Knowledge* 2 (1839): 260.
18 Andrew Johonnot, "The Johonnot Family," in *The New England Historical and Genealogical Register* (Boston: Samuel G. Drake, 1853), 7:141–142.
19 Frank A. Gardner, "Colonel John Glover's Marblehead Regiment," *Massachusetts Magazine*, 1903, 94.
20 David Hackett Fischer, *Paul Revere's Ride* (New York: Oxford University Press, 1994), 28–29.
21 Drake, *Tea Leaves*, 166.
22 *Boston Evening Post*, December 20, 1773.
23 John Adams to James Warren, December 17, 1773, in *The Adams Papers*, Papers of John Adams, vol. 2, *December 1773–April 1775*, ed. Robert J. Taylor (Cambridge, MA: Harvard University Press, 1977), 1–2.

CHAPTER 4: A VIRUS AND THE REVENGE OF THE LOYALISTS

1 *Journals of Ashley Bowen*, 344.
2 Ibid., 344–345.

3   Ibid., 352.

4   Ibid., 362.

5   *Essex Gazette*, October 19–26, 1773.

6   Nathaniel Bond to Joseph Warren, April 18, 1774, John Collins Warren Papers, Massachusetts Historical Society (MHS).

7   *Essex Gazette*, January 11–18, 1774.

8   *Essex Gazette*, January 18–25, 1774.

9   Ibid.

10 *Essex Gazette*, January 25–February 1, 1774.

11 Ibid.

12 Ibid.

13 *Essex Gazette*, February 22–March 1, 1774.

14 The scene of Glover defending his home comes from a Glover family member and is recorded in *Memorial of Uriel Crooker*, Boston, 1891, 21–22.

15 *Essex Gazette*, March 1–8, 1774.

16 Ibid.

17 Sam Adams to Elbridge Gerry, Boston, March 25, 1774, in James Trecothick Austin, *The Life of Elbridge Gerry: With Contemporary Letters to the Close of the American Revolution* (Boston: Wells and Lily, 1828), 1:36–37.

18 Marblehead Committee of Correspondence to Boston Committee of Correspondence, March 22, 1774, Bancroft Collection, New York Public Library.

19 George Billias, *Elbridge Gerry: Founding Father and Republican Statesman* (New York: McGraw Hill, 1976), 41.

CHAPTER 5: BOSTON PORT ACT

1   Thomas Hutchinson, *The Diary and Letters of His Excellency Thomas Hutchinson* (Boston: Houghton Mifflin, 1884), 497.

2   Hugh Percy, *Letters of Hugh Earl Percy from Boston and New York*, ed. Charles Bolton (Boston: Charles E. Goodspeed, 1902), 37–38.

3   Edmund Burke, "Conciliation," March 1775, House of Commons.

4   *Journals of Ashley Bowen*, 396.

5   He referenced the two Glover brothers and Azor Orne, who remained in Marblehead after the war. Gerry left the town for Boston.

6   William Bentley, *The Diary of William Bentley* (Salem, MA: Essex Institute, 1905), 3:130.

7   Marblehead letter, June 7, 1774, in Peter Force, *American Archives: Fourth Series, Containing a Documentary History of the English Colonies in North America from the King's Message to Parliament of March 7, 1774 to the Declaration of Independence of the United States* (Washington, DC: M. St. Clair Clarke and Peter Force, 1837), 1:391.

8   Richard Frothingham, *The Rise of the Republic of the United States* (Boston: Little, Brown, 1872), 323.

9   Ray Raphael and Marie Raphael, *The Spirit of 74: How the American Revolution Began* (New York: The New Press, 2015), 50.

10 John Andrews, "Letters of John Andrews of Boston, 1772–1776," *Proceedings of the Massachusetts Historical Society* 8 (1864–1865): 34.

11 Samuel Roads Jr., *The History and Traditions of Marblehead* (Boston: Houghton, Osgood, 1880), 103. The local newspapers also carried coverage of the incident.

12 Andrews, "Letters of John Andrews," 35.

CHAPTER 6: GUNPOWDER

1 Abigail Adams to John Adams, 16 June 1775, Adams Papers, MHS.

2 From John Adams to James Warren, 26 September 1775, in *The Adams Papers*, Papers of John Adams, vol. 3, *May 1775–January 1776*, ed. Robert J. Taylor (Cambridge, MA: Harvard University Press, 1979), 168–170.

3 David Rickard, *Pyrite: A Natural History of Fool's Gold* (New York: Oxford University Press, 2015), 51.

4 Meng Yuanlao, *Dreams of the Glories of the Eastern Capital* (ca. 1090–1150).

5 Rick Atkinson, *The British Are Coming* (New York: Henry Holt and Company, 2019), 1:126.

6 David Cressy, *Saltpeter: The Mother of Gunpowder* (Oxford: Oxford University Press, 2013), 154.

7 Patrick K. O'Donnell, *Washington's Immortals: The Untold Story of an Elite Regiment Who Changed the Course of the Revolution* (New York: Atlantic Monthly Press, 2016), 24.

8 Thomas Gage to Lord Dartmouth, August 1774. Thomas Gage Papers, American Series, vol. 122, William Clements Library, University of Michigan.

CHAPTER 7: ARMS RACE AND A FLEDGING GOVERNMENT

1 The Earl of Dartmouth to the Governors of the Colonies, October 19, 1774, in Peter Force, *American Archives: Fourth Series, Containing a Documentary History of the English Colonies in North America from the King's Message to Parliament of March 7, 1774 to the Declaration of Independence of the United States* (Washington, DC: M. St. Clair Clarke and Peter Force, 1837), 1:881.

2 Franklin Bowditch Dexter, *The Literary Diary of Ezra Stiles* (New York: C. Scribner's Sons, 1901), 480.

3 Ibid.

4 Ibid., 481.

5 *Proceedings of the Massachusetts Historical Society* (Boston: MHS, 1866), 8:353.

6 Edward Hill to John Adams, 4 August September 1774, Adams Papers, MHS.

7 Dirk Hoerder, "People and Mobs: Crowd Action in Massachusetts during the American Revolution, 1765–1780" (PhD diss., Freie Universität, Berlin, 1971), 487.

8 *Diary of Ezra Stiles*, 481.

9 Ibid.

10 Thomas Gage to Earl of Dartmouth on the powder alarm, September 2, 1774, in William Cobbett, *The Parliamentary History of England, from the Earliest Period to the Year 1803* (London: printed by T. C. Hansard, 1813), 18:100.

11 Hallowell to Grey Cooper, September 5, 1774, in *Documents of the American Revolution*, ed. K. G. Davies (Shannon: Irish University Press, 1972), 8:188.

12 Samuel Adams Drake, *History of Middlesex County, Massachusetts* (Boston: Estes and Lauriat, 1880), 1:342.

13 Thomas Gage to Earl of Dartmouth on the powder alarm, September 2, 1774, in Cobbett, *Parliamentary History of England*, 18:97.

14 Thomas Gage to Earl of Dartmouth, September 12, 1774, in Cobbett, *Parliamentary History of England*, 18:99–100.

15 Gage to Barrington, November 2, 1774, *Gage's Correspondence*, 2:659. The original Gage Papers are located at the William Clements Library, University of Michigan, Ann Arbor.

16 Articles of Association, October 20, 1774.

17 Joshua Coffin, *A Sketch of the History of Newbury, Newburyport, and West Newbury, from 1635–1845* (Boston: Samuel Drake, 1845), 340.

18 Rick Atkinson, *The British Are Coming*, 9.

19 Suffolk Resolves printed in the *Massachusetts Gazette*, September 15, 1775.

20 Reference Mass Provisional Congress Journals of the Committee of Safety and the Committee of Supplies, 504.

21 Thomas Amory Lee, *The Lee Family of Marblehead*, Essex Institute Historical Collections (Salem, MA: Essex Institute, 1916).

22 Joseph Gardoqui to Lee, Bilbao, February 15, 1775, in *Naval Documents of the American Revolution*, ed. William Bell Clark in collaboration with the US Department of the Navy, 13 vols. (Washington, DC: US Printing Office, 1964–), 1:401 (hereafter *NDAR*).

23 Ibid.

24 Elbridge Gerry to Sam Adams, October 9, 1775, in James Trecothick Austin, *Life of Elbridge Gerry: With Contemporary Letters to the Close of the American Revolution* (Boston: Wells and Lily, 1828), 2:115–119.

25 George Billias, *Elbridge Gerry, Founding Father and Republican Statesman* (New York: McGraw Hill, 1976), 126–128. Spain also utilized diplomat Arthur Lee to funnel supplies.

26 Ray Raphael and Marie Raphael, *The Spirit of '74: How the American Revolution Began* (New York: New Press, 2015), 145.

27 Thomas Hutchinson to Francis Bernard, January 29, 1772, MHS. Also see John Nagy, *Dr. Benjamin Church: A Case of Espionage on the Eve of the Revolution* (Yardley, PA: Westholme, 2013), 38–39, e-book.

CHAPTER 8: THE MARBLEHEAD REGIMENT

1 *Essex Gazette*, February 14–21, 1775.

2 *Essex Gazette*, December 6–13, 1774.

3 *Essex Gazette*, March 7–14, 1775; *Essex Journal*, March 15, 1775.

4 R. N. Tagney, *A County in Revolution: Essex County at the Dawning of Independence* (Manchester, MA: Cricket, 1976), 134–135.

5 *Essex Gazette*, November 22–29, 1774.

6 Thomas Amory Lee, *Colonel William Raymond Lee of the Revolution*, Essex Institute Historical Collections (Salem, MA: Essex Institute, 1917), 10–11.

7 B. P. Houges, *Firepower: Weapons and Effective Use on the Battlefield, 1630–1850* (New York: Charles Scribner's Sons, 1975), 26.

8 Maurice de Saxe, *Reveries on the Art of War*, trans. General Thomas R. Phillips (London, 1757), 32.

9 *Essex Gazette*, October 4–11, 1774.

10 Tagney, *County in Revolution*, 135.

11 Christopher Hill, *The World Turned Upside Down* (London: Penguin Books, 1972), 122.

12 Samuel Roads Jr., *The History and Traditions of Marblehead* (Boston: Houghton, Osgood, 1880), 106–107.

13 Ibid., 107–108.

14 Physical descriptions of individuals from various portraits of Caleb Gibbs.

15 *Journals of Ashley Bowen*, 372.

16 "Return of Capt. Glover's Company, 14th Continental Regiment," January 1, 1776, William Hawks Orderly Book, NARA.

17 Alexander Graydon, *Memoirs of a Life, Chiefly Passed in Pennsylvania with the Past Sixty Years* (Edinburgh: Blackwood, 1822), 146–147.

18 Massachusetts, Office of the Secretary of State, *Massachusetts Soldiers and Sailors of the Revolutionary War: A Compilation from the Archives*, 17 vols. (Boston: Wright and Potter, 1896–1908), 13:540 (hereafter *MSS*).

19 Pension application of Caesar Glover, S. 32738. All pension applications can be found at the National Archives. Fold3 or microfilm can be used to access them. Their location will not be repeated in the notes.

20 From *MSS*: (He is also named Emmanuel), Marblehead, Private, Capt. William Blackler's (6th) co. Col John Glover's 21st regiment; muster roll dated Aug 1, 1775; enlisted May 24th, 1775; service two months thirteen days; also, company return dated Cambridge, October 9, 1775; also, memorandum of firelocks received of sundry officers and soldiers; date of delivery, Feb 1, 1776; also, Private, Captain Nathaniel Lindsey's co; service from Dec. 10, 1776 to March 18, 1777, three months nine days; company raised in Marblehead to reinforce Continental Army; affidavit dated Marblehead, June 25, 1840, made by Nathaniel Lindsey, son of Capt. Lindsey, on reserve of roll, declares the same to be a true copy of the original found among his father's papers, and that the service was rendered at Rhode Island [see Manuel Soto].

21 The author spent months reconstructing the regiment using muster rolls, pension files, and a multivolume series of tomes titled *Massachusetts Soldiers and Sailors of the Revolutionary War*. Scores of African Americans, Indians, and a Spaniard fought in the Revolution on ships and on land from Essex County.

22 Lee, *Colonel William Raymond Lee*, 156.

CHAPTER 9: THE FORGOTTEN FIRST SHOTS

1 John Gerry to Portsmouth Committee of Correspondence, December 12, 1774, Landon-Whipple Papers, vol. 1, Athenaeum microfilm reel 115. The intelligence revealed that Marblehead might also be attacked by the British to seize the gunpowder and military supplies they had stockpiled.

2 William Cooper to Committee of Correspondence at Portsmouth, December 14, 1774, letter available at New Hampshire Historical Society, https://www.nhhistory.org/NHHS/media/NHHS-Media-Library/PDFs/Newsletter/NH_Historical_Society_Newsletter_Spring_2014.pdf.

3 Wentworth Letterbook. The New Hampshire State Archives has handwritten copies of the Wentworth's letters. The referenced letter is from Wentworth to Cochran, Portsmouth, 13 December 1774.

4 Letter to the editor dated December 20, 1774, *Rivington's New-York Gazetteer*, January 19, 1775, referenced in *Proceedings of the New Hampshire Historical Society*, vol. 4 (Concord, NH: New Hampshire Historical Society, 1906), 28.

5 Paul Wilderson, "The Raids on Fort William and Mary: Some New Evidence," *Historical New Hampshire* 30, no. 3 (Fall 1975): 178–202. Wilderson located the original depositions in the UK National Archives; the documents provide a detailed account of the events. Hereafter, each deposition outlined comes from this source. Deposition of Rockingham County sheriff John Parker, 187.

6 Cochran deposition, 189.

7 Ibid.

8 Paul Wilderson, "John Wentworth's Narrative on Fort William and Mary," *Historical New Hampshire* (Winter 1977): 236.

9 Cochran deposition, 190.

10 Ibid.

11 Cochran deposition, 190.

12 Cochran deposition, 190–191.

13 Ibid., 191.

14 Wilderson, "John Wentworth's Narrative on Fort William and Mary," 231.

15 Ibid.

16 Isaac Seveay deposition, 190.

17 Hall deposition, 200–201.

18 A portion of Wentworth's version of events is contained in a handwritten copy, located at the New Hampshire State Archives. The document is hereafter referred to as Wentworth. The quoted portion is contained on page 44.

19 Wilderson, "John Wentworth's Narrative on Fort William and Mary," 231.

20 Editor, "The Gunpowder from Fort William and Mary," *Granite Monthly: A New Hampshire Magazine* 38 (1906): 182–184. It's unclear how much powder at Bunker Hill came from Fort William and Mary; however, the evidence seems to suggest that gunpowder captured in this raid played a role.

21 John Wentworth to Thomas Gage, December 14, 1774, in *Provincial Papers: Documents and Records Relating to the Province of New-Hampshire*, ed. Nathaniel Bouton (Nashua, NH: Orren C. Moore, 1873), 7:420.

22 Charles P. Whittemore, *A General of the Revolution, John Sullivan of New Hampshire* (New York: Columbia University Press, 1961), 6–7.

23 Cochran deposition, 192.

24 Seavey deposition, 196.

25 Otis Hammond, ed., *Letters and Papers of Major General John Sullivan*, Collections of the New Hampshire Historical Society (Concord: New Hampshire Historical Society, 1930), 1:53; Peter Force, *American Archives: Fourth Series*

Containing a Documentary History of the English Colonies in North America in North America from the King's Message to Parliament of March 7, 1774 to the Declaration of Independence of the United States (Washington, DC: M. St. Clair Clarke and Peter Force, 1837), 1:1064–1065.

26 Samuel Ward to Richard Henry Lee December 14, 1774, Papers of the Lee Family, Stratford Hall, https://leefamilyarchive.org/papers/letters/transcripts -gw%20delegates/DIV0219.html.

CHAPTER 10: SALEM NEARLY IGNITES THE REVOLUTIONARY WAR

1 Joseph Tinker Buckingham et al., "Deaths, and Obituary Notices of Persons Lately Deceased," *New-England Magazine* 2 (January–June 1832): 177.
2 *Journals of Ashley Bowen*, 419. Trevett's raid is mentioned in Samuel Roads Jr., *The History and Traditions of Marblehead* (Boston: Houghton, Osgood, 1880) and other sources.
3 *Morning Chronicle and London Advertiser*, 8 April 1775.
4 James Duncan Phillips, *Salem in the Eighteenth Century* (Boston: Houghton Mifflin, 1937), 352.
5 Charles M. Endicott, *Leslie's Retreat at the North Bridge, in Salem* (Salem, MA: Wm. Ives and Geo. W. Pease Printers, Observer Office, 1856), 17.
6 Ibid., 19.
7 Phillips, *Salem*, 353.
8 R. N. Tagney, *A Country in Revolution: Essex County at the Dawning of Independence* (Manchester, MA: Cricket, 1976), 141.
9 Endicott, *Leslie's Retreat*, 24.
10 Ibid., 25.
11 Gravett's account in *Proceedings of the Essex Institute* (Salem, MA: William Ives and George W. Pease, 1856), 1:124–126.
12 Ibid. Also see Endicott, *Leslie's Retreat*.
13 Phillips, *Salem*, 356.
14 Endicott, *Leslie's Retreat*, 27.
15 D. Hamilton Hurd, *History of Essex County, Massachusetts, with Biographical Sketches of Many of Its Pioneers and Prominent Men* (Philadelphia: J. W. Lewis, 1888), 1085.
16 Timothy Alden, *A Collection of American Epitaphs and Inscriptions, with Occasional Notes* (New York: Whitig and Watson, 1812), 129.
17 Wallace Reed, "The Old Tavern," in "The Three Cods Tavern," *Marblehead Magazine*, http://www.legendinc.com/Pages/MarbleheadNet/MM /PeoplePlacesThings/ThreeCodTavern.html.
18 Endicott, *Leslie's Retreat*, 29.
19 Ibid., 38.
20 David Hackett Fischer, *Paul Revere's Ride* (New York: Oxford University Press, 1995), 64.
21 James Trecothick Austin, *The Life of Elbridge Gerry: With Contemporary Letters to the Close of the American Revolution* (Boston: Wells and Lily, 1828), 2:65–66.
22 Everett Watson Burdett, *History of Old South Meeting-House in Boston* (Boston: B. B. Russel, 1877), 79.

23 Ibid., 80.

24 Ibid.

25 J. L. Bell, *The Road to Concord: How Four Stolen Cannon Ignited the Revolutionary War* (Yardley, PA: Westholme, 2016), 111.

26 Lemuel Shattuck, *A History of the Town of Concord, Middlesex County, Massachusetts: From Its Earliest Settlement to 1832; and of the Adjoining Towns, Bedford, Acton, Lincoln, and Carlisle, Containing Various Notices of County and State History Not Before Published* (Boston: Russell, Odiorne, 1835), 97–98.

27 Church to Gage, "Intelligence of Military Preparations," March 4, 1775, in *Documents of the American Revolution*, ed. K. G. Davies (Shannon: Irish University Press, 1972), 8:63–65. Also see Thomas Gage Papers, American Series, vol. 123, William Clements Library, University of Michigan.

CHAPTER 11: PRELUDE TO WAR

1 Thomas Gage to Francis Smith, 10th Regiment Foot, April 18, 1775, Digital History, http://www.digitalhistory.uh.edu/active_learning/explorations/revolution/account2_lexington.cfm.

2 Ibid.

3 Ibid.

4 Richard Frothingham, *The Rise of the Republic of the United States* (Boston: Little, Brown, 1872), 318.

5 Frank Warren Coburn, *The Battle of April 19, 1775* (Lexington, MA: published by the author, 1912), 17.

6 Ibid., 16.

7 Gage to Smith, April 18, 1775.

8 Benjamin Cutter and William R. Cutter, *History of the Town of Arlington, Massachusetts, Formerly the Second Precinct in Cambridge, or District of Menotomy, Afterward the Town of West Cambridge, 1635–1879, with a Genealogical Register of the Inhabitants of the Precinct* (Boston: David Clapp and Son, 1880), 59.

9 Jonas Clarke, *Opening of the War of the Revolution 19th of April 1775: A Brief Narrative of the Principal Transactions of That Day*, appended to a sermon preached by Clarke on April 19, 1776 (repr., Lexington, MA: Lexington Historical Society, 1901), 1.

10 Henry W. Holland, *William Dawes and His Ride with Paul Revere* (Boston: John Wilson and Son, 1878), 14.

11 Elias Phinney, *History of the Battle of Lexington, on the Morning of the 19th April, 1775* (Boston: Phelps and Parnham, 1825), 17.

12 Elbridge Henry Goss, *The Life of Colonel Paul Revere* (Boston: Joseph George Cupples, 1891), 1:185.

13 Holland, *William Dawes*, 14.

14 Paul Revere, draft deposition, April 24, 1775, MHS.

15 Ibid.

16 David Hackett Fischer, *Paul Revere's Ride* (New York: Oxford University Press, 1994), 125.

17 Thomas Amory Lee, *Colonel Jeremiah Lee, Patriot* (Salem, MA: Essex Institute, 1916), 14.

CHAPTER 12: FIRST BLOOD AT LEXINGTON

1 Written record for Gage's orders to apprehend the Marbleheaders at the Black Horse Tavern does not exist, but obviously something happened to convince the men that the British were raiding the tavern. It's possible that members of the British column entered the tavern to apprehend the Patriots or for another, unknown reason.

2 Bennett Cuthbertson, *Cuthbertson's System for the Complete Interior Management and Oeconomy of a Battalion of Infantry* (Bristol, England: Rouths and Nelson, 1776), 190.

3 William Sutherland to Sir Henry Clinton, April 26, 1775, William Clements Library, University of Michigan, copy of letter via Don Hagist.

4 Ibid.

5 Paul Revere, deposition, ca. April 24, 1775, MHS; Elias Phinney, *History of the Battle at Lexington on the Morning of the 19th April 1775* (Boston: Phelps and Farnham, 1825), 19.

6 Elijah Saunderson, deposition concerning Lexington and Concord, April 1775, in *Journals of the Continental Congress, 1774–1789*, ed. Worthington C. Ford et al. (Washington, DC, 1904–1937), 2:29.

7 Robert Douglas, deposition, in Ezra Ripley, *A History of the Fight at Concord: On the 19th of April, 1775, with a Particular Account of the Military Operations and Interesting Events of That Ever Memorable Day . . .* (Concord, MA: Herman Atwill, 1832), 35.

8 Ibid.

9 *Report of the Committee on Historical Monuments and Tablets* (n.p., 1884). Carved on the boulder supporting John Parker's statue is a slightly different version: "If they mean to have a war, let it start here."

10 John Robins, deposition 5, April 24, 1775, in *Journals of the Continental Congress*, 2:31.

11 John Parker, deposition 4, April 24, 1775, in *Journals of the Continental Congress*, 2:31.

12 Lemuel Shattuck, *A History of the Town of Concord, Middlesex County, Massachusetts: From Its Earliest Settlement to 1832; and of the Adjoining Towns, Bedford, Acton, Lincoln, and Carlisle, Containing Various Notices of County and State History Not Before Published* (Boston: Russell, Odiorne, 1835), 103.

13 Thomas Fessenden, deposition 12, April 23, 1775, in *Journals of the Continental Congress*, 2:35.

14 Ebenezer Munroe, deposition 4, December 28, 1824, in Phinney, *History of the Battle at Lexington*, 37.

15 John Munroe, deposition 3, December 28, 1824, in Phinney, *History of the Battle at Lexington*, 20.

16 Paul Revere, deposition, ca. April 24, 1775, MHS.

17 "A British Officer in Boston in 1775," pt. 1, *The Atlantic*, April 1877, 399.

18 Frederick Mackenzie, *Diary of Frederick Mackenzie: Giving a Daily Narrative of His Military Service as an Officer of the Regiment of Royal Welch Fusiliers during the Years 1775–1781 in Massachusetts, Rhode Island and New York* (Cambridge, MA: Harvard University Press, 1930), 32.

CHAPTER 13: CONCORD

1 Thaddeus Blood, "Statement on the Battle of April 19," in Allen French, *The Day of Lexington and Concord* (Boston: Little, Brown, 1925), 157.

2 Lemuel Shattuck, *A History of the Town of Concord, Middlesex County, Massachusetts: From Its Earliest Settlement to 1832; and of the Adjoining Towns, Bedford, Acton, Lincoln, and Carlisle, Containing Various Notices of County and State History Not Before Published* (Boston: Russell, Odiorne, 1835), 111.

3 William Emerson, *Diaries and Letters of William Emerson, 1743–1776: Minster of the Church in Concord, Chaplain in the Revolutionary Army* (Madison: University of Wisconsin Press, 1972), 71.

4 Ephraim Jones, interview by Marquis de Castelleux, November 7, 1782, in *Travels in North America in the Years 1780, 1781, and 1782*, 2 vols., ed. Howard Rice (Chapel Hill: University of North Carolina Press, 1963), 2:481–482.

5 Shattuck, *History of the Town of Concord*, 105–106.

6 Interview with Mrs. Peter Barrett, November 3, 1831, Shattuck's Historical Notes, New England Historic Genealogical Society, Boston; Shattuck, *History of the Town of Concord*, 109; Robert A. Gross, *Minutemen and Their World* (New York: Hill and Wang, 1976).

7 *Proceedings at the Centennial Celebration of Concord Fight, April 19, 1875* (Concord, MA: published by the town, 1876), 104.

8 George Tolman, *Events of April 19* (Concord, MA, n.d.), 29; Douglas P. Sabin, *April 19, 1775: A Historiographical Study* (n.p.: Sinclair Street Publishing, 2011), 38.

9 Shattuck, *History of the Town of Concord*, 112, 366.

10 William Emerson's Diary, MHS, 75.

11 Frank Coburn, *The Battle of April 19, 1775* (Lexington, MA: Coburn, 1912), 86.

12 Ibid.

13 Ibid., 87.

CHAPTER 14: THE BLOODY GAUNTLET

1 James Trecothick Austin, *The Life of Elbridge Gerry: With Contemporary Letters to the Close of the American Revolution* (Boston: Wells and Lily, 1828), 2:68.

2 Glanville Evelyn, *Memoirs and Letters of Captain Glanville Evelyn of 4th Regiment (King's Own) from North America, 1774–1776*, ed. G. D. Scull (Oxford: James Parker, 1879), 54–55.

3 Lemuel Shattuck, *A History of the Town of Concord, Middlesex County, Massachusetts: From Its Earliest Settlement to 1832; and of the Adjoining Towns, Bedford, Acton, Lincoln, and Carlisle, Containing Various Notices of County and State History Not Before Published* (Boston: Russell, Odiorne, 1835), 115.

4 *Collections of the Massachusetts Historical Society*, 2nd ser., vol. 4 (repr., Boston: Charles C. Little and James Brown, 1846), 217.

5 Evelyn, *Memoirs and Letters*, 54–55.

6 Letter from Brigadier the Right Honorable Hugh Earl Percy to his father the Duke of Northumberland, April 20, 1775, in *Letters of Hugh Earl Percy*

from Boston and New York, 1774–1776, ed. Charles Knowles Bolton (Boston: Charles E. Goodspeed, 1902), 54.

7 Pension application of Gabriel Johonnot.

8 Various journal entries from Ashley Bowen confirm that they were fishing the Grand Banks.

9 *Journals of Ashley Bowen*, 431–433.

10 Ibid., 432.

11 Lord Percy to General Harvey Gage, April 20, 1775, in *Letters of Hugh Earl Percy from Boston and New York, 1774–1776*, 50.

12 Ibid., 51.

13 The author owns the original letter from Doctor Bond to Elbridge Gerry, dated April 26, 1775, Marblehead, Massachusetts.

14 Frederick Mackenzie, *Diary of Frederick Mackenzie: Giving a Daily Narrative of His Military Service as an Officer of the Regiment of Royal Welch Fusiliers during the Years 1775–1781 in Massachusetts, Rhode Island and New York* (Cambridge, MA: Harvard University Press, 1930), 20.

15 The Butterfield-Whittemore House and the Russell House still exist in Arlington, Massachusetts.

16 Lucius Paige, *History of Cambridge* (Boston, MA: H.O. Houghton, 1877), 414–415.

17 Ibid.

18 Daniel Putnam King, *An Address Commemorative of Seven Young Men of Danvers, Who Were Slain in the Battle of Lexington* (Salem, MA: W. and S. B. Ives, 1835), 23.

19 Samuel Smith, *West Cambridge 1775* (Boston: Mudge and Son, 1864), 37.

20 Ibid., 38.

21 Led by Moses Brown. Ibid., 96.

22 Frank A. Gardner, "Colonel John Glover's Marblehead Regiment," *Massachusetts Magazine*, 1903, 97.

23 Several days after the battle during a council of war, Pickering argued forcefully that American forces "ought act only on the defensive" and that offensive action against the British might "fatally prevent an accommodation."

24 Lord Percy to General Gage, April 20, 1775, 52.

CHAPTER 15: SIEGE, THE ARMY OF NEW ENGLAND, AND MR. GERRY

1 Richard Frothingham, *History of the Siege of Boston, and the Battles of Lexington and Concord and Bunker Hill* (Boston: Little, Brown, 1872), 94.

2 "Agreement between the Town of Boston and General Gage," in Peter Force, *American Archives: Fourth Series, Containing a Documentary History of the English Colonies in North America from the King's Message to Parliament of March 7, 1774 to the Declaration of Independence of the United States* (Washington, DC: M. St. Clair Clarke and Peter Force, 1839), 2:375–376.

3 *A Volume of Records Relating to the Early History of Boston: Miscellaneous Papers* (Boston: Printing Office, 1900), 321–332.

4 British Army regiments and strength via historian and authority Don Hagist.

5 Benjamin Rush on Gerry Sketches, ca. 1800, Center for the Study of the American Constitution, University of Wisconsin–Madison, https://csac .history.wisc.edu/multimedia/founders-on-the-founders/elbridge-gerry-in -mass-convention/.

6 Charles Thomson to Hannah Thomson, October 20, 1783, Center for the Study of the American Constitution, https://csac.history.wisc.edu/multimedia /founders-on-the-founders/elbridge-gerry-in-mass-convention/.

7 John Adams to James Warren, July 15, 1776, in *The Adams Papers*, Papers of John Adams, vol. 4, *February–August 1776*, ed. Robert J. Taylor (Cambridge, MA: Harvard University Press, 1979), 382–383.

8 Thomas Jefferson, ca. 1787, Center for the Study of the American Constitution. https://csac.history.wisc.edu/multimedia/founders-on-the-founders /elbridge-gerry-in-mass-convention/.

9 John Adams Autobiography, pt. 1, September 1774, 1–3, MHS.

10 William Lincoln, ed., *The Journals of Each Provincial Congress of Massachusetts in 1774 and 1775 and the Committee of Safety* (Boston: Dutton and Wentworth, 1838), 148.

11 Ibid., 152.

12 Ibid., 150.

13 Elbridge Gerry, for the Mass. Committee of Supplies, to José Gardoqui and Sons Bilbao, Spain, July 1775, *NDAR*, 1:818.

14 J. F. Jameson, "St. Eustatius in the American Revolution," *American Historical Review* 8, no. 4 (July 1903): 688.

15 Tristram Dalton to Elbridge Gerry, July 23, 1775, *NDAR*, 1:953–954.

CHAPTER 16: THE LOYALISTS

1 *Journals of Ashley Bowen*, 437.

2 Joseph Henry Stark, *The Loyalists of Massachusetts and the Other Side of the American Revolution* (Salem, MA: Salem Press, 1907), 222–224.

3 *Second Provincial Congress*, 249.

4 Ibid.

5 Ibid.

6 Author owns the original letter, which is dated April 26, 1775, from Doctor Nathaniel Bond to Elbridge Gerry.

7 Joseph Warren, *Essex Gazette*, April 26, 1775.

8 "Manuscript of the Letter from Col. Paul Revere to the Corresponding Secretary (Jeremy Belknap)" (original letter in the manuscript collection of the Massachusetts Historical Society), Paul Revere Heritage Project, http://www .paul-revere-heritage.com/ride-letter-to-Belknap.html. .

9 Ibid.

10 Ibid.

11 "Furnish Col. Benedict Arnold with ten Horses, two hundred pounds of Gunpowder, and two hundred pounds of lead balls." *Journal of the Provincial Congress*, May 3, 1775, vol. 31, Massachusetts Archives.

12 Warren to Elbridge Gerry, May 1, 1775, #GLC00782.23, Gilder Lehrman Collection, Gilder Lehrman Institute of American History, New-York Historical Society.

13 Justin Smith, *Our Struggle for Our Fourteenth Colony* (New York: G. P. Putnam, 1907), 139.

14 Ibid.

15 Benedict Arnold to the Massachusetts Committee of Safety, Crown Point, May 19, 1775, in Peter Force, *American Archives: Fourth Series, Containing a Documentary History of the English Colonies in North America from the King's Message to Parliament of March 7, 1774 to the Declaration of Independence of the United States* (Washington, DC: M. St. Clair Clarke and Peter Force, 1839), 2:646.

CHAPTER 17: TYRANNY, VICTIMS, AND THE AMERICAN NARRATIVE

1 *The Journals of Each Provincial Congress of Massachusetts in 1774 and 1775 and the Committee of Safety* (Boston: Dutton and Wentworth, 1838), 149.

2 John Adams to James Warren, July 15, 1776, *The Adams Papers*, Papers of John Adams, vol. 4, *February–August 1776*, ed. Robert J. Taylor (Cambridge, MA: Harvard University Press, 1979), 382–383.

3 *A Narrative of the Excursion and Ravages of the King's Troops under the Command of General Gage, on the Nineteenth of April, 1775: Together with the Depositions Taken by Order of Congress, to Support the Truth of It* (Worcester, MA: printed by Isaiah Thomas, by order of the Provincial Congress, 1775); *Journals of the Continental Congress, 1774–1789*, ed. Worthington C. Ford et al. (Washington, DC, 1904–1937), 62.

4 Judge Mellon Chamberlain interviewed Levi Preston in the 1830s. George Varney, *The Story of Patriot's Day, Lexington and Concord* (Concord, MA: Lee and Shepard, 1895), 77.

5 *Second Provincial Congress*; Robert Rantoul, *The Cruise of the "Quero": How We Carried the News to the King: A Neglected Chapter in Local History* (Salem, MA: Essex Institute, 1900), 19.

6 Rantoul, *Cruise of the "Quero,"* 3.

7 Orderly book of William R. Lee, MHS.

8 John Hancock to George Washington, October 5, 1775, *PGW: RW*, vol. 2, 533–535.

9 *The Journals of Each Provincial Congress of Massachusetts in 1774 and 1775 and the Committee of Safety* (Boston: Dutton and Wentworth, 1838), 338.

10 Author's exhaustive research of the regiment's muster rolls.

11 Pension application of Francis Grater, S10771.

12 "The Johonnot Family," in *New England Historical and Genealogical Register* (Boston: Samuel Drake, 1853), 7:141–143.

13 William Tudor to John Adams, August 18, 1776, Papers of John Adams (PJA), vol. 4, MHS.

14 Louise Pearsons Dolliver, *Lineage Book—National Society of the Daughters of the American Revolution* (Harrisburg, PA: Telegraph, 1907), 13:315.

15 Marblehead Regiment Muster Rolls and Returns, NARA.

CHAPTER 18: BUNKER HILL

1 Samuel Swett, *The History of Bunker Hill Battle with a Plan* (Boston: Munroe and Francis, 1826), 25.

2 Andrew Jackson O'Shaughnessy, *The Men Who Lost America* (New Haven, CT: Yale University Press, 2013), 214.

3 Pension application of Cuff Chambers (later named Blanchard), W23810.

4 Ibid.

5 Burgoyne to Germain, August 20, 1775, Germain Papers, William L. Clements Library, University of Michigan.

6 John Jennings, *Boston: Cradle of Liberty, 1630–1776* (Boston: Doubleday, 1947), 270.

7 Richard Frothingham, *The Battle of Bunker Hill*, booklet published by the Massachusetts Historical Society, 1875.

8 Ibid. Other historians record slightly different versions of Willard's words. Alexander Graydon's memoirs of his own time record his words, "As to his men, I cannot answer for them; but Colonel Prescott will fight you to the gates of Hell!" And William Prescott wrote a genealogy called *The Prescott Memorial*, in which Willard said, "That man will fight like hell, and if his men are like him you will have bloody work today."

9 Ibid., 160.

10 Samuel G. Drake, ed., *The New England Historical and Genealogical Register* (Boston: Samuel G. Drake, 1858), 12:230.

11 "Colonel Daniel Putnam's Letter Relative to the Battle of Bunker Hill and General Israel Putnam," in *Collections of the Connecticut Historical Society* (Hartford, CT: published for the Society, 1860), 1:247.

12 Ibid.

13 Richard Frothingham, *History of the Siege of Boston, and of the Battles of Lexington, Concord, and Bunker Hill* (Boston: Charles C. Little and James Brown, 1851), 170.

14 Margaret Wheeler Willard, ed., *Letters on the American Revolution, 1774–1776* (Port Washington, NY: Associated Faculty Press, 1968), 151.

15 "Judge Prescott's Account of the Battle of Bunker Hill," in *Proceedings of the Massachusetts Historical Society, 1875–1876* (Boston: MHS, 1876), 77.

16 William Heath, Henry Lee, James Wilkinson, and Henry Dearborn, *History of the Battle of Breed's Hill* (n.p.: William J. Cordon, 1831), 15.

17 Pension file of Samuel Gatchell, S348993.

18 Thomas J. Abernethy, "American Artillery Regiments in the Revolutionary War," vol. 1, "Col. Gridley's Regiment, 1775" (unpublished manuscript, MHS), 50.

19 Jared Sparks, *Lives of Eminent Individuals Celebrated in American History* (New York: Harper and Brothers, 1847), 2:227.

20 Samuel Trevett, letter, June 2, 1818, in William Heath, Henry Dearborne, Henry Lee, and James Wilkinson, *History of the Battle of Breed's Hill*, ed. Charles Coffin (Boston: William Gordon, 1831), 30–31.

21 Derek W. Beck, *The War before Independence: 1775–1776* (Naperville, IL: Sourcebooks, 2016), loc. 1963, Kindle.

22 Peter Force, *American Archives: Fourth Series, Containing a Documentary History of the English Colonies in North America from the King's Message to Parliament of March 7, 1774 to the Declaration of Independence of the United States* (Washington, DC: M. St. Clair Clarke and Peter Force, 1839), 2:1094–1095.

23 Robert Tomes, *Battles of America by Sea and Land* (New York: Virtue, 1861), 1:171.

24 John Fellows, *The Veil Removed* (New York: James D. Lockwood, 1843), 119.

25 Swett, *History of Bunker Hill*, 32.

26 Charles Francis Adams, "Contemporary Opinion on the Howes," in *Proceedings of the Massachusetts Historical Society, October 1910–June 1911* (Boston: published by the society, 1911), 99.

27 Fellows, *Veil Removed*, 120.

28 Pension file of Jabez Tarr, S30149.

29 "Sir William Howe Reports on Bunker Hill," History Central, http://www.historycentral.com/Revolt/battleaccounts/BunkerHill/Howereports.html.

30 Trevett, letter, June 2, 1818.

31 D. Hamilton Hurd, *History of Essex County, Massachusetts, with Biographical Sketches of Many of Its Pioneers and Prominent Men* (Philadelphia: J. W. Lewis, 1888), 1086.

32 "Judge Prescott's Account," 70.

33 Peter Brown to his mother, June 25, 1775, Massachusetts Historical Society, https://www.masshist.org/bh/brownp3text.html.

34 "Maynard's Account of the Battle of Bunker Hill," in Josiah Howard Temple, *History of Framingham, Massachusetts* (Framingham: published by the town of Framingham, 1887), 291.

35 "Judge Prescott's Account," 71.

36 "Letter Samuel Webb to Silas Deane," in *Proceedings of the Massachusetts Historical Society* (Boston: MHS, 1876), 14:81–82.

37 Lt. J. Waller to a Friend, June 21, 1775, Massachusetts Historical Society, https://www.masshist.org/bh/wallerp2text.html.

38 Paul Brown to Sara Brown, June 25, 1775, https://www.masshist.org/bh/brownp4text.html.

39 William Prescott to John Adams 25 August 1775, Papers of John Adams, MHS.

40 Frank Moore, *Diary of the American Revolution: From Newspapers and Original Sources* (New York: Charles Scribner, 1859), 1:97. Warren was appointed a major general before the battle.

41 Swett, *History of Bunker Hill*, 58.

42 Heath et al., *History of the Battle*, 22.

43 Samuel Roads Jr., *The History and Traditions of Marblehead* (Boston: Houghton, Osgood, 1880), 117.

44 "Sir William Howe Reports."

45 Frothingham, *History of the Siege of Boston*, 157.

46 "Massachusetts Provincial Congress, June, 1775," in Force, *American Archives*, 2:1438.

Chapter 19: General George Washington Arrives in Cambridge

1   George Washington Greene, *The Life of Nathanael Greene: Major General of the Army of the Revolution* (New York: G. P. Putnam and Son, 1867), 1:101.

2   "The Siege of Boston," *Atlantic Monthly* 37 (1876): 474.

3   Currently, the mansion is referred to as the Longfellow House, but Henry Vassall was the original owner.

4   William P. Upham, *A Memoir of General John Glover, of Marblehead* (Salem, MA: Charles W. Swasey, 1863), 41.

5   Washington and Kitman, *George Washington's Expense Account* (New York: Grove Press, 2001), 121.

6   Upham, *Glover*, 41.

7   William Heath, *Memoirs of Major-General William Heath*, ed. William Abbatt (New York: William Abbatt, 1901), 17.

8   *Williams Hawks Orderly Book*, NARA, unnumbered pages.

9   Pension application of William Beubier, R162.

10 William Lincoln, ed., *The Journals of Each Provincial Congress of Massachusetts in 1774 and 1775 and the Committee of Safety* (Boston: Dutton and Wentworth, 1838), 584.

11 Thomas C. Amory, *The Military Services and Public Life of Major-General John Sullivan* (Boston: Phillips, Sampson, 1859), 32.

12 Washington to Congress, August 4, 1775, in Peter Force, *American Archives: Fourth Series, Containing a Documentary History of the English Colonies in North America from the King's Message to Parliament of March 7, 1774 to the Declaration of Independence of the United States* (Washington, DC: M. St. Clair Clarke and Peter Force, 1840), 3:28.

13 *The Writings of George Washington*, ed. Worthington Chauncey Ford, vol. 3, 1775–1776.

14 From the Journal of Elias Boudinot, in Martin I. J. Griffin, *Stephen Moylan: Muster-Master General, Secretary, and Aide-de-Camp to Washington . . .* (Philadelphia, 1909), 32.

15 James Warren to John Adams, October 1, 1775, in *The Adams Papers*, Papers of John Adams, vol. 3, *May 1775–January 1776*, ed. Robert J. Taylor (Cambridge, MA: Harvard University Press, 1979), 178.

16 *Boston Weekly Post-Boy*, January 1775, quoted in Edward J. Witek, "Dr Benjamin Church Jr's Mistress," *Dr. Benjamin Church Jr.* (blog), September 30, 2017, http://drbenjaminchurchjr.blogspot.com/2017/09/dr-benjamin-church-jrs-mistress.html.

17 James Warren to John Adams, October 1, 1775, 3:178.

18 Elbridge Gerry to Robert Treat Paine, October 1, 1775, MHS.

19 George Washington to Massachusetts Committee of Supplies, August 1, 1775, in *PGW: RW*, vol. 1:211–212; Elbridge Gerry to Washington, August 1, 1775, in Force, *American Archives*, 3:5.

20 George Washington to Nicholas Cooke, August 4, 1775, *PGW: RW*, vol. 1, 221–223.

Chapter 20: Washington's Covert Navy

1 *Journals of Ashley Bowen*, 443.
2 *NDAR*, 1:674.
3 *NDAR*, 1:1115.
4 Abigail Adams to John Adams, 16 June 1775, Adams Papers, MHS.
5 *NDAR*, 1:1289. While it was not officially the "United States" yet, Glover captures the importance of the vessel.
6 Glover Contract for Wharf and Warehouse Benjamin Beckford, Beverly Historical Society, Beverly, MA (hereafter BHS).
7 Henry Waite, "Broughton: A Sketch of the Family," *New England Historical and Genealogical Register*, July 1883.
8 *NDAR*, 2:368.
9 George Washington's instructions to Broughton, September 2, 1775, *PGW: RW*, vol. 1, 398–401.
10 Ibid.
11 Ibid.
12 George Washington to John Augustine Washington, October 13, 1775, in *The Writings of George Washington from the Original Manuscript Sources, 1745–1799*, ed. John C. Fitzpatrick, vol. 4, *October, 1775–April, 1776* (Washington, DC: US Government Printing Office, 1931), 25–27.
13 *Journals of Ashley Bowen*, 2:45.
14 Dr. Holyoke to his wife, in *Essex Institute Historical Collections*, vols. 12–13 (Salem, MA: Essex Institute, 1874), 13:211.
15 Captain Nicholson Broughton to George Washington, September 7, 1775, *PGW: RW*, vol. 1, 428–429.
16 Ibid.
17 Ibid.
18 Ibid.
19 Log of the HMS *Lively*, PRO/Adm 51/546, UK National Archives.
20 Captain Nicholson Broughton to George Washington, September 7, 1775, *PGW: RW*, vol. 1, 428–429.
21 "Extract of a Letter from Cambridge to a Gentleman in New York," September 14, 1775, in Peter Force, *American Archives: Fourth Series, Containing a Documentary History of the English Colonies in North America from the King's Message to Parliament of March 7, 1774 to the Declaration of Independence of the United States* (Washington, DC: M. St. Clair Clarke and Peter Force, 1840), 3:713–714.
22 General Orders, September 22, 1775, *PGW: RW*, vol. 2, 35–36.
23 *NDAR*, 2:416.
24 Log of the *Nautilus*, PRO/ADM 51/629.
25 Ibid.

Chapter 21: Broughton's Odyssey

1 Instructions to Colonel John Glover and Stephen Moylan, October 4, 1775, *PGW: RW*, vol. 2, 90–92.
2 Reed to Glover and Moylan, October 4, 1775, PGW: RW, LC, NDAR, 2:399.

3 Martin I. J. Griffin, *Stephen Moylan: Muster-Master General, Secretary, and Aide-de-Camp to Washington* . . . (Philadelphia, 1909), 1–5.

4 "I should like vastly to go with full and ample powers from the United States of America to Spain." Stephen Moylan to Joseph Reed, January 2, 1776, quoted in Mariam Touba, "Who Coined the Phrase 'United States of America'? You May Never Guess," *From the Stacks* (blog), New-York Historical Society, November 5, 2014, http://blog.nyhistory.org/coined-phrase-united-states -america-may-never-guess/.

5 Instructions to Colonel John Glover and Stephen Moylan, October 4, 1775, *PGW: RW*, vol. 2, 90–92.

6 The ship is also referred to as the *Lynch* by Joseph Reed. "List of Armed Vessels and State of Them," October 29, 1775.

7 *NDAR*, 2:xi.

8 Langdon gave sixty dollars to Nicholson Broughton, forty dollars to John Glover Jr., and thirty dollars to John Devereaux.

9 *Journals of the American Congress from 1774–1788*, vol. 1, *From September 5, 1774, to December 31, 1776, Inclusive* (Washington, DC: Way and Gideon, 1823), 195.

10 Moylan to Reed, in Peter Force, *American Archives: Fourth Series, Containing a Documentary History of the English Colonies in North America from the King's Message to Parliament of March 7, 1774 to the Declaration of Independence of the United States* (Washington, DC: M. St. Clair Clarke and Peter Force, 1840), 3:1167.

11 Ibid.

12 Reed to Glover and Moylan, *PGW: RW*, LOC.

13 Reed to Broughton, *PGW: RW*, LOC, *NDAR*, 2:416.

14 Glover to Washington, *PGW: RW*, LOC, *NDAR*, 2:459–461.

15 Selman to Gerry, March 18, 1813, in *Extracts Relating to the Origin of the American Navy*, ed. Henry E. Waite (Boston: New England Historic Genealogical Society, 1890), 26.

16 Ibid.

17 A. N. Whitmarsh, *Our Flag: Its Origin and Symbolism* (1898), University of Illinois, Urbana-Champaign 4. Reed's original letter states: "Appeal to Heaven."

18 *NDAR*, 2:474.

19 Pension file of William Bean, W15575.

20 Selman and Broughton to George Washington, November 6, 1775, in Waite, *Extracts*, 18.

21 Ibid.

22 Selman to Gerry, March 18, 1813, 26–29.

23 Ibid.

24 Ibid.

25 Ibid.

26 Ibid.

27 "The Case of Philip Callbeck," *Salem Gazette*, July 22, 1856, in Waite, *Extracts*, 25.

28 Selman to Gerry, March 18, 1813, 27.

29 Pension application of John Teshew, S33786.

CHAPTER 22: "THIS INSTANCE OF DIVINE FAVOUR"

1 Washington to Hancock, December 4, 1775, *NDAR*, 2:1259.
2 Elbridge Gerry to John Adams, December 4, 1775, Papers of John Adams, vol. 3, MHS.
3 John Hannibal Sheppard, *The Life of Samuel Tucker, Commodore of the Revolution* (Boston: Mudge and Son, 1868), 44.
4 Stephen Moylan to William Bartlett, November 26, 1775, BHS and *NDAR*, 2:1142.
5 Robert Ephraim Peabody, *The Naval Career of Captain John Manley of Marblehead* (Salem, MA: Essex Institute, 1909), 5.
6 *London Chronicle*, December 30–January 2, 1775, describes the capture and cargo of *Nancy* and *Boston Gazette*, December 11, 1775.
7 Moylan to Reed, December 5, 1775, *NDAR*, 2:1284.
8 Washington to Lieutenant Colonel Joseph Reed, November 30, 1775, *PGW: RW*, 2:463–464.
9 Ibid.
10 Barlett Papers, BHS.
11 Vice Admiral Graves to Philip Stephens, December 4, 1775, *NDAR*, vol. 2, pt. 3, pp. 1266–1267.
12 Ekekiel Russell, *Manly, a Favorite New Song, in the American Fleet* (Salem, 1776).
13 Description of Coit found in "Captain William Coit," in P. H. Woodward, *Collections of the Connecticut Historical Society* (Hartford, CT: The Society, 1899), 7:5.
14 Coit to Samuel Blachley Webb, November 7, 1775, in *Correspondence and Journals of Samuel Blanchley Webb* (New York: Wickersham, 1893), 1:116–117.
15 George Washington to Joseph Reed, November 8, 1775, *PGW: RW*, vol. 2, 334–336.
16 William Bradford Reed, *Life and Correspondence of Joseph Reed* (Philadelphia: Lindsay and Blakiston, 1847), 1:137.
17 Frank Moore, *Diary of the American Revolution: From Newspapers and Original Sources* (New York: C. Scribner, 1860), 1:168.
18 Reed to Bowen, October 20, 1775, in Peter Force, *American Archives: Fourth Series, Containing a Documentary History of the English Colonies in North America from the King's Message to Parliament of March 7, 1774 to the Declaration of Independence of the United States* (Washington, DC: M. St. Clair Clarke and Peter Force, 1840), 3:1125.
19 Manvide's Journal, PRO, Admiralty 1/485; also in *NDAR*.
20 Ibid.
21 "Intelligence Received from Sion Martindale," PRO/ADM/1/485; also in *NDAR*, 3:64.
22 Ibid.
23 Graves to Captain Symons, December 8, 1775, PRO/ADM 1/485; also in *NDAR*, 3:9–10.
24 Ibid.

25 "John Walker's Appeal to Ben Franklin," Benjamin Franklin Papers, Part 13, 132, American Philosophical Society, PA.

26 George Washington to Lieutenant Colonel Joseph Reed, November 20, 1775, *PGW: RW*, vol. 2, 407–410.

27 Selman to Gerry, March 18, 1813, in *Extracts Relating to the Origin of the American Navy*, ed. Henry E. Waite (Boston: New England Historic Genealogical Society, 1890), 26–28.

28 "From John Adams to Elbridge Gerry, 11 February 1813," *Founders Online*, National Archives, https://founders.archives.gov/documents/Adams/99-02-02-5954.

CHAPTER 23: SNOWBALL FIGHT AND A DIVERSE REGIMENT

1 Israel Trask of Mansfield's Massachusetts Regiment, pension application.

2 Washington Irving, *The Life of George Washington* (New York: G. P. Putnam, 1876), 202.

3 Trask, pension application.

4 Documentation for the incident comes from several sources. However, it is entirely possible that Trask's account included events that took place in several time periods.

5 Alexander Graydon, *Memoirs of a Life, Chiefly Passed in Pennsylvania with the Past Sixty Years* (Harrisburg: John Wyeth, 1811), 131.

6 William Bentley, *The Diary of William Bentley* (Salem, MA: Essex Institute, 1914), 4:530.

7 Trask, pension application.

8 Irving, *Life of George Washington*, 202.

9 Trask, pension application.

10 Ibid.

11 Irving, *Life of George Washington*, 202.

12 William Lincoln, ed., *The Journals of Each Provincial Congress of Massachusetts in 1774 and 1775 and the Committee of Safety* (Boston: Dutton and Wentworth, 1838), 149.

13 George H. Moore, *Historical Notes on the Employment of Negroes in the American Army of the Revolution* (New York: Charles T. Evans, 1862), 7.

14 Ibid., 8.

15 Peter Oliver, *Peter Oliver's Origin & Progress of the American Revolution: A Tory View* (Stanford, CA: Stanford University Press, 1961), 89.

16 *The Triumph of the Whigs* (New York: James Rivington, 1775), 4.

17 Ibid.

18 Obituary, *Columbian Sentinel* (Boston), January 19, 1822, 2.

19 My research indicated that approximately fifty African Americans, Native Americans, and men with "dark complexions," who may or may not have been African American but likely were, served from Essex County. Many more probably served, but their service was not clearly documented. It is difficult to ascertain the race of some individuals because they are listed as "dark-complexioned" or "colored."

20 MSS, 5:381.

21 Revolutionary War Service Records, NARA.

22 Pension file of Francis Grater, S10771.

23 African Americans largely did not serve as officers. Officers were often chosen based on social status or leadership ability, and many had to raise their own units. Documentary evidence of black officers is sketchy. Most were not promoted beyond the rank of corporal.

24 MSS, 13:540. The author conducted original research using Massachusetts Soldiers and Sailors of the Revolution (MSS) muster rolls and National Archives pension files.

25 MSS, 7:1 (also spelled Habens).

26 MSS, 12:829.

27 MSS, 2:175.

28 MSS, 17:803 (also spelled Woodbery, Woodbry, or Woodbrry).

29 Charles L. Hill, "Slavery and Its Aftermath in Beverly, Massachusetts: Juno Larcom and Her Family," *Essex Institute Historical Collections* 116, no. 2 (April 1980): 118–119.

30 MSS, 977; Glenn A. Knoblock, *"Strong and Brave Fellows": New Hampshire's Black Soldiers and Sailors of the American Revolution, 1775–1784* (Jefferson, NC: McFarland, 2003).

31 MSS, 2:93.

32 MSS, 3:211.

33 Pension application of Cato Prince, S33514.

34 MSS, 10:866 (also spelled Mohigh) who served as a "Private, Capt. Francis Felton's (Marblehead) co.; enlisted July 18, 1775; service to Nov. 1, 1775, three mos. Twenty-two days."

35 MSS, 13:822.

CHAPTER 24: BEVERLY

1 Beverly Committee of Correspondence to George Washington, December 11, 1775, *PGW: RW*, vol. 2, 530–531.

2 William Bartlett to George Washington, December 11, 1775, *PGW: RW*, vol. 2, 530.

3 *The Journals of Ashley Bowen (1728–1813) of Marblehead*, ed. Philip Chadwick Smith, 2 vols. (Salem, MA: Peabody Museum of Salem and Colonial Society of Massachusetts, 1973), 2:470.

4 Daniel P. King, Address at Salem, MSS.

5 Glover's Orderly Book, Peabody Essex Museum, Salem, MA.

6 MSS, 1002 (served in Larkin Thorndike's company).

7 Moses Brown's Orderly Book, BHS.

8 William Raymond Lee, William R. Lee Orderly Books, 1775–1776, vol. 3, MS N-635, MHS.

9 Captain Brown's Orderly Book, BHS.

10 Ibid.

11 Ibid.

12 Ibid.

13 Ibid.

14 Orders and Instructions for John Morgan, April 3, 1776, Founders Online, National Archives, https://founders.archives.gov/documents/Washington /03-04-02-0023.

15 Elizabeth Rorke, "Surgeons and Butchers," Brandywine Battlefield Historic Site, https://www.ushistory.org/Brandywine/special/art06.htm.

16 Peter Force, *American Archives: Fourth Series, Containing a Documentary History of the English Colonies in North America from the King's Message to Parliament of March 7, 1774 to the Declaration of Independence of the United States* (Washington, DC: M. St. Clair Clarke and Peter Force, 1840), 3:1153.

17 Thomas Smith, *Extracts from the Journals Kept by the Rev. Thomas Smith* (Portland, ME: Thomas Todd, 1821), 52.

18 William Watson to George Washington, January 29–30, 1776, *PGW: RW*, vol. 3, 212–214.

19 George Washington to Captain John Manley, January 28, 1776, *PGW: RW*, vol. 3, 206–207.

20 Robert Ephraim Peabody, *The Naval Career of Captain John Manley of Marblehead* (Salem, MA: Essex Institute, 1909), 14.

21 Ibid.

22 *Journals of Ashley Bowen*, 2:478.

23 Ibid. The account of the damage comes from the log of the brig *Hope*.

24 Colonel John Glover to George Washington, January 3, 1776, Founders Online, National Archives, accessed April 11, 2019, https://founders.archives .gov/documents/Washington/03-03-02-0010.

Chapter 25: Washington's Life Guard and Lifting the Siege of Boston

1 Peter Force, *American Archives: Fourth Series*, (Washington, DC: M. St. Clair Clarke and Peter Force, 1844), 5:207–208.

2 Carlos E. Godfrey, *The Commander-in-Chief's Guard* (Santa Maria, CA: Janaway, 2014), 21.

3 George Washington to Captain Caleb Gibbs, April 22, 1777, *PGW: RW*, vol. 9, 236.

4 *Travels in North America in the Years 1780, 1781, and 1782*, 2 vols., ed. Howard Rice (Chapel Hill: University of North Carolina Press, 1963), 1:114; Harry Ward, *George Washington's Enforcers* (Carbondale: Southern Illinois University Press, 2006), 61.

5 Jefferson to Jones, January 2, 1814, *Niles Weekly Register*, August 16, 1828.

6 Pension application of Private Carswell Gardner.

7 Pension application of James Knox.

8 Benson Lossing, *Washington and the American Republic* (New York: Virtue and Yorston, 1870) 2:176.

9 Godfrey, *Commander-in-Chief's Guard*, 174.

10 Lossing, *Washington and the American Republic*, 2:177–178; Godfrey, *Commander-in-Chief's Guard*, 68–69.

11 New Jersey Historical Society, *Proceedings of the New Jersey Historical Society* (Edison, NJ: New Jersey Historical Society) 51 (1846): 152.

12 William Tudor to John Adams, September 30, 1775, in *The Adams Papers*, Papers of John Adams, vol. 3, *May 1775–January 1776*, ed. Robert J. Taylor (Cambridge, MA: Harvard University Press, 1979), 174–175.

13 *Proceedings of the New Jersey Historical Society* 51:152.

14 Details on dinner and Washington's day come from Arthur Lefkowitz, *George Washington's Indispensable Men* (Mechanicsburg, PA: Stackpole Books, 2018), 74–75.

15 Ibid.

16 Colonel Henry Knox to George Washington, January 5, 1776, *PGW: RW*, vol. 3, 29–30.

17 William Gordon, *History of the Rise, Progress, and Establishment of the Independence of the United States of America* (London: Charles Dilly, 1788), 2:189.

18 Rufus Putnam, *The Memoirs of Rufus Putnam* (Boston: Houghton, Mifflin, 1903), 57.

19 John Muller, *The Attack and Defense of Fortified Places*, 2nd ed. (London: J. Millin, 1775), 4.

20 Thomas Cushing to Elbridge Gerry, March 6, 1776, *NDAR*, 3:190–191.

21 Ibid.

22 Elbridge Gerry to James Warren, March 6, 1776, *NDAR*, 3:198–199.

23 Henry Dawson, *Battles of the United States: By Sea and Land: Embracing Those of the Revolutionary and Indian Wars, the War of 1812, and the Mexican War: With Important Official Documents* . . . (New York: Johnson, Fry, 1858), 1:94.

CHAPTER 26: DARK DAYS AND *HOPE*

1 Vice Admiral Molyneux Shuldham to Philip Stephens, May 20, 1776, PRO ADM 1/484.

2 William Bartlett to Major Artemas Ward, May 25, 1776, Ward Papers, MHS.

3 Charles Martyn, *The Life of Artemas Ward, the Commander-in-Chief of the American Revolution* (New York: Artemas Ward, 1921), 224; William Bartlett to Major Artemas Ward, April 26, 1776, Ward Papers.

4 Pension application of Moses Stacey, W19408.

5 *New-England Chronicle*, May 23, 1776, *NDAR*, vol. 5, pt. 1, p. 216.

6 Ibid., 217.

7 Ibid., 218.

8 *Collections, Historical and Miscellaneous: And Monthly Literary Journal*, ed. J. Farmer and J. B. Moore (Concord, MA: J. B. Moore, 1823), 2:385.

9 *New-England Chronicle*, May 23, 1776, *NDAR*, vol. 5, pt. 1, p. 218.

10 Farmer and Moore, *Collections*, 2:385.

11 Pension file of Moses Stacey, W19408.

12 Vice Admiral Molyneux Shuldham to Philip Stephens, May 20, 1776, PRO ADM 1/484.

13 *Journals of Ashley Bowen*, 487, via an endnote on the page that references "item 11242 of the Marblehead Historical Society" as a source.

14 Extract of a letter from Boston, July 1, *Pennsylvania Ledger*, July 27, 1776.

15 *NDAR*, 9:818.

16 John Hannibal Sheppard, *The Life of Samuel Tucker, Commodore in the American Revolution* (Boston: Mudge and Son, 1868), 22.

17 Ibid., 25.

18 Ibid., 106.

19 Pension application of John Howard, S. 29246.

20 Pension application of Marston Watson, W15454.

21 Sheppard, *Life of Samuel Tucker*, 29.

22 Ibid., 30–31.

23 Ibid., 59–60.

24 "Prizes and Captures," Library of Congress.

25 *NDAR*, 3:1.

26 O. W. Stephenson, "The Supply of Gunpowder in 1776," *American Historical Review* 30, no. 2 (January 1925): 271–281.

27 The National Park Service and other sources claim the Gardoquis "supplied the patriots with 215 bronze cannon - 30,000 muskets - 30,000 bayonets - 51,314 musket balls - 300,000 pounds of powder - 12,868 grenades - 30,000 uniforms - and 4,000 field tents during the war." In commemoration of the bicentennial, Spain presented a statue honoring Diego de Gardoqui to the city of Philadelphia.

28 John Adams to George Washington, January 6, 1776, *PGW: RW*, vol. 3, 36–38.

CHAPTER 27: KILLING WASHINGTON AND THE INVASION

1 Extract of a letter, June 24, 1776, in Peter Force, *American Archives: Fourth Series, Containing a Documentary History of the English Colonies in North America from the King's Message to Parliament of March 7, 1774 to the Declaration of Independence of the United States* (Washington, DC: M. St. Clair Clarke and Peter Force, 1846), 6:1054.

2 Dr. William Eustis to Dr. David Townsend, June 28, 1776, in *New England Historical and Genealogical Register* 23 (1869): 207–208.

3 Douglas Southall Freeman, *George Washington: A Biography* (New York: Scribner, 1975), 85.

4 David Hackett Fischer, *Washington's Crossing* (New York: Oxford University Press, 2006), 87.

5 "Proceedings of a General Court Martial of the Line . . . for the Trial of Thomas Hickey and Others, June 26th, A.D. 1776," in Force, *American Archives*, 6:1085.

6 Ibid.

7 Ibid.

8 Ibid., 6:1085–1086 (testimony of Isaac Ketchem).

9 Ibid. (testimony of Isaac Ketchem).

10 Ibid. (testimony of Isaac Ketchem).

11 Ibid. (testimony of Isaac Ketchem).

12 Frank Moore, *Diary of the Revolution: From Newspapers and Original Documents* (New York: Charles Scribner, 1860), 1:256–257n.

13 Dr. William Eustis to Dr. David Townsend, June 28, 1776, 207–208.

14 "Washington to New York Provincial Congress," May 1776, Force, *American Archives*, 6:1313.

15 P. K. Rose, "The Founding Fathers of American Intelligence," Central Intelligence Agency, last updated July 7, 2008, https://www.cia.gov/library/center-for-the-study-of-intelligence/csi-publications/books-and-monographs/the-founding-fathers-of-american-intelligence/art-1.html.

16 "To the Honourable Speaker in Provincial Congress from Isaac Ketcham," June 16 1776, Force, *American Archives*, 6:1410.

17 Letter dated June 24, 1776, in Force, *American Archives*, 6:1054.

18 Moore, *Diary of the Revolution*, 1:256–257n.

19 From court-martial proceedings dated June 26, 1776, in *The Writings of George Washington from the Original Manuscript Sources, 1745–1799*, ed. John C. Fitzpatrick, vol. 5, *May, 1776–August, 1776* (Washington, DC: US Government Printing Office, 1932), 182.

20 Carlos E. Godfrey, *The Commander-in-Chief's Guard* (Santa Maria, CA: Janaway, 2014), 32.

21 Dr. William Eustis to Dr. David Townsend, June 28, 1776, 207–208.

22 Ibid.

23 Ibid.

24 General Orders, June 28, 1776, *PGW: RW*, vol. 5, 129–130.

25 *American* (New York: National Americana Society, 1913) 8:724.

26 Daniel McCurtin, "Journal of the Times at the Siege of Boston since Our Arrival at Cambridge, Near Boston, August 9, 1775," in *Papers Relating Chiefly to the Maryland Line during the Revolution*, ed. Thomas Blach (Philadelphia: printed for the Seventy-Six Society, 1857).

27 Fischer, *Washington's Crossing*, 52.

28 Johann Ewald, *Diary of the American War: A Hessian Journal*, ed. Joseph Tustin (New Haven, CT: Yale University Press, 1979), 118.

29 Ambrose Serle, *The American Journal of Ambrose Serle, 1776–1778*, ed. Edward Howland Tatum Jr. (San Marino, CA: Huntington Library, 1940), 70.

30 Benjamin Rush to John Adams, July 20, 1811, Adams Papers, MHS.

31 Sylvanus Urban, *Gentleman's Magazine* (London: Nichols and Son, 1803), 177.

CHAPTER 28: "WE WISH TO GIVE THEM ANOTHER DRUBBING"

1 "Intelligence from New York," August 19, 1776, in Peter Force, *American Archives: Fifth Series, Containing a Documentary History of the United States of America, from the Declaration of Independence, July 4, 1776, to the Definitive Treaty of Peace with Great Britain, September 3, 1783* (Washington, DC: M. St. Clair Clarke and Peter Force, 1848), 1:983.

2 Ibid.

3 Captain James Wallace, August 16, 1776, Journal of HMS *Rose*, *NDAR*, vol. 6, pt. 2, p. 206.

4 George Washington to Jonathan Trumbull Sr., August 18, 1776, Founders Online, National Archives, https://founders.archives.gov/documents/Washington/03-06-02-0064.

5 Ibid.

6 Moses Brown's Orderly Book, 1775–1776, BHS.

7 Ibid.

8 Benj. Tupper to George Washington, August 3, 1776, *PGW: RW*, vol. 5, 553–555.

9 Patrick K. O'Donnell, *Washington's Immortals: The Untold Story of an Elite Regiment Who Changed the Course of the Revolution* (New York: Atlantic Monthly Press, 2016), 3–8. Marylander's original written oath is located in Maryland Historical Society, Gist Papers.

10 Paul David Nelson, *William Alexander, Lord Stirling* (Tuscaloosa: University of Alabama Press, 1987), 88.

11 Johnston, *Memoirs of the Long Island Historical Society* (Brooklyn, NY: The Society, 1867–1889), 2:357.

12 "Extract of a Letter from a Gentleman from Maryland," New York, August 30, 1776, in Force, *American Archives*, Fifth Series, 1:1231–1232; also referenced Papers of Mordecai Gist, MHS.

13 Ibid.

14 Unknown [Nathaniel Ramsay], "Extract of a Letter from New-York, Dated September 1, 1776," *Journal of the Transactions of August 27, 1776, upon Long-Island*, in Peter Force, *American Archives: Fifth Series, Containing a Documentary History of the United States of America, from the Declaration of Independence, July 4, 1776, to the Definitive Treaty of Peace with Great Britain, September 3, 1783* (Washington, DC: M. St. Clair Clarke and Peter Force, 1851), 2:107–108.

15 William Duer, *The Life of William Alexander, Earl of Stirling* (New York: Wiley and Putnam, 1847), 102.

16 "Extract of a Letter from a Gentleman from Maryland," 1:1231–1232.

17 Christopher Ward, *The Delaware Continentals, 1776–1783* (Wilmington: Historical Society of Delaware, 1941), 37.

18 Henry Onderdone, *Revolutionary Incidents* (New York: Leavitt & Co, 1849), 146.

19 Andrew Jackson O'Shaughnessy, *The Men Who Lost America* (New Haven, CT: Yale University Press, 2013), 249.

20 Lord Stirling to General Washington, August 29, 1776, in Force, *American Archives*, 1:1245. The author also consulted original correspondence in the Papers of William Alexander, Lord Stirling, N-YHS.

21 "Extract of a Letter from a Gentleman from Maryland" (Gist), 1:1231–1232.

22 Henry Whittemore, preface to *The Heroes of the American Revolution and Their Descendants: Battle of Long Island* (Brooklyn, NY: Heroes of the Revolution, 1897).

23 Walt Whitman, *Brooklyn Daily Eagle*, August 27, 1846.

24 Thomas Field, *The Battle of Long Island* (New York: Long Island Historical Society, 1869), 201.

25 Lord Stirling to General Washington, August 29, 1776, in Force, *American Archives*, 1:1245.

26 Unknown [Nathaniel Ramsay], "Extract of a Letter from New-York," 2:107–108.

27 "Extract of a Letter from a Gentleman from Maryland" (Gist) 1:1231–1232.

28 Ibid.

29 Onderdone, *Revolutionary Incidents*, 138.

30 Pension application of William McMillan.

31 *Maryland Gazette*, September 1776.
32 Letter from W. Smallwood, Camp of the Maryland Regulars, October 12, 1776, Smallwood Papers, Maryland Historical Society.
33 Smith's recollections of the battle, Samuel Smith Papers, Columbia University Library.
34 "Extract of a Letter from a Gentleman from Maryland" (Gist), 1:1231–1232.
35 Smith's recollections of the battle, Samuel Smith Papers, Columbia University Library.
36 John Thomas Scarf, *History of Maryland 1765–1812* (Hatboro, PA: Tradition, 1879), 247.
37 O'Donnell, *Washington's Immortals*, 3–8.

CHAPTER 29: THE DECISION

1 Alexander Graydon, *Memoirs of His Own Time: With Reminiscences of the Men and Events of the Revolution*, ed. John Stockton Littell (Philadelphia: Lindsay and Blakiston, 1846), 164.
2 Pension application of Philip Follet, W24751.
3 Benjamin Tallmadge, *Memoir of Col. Benjamin Tallmadge* (New York: Thomas Holman, 1858), 9–10.
4 William Howe, *The Narrative of Lieutenant General Sir William Howe in a Committee of the House of Commons, on the 29th of April, 1779* (London: Baldwin, 1781), 5.
5 Henry Whittemore, *The Heroes of the American Revolution and Their Descendants: Battle of Long Island* (Brooklyn, NY: Heroes of the Revolution, 1897), 24.
6 Tallmadge, *Memoir*, 10.
7 Ibid.
8 Ibid.
9 Henry Phelps Johnston, *The Campaign around New York and Brooklyn* (Brooklyn, NY: Long Island Historical Society, 1878), 218.

CHAPTER 30: AMERICAN DUNKIRK

1 Glover's men were assisted by the 27th Regiment from Massachusetts, which eventually formed part of Glover's Brigade.
2 William Gordon, *The History of the Rise, Progress, and Establishment of the Independence of the United States of America: Including an Account of the Late War, and the Thirteen Colonies, from Their Origin to That Period* (New York: Samuel Campbell, 1788), 2:102.
3 Gordon wrote account a few years after the Revolution based on personal conversations and letters from John Glover.
4 Ibid.
5 Pension file of Thomas Grant Jr., W19547.
6 Gordon, *History of the Rise*, 2:102.
7 Pension file of William Hawks, W11224, 17.
8 MSS, 7:44; Edwin Stone, *History of Beverly, Civil and Ecclesiastical: From Its Settlement in 1630 to 1842* (Boston: Dutton and Wentworth, 1843); and Moses Brown's Orderly Book, BHS.

9 Henry Phelps Johnston, *The Campaign around New York and Brooklyn*, 220–221.

10 Joseph Plumb Martin, *Narrative of a Revolutionary Soldier* (Hallowell, ME: Glazier, Masters, 1830; Mineola, NY: Dover, 2006), 17–18.

11 Henry Reed Stiles, *A History of the City of Brooklyn, Including the Old Towns of Brooklyn, Bushwick, and Williamsburgh* (Carlisle, MA: Applewood Books, 1867), 1:286.

12 Stephen M. Ostrander, *A History of the City of Brooklyn and Kings County* (Brooklyn, NY: published by subscription, 1894), 260–261.

13 Gordon, *History of the Rise*, 2:102.

14 Ibid.

15 Ibid., 2:103.

16 Stiles, *History of the City*, 1:286.

17 Pension application of Samuel Anthony.

18 Stiles, *History of the City*, 1:287.

19 Benjamin Tallmadge, *Memoir of Col. Benjamin Tallmadge* (New York: Thomas Holman, 1858), 10–11.

20 Gordon, *History of the Rise*, 2:102–103.

21 From the Memoir of Col. Benjamin Tallmadge, in Henry P. Johnston, *The Campaign of 1776 around New York and Brooklyn: Including a New and Circumstantial Account of the Battle of Long Island and the Loss of New York* (Brooklyn, NY: Long Island Historical Society, 1878), 2:77.

22 Gordon, *History of the Rise*, 2:103.

23 Ibid.

24 William Phineas Upham, *A Memoir of General John Glover, of Marblehead* (Salem, MA: Charles W. Swasey, 1863), 13.

25 Martin I. J. Griffin, *Stephen Moylan: Muster Master-General, Secretary, and Aide-de-camp to Washington . . .* (Philadelphia, 1909), 41.

Chapter 31: Kips Bay

1 *Freeman's Journal*, July 27, 1776, *NDAR*, 1236–1237.

2 David Chacko and Alexander Kulcsar, *Beggarman, Spy: The Secret Life and Times of Israel Potter* (Cedarburg, WI: Foremost, 2010), e-book.

3 George Washington, General Orders, September 4, 1776, Founders Online, National Archives, accessed August 27, 2020, https://founders.archives.gov/documents/Washington/03-06-02-0173.

4 George Washington to Lund Washington, October 6, 1776, Founders Online, National Archives, accessed August 27, 2020, https://founders.archives.gov/documents/Washington/03-06-02-0379.

5 John Adams, *The Works of John Adams* (repr., North Charleston, SC: Createspace, 1856), 9:242.

6 Ibid., 9:245.

7 Ibid.

8 Ibid.

9 William Raymond Lee, William R. Lee Orderly Books, 1775–1776, vol. 3, MS N-635, MHS.

10 George Washington, *The Writings of George Washington*, ed. Worthington Chauncey Ford (New York: G. P. Putnam's Sons, 1889), 403–404.

11 Frank A. Gardner, "Colonel John Glover's Marblehead Regiment," *Massachusetts Magazine*, 94–97).

12 William Gordon, *The History of the Rise, Progress, and Establishment of the Independence of the United States of America: Including an Account of the Late War, and the Thirteen Colonies, from Their Origin to That Period* (New York: Samuel Campbell, 1788), 2:110.

13 Ibid.

14 Ambrose Serle, *The American Journal of Ambrose Serle, 1776–1778*, ed. Edward Howland Tatum Jr. (San Marino, CA: Huntington Library, 1940), 103–105.

15 Joseph Plumb Martin, *Private Yankee Doodle* (repr., New York: Little, Brown, 1962), 34. The book was originally printed in 1830.

16 George Washington to John Hancock, September 16, 1776, Founders Online, National Archives, accessed August 27, 2020, https://founders.archives.gov /documents/Washington/03-06-02-0251.

17 From Brig. General Samuel Holden Parsons in report of the court of inquiry on Col. John Tyler, October 26, 1776, in Peter Force, *American Archives: Fifth Series, Containing a Documentary History of the United States of America, from the Declaration of Independence, July 4, 1776, to the Definitive Treaty of Peace with Great Britain, September 3, 1783* (Washington, DC: M. St. Clair Clarke and Peter Force, 1851), 2:1251–1254.

18 John Glover to Jonathan Glover, Fort Constitution (later Lee), October 6, 1777, Glover Papers, Peabody Essex Museum, Salem, MA; William P. Upham, *A Memoir of General John Glover, of Marblehead* (Salem, MA: Charles W. Swasey, 1863), 14.

19 William Hand Browne, ed., *Archives of Maryland, Journal of Correspondence*, vol. 12 (Baltimore: Maryland Historical Society [MHS], 1893), 342. The original letter is in Smallwood Papers, MHS.

20 Rufus Rockwell Wilson, ed. *Heath's Memoirs of the American War* (Wessels Company, 1798, repr., New York, 1904), 70.

21 Flexner, *George Washington*, 2:123.

22 Upham, *Memoir of General John Glover*, 14.

23 John Morgan, *A Vindication of His Public Character in the Station of Director General of the Military Hospitals, and Physician in Chief to the American Army* (Boston: Powers and Willis, 1827), 93.

24 George Washington to John Hancock, September 16, 1776.

25 Carlos E. Godfrey, *The Commander-in-Chief's Guard* (Santa Maria, CA: Janaway, 2014), 35.

26 John Glover to Johnathan Glover, October 6, 1776, John Glover Letterbook, 1776–1777, Philips Library/PEM, and Glover's orderly book located at MSS 314 at MHS.

27 Ibid.

28 Ibid.

29 Ibid.

30 Ibid.

31 Upham, *Memoir of General John Glover*, 14.
32 General Washington to Governor Cooke, September 17, 1776, in Force, *American Archives*, 2:367.
33 Revolutionary muster rolls, NARA.
34 David McCullough, *1776* (New York: Simon & Schuster, 2006), 222.
35 George Washington to Lund Washington, October 6, 1776.
36 Robert L. Tonsetic, *Special Operations in the American Revolution* (Philadelphia: Casemate, 2013), 85.
37 Consider Tiffany, manuscript, Library of Congress.
38 Hale's last words are not known for certain. He likely paraphrased *Cato*. One British officer who witnessed his execution, Lieutenant Frederick MacKenzie, noted, "[Hale] behaved with great composure and resolution, saying it was the duty of every officer, to obey any orders given him by his Commander-in-Chief; and desired the spectators to be at all times prepared to meet death in whatever shape it might appear." *Diary of Frederick Mackenzie Giving a Daily Narrative of His Military Service as an Officer of the Regiment of Royal Welch Fusiliers during the Years 1775–1781 in Massachusetts, Rhode Island and New York*, 2 vols. (Cambridge, MA: Harvard University Press, 1930), 1:46

CHAPTER 32: THE FORGOTTEN BATTLES
THAT SAVED WASHINGTON'S ARMY

1 Archibald Robertson, *His Diaries and Sketches in America, 1752, 1780* (New York: New York Public Library, 1971), 102.
2 Ibid.
3 Pension application of Marston Watson, W15454.
4 Pension application of Jabez Tarr, S30149.
5 Muster rolls, October 12, 1776, NARA.
6 The author found only a few documented incidents of desertion in the Marblehead Regiment, a very rare condition for American units during the Revolution.
7 Robertson, *Diaries*, 102–103.
8 John Glover, letter, October 22, 1776, in William P. Upham, *A Memoir of General John Glover, of Marblehead* (Salem, MA: Charles W. Swasey, 1863), 17. The letter was printed in the *New Hampshire Gazette* on November 26, 1776.
9 Thomas F. De Voe, *Genealogy of the De Veaux Family* (New York, 1885), 110–111.
10 John Glover, letter, October 22, 1776, 18.
11 De Voe, *Genealogy*.
12 William Abbatt, *The Battle of Pell's Point (or Pelham) October 18, 1776: Being the Story of a Stubborn Fight* (New York: William Abbatt, 1901), 11.
13 John Glover, letter, October 22, 1776, 18.
14 Robertson, *Diaries*, 103.
15 John Glover, letter, October 22, 1776, 18.
16 Abbatt, *Battle of Pell's Point*, 14.
17 Extract of a Letter from a Gentlemen in the Army . . . Nov 1, 1776, in Peter Force, *American Archives: Fifth Series, Containing a Documentary History of the*

United States of America, from the Declaration of Independence, July 4, 1776, to the Definitive Treaty of Peace with Great Britain, September 3, 1783 (Washington, DC: M. St. Clair Clarke and Peter Force, 1853), 3:473.

18 Abbatt, *Battle of Pell's Point*, 15.
19 Extract of a Letter from Col. John Glover, Mile Square, October 22, 1776, in Force, *American Archives*, 2:1188. Hereafter, Glover letter, October 22, 1776.
20 Copy of the Will of Captain William Glanville Evelyn, June 17, 1775, *Memoir and Letters of Captain W. Glanville Evelyn of the 4th Regiment*, ed. G. D. Scull (Oxford: James Parker, 1879), 90.
21 Glover letter, October 22, 1776.
22 *Westfield's Quarter Millennial Anniversary Official Souvenir Program*, ed. Edgar Holmes Plummer (Westfield, MA: Westfield's 250th Anniversary Association, 1919), 23.
23 Glover letter, October 22, 1776.
24 Ibid.
25 Letter from Loammi Baldwin, in Abbatt, *Battle of Pell's Point*, 17; Loammi Baldwin to Mary Baldwin, October 20, 1776, MS Am 1811, Houghton Library, Harvard University.
26 Abbatt, *Battle of Pell's Point*, 20 (Abbatt cites a Dawson for this quote).
27 Glover letter, October 22, 1776.
28 William R. Lee's Orderly Book, MHS.
29 Henry Dearborn, "Dearborn's Life of Col. W. R. Lee," manuscript, Boston Public Library (unpublished, handwritten manuscript from Raymond Lee's son-in-law that's never been fully transcribed).
30 William R. Lee's Orderly Book, MHS.
31 Ibid.
32 Extract of a letter from East-Chester, October 23, 1776, *Independent Chronicle*, October 31, 1776. Via Todd Braisted.

CHAPTER 33: WHITE PLAINS

1 John Glover, letter, October 22, 1776, in William P. Upham, *A Memoir of General John Glover, of Marblehead* (Salem, MA: Charles W. Swasey, 1863), 18–19. Also see Glover's Letterbook, Peabody Essex Museum, Salem, MA, and his Orderly Book at the MHS.
2 John Glover, letter, October 22, 1776.
3 Ibid.
4 Ibid.
5 William R. Lee's Orderly Book, MHS.
6 William Heath, *The Revolutionary War Memoirs of Major General William Heath*, ed. Sean M. Heuvel (Jefferson, NC: McFarland, 2014), 54.
7 Pension application of Thomas Grant, W19547.
8 Pension application of Jabez Tarr, S30149.
9 Carlos E. Godfrey, *The Commander-in-Chief's Guard* (Santa Maria, CA: Janaway, 2014), 36.
10 William Gordon, *The History of the Rise, Progress, and Establishment of the Independence of the United States of America: Including an Account of the Late War,*

and the Thirteen Colonies, from Their Origin to That Period (New York: Samuel Campbell, 1788), 2:341; Glover, letter, November 14, 1776, North Castle, via William Upton, *A Memoir of General John Glover*, 19–20.

11 Ibid.

12 Loammi Baldwin to Samuel Blodgett, November 9, 1776, Loammi Baldwin Papers, MS Am 1811, Houghton Library, Harvard University.

13 Pension application of John Savage, W22147.

14 Pension application of John Teshew, S33786.

15 Pension application of Marston Watson, W15454.

16 Pension application of Moses Stacey, W19408.

17 Pension application of William Hawks, W11224.

18 Loammi Baldwin to Samuel Blodgett, November 9, 1776.

CHAPTER 34: THE DARKEST DAYS

1 Johannes Reuber, Journal, December 25 [26], 1776, in David McCullough, *1776* (New York: Simon & Schuster, 2006), 242.

2 Pension application of Athelston Andrews, S1620.

3 Pension application of Lawrence Everhart.

4 Pension application of Richard Thomas Aktinson. Aktinson was placed "in a sugar house, and then on a vessel of war, that he soon after taken sick & removed to the hospital, on his recovery he was compelled to attend the sick in the hospital, and subsequently permitted to go in and out as he pleased, that at length his escape about the month of June (1777)."

5 American prisoner numbers come from Edwin G. Burrows, *Forgotten Patriots: The Untold Story of American Prisoners during the Revolutionary War* (New York: Basic Books, 2008), xi.

6 Washington Irving, *The Life of George Washington* (New York, 1855–1859), 2:424.

7 Henry Dearborn, "Dearborn's Life of Col. W. R. Lee," manuscript, Boston Public Library (unpublished handwritten manuscript from Raymond Lee's son-in-law. Author transcribed the MS).

8 Ibid.

9 John Adams to James Warren, July 24, 1775, in *The Adams Papers*, Papers of John Adams, vol. 3, *May 1775–January 1776*, ed. Robert J. Taylor (Cambridge, MA: Harvard University Press, 1979), 89–93.

10 Charles Lee, *The Lee Papers* (New York: New-York Historical Society, 1872), 1:207.

11 William S. Baker, "Exchange of Major-General Charles Lee," *Pennsylvania Magazine of History and Biography* 15, no. 1 (1891): 26.

12 George Washington to Major General Charles Lee, November 21, 1776, Founders Online, https://founders.archives.gov/documents/Washington/03-07-02-0137.

13 James M. Van Valen, *History of Bergen County, New Jersey* (New York: New Jersey Publishing and Engraving, 1900), 64.

14 George Billias, *Elbridge Gerry: Founding Father and Republican Statesman* (New York: McGraw Hill, 1976), 72.

15 Charles Willson Peale, *The Selected Papers of Charles Willson Peale and His Family*, ed. Sidney Hart and David Ward (New Haven: CT: Yale University Press, 2000), 50.

16 Christopher Ward, *The Delaware Continentals, 1776–1783* (Wilmington: Historical Society of Delaware, 1941), 104

17 Catherine Read Williams, *Biography of American Heroes: Containing the Life Brig. Gen. Barton and Stephan Olney* (New York: Wiley and Putnam, 1839), 184.

18 Amandus Johnson, *The Journal and Biography of Nicholas Collin* (Philadelphia: New Jersey Society of Philadelphia, 1936), 236–237.

19 George Washington to Lund Washington, December 10–17, 1776, *PGW: RW*, vol. 7, 289–292.

20 Thomas Paine, "The Crisis," December 23, 1776.

21 Ibid.

22 Benjamin Rush to John Adams, July 13, 1780, Founders Online, National Archives, https://founders.archives.gov/documents/Adams/06-09-02-0311.

23 Samuel Adams to John Adams, January 9, 1777, Founders Online, National Archives, https://founders.archives.gov/documents/Adams/06-05-02-0036.

24 William Raymond Lee, William R. Lee Orderly Books, 1775–1776, vol. 3, MS N-635, MHS

25 Ibid.

26 John Glover, Orderly Book #2, 1775–1776, MSS 314, MHS. Collection includes orderly book of Thomas Fosdick.

27 William Raymond Lee, Orderly Book, MHS.

28 George Washington to Charles Lee, November 27, 1776, *PGW: RW*, vol. 7, 224–225.

29 George Washington to Charles Lee, December 1, 1776, *PGW: RW*, vol. 7, 249–250.

30 George Washington to Charles Lee, December 10, 1776, *PGW: RW*, vol. 7, 288–289.

31 Charles Lee to Horatio Gates, December 13, 1776, American Archives, Northern Illinois University Libraries Digital Collections and Collaborative Projects.

32 The British force included thirty members of the 16th Light Dragoons, which was commanded by Colonel William Harcourt.

33 McCullough, *1776*, 265.

34 Joseph Reed to George Washington, December 22, 1776, *PGW: RW*, vol. 7, 414–417.

CHAPTER 35: COUNTERATTACK

1 Benjamin Rush, *A Memorial Containing Travels through Life or Sundry Incidents in the Life of Dr. Benjamin Rush* (privately published by Louis Alexander Biddle, 1905), 94.

2 *The Writings of George Washington*, ed. Jared Sparks (Boston: Ferdinand Andrews, 1838), 4:217–218.

3 Ibid.

4 Bruce E. Burgoyne, *Enemy Views: The American Revolutionary War as Recorded by the Hessian Participants* (Bowie, MD: Heritage Books, 1996), 116–117.

5 William Scudder Stryker, *The Battles of Trenton and Princeton* (Boston: Houghton, Mifflin, 1898), 198.

6 Ibid., 116, additionally, see 404–410 for Hessian investigation.

7 Samuel S. Smith, *Battle of Trenton* (Monmouth Beach, NJ: Philip Freneau Press, 1965),

8 Colonel Rall to Colonel Donop, December 21, 1776, in Stryker, *Battles of Trenton and Princeton*, 332.

9 "The Affair at Trenton, Finding of Hessian Court Martial, Colonel's Report," Lidgerwood Transcripts, Morristown National Historical Park Library, NJ; David Hackett Fischer, *Washington's Crossing* (New York: Oxford University Press, 2006), 427. Additionally, see Stryker, *Battles of Trenton and Princeton*, 404–410 for Hessian investigation.

10 Don Higginbotham, *The War of American Independence: Military Attitudes, Policies, and Practice, 1763–1789* (New York: Macmillan, 1971), 163.

11 William L. Kidder, *Ten Crucial Days* (Lawrence Township, NJ: Knox, 2018), 87.

12 Henry Knox, "A Plan for the Establishment of a Corps of Continental Artillery, Magazines, Laboratories," December 18, 1776, enclosed in Washington's letter to Congress, December 20, 1776, *PGW: RW*, vol. 7, 381–389.

CHAPTER 36: THE CROSSING

1 David Hackett Fischer, *Washington's Crossing* (New York: Oxford University Press, 2006), 203.

2 John Greenwood, "A Massachusetts Fifer at Trenton," in *Americans at War: Eyewitness Accounts from the American Revolution to the 21st Century*, ed. James R. Arnold (Santa Barbara, CA: ABC-CLIO, 2018), 20–22.

3 William Scudder Stryker, *The Battles of Trenton and Princeton* (Boston: Houghton, Mifflin, 1898), 362.

4 Greenwood, "Massachusetts Fifer at Trenton," 20–22.

5 Pension application of Henry Wells (Wales).

6 William L. Kidder, *Ten Crucial Days* (Lawrence Township, NJ: Knox, 2018), 106–107.

7 Henry Knox to his wife, December 28, 1776, in Arnold, *Americans at War*, 23.

8 Pension application of Marston Watson, W15454.

9 James Wilkinson, "The Battle of Trenton," in Arnold, *Americans at War*, 18.

10 Pension application of Thomas Grant, W19547.

11 Pension application of Jabez Tarr, S30149.

12 Henry Knox to his wife, December 28, 1776, 23.

13 Alexander Graydon, *Memoirs of His Own Time: With Reminiscences of the Men and Events of the Revolution*, ed. John Stockton Littell (Philadelphia: Lindsay and Blakiston, 1846), 148–149.

14 The author referenced pension applications and muster rolls portions of the regiment were rebuilt over the course of two years utilizing this method.

15 George Cabot to George Washington, 16 July 1790, *PGW, PS*, vol. 6, 87.

16 Glover to George Washington, June 15, 1777, Papers of George Washington, digital edition, Rotunda.

17 Pension application of John Savage, W22147.

18 Daniel Morgan to William Swihers, January 26, 1778, New-York Historical Society.

19 George Washington, General Orders: Bucks County, December 25, 1776, *PGW: RW*, vol. 7, 434–437.

20 Greenwood, "Massachusetts Fifer at Trenton," 20–22.

21 Pension application of Caesar Glover, S32738.

22 Graydon, *Memoirs of His Own Time*, 148–149.

23 Pension application of Oliver Cromwell, S34613.

24 Stryker, *Battles of Trenton and Princeton*, 362.

25 George Washington to John Hancock, December 27, 1776, *PGW: RW*, vol. 7, 454–455.

26 Ibid.

27 Christopher Ward, *The Delaware Continentals, 1776–1783* (Wilmington: Historical Society of Delaware, 1941), 121.

28 Greenwood, "Massachusetts Fifer at Trenton," 20–22.

29 Ibid.

CHAPTER 37: TRENTON

1 Pension application of John Boudy (Bondy, Bodray).

2 Samuel Roads Jr., *The History and Traditions of Marblehead* (Boston: Houghton, Osgood, 1880), 155.

3 Hugh Scheer and George Rankin, *Rebels and Redcoats* (Cleveland, OH: World Publishing Company, 1957), 212.

4 William S. Powell, "A Connecticut Soldier under Washington: Elisha Bostwick's Memoirs of the First Years of the Revolution," *William and Mary Quarterly* 6, no. 1 (January 1949): 102.

5 James Wilkinson, *Memoirs of My Own Times* (Philadelphia: Abraham Small, 1816), 1:129.

6 Christopher Ward, *The Delaware Continentals, 1776–1783* (Wilmington: Historical Society of Delaware, 1941), 121.

7 "No. 49 Memorandum in General Robert Anderson's Letter Book," in William Scudder Stryker, *The Battles of Trenton and Princeton* (Boston: Houghton, Mifflin, 1898), 373–374.

8 W. W. H. Davis, "Washington on the West Bank of the Delaware, 1776," *Pennsylvania Magazine of History and Biography* 4, no. 2 (1880): 153.

9 Stryker, *Battles of Trenton and Princeton*, 116.

10 David Hackett Fischer, *Washington's Crossing* (New York: Oxford University Press, 2006), 205.

11 John Greenwood, *The Revolutionary Services of John Greenwood of Boston and New York, 1775–1783* (New York: De Vinne, 1922), 41.

12 Washington Irving, *The Life of George Washington* (New York, 1855–1859), 2:555.

13 Pension application of James Knox.

14 Stryker, *Battles of Trenton and Princeton*, 144.

15 Testimony of Jakob Piel, Hessian court-martial, transcript, in Stryker, *Battles of Trenton and Princeton*, 364.

16 Wiederholt Diary, in Bruce E. Burgoyne, *Enemy Views: The American Revolutionary War as Recorded by the Hessian Participants* (Bowie, MD: Heritage Books, 1996), 120.

17 Fischer, *Washington's Crossing*, 244.

18 Greenwood, *Revolutionary Services of John Greenwood*, 41.

19 Journal of Johannes Reuber, December 25, 1776, in Fischer, *Washington's Crossing*, 246.

20 Joseph White, *A Narrative of Events, as They Occurred from Time to Time, in the Revolutionary War, with an Account of the Battles of Trenton, Trenton-Bridge, and Princeton* (Charlestown, MA, 1833).

21 Knox to his wife, in Stryker, *Battles of Trenton and Princeton*, 371–372.

22 Wilkinson, *Memoirs of My Own Times*, 131; White, *Narrative of Events*, extract reproduced in American Heritage.

23 Pension application of Moses Brown, W14400.

24 General Orders: Bucks County, December 25, 1776, provide marching order of the brigades, *PGW: RW*, vol. 7, 434–437.

25 Stryker, *Battles of Trenton and Princeton*, 167.

26 Ibid., 168; Wilkinson, *Memoirs of My Own Times*, 129.

27 Reference to the blunderbuss is found in various naval documents relating to the regiment including an attack involving John Mugford.

28 Johann Ewald, *Diary of the American War: A Hessian Journal*, ed. Joseph P. Tustin (New Haven, CT: Yale University Press, 1979), 31, 34, and 44–45.

29 Greenwood, *Revolutionary Services of John Greenwood*, 83.

30 William Dwyer, *The Day Is Ours! An Inside View of the Battles of Trenton and Princeton, November 1776–January 1777* (New York: Viking, 1983), 259.

31 Ibid.

32 Ibid.

33 Adelbert Milton Dewey, *Life of George Dewey, Rear Admiral: And Dewey Family History* (Westfield, MA: Dewey, 1898), 280.

34 Fischer, *Washington's Crossing*, 252.

35 Washington Irving, *The Life of George Washington*, vols. 1 and 2 (New York: Fred DeFau, 1898), 234.

36 Ibid., 192.

37 Ibid.

38 Ron Chernow, *Washington: A Life* (New York: Penguin, 2010), 282.

39 Letter from John Adams to Abigail Adams, dated February 17, 1777, in *Familiar Letters of John Adams and His Wife Abigail Adams during the Revolution*, ed. Charles Francis Adams (New York: Hurd and Houghton, 1876), 247.

40 Joseph Reed, "General Joseph Reed's Narrative of the Movements of the American Army in the Neighborhood of Trenton in the Winter of 1776–77," *Pennsylvania Magazine of History and Biography*, December 1, 1884, 390–391.

41 "Washington's Dispatch to the President of Congress," letter, December 27, 1776, in Henry Barton Dawson, *Battles of the United States, by Sea and Land* (New York: Johnson, Fry, 1858), 1:201.

42 Pension application of Marston Watson, W15454.

CHAPTER 38: THE EPIC STAND AT ASSUNPINK CREEK

1 John C. Clyde, *Rosbrugh, a Tale of the Revolution* (Easton, PA, 1880), 54.

2 Sergeant R——, "The Battle of Princeton," from *The Phenix*, March 24, 1832, reprinted in *Pennsylvania Magazine of History and Biography* 20, no. 4 (1896): 515–516.

3 Ibid.

4 Ibid.

5 Ibid.

6 Pension applications, Marston Watson Archbald is cited in General Orders August 1776, *PGW: RW*, Letter. William Courtis to George Washington April 28, 1778 his three years of continual service in the Continental Army.

7 Pension application of William Curtis, W14551. William Thompson provides an affidavit of William Curtis's service and states that Thompson and Courrtis fought in Princeton and later were discharged in the middle of February 1777 in Morristown, New Jersey.

8 *Journals of Ashley Bowen*, 510.

9 The author scoured the archives for all available muster rolls and rebuilt the regiment using their pension applications. The muster rolls of Lee's Additional Continental Regiment were compared with prior muster rolls from the 21st Continental Regiment and 14th Continental Regiment during the relevant time periods during the war.

10 Sergeant R——, "Battle of Princeton," 515–516.

11 George Washington's orders to Bond have not been found. But a letter from George Washington to William Shippen Jr. on February 6, 1777, states, "I have directed Doctr Bond to prepare immediately for inoculating in this Quarter." *PGW: RW*, vol. 8, 264.

12 "From George Washington to the Executive Committee of the Continental Congress, 1 January 1777," *PGW: RW*, vol .7, 499.

13 Congressional Committee in Philadelphia to George Washington, December 28, 1776 (extract), in *NDAR*, vol. 7, *American Theatre: Nov. 1, 1776–Dec. 31, 1776; European Theatre: Oct. 6, 1776–Dec. 31, 1776; American Theatre: Jan. 1, 1777–Feb. 28, 1777*, pt. 4 of 9

14 Pension application of Gabriel Johonnot; statement made April 1818.

15 A few men were from nearby towns such as Lynn, Danvers, and Plymouth.

16 John Greenwood, *The Revolutionary Services of John Greenwood of Boston and New York, 1775–1783* (New York: De Vinne, 1922), 44.

17 Elbridge Gerry to Joseph Hawley, January 1, 1777, in *Letters of the Delegates to Congress, 1774–1789*, vol. 6, *January 1–April 30, 1777*, ed. Paul H. Smith (Washington, DC: Library of Congress, 1980), 4–5.

18 The British talked of capturing Philadelphia in late 1776 and early 1777, but they did not seize the town until September 26, 1777.

19 Johann Ewald, *Diary of the American War: A Hessian Journal*, ed. Joseph Tustin (New Haven, CT: Yale University Press, 1979), 44.

20 Thomas Sullivan, *From Redcoat to Rebel: The Thomas Sullivan Journal*, ed. Joseph Lee Boyle (Bowie, MD: Heritage Books, 1997), 98.

21 General Orders, Trenton, December 30, 1776, Papers of George Washington, digital edition, Rotunda.

22 James Wilkinson, *Memoirs of My Own Times* (Philadelphia: Abraham Small, 1816), 1:135.

23 Ibid.

24 Clyde, *Rosbrugh*, 59.

25 Wilkinson, *Memoirs of My Own Times*, 1:138.

26 Harry Ward, *Charles Scott and the Spirit of '76* (Charlottesville: University Press of Virginia, 1988), 27.

27 Wilkinson, *Memoirs of My Own Times*, 1:138.

28 Edwin Martin Stone, *The Life and Recollections of John Howland* (Providence, RI: George Whitney, 1857), 74.

29 Ward, *Charles Scott*, 27.

30 Wilkinson, *Memoirs of My Own Times*, 1:135.

31 Benjamin Cowell, *Spirit of '76 in Rhode Island: Or, Sketches of the Efforts of the Government and People in the War of the Revolution* (Boston: A. J. Wright, 1850), 309.

32 Ibid.

33 Eyewitness account of the Battle of Assunpink, *Princeton Whig*, November 4, 1842, reprinted in John Barber and Henry Howe, *Historical Collections of the State of New Jersey* (New York: S. Tuttle, 1844), 300–301.

34 Ibid.

35 Ibid.

36 William White, "The Good Soldier White" (Revolutionary War memoir), *American Heritage*, June 1956, 75–79.

37 Ibid.

38 Wilkinson, *Memoirs of My Own Times*, 1:139.

39 William Scudder Stryker, *The Battles of Trenton and Princeton* (Boston: Houghton, Mifflin, 1898), 268.

Chapter 39: Princeton

1 James Wilkinson reveals Washington's words in his memoir and Washington Irving, *Life of George Washington* (New York: G. P. Putnam, 1875), 317.

2 Arthur St. Clair, *A Narrative of the Manner in Which the Campaign against the Indians, in the Year One Thousand Seven Hundred and Ninety-One, Was Conducted . . .* (Philadelphia: printed by Jane Aitken, 1812), 242.

3 Ibid.

4 Sir George Otto Trevelyan, *The American Revolution, Part 3* (New York: Longmans, Green, 1905), 133.

5 Catherine R. Williams, *Biography of Revolutionary Heroes: Containing the Life of Brigadier Gen. William Barton, and Also, of Captain Stephen Olney* (Providence, RI: Mrs. Williams, 1839), 193–194.

6 Pension application of Marston Watson, W15454.

7 William Henry Smith, *The Life and Public Services of Arthur St. Clair, Soldier of the Revolutionary War; President of the Continental Congress; and Governor of the North-Western Territory with His Correspondence and Other Papers* (Cincinnati: Robert Clarke, 1882), 38.

8 Walter Harold Wilkin, *Some British Soldiers in America* (London: Hugh Ress, 1914), 223.

9 Samuel Stelle Smith, *The Battle of Princeton* (Monmouth Beach, NJ: Philip Freneau, 1967), 21.

10 Ibid., 24.

11 William Scudder Stryker, *The Battles of Trenton and Princeton* (Boston: Houghton, Mifflin, 1898), 447.

12 Wilkin, *Some British Soldiers in America*, 223.

13 James Reed to his wife, 1777, in "Notes and Queries," *Pennsylvania Magazine of History and Biography* 16, no. 4 (1893): 466.

14 Pension file of Marston Watson.

15 Sergeant R——, "The Battle of Princeton," from *The Phenix*, March 24, 1832, reprinted in *Pennsylvania Magazine of History and Biography* 20, no. 4 (1896): 517.

16 James Wilkinson, *Memoirs of My Own Times* (Philadelphia: Abraham Small, 1816), 1:145.

17 Smith, *Battle of Princeton*, 27.

18 Francis Samuel Drake, *Life and Correspondence of Henry Knox: Major-General in the American Revolutionary Army* (Boston: Samuel G. Drake, 1873), 40.

19 St. Clair, *Narrative of the Manner*, 243.

20 Washington to John Hancock describing victory at Princeton, January 5, 1777, *PGW: RW*, vol. 7, 519–530.

21 Moylan to Morris from Morristown, January 7, 1777, in Martin I. J. Griffin, *Stephen Moylan: Muster-Master General, Secretary, and Aide-de-Camp to Washington* . . . (Philadelphia, 1909), 48.

22 Stryker, *Battles of Trenton and Princeton*, 464.

CHAPTER 40: HOME AND BACK

1 Ashley Bowen notes the arrival of "some of his regiment" on Monday, January 20, 1777. *Journals of Ashley Bowen*, 510.

2 Molly Gutridge, *A New Touch on the Times: Well Adapted to the Distressing Situation of Every Sea-Port Town* (Danvers, MA: Ezekiel Russell, 1779). Unfortunately, little is known about Gutridge; her suspected birth is around 1749.

3 Brigadier General John Glover to George Washington, April 1, 1777, *PGW: RW*, vol. 9, 34–35.

4 George Washington to Brigadier General John Glover, April 26, 1777, *PGW: RW*, vol. 9, 274.

5 Ibid.

6 John Glover to Jonathan Glover and Azor Orne, September 21, 1777, in William P. Upham, *A Memoir of General John Glover* (Salem, MA: Charles Swasey, 1863), 28–29.

7 Brigadier General John Glover to George Washington, May 15, 1778, *PGW: RW*, vol. 15, 124–125.

8 John Glover to George Washington, June 18, 1782, Founders Online, National Archives, https://founders.archives.gov/documents/Washington/99-01-02 -08720.

9 Pension application of Caesar Glover, S32738.

10 *Hampshire Federalist* (Springfield, MA), April 8, 1806, 3.

11 The regiment was known as Lee's Additional Continental Regiment.

12 Francis Bernard Heitman, *Historical Register of Officers of the Continental Army* (Washington, DC: Rare Book Shop, 1914), 280.

13 From George Washington to William Shippen, Jr., February 6, 1777, *PGW: RW*, vol. 8, 264.

14 Ibid.

15 Joseph Ellis, *His Excellency: George Washington* (New York: Vintage Books, 2005), 57.

16 George Billias, *Elbridge Gerry: Founding Father and Republican Statesman* (New York: McGraw Hill, 1976), 332.

17 Elbridge Gerry to John Adams, April 25, 1785, *The Adams Papers*, vol. 17, 45–47.

18 John Fiske, *The Critical Period of American History, 1783–1789* (New York: Houghton, Mifflin, 1889), 184.

19 Robert Ephraim Peabody, *The Naval Career of Captain John Manley of Marblehead* (Salem, MA: Essex Institute, 1909), 23.

20 Madison Papers, 3:1388, et seq.

21 Based on their muster rolls, the regiment had one of the lowest rates of desertion the author has ever seen in an American unit.

22 Roads, *History and Traditions of Marblehead*, 133.

23 L. P. Hartley, *The Go-Between* (London: Harmondsworth, 1953), 1.

24 George Trevelyan, *American Revolution* (New York: Longman, Green, 1903), part 2, 2:113.

25 Extract from speech in Massachusetts Legislature by General Knox, *Historical Collections of the Essex Institute* (Salem, MA: G. M. Whipple and A. A. Smith, 1863), 5:69.

INDEX

Praise for *The Indispensables*

"Historian Patrick K. O'Donnell sets forth in a gripping narrative the transformation of this New England town as it moves from protest to armed Revolution. It is a fascinating, unique journey of a band of Massachusetts rebels who play a critical role in George Washington's and America's success and independence." —Todd W. Braisted, author of *Grand Forage 1778*

"Broadly conceived and beautifully written, *The Indispensables* is an absolutely gripping book. Authored by the highly respected historian Patrick K. O'Donnell, it explores the story of the community of Marblehead, MA, and its famous Mariners Regiment, led by the determined John Glover, whose sailors and soldiers made a host of valuable military contributions through the critical battles of Trenton and Princeton. Highly recommended reading for anyone wanting to learn more about the real realities of the Revolutionary War." —James Kirby Martin, co-author of *A Respectable Army: The Military Origins of the Republic, 1763–1789*